A Lost Left

**Three Studies in
Socialism and
Nationalism**

For Alan

David Howell

A Lost Left

**Three Studies in
Socialism and
Nationalism**

The University of Chicago Press

The University of Chicago Press, Chicago 60637
Manchester University Press, Oxford Road, Manchester M13 9PL
© 1986 by David Howell
All rights reserved. Published 1986
Printed in Great Britain

95 94 93 92 91 90 89 88 87 86   54321

Library of Congress Cataloging-in-Publication Data

Howell, David, *1945–*
  A lost left

  Bibliography: p. 326
  Includes index.
  1. Nationalism and socialism—Great Britain—History.
2. Nationalism and socialism—Ireland—History.
3. Scotland—History—Autonomy and Independence movements. 4. Ireland—History—Autonomy and Independence
movements. 5. Maclean, John, 1879–1923. 6. Wheatley,
John, 1873–1930. 7. Connolly, James, 1868–1916.
I. Title.
HX550.N3H68   1986   320.5'31'0941   86-6968

ISBN 0-226-35513-6
ISBN 0-226-35514-4 (pbk.)

Contents

Acknowledgments	*page*	vii
Threads		1

Part I   James Connolly

	The red and the green	17
1	Edinburgh	19
2	Dublin	28
3	Sectarianism	42
4	Syndicalism	53
5	Socialism and the *Gael*	74
6	Unionism and the working class	93
7	Lock Out	107
8	The choice	128
9	Might-have-beens	140

Part II   John Maclean

	A disputed legacy	158
1	A model Social Democrat	161
2	Internationalism	172
3	Revolution?	184
4	Retrenchment	195
5	Isolation	203

Part III   John Wheatley

1	Roots	229
2	Labour and the nation	244
3	Radicalisation	252
4	Defeat	265

A past for a future		281
Notes		288
Bibliography		326
Index		341

Acknowledgments

The justification for this book and a discussion of the political events that influenced its writing can be found in the first chapter. All that needs to be added is that this is a book by an Englishman about the complex relationship between Socialism and the Nationalisms of the British Isles. This in itself is unusual; hopefully its value will extend beyond its relative novelty.

The book could not have been written without the insights provided by the vast collection of Connolly material in the National Library of Ireland and by the Maclean Papers and other collections in the National Library of Scotland. I wish to thank the staff of both institutions for their unfailing courtesy and valuable advice. Other institutions provided important material – the Mitchell Library, Glasgow, the British Newspaper Library, the Working Class Movement Library, Manchester, Independent Labour Publications, Leeds, the City of Manchester Central Reference Library and the University of Manchester John Rylands Library. I am fortunate to have had the assistance of the efficient Inter-Library Loans service at the last-named institution.

Several colleagues have discussed this topic with me and students have listened and contributed to digressions on the politics of Connolly, Maclean and Wheatley. Papers covering aspects of the argument have been given at the University of Liverpool, Portsmouth Polytechnic, Manchester History Workshop Seminar and the University of Sheffield. My thanks go to all who were involved in the discussions on these occasions. David Beetham commented on an earlier draft on this theme, Austen Morgan exchanged ideas with me on Connolly, Peter Mair scrutinised much of the final version. I also obtained useful encouragement and advice from the two referees utilised by Manchester University Press. My most basic intellectual debt is to Dylan Morris who helped me to see that the question was important.

Lynn Dignan typed successive versions with enthusiasm. Since she is no longer employed by the University of Manchester, perhaps this is an appropriate place to record my thanks for the support that she has always given to my work. Alec McAulay has been an encouraging and understanding editor.

The most fundamental debts lie at home. Katie's advent paralleled the writing of the final draft; Judith offered support, encouragement and so much else at the busiest of times; Alan has just acquired a new sister: now he has his own book.

D.H.
Disley
November 1985

Threads

One strand begins with the image of a man's face. The television screen on the night of 9 June 1983 presented Michael Foot, leader of the Labour Party, as the statistical confirmation of Labour's electoral disaster accumulated. The face of defeat provided a poignant epitaph not just to a failed campaign but to the destruction of a family of political assumptions. Already there had been debate about Labour's electoral prospects. Some had claimed the halting of Labour's Forward March; others had clung to a cosy 'wisdom' about class and voting loyalties and had preferred not to consider inconvenient facts.[1] But as the dimensions of disaster became apparent, Labour did not seem so much to have halted, as to have come close to destruction as a credible political force. Analysts set to work providing diverse diagnoses and remedies.

This exercise begins with a focus on the Party Leader, not because of any distinctive culpability, but because he epitomised one significant aspect in a particularly clear fashion. If ever a politician was trapped in a web of images spun by himself, then that fate befell Michael Foot. In the summer of 1940, he contributed to *Guilty Men*,[2] that polemic which symbolised a moment of popular disgust with the conservatism and incompetence of British ruling circles. Its argument was devoid of Socialist content; rather it was a radical condemnation of the 'little men' who had dominated British politics between the Wars. Its heroes were the iconoclasts, notably Churchill and Lloyd George, who had not accepted the crippling constraints of party orthodoxy and discipline. The consequences in national terms had been disastrous, but radicalism and patriotism could come together now, in a People's War. Such a synthesis allegedly contributed to Labour's 1945 electoral victory. The argument was absorbed by at least one historian who shared Foot's Radical–Liberal sentiments:

In the Second World War the British people came of age. This was a people's war. Not only were their needs considered. They themselves wanted to win ... Traditional values lost much of their force. Other values took their place. Imperial greatness was on the way out; the welfare state was on the way in.[3]

This celebration was underpinned by a self-congratulatory assessment of the British – or perhaps the English – character: 'a peaceful and civilised people, tolerant patient and generous'. In the mid-1960s, when

Alan Taylor provided this climax to his *English History 1914–1945*, such a hymn of praise provoked little scepticism. The apparent durability of the post-war settlement might appear to license a claim that Progressive politics had been married with well-established national procedures and sentiments. Often this combination could appear as 'commonsense' that seemed to require no discussion.

But beneath the Pecksniffian facade, the predictable world of British politics was altering. Socialists might show a reverential attitude to the achievements of the Attlee Government; even the most myopic Labour loyalist could hardly respond with similar enthusiasm to the records of the Wilson and Callaghan administrations. Any expectation of continuing progress founded on a significant degree of political consensus seemed increasingly tenuous. Equally the synthesis of left politics with a particular characterisation of the 'nation' came under pressure. From the late 1960s there were successive reminders that British Governments presided over a multinational State. The harshest testimony came with the escalating violence in Northern Ireland. British politicians ended almost half a century of amnesia, as they were forced to acknowledge their own involvement in an unresolved National Question; less dramatically, the failures of Labour Governments led significant numbers of Scottish and Welsh voters to sample the Scottish National Party and Plaid Cymru. Sometimes the shift became permanent, and although both parties encountered problems after 1974, Labour's plausibility as the representative of Scottish and Welsh claims within the British State had diminished. Within England the growth and the attraction of racist propaganda yoked to a populist rhetoric suggested doubts about traditional celebrations of tolerance.[4]

The political agenda of the late seventies had been moulded by such developments – deflationary policies, a draconian regime in Northern Ireland; clashes between the National Front and anti-racists in English cities; all presided over by a Labour Government. It was far removed from that once persuasive hope for Progressive politics founded on the tolerance of the civilised British. This however was merely an overture; from May 1979 the Thatcher Government proclaimed its willingness to break with the post war consensus, and to do so in the name of an alternative national identity.

The early consequences for many working-class people were devastating. Unemployment rocketed especially in areas of traditional heavy industry. In itself this eroded trade union strength, but alongside this, unions suffered major defeats. Sometimes these involved set-piece confrontations, as in the steel strike early in 1980, but unions also found themselves the object of legislative initiatives wrapped in populist rhetoric. Amidst all this regression from the image of a 'Progressive nation' the Labour Party offered little effective response. An introverted post-mortem on its earlier failures left little energy for combating the Government and provided few strategic suggestions. Against this backcloth of deprivation, lacking a credible political response, it was hardly surprising that inner-city communities in London, Liverpool and Manchester experienced riots during the 1981 summer. These provided a bitter pyrotechnic commentary on an official national image constructed around the theatre of a royal wedding. The flames afforded a brief illumination of institutionalised racism and of unemployment as a way of life.

Then came the crisis in the South Atlantic. Michael Foot attempted to conjure up the spirit of *Guilty Men*. Once again a reactionary incompetent government had presided over a national humiliation; once again radical-ism could unite with patriotism. But this time the outcome was very different. The adversary was not a military machine dominant through-out much of Western Europe, but much more a symbolic challenge to the Government's image of itself and of 'the British nation'. As such it provoked a murderously theatrical response. Foot's argument about competence was checkmated by a military victory. This provided a stern authorisation for the Government's version of national characteristics. Margaret Thatcher presented an interpretation to set against those who had seen 'the British nation' in progressive terms. The liberal doubters had been routed:

they ... had their secret fears that it was true; that Britain was no longer the nation that had built an Empire and ruled a quarter of the world. Well they were wrong. The lesson of the Falklands is that Britain has not changed and that this nation still has those sterling qualities which shine through our history.[5]

For Labour the road led through a landscape of reaction to electoral catastrophe. The face on the screen told it all.

The South Atlantic episode and the associated political debacle provoked widespread debate on the left. Inevitably, arguments involved assessments of the historically complex relationships between Socialism, Nationalism and working-class organisations and of the inventory of relevant ideas within the Socialist tradition.[6] Here is the start of another strand. At a rhetorical level, a tradition of Socialist Internationalism has remained a compelling one, based on familiar claims about the common interests of workers across national frontiers and buttressed in the case of the British Labour Movement by a durable anti-militarist sentiment derived from Radical Liberalism. Although Socialists have often employed the language of Internationalism, they have frequently abandoned it when compelled to move from rhetoric to action. However much inter-nationalist principles have been protected by warnings about the favoured use of nationalist sentiments as a powerful element within bourgeois ideology, some of the most poignant images in the history of Socialist and working-class movements demonstrate the power of nationalist priorities at critical moments. The most sombre examples occurred in August 1914. Several Labour MPs joined vigorously in a chorus of 'Rule Britannia' on the floor of the House of Commons; most devastating for the dreams of Second International Socialists, German Social Democrats decided to vote for War Credits in the Reichstag.

The common contrast between language and action can provoke a sceptical response. The divergence demonstrates the fundamental utopianism at the heart of any socialist project. The sometimes violent almost always decisive appeals of twentieth century nationalisms have played a critical role in shattering earlier hopes of socialist progress. In particular, sceptics would claim that the hopes invested in the industrial working class as the prime agent of any socialist transformation have been blighted consistently by the commitment of that class to national symbols and priorities.

Such scepticism provokes and in turn gains credibility from a purist strand in Socialist assessments of nationalism. This stigmatises nationalist sentiments as introverted and irrational, concerned only with the emancipation of a specific self-defined community, devoid of any more inclusive perspective on the bases for oppression and often blind to injustices suffered by minorities within the designated territory. The typical outcome is portrayed as a series of superficial but often vicious animosities which are destructive and distract attention from more fundamental problems.

Both purist and sceptic base their cases on an image of undiluted Socialist Internationalism. One embraces the ideal. A mass of inconvenient facts are ignored or discounted. The other lets the facts decide and pronounces the ideal redundant. Yet arguably this is an inappropriate starting point for consideration of this complex issue. Historically, Socialists have had to come to terms with the facts of nationalist movements; often they have had to operate within the political institutions of nation-states. Although *The Communist Manifesto* is portrayed often as an expression of internationalism, Marx was in no doubt about the appropriate arena for forthcoming Socialist activities:

In form though not in substance, the struggle of the proletariat against the bourgeoisie is primarily national. Of course, in any country, the proletariat has first of all to settle accounts with its own bourgeoisie.[7]

Even a frequently quoted passage on nationalism and the working-class has its complexities:

The workers have no country. No one can take from them what they have not got. Since the proletariat must first of all win political power, must make itself the ruling class, must raise itself to the position of a national class, must establish itself as the nation − it is, so far, still national, though by no means in the bourgeois sense of the term.[8]

This elliptical passage does not dismiss all idea of the 'nation' as a bourgeois illusion; rather it suggests perhaps the need for the working-class to emerge as the advocate of genuine national interests. The quality of such a partnership remained obscure but clearly Marx, even in this generalising polemic did not hide from the issues raised by the location of Socialist organisations within national communities.

The emergence of mass Socialist and Labour Parties from the 1880s underlined this situation. Practically every independent nation that experienced capitalist industrialisation down to the 1920s developed such a party. These national organisations were the building blocks of the Second International; the relationship between Socialism and Nationalism was institutionalised in its organisational structure.[9]

In fact the pre-1914 situation was even more complicated since both the Russian and the Austro-Hungarian Empires were multinational. Socialists under these regimes not only had to relate to the existing State, they also had to consider the claims for self-determination made by various groups. Thus Marx and Engels supported Polish demands for national independence, largely as an instrument for weakening reactionary Russia.[10] This instrumentalist argument placed a premium on an assessment of revolutionary significance. The grievances of Polish — or other nationalists — should be regarded as potential gunpowder directed against established institutions. Eventually Engels claimed that Socialists should show more general support for national self-determination. Only when this demand was met, could the Socialist movement flourish:

An international proletarian movement ... can only grow out of the existence of independent nations.[11]

This pronouncement was made during a discussion of the Polish case; it was rejected by Poland's most eminent Marxist. Rosa Luxemburg argued forcefully against any involvement of Socialists with Nationalist movements. In her view, claims for self-determination ranked no higher than the abstract empty arguments that in other contexts Marxists loved to deride. Participation in a nationalist agitation was a surrender to a bourgeois perspective. To talk of 'the nation' and to take its independence as one indice of emancipation was to relegate Socialist claims about the centrality of class interests. Moreover such involvements were utopian. Small nations had no independent future since economic developments would necessitate the creation of large States. These should be the appropriate battle grounds for class-conscious Socialists.[12]

For Luxemburg as for many Second International Socialists, national differences were in the final analysis, epiphenomenal. Her distinctiveness lay in carrying the practical implications of this position to its logical conclusion. One of the few pre-1914 Socialists who opposed the underlying position was Otto Bauer of the Austrian Social Democrats.[13]

His awareness of the importance of national differences within the
Habsburg Empire produced some revision of conventional views:

> they all had to learn in the old Austria rent by national struggles, how to apply
> the Marxist conception of history to very complicated phenomena which defied
> analysis by any superficial or schematic use of the Marxist method.[14]

The significant aspect of Bauer's policy on nationalism was that although
he did not initially support separate states for each nationality within
the Empire, he did advocate cultural autonomy. His position was supported by two significant claims. This national–cultural diversity would
not disappear once capitalism was abolished. Although Bauer argued in
orthodox terms that the end of class conflict would end disputes between
nations, it would not abolish national differences. Indeed, working-class
emancipation would enrich each national culture by making it more
representative of the whole population. The expectation required a
further claim. Nations had to be seen as entities in their own right which
were not reducible to class terms. Bauer presented nations as 'communities of fate'. Their members were likely to have similar qualities
produced by the demands of their environment. These traits would be
reflected in a distinctive culture which could change over time as the
relationship between members and environment altered. The analysis
saw national differences as the consequences of historical forces but
nevertheless as a feature that had to be considered in its own terms.

Bauer's work has significance as a rare attempt to analyse national
differences within a Marxist framework. It is a reminder that Second
International Socialism contained a rich variety of individual thinkers.
They were largely optimistic, for many their world collapsed in August
1914: often their reputations and their insights were buried beneath
comradely vituperations. Soon the Marxist orthodoxy on Socialism
and Nationalism became heavily influenced by Lenin.[15] He was acutely
aware of how far Russian Socialists might be insensitive to the demands of
other 'nations' within Greater Russia. Emphasis was placed on the democratic content of demands for self-determination and as a consequence,
their corrosive potential for other groups. In such terms Lenin would
defend the 1916 Easter Rising. Much of what he wrote on nationalism was
informed by the expectation that a widespread socialist revolution would
occur sooner rather than later. Subsequently his canonised arguments
were applied mechanically to very different situations.

The Marxist tradition has prided itself on its theoretical rigour and
ambition, yet in the historically critical area of the relationship between
nationalist and socialist politics, achievement has been both limited and
discordant. One gordian response might be that such uncertainties and
lacunae have minimal relevance for the politics of the British Left, where
debates have been influenced only marginally by major Marxist polemics.

Disputes over nationality and class have had relevance only in the tortuous political and cultural geography of Central and Eastern Europe.

This response would be historically simplistic. This analysis began with a claim about the significant contribution made to Labour Party politics and to historiographical images by a particular characterisation of British nationality. From some point in the 1920s, most Socialists within Britain were also British Socialists. They sought a political mobilisation on an all-British basis. Their objective was to capture the British State for Socialist purposes. The apotheosis of this strategy came in the years after 1945; its optimism rested on the assumption that the British State could be used for Socialist objectives. This belief fitted snugly alongside other features of British Labour politics: optimism about liberal institutions, faith in parliamentary practices, perhaps a dash of arrogance about the good fortune of the British living in a society where peaceful gradual transition was possible. Common values and memories could be employed for radical purposes, if only conservatives were removed from decisive positions. Orwell epitomised the limits of such radicalism and also demonstrated a typical uncertainty about the identity of the national community:

A family with the wrong members in control – that, perhaps, is as near as one can come to describing England in a phrase.[16]

Such a constrained criticism could license a political strategy that accepted an institutional framework whose impact was heavily conservative – although often discreetly so. Despite the disillusionments of the years after 1964, many still regarded Britain as peculiarly fitted for Socialist advance. The campaign against British membership of the European Economic Community often hinted that somehow it would be easier to move towards Socialism on supposedly congenial British terrain. Proposals for devolution and separation within Great Britain were dismissed patronisingly as evasions of problems that should be resolved on an all-British basis. The Communist Party continued to title its political programme: 'The British Road to Socialism'. Even the iconoclasm of Tony Benn on institutional issues has not been applied thoroughly to the question of the appropriate national community. He has written of the need for a programme that would liberate Britain from the grip of both national and international capitalism.[17]

Yet such near-unanimity had not always been the case. Until shortly after the First World War, there existed significant currents of Left-opinion in Scotland, to a lesser degree in Wales, but most crucially of course in Ireland, which advocated Home Rule, or in a few cases, national independence as a necessary or valuable contribution to the achievement of socialism. By the mid-twenties such arguments had ceased to register on what had become defined as the British Left. In much of Ireland, separatism, but emphatically not socialism, had triumphed; elsewhere Home Rule aspirations had lost out. Both the Labour Party and the Communists organised on an all-British basis.

The resulting orthodoxy survived on the left for more than four decades until neglected questions of national identity were pushed back onto the political agenda, at least in the non-English parts of the United Kingdom. But if links are made back to the years before this orthodoxy was established then the politics of the left in Britain appear as profoundly affected by the multinational character of the British State. Whilst it would be an excessive compensation to present the years from say 1922 to 1966 as a 'British' deviation from a more complex norm, it is important to grasp the richness of the earlier situation, and through this to appreciate the factors that generated the subsequent orthodoxy.

Within this complexity, Ireland played a vital role. Debate over a British response to Irish demands had restructured party politics in the 1880s, and had often dominated it during subsequent decades. Sometimes Irish issues and images had a powerful grip on the emotions of British Socialists and Radicals. This was certainly true on 13 November 1887 when a demonstration was held in Trafalgar Square, despite a police ban. The consequences were three deaths, hundreds of injuries and a *Times* leader applauding the police response.[18] The confrontation became a familiar item in the chronicles of the British Left, but the underlying issue could be obscured. This was not an economic grievance but opposition to the Salisbury Government's policy of coercion in Ireland, in particular the prison treatment of a Nationalist MP.

Irish Nationalism could not only precipitate a confrontation between the Left and the Metropolitan Police; it also left a significant imprint on Marx's political ideas. Initially his views seem to have been structured by the belief that a working-class triumph in developed Britain was a decisive requirement for change in agrarian Ireland. But in the late 1860s, in the context of Fenianism, a limited enfranchisement of urban working-class males and the failure of British Labour to develop independent political initiatives, Marx presented a sharply different diagnosis. He claimed that 'a preliminary condition' for an English proletarian revolution was the destruction of the English landed aristocracy. This project could be initiated more easily in Ireland, where the withdrawal of the English army and the police would produce a rapid agrarian revolution.

Marx's explanation emphasised a fusion of economic and national grievances:

in Ireland *the land question* has hitherto been the *exclusive form* of the social question, because it is a question of existence, of *life and death*, for the immense majority of the Irish people, and because it is at the same time inseparable from the *national* question.

The status of 'the nation' within Marx's argument remains obscure. This is precisely the kind of gap that Bauer later attempted to fill. At least it is clear that Marx accepted one stereotyped 'national' contrast. The Irish were 'more passionate and revolutionary in character than the English'.

Whatever the opacity within his explanation Marx was unequivocal about its practical significance. Irish landlordism was of considerable material benefit to the English aristocracy; it was also 'its greatest *moral* strength'. Thus, aristocratic defeat in Ireland would involve 'as a necessary consequence' its overthrow in England. There would be consequences also for the English bourgeoisie. The present situation was economically advantageous:

Ireland steadily supplies her own surplus to the English labour-market and thus forces down wages and lowers the moral and material condition of the English working class.

The implications for any hope of working-class political unity were discouraging. Antagonisms were fed by perceptions of economic rivalry, but also by English workers' sense of superiority:

In relation to the Irish worker he feels himself a member of the *ruling nation* and so turns himself into a tool of the aristocrats and capitalists of his country *against Ireland*, thus strengthening their domination *over himself*.

Marx saw this sentiment as nurtured by a variety of ideological techniques: 'the press, the pulpit, the comic papers'. He claimed that the consequence was far reaching:

This antagonism is the secret of the impotence of the English working class, despite its organisation.

A solution to the Irish national question would remove therefore a crucial obstacle to working-class revolution in England. The blockage had heightened significance given Marx's belief that the latter was:

for the present the most important country for the workers' revolution, and moreover the *only* country in which the material conditions for this revolution have developed up to a certain degree of maturity.[19]

The analysis made no claims about socialist prospects in Ireland. There was no suggestion of the kind made by Marx in the 1870s that a particular type of agrarian structure could lead, as for example in Russia, to a socialist breakthrough provided that equivalent advances occurred in more developed European societies.[20] Rather, Marx's point about Ireland was that an agrarian campaign combined with a nationalist agitation would have a decisive impact on the prospects for Socialism in Britain.

The problems with the analysis are obvious.[21] Marx implied a homogeneity about Irish economic experiences in the 1860s which ignored inconvenient facts. The rural social structure was complex; the possibilities for division already existed amongst the peasantry. Like many socialists who have commented on Ireland, Marx seemed oblivious to the development of Belfast as an industrial city, with a working-class divided by competing perceptions of nationality. Over-simplification about Ireland was complemented by excessively parsimonious arguments about British implications. Marx placed far too much weight on the economic importance of the Irish connection for the English aristocracy. Eventually it could be sacrificed without radical consequences. Fundamentally, any attempt to explain the quiescence of British workers through the Irish connection was to seek the illumination of a vast territory equipped with only a small torch. The roots of working-class reformism extended far beyond the factors emphasised by Marx. Working-class British nationalism and xenophobia could not be reduced simply to an anti-Irish sentiment which would be exorcised once the underlying causes were removed.

Marx's comments have significance despite their limitations. They were immediate responses to the specific circumstances of the late 1860s; a status ignored in their later fossilisation into a misleading orthodoxy. As such they demonstrate how a major political crisis for the nineteenth-century British State raised the question of national identity, and thus for a Socialist, precipitated problems over the relationship between national and class-based mobilisations. Even in 'advanced' Britain there seemed a possibility that a relatively 'backward' sector could play a decisive role in promoting significant changes in more 'developed' areas – and in that anticipated sequence, nationalist agitation would form a crucial link.

Such emphases on uneven development, cultural diversity and nationality form a contrast with the orthodoxy that dominated the British Left from the 1920s. The later perspective concentrated on action through the British State, for economic and social benefits. The earlier dispensation was much less tidy. Even for the conceptually-aware Marx, types of economic system, perceptions of nationality, even ascribed national characteristics jostle together as components of a would-be explanation. Prior to 1914, there was no widely accepted Socialist position on the relationship between nation, class and any Socialist project. Within this confusion the British Isles should not be seen as a remote group of offshore islands insulated from European doctrinal disputes by a Sea of Pragmatism. Rather these issues were central to the politics of the British Left. Once this is appreciated, then subsequent political developments become more complex and less inexorable than conventional renditions might suggest. What follows is not an alternative analysis; rather it is a counterpart to a well-established melody.

Perhaps these complexities can be approached through studies of three significant individuals. Their careers, their decisive choices, the constraints on their activities can illuminate a more general history. Each of them typically secures an honourable mention in the standard histories of the British Left. An emphasis on the connection between socialism and nationalism moves them towards the centre of the stage.[22] The intention is to provide not detailed biographies but critical analyses of three Socialists' ideas and political activities.

James Connolly was born in an Edinburgh slum in 1868; his parents were Irish. This family history suggests how the development of British capitalism induced mass movements of people that generated novel perceptions of class and of national identity. Connolly's childhood and youth were poverty-stricken. After military service, he returned to Scotland at the end of the 1880s and entered the Socialist movement. The remainder of his life was constructed around his commitment to Socialist propaganda. An irregular income came from unskilled jobs or from periods as a political or trade union organiser. Nearly always his political commitment had to be maintained against the pressures of family hardship. This necessity produced geographical mobility. Within the British Isles, Connolly's Socialism was a Tale of Three Cities: Edinburgh, Dublin and Belfast. His first sojourn in Dublin from 1896 until 1903 forced him to consider the relationship of a Socialist to Irish Nationalism. He responded by a commitment to Irish independence, but his prime concern was that of developing support for Socialism amongst the Irish working class. Poverty also led to a seven year sojourn in the United States – a period of vital significance for the development of his politics. It was there between 1903 and 1910 that he abandoned a Socialist sectarianism and accepted the basic tenets of Syndicalism.

In several respects Connolly typified the Socialism of the Second International. For most of his political life, he evinced a basic optimism about the growth of Socialist consciousness through the hard grind of economic experience and the inspiration of agitation and propaganda. But in 1914, this universe of expectations collapsed. He reacted neither with passive pessimism nor apologetic chauvinism, but with an attempt to link the prospects for Socialism to those for Physical Force – Irish Nationalism. Certainly this Nationalism was radical in method. Its advocates saw armed insurrection as the way forward out of a stagnation attributable in part to the decadent politicking of the Irish Parliamentary Party. Whether such a Nationalism could offer anything for Socialists was another matter.

John Maclean's family history was another reflection of the upheavals precipitated by the economic changes of the nineteenth century. This time the shift had been from the depopulated crofting society of the Western Highlands to industrial Central Scotland. Maclean was born in 1879. His childhood in Pollokshaws near Glasgow was hardly affluent but he did not suffer the same physical and educational deprivations as Connolly. Maclean's early life was a testimony to the relative openness of the educational system in late nineteenth-century Scotland. He trained as a teacher then registered as a part-time student at Glasgow University. As a Socialist propagandist his pamphlets and posters carried the heading, 'John Maclean MA'.

His cultural background contrasted with Connolly's Catholicism. Although his initial strict Calvinism was replaced firstly by secularism and then by socialism, his style retained the austere quality of his religious roots. Organisationally he gave his commitment to the Social Democrats; down to 1914 he shared Connolly's Socialist optimism. He had little interest in specifically Scottish projects. Socialist activities should be carried out on a British basis. Maclean reacted to the outbreak of war with a thorough Socialist internationalism. He was imprisoned twice. By 1919 two developments had fundamentally affected his politics. His enthusiasm for the Bolshevik Revolution was typical of the European Revolutionary Left; his interest in the Irish War of Independence was much more distinctive. He combined revolutionary zeal, a belief in the radical potential of separatist movements within the British Isles, and a deepening suspicion of the motives and effectiveness of those who sought the formation of a British Communist Party. All this was against the backdrop of a deteriorating prospect for working-class industrial organisation. In this predicament, he brought together arguments for revolution and for Scottish independence.

Connolly was shot by a British Army firing squad; Maclean died in acute poverty. Connolly was 47; Maclean, 44. The third figure, John Wheatley died a prosperous Glasgow businessman; his origins had been similar. He had lived through the abrupt shift from agrarian to industrial society. Born in County Waterford in 1869, his family migrated to the Lanarkshire coalfield; much of his childhood was spent in the harsh environment of a mining village. As an adolescent he went into the pits and worked there for twelve years. His eventual escape utilised channels available to the Irish community in the West of Scotland – the encouragement of a priest, evening education classes, the liquor trade, a grocery business, employment with the Catholic newspaper the *Glasgow Observer*, and eventually a printing and publishing firm. This business proved lucrative, not least because of its contracts for Catholic devotional literature.

Superficially, he became just a successful Glasgow Catholic businessman. Rotund and neat in appearance, he owned a sizeable detached house; his children entered higher education and at his death in 1930 his assets were considerable. The contrasts with Connolly's perennial financial insecurity and Maclean's descent from professional respectability to penury were acute. Although Wheatley's own economic success might have seduced him into accepting a benign characterisation of existing society, this did not happen. A political radicalisation accompanied his growing prosperity. This involved developments on the theme of nationality and socialism that were distinctive, and yet illuminated more general tendencies.

His involvement in Irish Nationalist politics gave way by 1906–7 to membership of the Independent Labour Party. He remained a practising Catholic; his political loyalty was given not to a Marxist organisation but to a party concerned more with community and less with class, expressing broad ethical sentiments rather than a studied doctrine.

He could appear as a respectable moderate Labour politician – County Councillor, City Councillor, returned as an MP in the 1922 Election, a Minister in the first Labour Government. But beneath these conventional successes, there were significant political shifts. The experience of the Wartime State and then of post-war austerity led him from municipal to national politics. The ex-Irish Nationalist saw the 'nation' as Britain. His search for influence within the British State – and his growing frustration with the supine character of MacDonald's Labour Party – led to his becoming a central figure in the Leftward shift of the ILP. In his view the Left's developing enthusiasm for State planning was incompatible with Free Trade. Effective political action to defend the British working-class meant facing the problem of Socialism in One Country. Frequently, from 1922, he was presented as the political partner of James Maxton. Wheatley's affluent respectability contrasted sharply with Maxton's austere revolutionary style. Both images were misleading. Although Wheatley was one of the most prestigious individuals in the ILP of the late twenties he was not a representative figure. He held distinctive positions on both strategy and policy. Sometimes these reflected his blend of Socialist and Nationalist priorities.

The similarities and the divergences between these three figures can hopefully illuminate the complex history of the British Left on the question of nationalism and socialism. Any insights will amend conventional historiographical images and in so doing carry relevance for contemporary arguments. Yet even a cursory examination demonstrates that any illumination cannot be restricted readily to a consideration of the nationalist theme. These individuals responded very differently to the strategic problems faced by Edwardian Socialists. Moreover, the politics of Connolly and Maclean provided sharp reminders that two of the few within the British Isles who have attempted to take Socialist precepts to a revolutionary conclusion and who suffered the costs of doing so, also supported separatist nationalisms. Considerations on socialism and nationalism seemed inseparable from the discussion of socialist strategy; a complex history threatened to become even more untidy.

And then in the Spring and Summer of 1984, there came the answer to the problem, in the shape of another image – or rather host of images. This time, it was not a tired political leader faced with electoral disaster, but thousands of miners on picket lines confronting the police, the Government, the etiquette of respectable society, the arithmetic of the Coal Board, the calumnies of the media, and the cool distancing of some who proclaimed themselves as Socialists. Here was a confrontation expressed in terms of community and class to set against the populist Nationalism of the South Atlantic War.

A little thought showed that this was nothing new. The Cambrian Combine dispute of 1910–11 symbolised by the Tonypandy riot had highlighted aspects of Welsh industrial society that respectable Welsh bourgeois Liberals preferred not to notice.[23] The disorders that marked the Dublin Lock Out of 1913 disturbed the thoughts of some Irish Nationalists who believed Home Rule to be imminent. In each case a self-congratulatory and politically significant celebration of national virtues was rudely interrupted as some who were meant to have walk-on parts or to be part of the admiring audience not only invaded the show, but began to suggest a new script. So it was in the 1980s. The Battle of Orgreave provided a discordant counterpoint to the harmonies of a British – or English – identity, blind to deprivation, buttressed by militarism and employed for political advantage – one more significant strand in the unravelling of this complex web.

Part I

James Connolly

The red and the green

Railway stations in the capital cities of Western Europe are not usually named after left-wing socialists. Passengers from London to Manchester do not depart from the Engels station, nor is it likely that their counterparts from London to Sheffield will ever depart from Scargill station. Yet in Dublin, the capital of a State with a weak Socialist movement, passengers for Belfast must go to the Connolly station. This terminus is named after a Marxian Socialist and Syndicalist, the accomplice of Larkin in the 1913 Lock Out that had alarmed respectable Dublin opinion.

The name of a railway station offers an insight into the difficulties in analysing Connolly's career. He is commemorated there not as a Socialist, but as a leading actor in the Easter Rising, the initiative which forms such a fundamental element in the ideology of the modern Irish State. Any approach to his politics requires a journey through a quagmire of claims and counter-claims. Their content has reflected the political achievements that followed 1916, but also a Socialist insistence that this institutional revolution was not accompanied by any economic and social radicalism. The political divisions of the Free State, and then the Republic have borne the imprint of the unfinished political business of 1921. Inevitably, the durability of Partition, and more recently the re-emergence of violent conflict in the Six Counties have influenced assessments of Connolly.

Official eulogies have often ignored or played down his Socialism. In response those Socialists who characterise the Easter Rising as a progressive initiative suggest that Connolly provided an effective synthesis of nationalist and socialist precepts.[1] Sometimes, it is claimed that his writings offer unambiguous and relevant guidance for contemporary Irish Socialists. This commendation may be fuelled by a concern with the Social Revolution That Never Happened; that it is possible to go back to Connolly's ideas and then apply them to the politics of the Republic. Such anachronism is over-shadowed however by the suggestion that he also offers guidance to the politics of the Six Counties. His supposed blending of National and working-class claims is then applied as a general precept without asking those awkward questions: 'which nation, which working class?'.[2]

Such hagiographies have inevitably provoked anti-heroic responses.

Sean O'Casey offered an early polemical portrait of Connolly abandoning Socialism for what proved to be a conservative Nationalism.[3] More recently, some Irish writers influenced by working-class divisions in the Six Counties, have taken a hostile view of Socialists who see traditional Republicanism as progressive. The traditional celebrations of Connolly are indicted for their contribution to such an identification. This revolution is significant in that it offers not an idealised Nationalist – Socialist, but a substantive historical figure who faced difficult decisions and inevitably made many mistakes. At least such analyses present Connolly's political choices in terms that permit reasoned historical discussion.[4]

Such will be the style of this analysis. Connolly's writings and actions will be located in their varied contexts. His judgements will be subjected to the demanding interrogation posed by available evidence. The answers may be debatable, but at least they will be responses to significant historical and political problems. He was too important to be left to the myth-makers.

Chapter 1

Edinburgh

The class structure of the city in which Connolly served his Socialist apprenticeship bore the imprint of Edinburgh's status as the Scottish capital.[1] Its professional middle class was unusually large; its industrial base was relatively limited.[2] This environment left its mark on one of his first pieces of journalism:

The population of Edinburgh is largely composed of snobs, flunkeys, mashers, lawyers, students, middle-class pensioners and dividend hunters. Even the working-class portion of the population seemed to have imbibed the snobbish would-be respectable spirit of their 'betters', and look with aversion upon every movement running counter to conventional ideas.

Yet Connolly was optimistic about the prospects for Socialism in Edinburgh. It:

is now recognised as an important factor in the life of the community, a disturbing element which must be taken into account in all the calculations of the political caucuses.[3]

This was an exaggeration, but it pointed to a significant development in the politics of the Edinburgh Left. Despite the relative importance of traditional consumer crafts within the local economy, Edinburgh trade unionism faced similar pressures to those found in other urban centres. Artisans found their positions threatened by technical changes and by managements' desire to strengthen their authority in the workplace. Organisation of the semi-skilled and unskilled had made a significant advance in the late 1880s amongst many sectors including the Leith waterfront. As elsewhere, 'New Unionist' gains were eroded as local firms gained important victories and the Leith dockers were hit by the aggressive anti-unionism of the Shipping Federation. Increasingly, Edinburgh disputes either reflected or were part of wider conflicts. This widening of perspectives was emphasised in the Winter of 1890–1, when the Trades Council intervened in the unsuccessful Scottish railway strike.[4]

This process meant that some of the divisions between craft workers and the semi- or unskilled began to decline. The conception of a broadly based labour movement began to make more sense, at least as an ideal. The political allegiances of trade unionists and of the Trades Council also began to shift. Trades Council commitment to the Legal Eight Hour Day became firmer and in 1893 the Council held a joint May Day demonstration with the Socialists. There were still tensions. Co-operation in municipal elections often remained a frustrated hope. Socialists could still take a dim view of the value of industrial action but essentially the Edinburgh labour movement of the 1890s followed a similar path to its counterparts elsewhere.

Local Socialism was organisationally complex. There had been a Socialist presence since the early days of the Social Democratic Federation. The branch had quickly adopted the title, Scottish Land and Labour League, reflecting thereby a dominant preoccupation of Scottish Radicals. Under the guidance of the Austrian, Andreas Scheu, many from the branch had joined the Socialist League and this organisation maintained a relatively strong presence for the next four years. Eventually moves towards re-unification produced the formation of a Scottish Socialist Federation in September 1889. Although this was intended as a broad Scottish initiative, it was effective only in Edinburgh, and with the demise of the Socialist League, the SSF became essentially a branch of the SDF.[5] This body was the focus for much of Connolly's political work – outdoor propaganda meetings, studying the few Marx texts available in English, and eventually in 1894–5 contesting local elections. This educational experience was likely to incorporate a strongly deterministic emphasis into any prognostication about the future of capitalism. This strand can certainly be found in many of Connolly's writings. Yet the strength of the Socialist League connection could generate a less reductionist emphasis; arguably the strongly normative element in some of Connolly's later work owes something to this influence.[6]

The Scottish Socialist Federation did not stand alone on the Edinburgh Left. The Scottish Labour Party had a presence in the city, and after initial problems managed to work in relative harmony with the Trades Council. Thus in July 1892, a broad alliance of trade unionists, socialists and temperance enthusiasts supported the parliamentary candidacy of the Broxburn Miners' Agent, John Wilson, in Edinburgh Central. The following summer, the SLP's Edinburgh Central branch took the title of 'Independent Labour Party', with James Connolly serving for some months as Secretary.[7]

Such developments and organisations – a Trades Council moving away from Liberalism as a result of industrial experiences, an explicitly Socialist body, a less clear-cut Labour group – highlight general themes of the 1890s. Despite the distinctive character of Scottish politics leaving its mark in the title, Scottish Land and Labour League, and in the formation of the Scottish Labour Party, this was an essentially British Movement. What was noticeable about Edinburgh, and distinguished it from many, although not all centres of Socialist development, was its ecumenism. Connolly imbibed Marxism within the SSF and organised within both the Federation and the ILP. He was already emphasising the centrality of a Marxist understanding, but equally, he was committed to the search for a broadly-based mobilisation for immediate objectives.

Despite his underlying optimism about the prospects for Socialism, Connolly soon felt the frustration of propagandising amongst an unreceptive working class. Although he claimed some progress in fashionable Edinburgh, he saw little ground for satisfaction in proletarian Leith. Conventional Socialist expectations seemed to be unfulfilled and Connolly fell back on the characteristic explanation of the chastened Social Democrat:

Whatever be the reason whether it be for lack of backbone, or for want of knowledge, or through sheer unadulterated cowardice, it is hard to say.

But attempts at Socialist propaganda seemed to have achieved little:

there are only a few Socialists in Leith, in spite of all the educational work performed at our open-air meetings during the summer months.[8]

All he could offer was a renewed exercise in propaganda – this time with more determination and hopefully more success. It was the perennial response of the Socialist evangelist to the problem of securing and maintaining support.

Orthodox Social Democrats had another strategy for expanding their influence; they could contest elections. Inevitably Connolly with his commitment and his organisational zeal became involved in electoral politics. During the spring and summer of 1894, he was involved in ultimately abortive negotiations for an ILP candidate for Central Edinburgh and a few months later in November, he stood as a 'Socialist' municipal candidate in the St Giles Ward. The contest was four-cornered with an Independent, as well as a Tory and a Liberal. Connolly argued for the displacement of confusing side-issues: Liberal and Independent with their claims to represent the working class should withdraw and:

leave the ground clear for the real battle of the Election betwixt the representative of rankest Toryism and the representative of militant Social Democracy.[9]

In fact, the Liberal was victorious, and with this knowledge, Connolly argued an amended version of the same thesis, that the basic battle lay between Social Democracy and the Liberal as the stronger capitalist party.[10] Yet, as he acknowledged, the Liberals retained a deceptively progressive image, and in a complex contest, electors could be persuaded to vote Liberal to keep the Tory out:

hundreds of men who would otherwise have voted Socialist, cast their votes reluctantly for Mr Mitchell as the candidate most likely to ensure the defeat of the Tory.[11]

The wasted vote argument was a perennial problem for Socialists. Their response tended to assume that there existed a group of naturally Socialist voters who could be persuaded by an unambiguous policy. Some of the emphases in this first campaign of Connolly were to be constants in his strategic thinking – the desire to have a clean-cut issue as between Socialist and capitalist politicians; the claim that Liberal progressive blandishments were illusory with the implication that Socialists must keep well clear of Liberal overtures. Conventional politics were a damaging distraction for the working class:

I know several working men who will not be able to rest in their beds at night until the Town Council decides who is to be Lord Provost. It is a most momentous question no doubt. And yet it seems to me that we will still be rack-rented and sweated, over-worked and under-paid, insulted and bullied, humiliated and despised, ground beneath the heel of landlord and capitalist, foreman and manager, whether the honours go round or remain in the hands of the Liberal ring.[12]

It was an argument that Connolly would apply to all manner of politicians – most persistently of course to the Irish National Party.

His judgement of the significance of Socialist electioneering was as yet firmly within the conventional Social Democratic wisdom. During his campaign he emphasised immediate questions such as housing and the inclusion of fair wages' clauses in council contracts,[13] but he viewed the short-term significance of any Socialist election success as propagandist:

The election of a Socialist to any public body at present, is only valuable in so far as it is the return of a disturber of the political peace.[14]

Until a Socialist majority was a realistic hope, the task must be to cast a searching light on Tory and Liberal activities. For Connolly this was not simply a question of muck-raking: the disturbance of the peace would involve the propagating of an alternative set of priorities that could generate a mass Socialist following:

by constantly placing our doctrines and our efforts upon the same platform as the class interests of the workers, to create such a public feeling in our favour as shall enable us to bridge the gulf between the old order and the new, and lead the people from the dark Egypt of our industrial anarchy into the Promised Land of industrial freedom.[15]

Connolly's vote in November was respectable – 263 – and he looked forward with optimism to the Spring 1895 inaugural elections for the Poor Law authorities:

The workers will then have an opportunity of humanising this iniquitous system by placing upon every Parish Council, a sufficient number of Social Democrats to counteract the despotic tendencies of our Liberal and Tory taskmasters.[16]

This time however his vote was much lower – 169. The frustrations of Socialists seeking to expand support beyond the committed few were all too apparent. Propaganda plus elections as a strategy made far-reaching assumptions about workers' receptivity to Socialist argument. These were backed by claims about the radicalising impact of expected economic changes. Despite disappointments, Connolly adhered to this strategy and it was as a conventional Social Democrat that he left Edinburgh for Dublin in May 1896.

As yet, he was far from developing a cogent position linking his Socialism, to his Irish identity. But, inevitably, the fact of that identity plus the attempts by Edinburgh Socialists to establish links with Irish workers left an important and early legacy for his politics. It was not just an Irish working-class Socialist who would be bemused by the role of the Irish in British politics in the 1880s and 1890s. To many Socialists, Irish agrarian agitations and parliamentary strategies seemed the prime radical hope. Here was a mass movement that had confronted the British State, a parliamentary group that had pressurised the Liberal Party into adopting Home Rule and in so doing had effectively remoulded British politics. The exemplars for radical agitation and electoral and parliamentary organisation were attractive. Yet there was another side. The Irish in Britain were overwhelmingly working class. They seemed natural recruits for a Socialist organisation, but attached as they were to the Irish National League; involved in distinctive religious and cultural bodies, they could appear as a divisive sectarian grouping. When INL pressure was in favour of a Liberal vote, then recriminations between Irish leaders and Socialists could become bitter.[17]

In Edinburgh, as elsewhere in Scotland, an effective alliance between Irish and Scottish workers could be undermined by divisions of ethnicity, religion and skill. When the President of the Edinburgh Trades Council, the Carpenter, A.C. Telfer, was asked during evidence to the Royal Commission on Housing in Scotland, about the attitude of slum dwellers to their living conditions, his reply was revealing:

Properly speaking it is generally the Irish element, labourers and what not, who live in that locality, and I must confess that I do not come into communication with them as a rule, so as to feel as it were the touch of their inner feelings in that respect.[18]

In the industrial circumstances of the 1890s, many of the Edinburgh trade unionists who shifted into the Socialist movement were skilled workers. Connolly, as a carter, was perhaps exceptional;[19] Connolly as an Irish-Catholic carter most certainly was. The gap between Edinburgh Socialists and the local Irish working class should not be attributed simply to the politics of the latter's organisations.

During his Edinburgh years, Connolly's references to the Irish dimension are scattered through his journalism and correspondence. His principal emphasis was on the relationship between the Irish vote in Britain, and Socialist and Labour organisations, but consideration of this led to some suggestions about Labour politics in Ireland. As yet, he did not develop any cogent arguments about Socialist attitudes to the National Question as such. Nevertheless one of his Edinburgh comrades, John Leslie had given some thought to this issue during the Winter of 1893–4, and the results of Leslie's work provide a useful context for the analysis of Connolly's early ideas.

As a former member of the Irish National League and a leading figure in the Scottish Socialist Federation, Leslie had possibly been led to consider the problem on account of Irish organisational opposition to Edinburgh's first Labour municipal candidate in November 1893. He subsequently lectured to the SSF on the National Question, wrote a series of articles for *Justice* under the title 'Passing Thoughts on the Irish Question', and then published them as a pamphlet, *The Present Position of the Irish Question*.[20]

This was, in several respects, an occasional piece. It bore the stamp of its immediate origins – the defeat of the Second Home Rule Bill in the Lords, and the electoral tensions between Irish and Socialist organisations. Nevertheless it offered an insight into the discussion of some Edinburgh Socialists, and some themes emerged that found echoes in Connolly's subsequent writings. One was the view stated sharply at the start that political independence is insufficient. In a phrase, close to one employed later by Connolly, Leslie denied that:

the Alpha and the Omega of the Irish Question consists in the hoisting of the green and gold banner above the old Parliament House in Dublin.[21]

Instead, the root of Ireland's problem was located in the institution of private property:

Let there be no mistake about it, the cause of Irish misery is not to be found in the incorporation of the Irish Parliament in that of England, (although such incorporation undoubtedly tends to aggravate the evil), but it is to be found in the fact that the means by which the Irish people must live are in possession of a class, which class will not allow the people to use these means unless by so doing a profit will accrue to this class.[22]

Here was a theme that would secure much more elaboration in Connolly's writings, culminating in his *Labour in Irish History*. It would be supported by some of Leslie's emphases. Thus the latter viewed critically the 'revolutionaries' of 1848 with the exception of James Fintan Lalor. The Fenians as a spontaneous democratic movement were regarded more favourably,[23] but the paradigm of Irish democratic organisation was presented as the Land League:

the new doctrine ... obliterated all narrow sectarianism, and it forms an instructive object lesson for the Socialist inculcating the necessity of unceasing watchfulness for the opportune moment ...[24]

It was an initiative seen as destroyed by the Kilmainham Treaty which replaced the land agitation by the single plank of Home Rule.[25] Despite this, Leslie's – and later Connolly's – view of Parnell was positive, a leader who was committed to the Nationalist viewpoint and who developed an effective political organisation.[26] The legacy of the Parnellite split was viewed as a chance for Irish Labour to seize the initiative. The advent of the Irish Trades Union Congress led Leslie to take an optimistic view of the prospects for an Irish Labour Party:

Is it not time the Irish working class asked themselves the question for whose benefit it has all been? They have fought the fight, while others have gathered the fruits of such victory as there may have been. The recent Irish Trades Unions Congress declared in favour of the necessity for a working-class party in Ireland. There is shortly to be held an Irish *Labour* Congress ... Is one too sanguine in expecting that this Congress will mark the point of a new departure, and that the banner of a new Land and Labour League in which the green – and for that matter the orange – will shade off and merge into the red, will be displayed ...?[27]

The claim that Labour was the proper champion of the national cause would be a central element in Connolly's position and would be backed by continuing optimism about the development of a non-sectarian working-class party. In such a perspective, the proper ally for Irish Labour was its British equivalent; the internationalism of the Socialist movement would not detract from the identity of Irish Labour.

During his Edinburgh years Connolly approached the complexities of this question through specific strategic problems. When he became involved in correspondence with Keir Hardie on the possibility of a parliamentary candidate for Edinburgh Central, his mind naturally turned to the possibility of Irish support. Initially he hoped that Socialists could benefit from the Nationalist split and that the Parnellites would be sympathetic. He suggested that Hardie discuss the question with John Redmond.[28] But disappointment led quickly to a more hostile view of both Irish parliamentary groups – their radicalism was an accident.

Both of them are essentially middle-class parties interested in the progress of Ireland from a middle-class point of view. Their advanced attitude upon the land question is simply an accident arising out of the exigencies of the political situation and would be dropped tomorrow, if they did not realise the necessity of linking the Home Rule agitation to some cause more clearly allied to their daily wants than a mere embodiment of national sentiment of the people.

Already Connolly was suggesting a strategy for British Labour which would by-pass the Irish MPs and their local organisations. Instead,

Leslie's analysis should be applied and a link should be struck with the Irish Labour Movement. Optimistically Connolly suggested:

There is a nucleus of a strong Labour movement in Ireland, which only needs judicious handling to flutter the doves in the Home Rule dovecote.

As will become clear, such a prognostication exaggerated both Irish Labour's strength and its willingness or ability to criticise the Parliamentary factions. Connolly's proposal was that Hardie should visit Dublin to speak under labour auspices:

putting it in strong and straight, without reference to either (of) the two Irish parties; but rebellious anti-monarchical and outspoken on the fleecings of both landlord and capitalist, and the hypocrisy of both political parties for a finale.[29]

This proposal should be placed in context. Connolly's knowledge of Irish politics in 1894 was limited; his object at that point was to pressurise the Parnellites to support Labour candidates in Britain, despite their private inclinations. Yet already against the background of Leslie's writings there were the beginnings of Connolly's position on the relationship between the British and Irish Labour movements. Most centrally there was the implication that it was *this* relationship that should matter to Socialists. Workers and Socialists from each society should ally with one another, and not with the bourgeois politicians.

Connolly experienced the complexities of the relationship for himself during his municipal election contests in a ward with a sizable Irish population. The local branch of the Irish National League denounced his candidacy in the customary terms as serving Unionist interests. In fact, it seems likely that he secured a significant part of the Irish vote. Nevertheless the lesson seemed clear. Irish working class voters could be blinded to the facts of capitalist exploitation by the manipulative use of a national appeal. Liberal Government was still capitalist government; ethnic tensions could divide the working class:

Perhaps they will learn how foolish it is to denounce tyranny in Ireland, and then vote for tyrants and the instruments of tyrants at their own door. Perhaps they will begin to see that the landlord who grinds his peasants on a Connemara estate and the landlord who rack-rents them in a Cowgate slum, are brethren in fact and deed. Perhaps they will realise that the Irish worker who starves in an Irish cabin and the Scotch worker who is poisoned in an Edinburgh garrett are also brothers with one hope and one destiny. Perhaps they will observe how the same Liberal Government which supplies police to Irish landlords to aid them in their work of exterminating the Irish peasantry also imports police into Scotland to aid Scottish mineowners in their work of starving the Scottish miners.[30]

But in terms of Scottish politics, the change would be slow. Connolly experienced a speedy reminder of the difficulties involved in his 1895 Parish Council contest. He experienced the hostile pressure of the Irish organisation; his reduced vote could be ascribed in part to the candidacy of a Catholic priest.

When poverty forced Connolly to leave Edinburgh for Dublin in the Spring of 1896, he went in Socialist terms as an orthodox Social Democrat. Cogent claims about his position on the National Question are more elusive. Leslie's ideas had clearly been significant, as had his own conflicts with the Edinburgh Irish caucus. Inevitably, conscious of being an Irishman in Scotland, he had not yet made an overt commitment to nationalism. The Dublin years would see not just the elaboration and publicising of such a commitment, but the linking of this with the Social Democratic framework that was the legacy of his Edinburgh apprenticeship. It would be a vital period in the development of his thought.

Chapter 2

Dublin

Connolly arrived in Dublin to find himself amongst a working-class whose condition was noticeably worse than that of its counterpart in British urban centres. Although Dublin workers included a minority in craft-based occupations, they were primarily semi- and unskilled, often casually employed, poorly paid and living in horrendous conditions. Glasgow's housing was regarded in British terms as poor; in 1903, the proportion of Glaswegian families living in a single room was 24%. The comparable figure for Dublin was 36.6%. By any yardstick – income, housing standards, death rates per thousand – the predicament of the Dublin working-class was appalling.[1]

The organised labour movement made but a slight impact on this ocean of deprivation. Unlike Edinburgh, the leaven of New Unionism had had minimal significance. Craft unions had undergone little radicalisation, since in Dublin with its relatively stagnant economy, the traditional position of their members had come under relatively little pressure. Cautious craft unionists continued to dominate the Dublin Trades Council until well after 1900. The formation of the Irish Trades Union Congress in 1894, welcomed by John Leslie as the harbinger of a vigorous Irish labour movement tended in the early years to strengthen these cautious sectional sentiments. Thus, the new body was dominated initially by skilled localised groups, increasingly insulated from relatively progressive developments within British trade unionism.[2]

In time, this conservatism and limited influence would change, but in the late 1890s the meagre radicalism of the Dublin labour movement was reflected not just in the passivity of the ITUC but also in the lack of socialist organisations. The Edinburgh activists might have met frustrations in some of their dealings with the Trades Council, they might have seen the blunting of initially optimistic electoral ambitions, but they could look back on some successes. Edinburgh Socialists achieved some wider support in municipal elections, and more crucially they secured the backing of several trade union activists. An early attempt to develop an ILP presence in Dublin had languished; a faithful few had kept afloat the Dublin Socialist Club. Then Connolly arrived.[3]

The Dublin Socialist Club became the Irish Socialist Republican Party. In a real sense throughout its seven year life, the ISRP remained Connolly's party – in William O'Brien's recollection he 'was of course the presiding genius of the whole business'.[4] This was despite the party's formal claim that it rejected the cult of the leader in order to introduce members to the democratic practices of a socialist society.[5] Under Connolly's guidance, the organisation followed the same political strategy as the Edinburgh Socialist movement, open air propaganda meetings, backed up from August 1898 by a newspaper – *The Workers' Republic* – and a few election contests.[6] Throughout its life, the ISRP remained small. O'Brien retrospectively assessed the average weekly turnout at meetings as twelve to fifteen, the number of enrolled members as around fifty and the number of activists as about half this figure.[7] The party remained essentially a Dublin organisation. Attempts to develop branches elsewhere failed, in part due to local problems but also due to the absence of any overall structure. The apparent lack of progress could erode the enthusiasm of members. As the Party minute book noted for 12 February 1900:

The usual public meeting was held on Sunday 10th ... There was an improvement in the number of outsiders present, but no improvement in the attendance of members.[8]

The state of the Dublin labour movement was part of the problem. Trade union organisation was both limited and cautious and could not be utilised easily by Socialists, but beyond this both Socialist and Labour groups faced the problem posed by the National Question's dominance of Irish politics.

Connolly's early response can be found in the programme of the ISRP. He had arrived in Dublin essentially as a Social Democrat, obviously with an awareness of his Irish identity, but with no history of involvement in Nationalist politics; indeed his Edinburgh experiences had afforded abundant scope for strictures on the conservative and manipulative practices of the Nationalist caucus. Yet when an ISRP programme emerged it reflected conventional Social Democratic emphases in all significant aspects but one.[9] The SDF positon of 'legislative independence for all parts of the Empire' was replaced by complete separation from Britain, and a commitment to an Irish Socialist Republic.[10] Such an emphasis could be seen as Connolly's response to the problems facing a Socialist propagandist in Ireland, but it would become a principled commitment.

The quest for an effective combination of Socialist and Nationalist sentiments faced serious difficulties. Most obviously, the vast majority of Irish electors outside the North East continued to give their support to the Parliamentary Party, despite the divisions that followed Parnell's fall.[11] There seemed little scope for a credible challenge by Irish Labour at the parliamentary level, given the weakness of the industrial working class and the prior occupation of much of the available political space.

But in municipal politics following the democratisation of Irish local government in 1898, the outlook seemed more promising. Perhaps Nationalist organisation could not utilise the same loyalties when the prize was a seat on the local council rather than representation of the claims of a nation. Socialist and Labour politicians entered early municipal contests with optimism. Yet they soon found that national and religious sentiments could be utilised with powerful effect against labour and Socialist municipal campaigns backed by limited trade union machinery and even weaker party organisation.

If Dublin's small group of Socialists had to come to terms with the still potent organisational and rhetorical legacies of Parnell's party, there were other innovations in the Nationalist movement in the 1890s that provided both further obstacles and some opportunities. The complex developments that produced the Gaelic Athletic Association, the Gaelic Literary Revival, and the politics of Sinn Fein, at a time when the Parliamentary Party seemed impotent, and agrarian radicalism tamed, are viewed typically through their eventual political implications. But it is too simple to contrast the problems facing the Parliamentary Party in the 1890s, with these vivid developments, and thus to paint a signpost towards the collapse of old-style Home Rule nationalism. This sequence has a misleading coherence. At the time of Connolly's first political sojourn in Dublin, the new movements could not agree on a conception of Irish nationality. That the dominant one would be that of 'Irish Ireland' still lay in the future. This tangled web was nevertheless an alternative to that of the Dublin Socialists. Younger men and women disillusioned with the wranglings and sterility of the Parliamentary Party had an alternative – culturally stimulating, perhaps politically radical, most certainly national.[12] Elsewhere, Socialism often flourished in the 1890s as an alternative to discredited older organisations, but compared with a Gaelic alternative it could seem less attractive and less relevant.

Yet if Irish Socialists were handicapped by the fact that the battle between radicals and conservatives was confined largely to the Nationalist household, nevertheless the fact that radical Nationalists made converts amongst the young could have benefits for Socialists. At least the hegemony of the older conservative elements was threatened. Socialists could combine with the more radical Nationalists on campaigns where Socialist and Nationalist precepts pointed in the same direction. Some Nationalists might be led to accept the validity of some Socialist arguments, perhaps as a result of collaboration, perhaps also as a consequence of a fear that labour organisation could divide the Nationalist movement. The Nationalist journal *Shan Van Vocht* was concerned in October 1896 that:

A great proportion of the intelligent and thinking element among the artisan population is liable to drift away from sharing in the National movement proper and become absorbed in the labour party.[13]

The journal responded by taking a sympathetic view of Socialist positions on economic and social policy and gave Connolly space to expound his views. In the short run, the fear was unfounded, but in a longer perspective the complex relationship between Socialists and radical Nationalists afforded abundant scope for both tensions and points of growth. If the focus is to be limited firmly to Connolly's ISRP period however, the most basic feature is the marginality of his political organisation. Assessment of his writings must begin with that perception.

Connolly's views during his Dublin years show a decisive development from his Edinburgh period. From one perspective, his analysis can be characterised as an attempt to apply the conventional Social Democratic outlook that he had brought with him to his perception of the distinctively Irish situation. From another, these years were crucial for the development of propositions that remained relevant to Connolly's position until 1916. Much would shift, priorities would change but some claims formulated during these years remained. Yet again his position can be viewed as the remarkable achievement of a self-educated worker, adding lengthy studies in Ireland's National Library to the apprenticeship in Scottish Socialism. Most fundamentally, from 1896 onwards, distinctive Irish concerns were at the centre of his Socialist activities.

The complex significance of these preoccupations for his hitherto orthodox Social Democratic view on political change can be traced by analysing an important section of his pamphlet *Erin's Hope: The End and the Means*.[14] Characteristically, Connolly began his analysis with an immediate political problem; he argued that the conventional way of presenting the Anglo–Irish argument as centred on forms of government, was superficial, indeed erroneous. It followed that any belief in the adequacy of Home Rule as an adequate solution was fallacious. Instead the underlying conflict originated in divergent conceptions of property in land – a claim that was linked to recent anthropological work. This argument carried sharp implications for influential images of 'progress'. Connolly presented the economic liberal, 'the adherent of the present order of society'. This protagonist would view the Irish tradition of communal ownership:

as proof of the Irish incapacity for assimilating progressive ideas ... this incapacity is the real source of Ireland's misery since it has unfitted her sons for the competitive scramble for existence, and so foredoomed them to the lot of hewers of wood and drawers of water.

But then, Connolly considered a second stereotype, the belief that:

the progress of the human race through the various economic stages of communism, chattel slavery, feudalism, and wage slavery, has been but a preparation for the higher ordered society of the future.

Within such a perspective there was a temptation to view:

the Irish adherence to clan ownership at such a comparatively recent date as the Seventeenth Century as evidence of retarded economical development, and therefore a real hindrance to progress.

But Connolly proclaimed an alternative, carrying radical implications for any deterministic view of social development:

the possibility of a people by political intuition anticipating the lessons afterwards revealed to them in the sad school of experience ...

This provided scope for a Nationalist–Socialist alliance. The latter could:

join with the Irish patriot in his lavish expressions of admiration for the sagacity of his Celtic forefathers who foreshadowed in the democratic organisation of the Irish clan the more perfect organisation of the free society of the future.[15]

Already in Connolly's writings, there was a theme – Celtic Communism – which would be central to *Labour in Irish History* and which would find Scottish echoes in the collaboration between John Maclean and Erskine of Mar. Historically, it had its problems: 'the democratic organisation' of the Irish clan did not include the slaves. The more fundamental difficulty concerns the status of the argument. The writings of Marx and Engels from the mid 1870s had suggested the possibility of a potential for communist development, within the threatened – but still existing – Russian peasant communes, and its survival dependent on support from working-class revolutions in Western Europe.[16] The Irish case involved no institutional inheritance – only a historical memory with a substantial accretion of myth. Connolly subsequently acknowledged the brittle quality of the legacy:

The clans are now no more and could not be revived, even if it were desirable to do so, which is more than questionable, but the right of ownership still lives on, and should now be established in the modern Corporate embodiment of the life of the Irish nation – our public boards, municipality and independent Irish Congress when we are men enough to win one.[17]

Despite the restriction of the communal inheritance to the realm of ideas and the unanalysed but highly problematic concept of 'the Irish nation' this argument did provide the suggestion that national and socialist emancipation in Ireland must advance together. There was a hint that paralleled Marx's explicit claims on Russian prospects. The path to socialism need not be the same everywhere; the histories and the contemporary situations of societies make a difference.

This was an important and tantalising claim with radical implications for the coherence of a conventional Marxist image of political change. Already equipped with such an orthodox position from his Edinburgh years, Connolly in the late 1890s ignored the potential for disparity. He frequently argued the epochal case that he criticised in *Erin's Hope*. Socialism was:

the legitimate child of a long drawn-out historical evolution ... its consummation will only be finally possible when that evolutionary process has attained to a suitable degree of development ... (ie) ... when the development of capitalism in its turn renders the burden of a capitalist class unbearable and the capitalist system unworkable.[18]

This reasoning could lead him to take a strongly reductionist view of political institutions. They could be presented as 'but the reflex of the economic forms which underlie them'.[19] Decisions by governments had to be viewed as the products of underlying economic forces:

The Cabinets who rule the destinies of nations from the various capitals of Europe are but the tools of the moneyed interest.[20]

This judgement did not exclude the claim that political forms mattered. Connolly declared that 'Socialists cannot be indifferent to monarchy'.[21] The achievement of a republican system even under capitalism would remove one significant obstacle.

These starting points, albeit with their potential tensions, provided Connolly with a basis for deflating the pretensions of middle class Nationalist politicians. They supported capitalism and thereby denied the merits of traditional Irish social organisation. Their support for the existing economic order was also anti-national. They had:

so far compounded with the enemy, as to accept the alien social system, with its accompanying manifestations, the legal dispossession and economic dependence of the vast mass of the Irish people, as part of the natural order of society.

Accordingly, they achieved a political reputation based on an illusory prospectus:

Their political influence they derived from their readiness at all times to do lip service to the cause of Irish nationality, which in their phraseology meant simply the transfer of the seat of government from London to Dublin ...[22]

This diagnosis was reflected and extended in an emphasis similar to that presented three years earlier by John Leslie:

If you remove the English army tomorrow, and hoist the green flag over Dublin Castle, unless you set about the organisation of the Socialist Republic, your efforts would be in vain.

England would still rule you. She would rule you through her capitalists, through her landlords, through her financiers ...[23]

This narrowness of vision had led Irish politicians into a succession of disasters. The 'Young Ireland' movement of the 1840s had failed because it attempted to mobilise support simply on the principle of nationality. This could never be sufficient. It brought together people of divergent economic views;[24] the idea of a 'United Nation' was an illusion in a capitalist society.[25] The Home Rule policy continued to link the well-being of Ireland with the fate of the British Empire. As such most Irish people would gain nothing: only capitalists and officials benefiting from the shift of administrative functions to Dublin would be advantaged. Home Rule was characterised by Connolly as against national independence, but in favour of capitalism and of imperialism. Only the myopic conservatism of many British politicians could lend it credibility as a radical strategy.[26]

Connolly's dismissive attitude towards Home Rule politicians was not extended to more radical Nationalists. He contributed to the journal, *Shan Van Vocht* – he collaborated with Republicans such as Maud Gonne[27] in the anti-Jubilee demonstrations of June 1897 and was arrested. Attempts to give a radical content to the Wolfe Tone centenary celebrations failed however when parliamentarians came to dominate the preparations, and Connolly's group withdrew.[28] Reflecting on these experiences, Connolly could see a distinction between Home Rulers who accepted the monarchy and the British connection, and the Republicans who wished for complete political independence. Despite his strictures about political independence being insufficient, he nevertheless saw it as a vital basis for a Socialist advance. The illusions that created superficial political divisions and blurred the essential ones would be exorcised by an Irish Republic:

the only power which would show in full light of day all the class antagonisms and lines of economic demarcation now obscured by the mists of bourgeois patriotism.[29]

Thoroughgoing Nationalists should therefore be supported:

... even when he is from the economic view intensely Conservative, the Irish Nationalist ... is an active agent in social regeneration, in so far as he seeks to invest with full power over its own destinies a people actually governed in the interests of a feudal aristocracy ...[30]

It was a distinction and a claim that would have decisive implications.

The relevance of a Socialist strategy for an independent Ireland could be demonstrated by highlighting the illusory character of Home Rule expectations. Connolly saw the restless search for markets as posing problems for an already industrialised society, let alone a newcomer. The search for a competitive Irish industry would be disastrous for the working class that would be created:

our one hope of keeping our feet as a manufacturing nation would depend upon our ability to work longer and harder for a lower wage than the other nations of Europe ... This is equivalent to saying that our chance of making Ireland a manufacturing country depends upon us becoming the lowest blacklegs in Europe.[31]

In his opinion, even this harsh hope would be frustrated by Chinese and Japanese competition.

If the hope of an industrial capitalist Ireland seemed both horrific and unattainable, then how about the dream of a peasant proprietorship that had done so much to fuel the radicalism of the Land League? His initial pronouncements on the agrarian issue depended on second-hand evidence, but in the Spring of 1898, he toured Kerry, then under threat of famine, equipped with a leaflet arguing that starving people had a moral right to food that overrode any legal prohibition.[32] Prior to this experience, Connolly had already emphasised the partiality of the proprietorship demand. Not only would it legitimise the private property system by extending its base, it would also strengthen a significant social division:

The private ownership of land by the landlord class is an injustice to the whole community, but the creation of a peasant proprietary would only tend to stereotype and consecrate that injustice, since it would leave out of account the entire labouring class.[33]

The only just solution was land nationalisation. Connolly recognised that 'peasant proprietary is somewhat of a hindrance to the spread of socialist ideas'.[34]

But it could not be a long-term pillar of capitalism since a viable peasant proprietorship was ceasing to be feasible in the face of competition from cheap North American and Antipodean producers:

Every perfection of agricultural methods or machinery lowers prices; every fall in prices renders more unstable the position of the farmer, whether tenant or proprietor; and every year – nay every month – which passes sees this perfection and development of machinery going more and more rapidly on. We are left no choice but socialism or universal bankruptcy.[35]

This dichotomous choice allowed Connolly to develop a largely orthodox Social Democratic diagnosis and remedy. Production should be for use, not for profit; workers were robbed by the need to sell their labour on a competitive market; similarly, tenant farmers found rents forced upwards by competition for land. The solution was the Irish Socialist Republic. If Irish agriculture could not compete internationally, then it must cease competing and instead organise communally. Its structure should be democratic with boards of agriculture elected by those who work on the land. Similarly, industries should be administered according to co-operative precepts.[36]

This emphasis on democratic control of organisations by the workers concerned, was already an important part of Connolly's Socialist vision. He responded to increasing evidence of capitalist support for State intervention:

Socialism properly implies above all things the cooperative control by the workers of the machinery of production; without this cooperative control the public ownership by the State is not Socialism – it is only State Capitalism.[37]

The democracy of Parliament was characterised as 'the democracy of Capitalism'. Reflecting relationships in the workplace, it implied the workers':

continued subjection to a ruling class once his choice of the personnel of rulers is made.

The revolutionary alternative included the direct involvement of the people in law making; 'the appointment of reliable public servants under direct public control'. In Connolly's phrase, here was 'the industrial democracy of the Socialist Republic'.[38] It was a vision that contained echoes of Marx's praise of the Paris Commune,[39] and also anticipated Connolly's later syndicalism.

His portrait of the Irish Socialist future involved a suggestion that a proper balance between rural and urban society could be maintained. It was a characteristic elaboration of the frequently-voiced Socialist view that capitalist development distorted the relationship between town and country. Instead:

Let the produce of Irish soil go first to feed the Irish people, and after a sufficient store has been retained to insure of that being accomplished, let the surplus be exchanged with other countries in return for those manufactured goods Ireland needs but does not herself produce.[40]

Such a strategy with its abandonment of unregulated Free Trade could help Ireland avoid the horrors of large-scale industrialisation.

Connolly's case saw Socialism and national independence as necessarily interrelated aspirations. Already it raised a series of difficult problems. One was obviously how far the prospects for developments within a single society could be decisive. His comments on Poland which he saw as in several respects analogous to Ireland were not optimistic, even on the narrow question of political independence:

In view of the enormous strength of modern armaments I fear the conquest of its National Freedom by Poland is not at present practicable, except the effort at attaining it be made in conjunction with a proletarian revolt in the ruling Empires.[41]

Such a verdict inevitably raised for any Irish Socialist the question of the appropriate relationship with the British Socialist movement.

The awareness of the common interests of workers in all societies did not entail a uniform strategy for Socialism:

The interests of labour all the world over are identical ... but it is also true that each country had better work out its own salvation on the lines most congenial to its own people.

Separate paths were justified as between England and Ireland:

The national and racial characteristics of the English and Irish people are different, their political history and traditions are antagonistic, the economic development of the one is not on a par with the other.[41]

This claim provoked hostile reactions from some British Socialists who defined – or claimed to define – their Socialism in sharply international-ist terms. Part of Connolly's response paralleled a view expressed almost thirty years earlier by Marx regarding the British end of the relationship:

there is between the two nations an incompatibility of temper which has been, is now and will be exploited in the interests of reaction by the possessing classes of both countries, until the Gordian Knot which binds us together is finally severed, and each nation left free to settle accounts with its own native oppressors.[42]

Connolly went on to develop two points that would have a long-term importance within his politics. In dealing with the criticism that the ISRP programme would necesitate the use of violence, his response was sharp. This was:

not so much an argument against our propaganda as an indictment of the invincible ignorance and unconquerable national egotism of the vast mass of the British electorate, and as such concerns the English socialists more than the Irish ones.

The question of how Irish Socialists should relate to a more numerous labour movement in a centre of imperialism would be a persistent theme until – and after – Easter 1916. Moreover, British Socialists attracted by Home Rulers' attacks on British politicians and conventional preju-dices, could be tempted into a naive assessment of Irish Members' radicalism. This response could be bolstered by a desire to secure the electoral support of the Irish in Britain through developing a Labour–Irish alliance. It was a temptation which Connolly warned against; Socialists should not support Home Rule politicians whose sole objective:

is to reproduce in Ireland all the political and social manifestations which accompany capitalist supremacy in Britain.[43]

The suggestion that Socialists should ally with Socialists and no others was to have a crucial impact on Connolly's view of Socialist strategy.

The working class would play the crucial role in both the national and economic struggles in Ireland. The terminology within which Connolly justified this claim had a considerable similarity to Marx's justification for the proletariat as the agent of universal emancipation. The working classes were:

the only secure foundation on which a free nation can be reared ... which has borne the brunt of every political struggle and gained by none ... the only class in Ireland which has no interest to serve in perpetuating either the political or social forms of oppression – the British connection or the capitalist system.

In keeping with his Social Democratic politics, Connolly argued that prior to the decisive break with capitalism, there remained abundant scope for pursuing immediate objectives such as state-financed agricultural co-operatives, the nationalisation of Irish railways, eight hours' legislation and free meals for school children.[44] Such a growth of Socialist influence would provoke conflict with the British Government and thus Irish Socialists would achieve the position of a dominant national party.[45]

Even the growth of significant Socialist support in the Ireland of the late 1890s seemed highly optimistic, let alone the hope that such resources could be put to effective use. Yet Connolly expressed a buoyant confidence about such an expansion that was founded upon his view of historical developments:

The power of unconquerable optimism of the Socialist Party is due to their recognition of the materialist basis of history ... they know that the needs of the workers, who are the majority, will impel them into line with the social revolutionary forces.[46]

This progressive development would not be undermined by the fact that 'the self interest (of the workers) may sometimes be base'.[47]

This optimism about the experiences of the working class helping to develop a Socialist consciousness was allied with a positive verdict on recent developments within capitalist industry. The economic system not only produced the need and desire for revolt; it also provided the conditions that could make such a revolt successful.[48] Capitalists were becoming superfluous; salaried managers were becoming crucial:

the first step in the Socialist organisation of industry is illustrated by the last step in capitalist organisation.[49]

The suggestion that Socialists were working with the grain of contemporary developments, indicates that Connolly had hopes of a peaceful transition to Socialism based upon education and widespread support.

This was clearly his position in 1898, when he expressed a commitment to the electoral road forward, characteristic of the innocent optimism of much Second International Socialism:

Since the abandonment of the unfortunate insurrectionism of the early Socialists whose hopes were exclusively concentrated on the eventual triumph of uprising and barricade struggle, modern Socialism relying on the slower but surer method of the ballot box has directed the attention of its partisans towards the peaceful conquest of the forces of Government in the interests of the revolutionary ideal.[50]

This view of the transition was paralleled in the National dimension by his argument that Republicans should enter electoral politics; only through this method could the moral consent be developed for the policy of a break with Britain that in the final analysis might need armed force.[51] Nevertheless, along with his optimism about the prospects for Socialist advance, and his view that a Socialist like a Republican transition needed widespread consent, there were very exacting specifications for the use of violence. Only if a Socialist Party found itself backed by an informed majority, blocked by a minority and with all peaceful means exhausted, could it reasonably employ force to impose the majority's views.[52]

This essentially optimistic perspective with its attempt to integrate Nationalist and Socialist strands had little purchase on the realities of Irish politics in the late 1890s. Yet several of the themes and emphases remained important for Connolly to be applied in circumstances that offered more encouragement. At this point, two features can be reasonably noted. Already Connolly was writing as if the idea of an Irish national identity was unproblematic. Presumably it included all those who lived or wished to live on the island of Ireland. Yet at precisely that moment, the idea of Irish nationality was being contested sharply amongst some who rejected the Union – quite apart from those, including the Protestant working class of the North East, who remained fiercely attached to the British connection.

His 1890s writings on Socialist strategy contain one obvious lacuna; references to the role of trade unions are few. He was initially optimistic about the Socialist potential of labour candidates for the Dublin City Council, but it was a hope soon deflated by the conservatism of those elected.[53] In part, this absence could reflect the weak, cautious quality of Dublin trade unionism, but beneath this, there probably lay the orthodox Social Democrats' belief that trade unions could contribute little to the abolition of capitalism, and little to the short-term amelioration of the workers' plight. The Dublin labour movement offered little grounds for revising such a belief.

Although Connolly's perspective contained what were to prove durable elements, it was soon pressurised by political developments. Most crucially, these centred around international crisis. Connolly had developed an orthodox position on the causes of international conflict:

The influence which impels towards war to-day is the influence of capitalism. Every war is now a capitalist move for markets and it is a move capitalism must make or perish.[54]

When war between Britain and the Boer Republics seemed imminent, Connolly's opposition was unequivocal, fusing together nationalist and socialist themes. It was a war waged:

by a mighty empire against a nation entirely incapable of replying in any effective manner, by a government of financiers upon a nation of farmers, by a nation of fili-busterers upon a nation of workers, by a capitalist ring who will never see a shot fired during the war, upon a people defending their own homes and liberties ...

These emphases were shared by critics of the war within the British Socialist movement, but with one exception. British Socialists typically shrank from condemnation of the British people, preferring to concentrate their fire on a narrow group of financiers, politicians and journalists who were misleading essentially decent citizens. Connolly had no such inhibitions. The English were:

doing their utmost to justify the low estimate in which their rulers hold them; a people who for centuries have never heard a shot fired in anger upon their shores, yet who encourage their government in its campaign of robbery and murder against an unoffending nation; a people who, secure in their own homes permit their rulers to carry devastation and death into the homes of another people, assuredly deserve little respect, no matter how loudly they may boast of their liberty-loving spirit.[55]

It was a condemnation that led Connolly to take a critical view of several British Socialists. Predictably Robert Blatchford's support of the War was castigated; he was a 'chauvinist' supplying:

a brutal endorsement of every act of brigandage and murder in which the capitalists of England may involve their country.

He coupled this with a criticism of Hyndman's view that on Socialist grounds, Britain should not have given way to 'less-developed' Russians over Port Arthur. In this case, his argument was strongly determinist. Hyndman's preference for Britain over Russia was that of a 'political radical'. But Socialist revolution could be advanced only if Russian capitalism was allowed to grow, generating its own proletariat. For Connolly, as for Marx in the 1850s, the road to Socialism led between the iron limitations of imperialist development; a path that had to be reconciled albeit uneasily, with Connolly's concern for national self-determination:

Drive the Russians out of Poland! By all means! Prevent his extension towards Europe! Certainly, but favour his extension and his acquisition of new markets in Asia (at the expense of England if need be), if you would see Capitalism being hurried onward to its death.[56]

Although his attachment to a deterministic perspective remained strong, the facts of imperialist war led him to take a more sceptical view of the feasibility of a peaceful evolution from capitalism to socialism.

For some British Socialists, the South African conflict bruised their essentially liberal optimism by demonstrating what they characterised as the gullibility of sections of the working class;[57] for Connolly, the lesson concerned the brittleness of rulers' attachments to liberal precepts. He still adhered to the view that it would be 'the enemies of progress' who would determine whether the transition to socialism would be peaceful. But contemporary evidence was not encouraging:

> If, then, we see a small section of the possessing class prepared to launch two nations into war, to shed oceans of blood and spend millions of treasure in order to maintain intact a SMALL PORTION of their privileges, how can we expect the entire propertied class to abstain from using the same weapons, and to submit peacefully, when called upon to YIELD UP FOR EVER ALL THEIR PRIVILEGES? ... the capitalist class is a beast of prey, and cannot be moralised, converted or conciliated but must be extirpated.[58]

Possibly Irish workers could take a significant step forward for themselves and also influence developments in the Transvaal by taking actions that would occupy the attention of a sizeable section of the British Army.

This emphasis was to reappear in Connolly's arguments from 1914 onwards; in 1899–1900, the one concrete development was the coming together in the Irish Transvaal Committee, of the ISRP, the radical Nationalists symbolised by the involvement of Maud Gonne, and the separatists involved with Arthur Griffith's recently launched newspaper – the *United Irishman*.[59] Connolly played a significant part in anti-War demonstrations, but given the balance of political forces, the Nationalists came predictably to dominate the anti-War agitation. Indeed, the conflict gave the newly reunited Parliamentary Party the chance to recover some radical credibility.

The ISRP remained weak; radical politics in Ireland were easily dominated by Nationalist arguments. Although the national–socialist connection, established within Connolly's thought during these years would remain significant in his ideas, he was about to enter onto a decade of wanderings, a renewed involvement in Scottish politics, and then a seven-year sojourn in the United States. During this period, he was continually concerned with the question of Socialism for the Irish people, whether for those who remained in Ireland, or for the first significant Irish urban working class, that he encountered in the United States. Such a concern raised questions of strategy; Connolly was about to move far not just in terms of geography, but in terms of the route to Socialism.

Chapter 3

Sectarianism

A new edition of *Erin's Hope* was published in 1902. One section had been rewritten to emphasise the necessary connection between the emancipation of the Irish working class and the liberation of Ireland. The flowering of this relationship would require an assertion of self-reliance:

The Irish working class must emancipate itself, and in emancipating itself, it must, perforce, free its country ... The freedom of the working class must be the work of the working class.

This was coupled with a heightened concern about the corrosive effects of political alliances. Arrangements to achieve immediate objectives could produce damaging long-term entanglements:

the first action of a revolutionary army must harmonise in principle with those likely to be its last and ... therefore, no revolutionists can safely invite the co-operation of men or classes, whose ideals are not theirs, and whom, therefore, they may be compelled to fight at some future critical stage of the journey to freedom.[1]

Such a precept carried implications for co-operation with radical National-ists, or with trade unionists who were not socialists.

This note had been present in Connolly's writings for some time. As early as 1899, reflecting on his Dublin experiences, he concluded that:

in the uncompromising spirit, the rigid intolerance, and stern exclusiveness shown by the Socialist Republican Party are to be found the only true methods whereby an effective revolutionary movement may be built up ...[2]

In part, this perhaps reflected the complex relationship with the more radical Nationalists, but it stemmed also from a shifting assessment of the politics of Dublin trade union leaders. Connolly had responded positively to the Trades Council decision to run candidates in the 1899 municipal elections.[3] Admittedly the nominees would not be Socialists but the logic of events would prove decisive:

every working man elected to the Municipal Council of Dublin, if he be true to his class when elected, will find that every step he takes in the Council in furtherance of the interests of his class, must of necessity take the form of an application of Socialist principles.[4]

The trade unionists' pursuit of socialist palliatives would not only radicalise them; it would restructure the party system so as to reflect the fundamental division between capital and labour. This was the argument favoured by those British Socialists who sought a political alliance with trade unionists, an ambition realised early in 1900.

Yet before conferences in Edinburgh and in London helped to establish dominant institutions for British working class politics, Connolly was criticising the Dublin Labour councillors:

From the entry of the Labour Party into the Municipal Council to the present day, their course has been marked by dissension, squabbling and recrimination. No single important move in the interest of the worker was ever mooted, the most solemn pledges were incontinently broken, and where the workers looked for inspiration and leadership, they have received nothing but discouragement and disgust.[5]

For Connolly, the supine behaviour of the labour representatives was a betrayal of 'the splendid class spirit' demonstrated by Dublin workers at the municipal elections. His analysis included a firm belief in the inherent radicalism of the working class. The problem centered around the means by which such radical potential was diverted into 'safe' channels.

His response carried implications beyond the specificities of Dublin municipal politics, and led to criticism of the strategy followed by many British Socialists, most significantly the leadership of the ILP. Connolly opposed any weakening of Socialist commitment in order to court trade union or Radical Liberal support. Instead the proper tactic must be to proclaim the centrality of the class struggle; then workers could be won for Socialist politics.

But where the principle is obscured or denied, the organisations of the working-class, even when professedly Socialist, only serve as decoy ducks to the politics of their masters.

One such cul-de-sac was Fabianism, a strategy which could:

emasculate the working-class movement, by denying the philosophy of the class struggle, weakening the belief of the workers in the political self-sufficiency of their own class, and by substituting the principle of municipal capitalism, and bureaucratic State control for the principle of revolutionary reconstruction involved in Social Democracy.[6]

Clearly, by 1900 Connolly was increasingly out of sympathy with the political developments that were beginning to dominate the British Labour Movement. The option of a union of the ILP and the SDF under a Socialist banner had been defeated in favour of an alliance dominated by the trade unions. Added to this, there was the depth of Connolly's hostility to British policy in South Africa. This made no excuses for the support, passive or enthusiastic of sizeable sections of the British working class. Both his Socialism and his Nationalism were separating him from the politics of the Labour Alliance.

This distance was increased by the willingness of some British Socialists to seek electoral support from the United Irish League, a tactic given plausibility by Irish MPs' opposition to the War, and Liberal Imperialists' readiness to jettison Home Rule. In the light of Connolly's analysis in *Erin's Hope* and elsewhere, this strategy was unacceptable. By March 1901, he was attacking the *Labour Leader's* position on this as 'the veriest treason to the cause of International Socialism'.[7] Later that year, Bob Smillie secured UIL support at the North-East Lanarkshire by-election, in preference to a Liberal Imperialist. Connolly returned to the attack. Hardie's intention in seeking Irish support through the Home Rule Party machinery might be honest, but the strategy should be opposed by Socialists.[8]

Connolly's reactions to political developments within the Labour Movement seemed to reflect his longstanding identification with the basic position of the Social Democratic Federation. In August 1901, the SDF withdrew its national affiliation to the Labour Representation Committee, claiming that the latter lacked commitment to class conscious action for a socialist objective. Yet Connolly was increasingly critical of the Federation. In part, this reflected the SDF's attitude on Irish issues. The divergence between its policy and that of the ISRP has been noted already. At the Paris Congress of the Socialist International in September 1900, the SDF delegates unsuccessfully opposed the ISRP claim that Irish Socialists should be regarded as a separate national group.[9] Moreover, the Federation were happy to seek UIL support in elections; the search for votes led them down the same path as the ILP.[10]

His dissatisfaction went far deeper than the SDF's responses to Irish issues. The Federation had always had a complex political personality. Criticisms – both contemporary and retrospective – tended to focus on the idiosyncracies of H. M. Hyndman and his supporters, and ignored the fact that in some communities, the organisation had developed a significant working-class presence. Yet the SDF's achievements were limited: membership remained stagnant; electoral contests ended in disappointment.[11] Despite its secession from the LRC many within the Federation felt a need to establish connections with other groups. But some members saw such flexibility as evidence of a damaging deradicalisation.

Such critics had acquired a focus for their grievances at the Paris Congress of the Socialist International. Whatever the weaknesses of British Socialism, its place within a wider movement ensured that significant socialist controversies left their marks. The Congress fiercely debated the acceptability of French Socialists joining the Waldeck–Rousseau Government in order to defend the Third Republic against reactionaries. This raised the fundamental issue of whether

Socialists should participate in capitalist administrations in a particularly sharp form, since the Waldeck–Rousseau Cabinet included General Gallifet, active thirty years before in the butchery of the Communards. The debate was terminated with a resolution from Karl Kautsky, proclaiming the principle that Socialists should stay out of capitalist governments, but accepting that there could be exceptions. This qualification was opposed by a small section of the Congress, including the ISRP delegation of two. The Kautsky compromise was rejected also by a minority within the SDF who viewed their leader's acquiescence as evidence of the organisation's degeneration.[12]

It was hardly surprising that this SDF faction – based primarily in some of the Scottish branches – should seek a link with the ISRP. This functioned essentially through Connolly who propagandised for sympathetic SDF branches in the Summers of 1901 and 1902, thereby re-establishing his links with a section of the Scottish Socialist movement. Throughout his tours, he emphasised the need for class-conscious, explicitly Socialist propaganda.[13] On occasions, he spoke of the SDF as the body able to carry this through, but privately his doubts grew. Aberdeen had been a relative stronghold of the SDF for several years but Connolly was concerned about the branch's practice of collaborating with ILPer's, trade unionists, temperance organisations and a 'whole string of other faddists'.[14] Lancashire contained several branches unhappy about the SDF's breach with the LRC; he was sceptical about the prospects there. They were:

so much admirers of Quelch and Hyndman that little can be done with them.[15]

Yet Salford offered more encouragement. One member agreed with his diagnosis:

this conflict between theory and practice was ruinous and explains the little progress the SDF is making ... the impossiblists were the only logical body in the SDF.[16]

This last sentiment gradually drove Connolly and other critics to a breach with the Federation.

In August 1902, the Scottish District Council of the Federation initiated its own journal, *The Socialist*.[17] Over the next few months, its content helped to ensure a split. Early in 1903, Connolly prognosticated with partial accuracy on the likely outcome to a regular correspondent, the Falkirk schoolteacher John Carstairs Matheson:

I think that you will all be fired at the Conference, and that the ILP and SDF will rush into each others' arms. Are you strong enough to stand alone?[18]

During these months, Connolly's world changed dramatically. In the Autumn of 1902, he toured the United States under the auspices of Daniel

De Leon's Socialist Labor Party to raise money for the ISRP, but he returned to Dublin to find the latter in the process of disintegration.[19] When the SDF expelled its Scottish critics in April 1903, Connolly played a leading role in setting up a new organisation, and presided over part of its inaugural meeting.[20] He provided the new body with a name, the Socialist Labour Party,[21] and served for three months as its organiser. He also developed an indictment of the SDF which illuminated his position on Socialist strategy.

Part of his condemnation concerned the quality of the Federation's opposition to the South African War. As with ILP and Radical propagandists, *Justice* had taken the easy and discreditable path of relying on a xenophobic stereotype; it strove:

to divert the wrath of the advanced workers from the capitalists to the Jews ... its readers were nauseated by denunciations of 'Jewish millionaires' and 'Jewish plots', 'Jewish controlled newspapers', 'German Jews', 'Israelitish schemes', and all the stock phrases of the lowest anti-semitic papers until the paper became positively unreadable to any fair-minded man who recognised the truth, viz that the war was the child of capitalist greed and inspired by men with whom race or religion were matters of no moment.

Beyond this, he condemned the SDF for the persistent dualism between rhetoric and action. It claimed to be a separate Socialist Party but it always sought electoral backing from the ILP and pursued Radical votes; it denounced trade unionism as 'played out', but opposed any attack on labour leaders who presented trade unionism as the vital weapon for working-class improvement; it was dismissive of the Labour Alliance but it opposed criticism of LRC candidates. Once again Connolly saw this as a case of a radical rank and file betrayed by its leadership:

There was revolutionary activity in the SDF once, but their leaders, Hyndman, Quelch, Burrows etc have led it indeed as a lightning conductor leads lightning – into the earth to dissipate its energy.[22]

One problem was raised repeatedly – the degeneration of a professedly Socialist organisation.

In the Summer of 1903, Connolly provided a sharply sectarian answer. The model for an effective Socialist Party could be found in the United States, in the strategy of De Leon's Socialist Labor Party. The link went back some years. Correspondence had begun soon after the ISRP's formation; Connolly had advised Irish voters in the USA to vote for the SLP; the latter had given financial support to the ISRP;[23] in 1898 he had written articles on the agrarian depression in the West of Ireland for the SLP's *Weekly People*.[24] He began to believe that aspects of SLP doctrine fitted the Irish and British experiences. When De Leon denounced collaboration with trade unions affiliated to the American Federation of Labor, Connolly responded sympathetically:

If those leaders are helping to keep their followers chained to the chariot wheels of capitalist parties, it is a crime to coquet with them and a virtue to fight them.[25]

As he was about to begin his SLP-sponsored American tour, he commented in August 1902 that 'our ideas upon policy and tactics generally were practically identical'.[26] The experience of seeing the SLP in action did not erode this estimate. His verdict from Bridgeport Connecticutt was:

The SLP comrades impress me very favourably; there is a good sprinkling of Irish in all the sections.[27]

When he returned across the Atlantic his enthusiasm was tinged only by a slight hint of unease about the Party's sectarianism:

... I came back stronger than ever in my belief in our position, and in the general SLP analysis of its own enemies. Of course it exaggerates sometimes.[28]

The significance of this model requires a brief assessment of the SLP's dominant figure, Daniel De Leon.

The former Columbia professor had been born into a Jewish family in Curaçao in 1852. During the 1880s, he had progressed through the radical politics of New York City – the Henry George mayoral campaign, public support for those convicted of the Haymarket killings, the Nationalist movement of Edward Bellamy, the Knights of Labor – and then late in 1890, the Socialist Labor Party. He brought with him the gifts of a scholar, of a highly effective speaker, and of a zealous convert. Within less than a year, he was editor of the *People*; he would be the Party's dominant figure until he died in 1914.[29]

For most contemporaries and many historians, De Leon epitomised the theoretically adroit but inflexible sectarian. Under his leadership splits and the appeal of more flexible alternatives reduced the SLP to an irrelevant rump. This image had dominated judgements as even one of his political opponents subsequently acknowledged:

Daniel De Leon was intensely personal. Almost immediately upon his entry in the Socialist arena he divided the movement into two antagonistic camps – his devoted admirers and followers, and his bitter critics and opponents ... (Thus) it is not easy to formulate a just and objective evaluation of his personality, and of the part he played in the history of American Socialism.[30]

De Leon's view of Socialist strategy had developed two distinctive emphases by the time that Connolly became familiar with it. Both were evident in the latter's analysis in the Summer of 1903. On the political front, De Leon's Party was:

the only genuine Socialist Party in the United States, and acting on that belief, it opposes every other party and fights them at every election.[31]

A basis for such separatism was provided by De Leon's claim that Socialist politics was founded on propositions that had the same status as those in the biological sciences:

The laws that rule sociology run upon lines parallel with and are the exact counter-parts of those that natural science has established in biology.[32]

Many contemporary Socialists made a similar biological emphasis, but much more at the level of metaphor, than of a theory that determined actions. But for De Leon, Socialist organisation must be 'as intolerant as science';[33] there must be unvarying obedience:

Organisation must be the incarnation of principle ... obedience is the badge of the civilised man ... you will never find the revolutionist putting himself above the organisation.[34]

A disciplined organisation based on a scientific analysis could look forward with optimism; capitalist development would heighten and simplify class divisions. Socialist rectitude would reap its reward. It was a position that could appeal to the Socialist disenchanted by ILP and SDF manoeuvres.

This emphasis on the political was seen by De Leon as crucial:

The Social Question, and all such questions, are essentially political. If you have an economic organisation alone, you have a duck flying with one wing; you must have a political organisation, or you are nowhere.[35]

Yet the SLP had to develop a response in the trade union field, and this once again was accepted by Connolly. He accepted the Party's view that 'pure and simple trade-unionism' was finished as a positive force, and that therefore the 'treacheries and sophistries' of such organisations' leaders should be consistently exposed. Moreover he embraced the Party's alternative dual unionist strategy. The SLP:

seeks to make Socialism a guiding principle in the daily life of the workers by organising trade-unions on Socialist lines, and by refusing membership to anyone who identifies with its antagonists by accepting office in a pure and simple trade union.[36]

It was strategy pursued by the SLP through the formation of the Socialist Trades and Labor Alliance.

The British SLP might appeal to Connolly as ideologically acceptable; but it offered no reliable income for him as a political organiser.[37] In September 1903, he sailed once more for the United States, as a committed supporter of De Leonite Socialism, and this time with no return envisaged. Before considering subsequent developments in Connolly's views on Socialist strategy, it is useful to locate De Leon's Party within the wider American context.

The SLP now had a rival, the Socialist Party of America, formed after much debate, from disparate groups in 1901. It was an alternative dismissed by Connolly as an American equivalent of the SDF:

Inconsistency and sacrifice of principle for the sake of votes mark both organisations, and 'Be all things to all men' might be the watchword of either.[38]

Yet even before unity had been achieved, this tendency had contested the 1900 Presidential election, and had secured 96,878 votes compared with 34,191 for the SLP ticket. The expectation that Socialist rigour would be electorally attractive was hardly borne out. In 1904, the contrast would be even more stark; the SPA vote more than quadrupled to 402,283; the SLP fell to 31,248. The organisation with which Connolly had identified himself was already marginal to the American Left.

A parallel claim could be made, albeit even more sharply about the SLP's Dual Unionist strategy. During his earlier American tour, he had seen the legacy of a thirty four week weavers' strike in Massachusetts and Rhode Island, conducted under ST and LA leadership. He felt that this had made a significant difference:

A strike conducted by Socialists even when unsuccessful does not leave the workers as despairing and disheartened, as a strike conducted by non-Socialists generally does.[39]

Yet this disregarded the chronic weakness of the ST and LA.

The tactic of attacking all AFL organisations without any sensitivity towards their diverse political positions alienated even those union leaders who had some sympathy for De Leon's Socialist message. Thus the Boot and Shoe Worker's Union, like their British counterpart, developed significant Socialist sympathies during the 1890s.[40] Pressures for mechanisation could evoke responses that built on traditional co-operative sentiments within the industry; the union acquired a socialist objective; but the desire to build up a strong organisation pointed away from isolation. As one union activist claimed in 1898:

the present form of trades unions will for a long time be with us. I consider it our duty to organise in them, get the benefits and advantages that result from large numerical strength and that cannot be had outside of the American Federation of Labour.[41]

Socialist trade unionists faced with such a prospect would be likely to transfer their loyalty from the SLP to the Socialist Party.

The activities of ST and LA affiliated organisations did not of themselves offer a radical alternative. Their industrial strategies were typically indistinguishable from those of AFL unions; what mattered was that they should engage in appropriate political propaganda. The ST and LA was emphatically not a precursor of the Industrial Workers of the World that would influence Connolly's views from 1905. Indeed, many of the affiliates were craft organisations.[42] For De Leon the issue was not the type of worker enrolled, nor the organisational structure, but availability for Party education. It is perhaps not surprising that the ST and LA – industrially divisive but not distinctive, linked to a party with slight and declining membership and support – should wither away. Initially, more than two hundred affiliates had enrolled 30,000 members. In 1898, a dispute over intensified Party control had produced a spate of withdrawals and expulsions. In 1905, prior to its demise, it had less than 1500 members. Its claim to be an effective Socialist trade union organisation was vacuous. As Connolly became more critical of De Leon's politics, he characterised the ST and LA as 'little else than a mere ward-heeling club for the SLP'.[43]

This remark had been made in the context of a controversy with De Leon that Connolly had initiated unwittingly in the Spring of 1904. He had queried SLP attitudes on a range of topics – religion, marriage, the iron law of wages, expecting a reasoned discussion but finding himself the target of De Leonite polemic and organisational manipulation. His verdict on De Leon's utilisation of the party organisation was sharp:

Dan played a smart trick at the Conference. Of course I could not be present; was not a delegate, and had my nose too close to the grindstone of exploitation to attend anyway. So Dan read my correspondence, paragraph by paragraph, *adding his own criticism in between*, so delegates could not discern where I ended and *my quotations* began, and lost sight of one sentence before he began to read the one that pointed its moral. As a result he had no difficulty in tearing me to pieces – and thus succeeded by this trick, worthy of a shyster lawyer – in preventing the publication of the letters, and in preventing the delegates and the party at large from having the opportunity of studying and calmly reviewing the evidence in cold print. It was a 'great victory'.

Such an experience of oligarchic control produced a general reflection on Socialist leadership, with a hint that the SLP's revolutionary zeal was not of itself a solution to the problem of de-radicalisation. The dominance of apparently revolutionary bodies by bourgeois leaders could have damaging consequences:

Of course there is not hero-worship amongst *us*. We believe that the emancipation of the working class must be the achievement of the working class, but neither in Great Britain nor America can a working-class Socialist expect common fairness from his comrades if he enters into controversy with a trusted leader from a class above them. The howl that greets every such attempt whether directed against a Hyndman or a De Leon in America (excuse the comparison) sounds to my mere proletarian ear wonderfully alike, and everywhere is but the accents of an army, not of revolutionary fighters, but of half emancipated slaves.[44]

This experience did not destroy Connolly's faith in the political principles central to the SLP but over the next three and a half years his commitment to this instrument, and then to some of the underlying assumptions was challenged both by political events and by the mounting evidence of the damage wrought by De Leon's methods. Late in November 1905, Connolly acknowledged the Party's current weakness but expressed optimism about the future:

The SLP is weaker to-day both financially and politically than it has ever been; it can scarcely reckon on many votes outside its own membership; but the absolute correctness of its tactics and its analysis of the industrial situation is now being admitted by thousands of the working-class who a year ago were its bitter enemies, and a year hence may be its staunchest political supporters.

But too many within the Party were ready to ignore uncomfortable facts:

I have nothing but contempt for the men who, now, echoing De Leon like parrots, pretend that the vote is of no importance ...[45]

The myopia indicated De Leon's continuing domination. His principles might be impeccable, but his management of the Party was disastrous:

We are not treated as revolutionists capable of handling a revolutionary situation but as automatons whose duty it is to repeat in varying accents the words of our Director-General. Everything must filter through Dan.[46]

This style made alliances with other radical organisations very difficult, since it provoked claims that the SLP used broader movements for its own purposes. But as Connolly eventually acknowledged, elitism and suspicion were central to De Leon's politics:

he can't trust the revolutionary working class movement unless it is in the control of his creatures.[47]

The party's isolation was inevitably heightened:

Whilst the SLP remains in De Leon's hands it will never have a future except that of a church.[48]

Early in 1908, Connolly finally left the SLP. Before doing so, he characterised the Party without illusions:

A Socialist party that holds no meetings except during election times, that repeats like a parrot whatever is said by one man, whose sections go for years without entering a new name upon its books, that in a number of the largest cities in the country was not able to put up a ticket after twenty years of activity ... that has a daily paper that after seven years existence has less than 2000 readers, although it is pushed from Maine to California, and bought by every one of its members ... such a party is ... a fraud and a disgrace to the revolutionary movement.[49]

Soon afterwards, he widened the indictment to incorporate not just the leadership style of De Leon but his excessive emphasis on Socialist rectitude. In so doing, Connolly abandoned the position that he had adopted in 1903. Essentially, the SLP had refused to acknowledge any positive growth in the Labour Movement; its dichotomous view had been absurd. Instead, revolutionary socialists should recognise that:

the developing consciousness of the labour movement in Britain is healthier and more potent for good than the 'clearness' of a sect which insists on cutting the umbilical string uniting it to the general movement of the working class.[50]

Valid political principles had been taken over by

a number of sectarians, narrow-minded doctrinaires, who have erected Socialism into a cult with rigid formulas which one must observe or be damned.

So Connolly reflected on his years as a De Leonite:

It is a biter lesson to learn but it is better to learn it than to persist to the end in endeavouring to make statesmanlike Socialists out of a covenanting clique.[51]

But in rejecting isolation, Connolly retained the commitment to Socialist principles that had led to De Leonism in the first place. How could such principles be realised within a broader movement? That would be the positive legacy from his American years.

Chapter 4

Syndicalism

Connolly's views on socialist strategy were influenced decisively by the emergence of the Industrial Workers of the World.[1] This body had been formed in Chicago in June 1905 as a revolutionary alternative to the American Federation of Labor. When Connolly abandoned the Socialist Labor Party, he offered the IWW as a partial solution to the problem of connecting revolutionary principles to immediate working class demands. The organisation:

will further the clean policy that the SLP stood for far better than it could do itself.

The secret of revolutionary effectiveness lay in the basing of IWW activity in the workplace:

it is a body of men and women at once intensely practical and uncompromisingly revolutionist; it can never degenerate into a mere sect as the SLP has done but palpitates with the daily and hourly pulsations of the class struggle, as it manifests itself in the workshop.

Equipped with such a basis, the IWW could avoid the danger of deradicalisation through control by middle-class politicians:

when it moves onto the political field, as move it will, its campaign will indeed be the expression of the necessities of the working class, not the result of the theories of a few unselfish enthusiasts.[2]

This assessment came out of Connolly's involvement with the organisation, especially his attempts to recruit a variety of New York workers into the 'Wobblies'. His activities not only produced conflict with organisations affiliated to the AFL; they also provided one more strand in the deepening conflict with De Leon.[3]

Yet initially Connolly's enthusiasm for the IWW seemed wholly compatible with membership of the SLP. De Leon played a significant part at the founding convention of the 'Wobblies' and remained active in the organisation until his eviction in September 1908. Such an association indicated a shift in De Leon's views compared with his ST and LA period. Although he had been interested in syndicalist doctrines for some years, he now made a clear commitment to the principle of Industrial Unionism and adopted a much more positive perception of the function that such industrial organisations could fulfil within a revolutionary strategy. Purely political gains by a socialist party would encounter a decisive obstacle in the continuing capitalist control of the means of production. This challenge could be met only by an appropriate industrial organisation. The 'vital act' was the taking and holding of industrial plants, and for this 'lock out' of the capitalists a political party was irrelevant.[4]

Moreover, De Leon's support for industrial unions was not restricted to a claim for their effectiveness against capitalist obstruction. He clearly envisaged them as anticipating the administrative structures of a socialist society:

> The mining, the railroad, the textile, the building industries ... each of these regardless of former political boundaries will be the constituencies of that new central authority ... Where the General Executive Board of the Industrial Workers of the World will sit, there will be the nation's capital.[5]

It was a theme hinted at by Connolly in some of his earlier Irish writings.

The enthusiasm evinced by De Leon even included an acceptance of the IWW's refusal to commit itself to any specific political party. Its original constitution acknowledged that agitation must be developed:

> on the political as well as on the industrial field ... without affiliation to any political party.[6]

This was significantly different from the earlier ST and LA insistence that its affiliates must accept the correctness of SLP strategy. Arguably De Leon still believed that revolutionary trade unionists would be led towards the SLP; perhaps this formulation was the best obtainable in a convention that included a significant anti-political tendency. At least his acceptance of this position suggests some amendment to the stereotype of De Leonite inflexibility.

The views of De Leon left a lasting mark on Connolly, despite the latter's eventual break with the SLP. As he moved towards more intensive involvement in the IWW Connolly became increasingly sceptical about the value of any link between the 'Wobblies' and the SLP. His initial concern had been that of a Party loyalist, lest involvement of SLP members in the new organisation lead to neglect of political work.[7] Yet, more significantly, it became clear that recruitment to the IWW seemed to bring no benefits for the SLP. He reflected on developments in a town which would become celebrated in IWW history:

> In Paterson, New Jersey where the IWW has gained thousands of members, the SLP is not one man stronger than before.[8]

Indeed, many 'Wobblies', dubious about De Leon's methods were hostile to the SLP:

> Most of us here in New York think that the election of so many SLP men to the Executive Board was a criminal mistake, as it tends to foster the suspicion that we control and 'boss' the IWW ...[9]

Such antagonism was one factor behind the withdrawal of the relatively strong Western Federation of Miners.[10] This Federation was responsible for whatever credibility the IWW had as a popular organisation. Yet as early as August 1906, before the SLP presence on the 'Wobblies' Executive became dominant, John O'Neil, editor of the *Miners' Magazine* gave a sharp warning:

It is now apparent to us that SLPism has hooked itself to the Industrial Workers of the World, in order that it might gather sustenance to prolong the life of an invalid that is almost a corpse. The convention at Chicago must either get rid of the fanatics and disrupters or the IWW is slated for destruction.[11]

Connolly claimed to be unconcerned about the secession of the Western Federation,[12] yet this departure left the 'Wobblies' with little presence in the American working class. His increasing emphasis on Industrial Unionism as the basis for revolutionary action on both industrial and political levels must be placed in context. How credible was the early IWW when measured against Connolly's claims?

The inaugural convention was a heterogeneous gathering. SLP members who hoped that the new organisation would benefit their ailing party combined with some left-wing members of the Socialist Party of America, who had written off the AFL. The most significant of these was Eugene Debs who for a short time seemed to establish comradely relations with De Leon. In contrast to the politicians, delegates from the Western Federation of Miners and other unions had, as their priority, the creation of an effective industrial unionism. Eventually this might develop a 'political reflex', but for the moment politics could wait. Besides these ideological differences, the Chicago meeting included some would-be trade union leaders who had failed to secure a niche elsewhere. One of these, Charles Sherman, became the IWW's first and only President. His murky financial dealings and lack of radicalism generated sufficient opposition by September 1906 to depose him and to abolish the office of president. It was hardly an auspicious start.[13]

This incompetently-led organisation rapidly encountered hostility from the AFL. Support from within the Socialist Party declined as the underlying hostility to De Leon reasserted itself. Connolly portrayed the dilemma facing Eugene Debs – he is:

in a strange fix; his instincts are all revolutionary, but he balks at swallowing De Leon and the latter's followers insist that to accept the IWW in its entirety is to accept Dan.[14]

More crucial than the disenchantment of politicians was the loss of the WFM, as official claims about membership in transport and metal manufacture had little reality. The early record of defeat in strikes was depressing yet the IWW began to apply its belief that previously unorganised workers could be brought into effective trade union organisation. As yet claims of effectiveness were largely rhetorical, yet in those early years the IWW survived not just organisational rivalries and administrative chaos, but also the economic depression of 1907–8. That it survived as an alternative to the AFL gave radicals such as Connolly hope for the future, yet the impact of depression raised a serious problem.

The 'Wobblies' optimism was based on the expectation that revolutionary aspirations and opportunities would grow out of workers' power at the point of production. Yet Connolly acknowledged in April 1908 that:

the only danger confronting the IWW is the almost universal bankruptcy through unemployment of its members.[15]

Obviously, this was not the only peril. Repression by Federal, State and local authorities, non-recognition and coercion by employers, hostility from the AFL, the likelihood that such pressures would intensify if the 'Wobblies' influence seemed to be increasing: all these difficulties were already visible. But beneath them, there was the fundamental point that a revolutionary strategy founded on power in the workplace required that workers should have jobs. Mass unemployment devastated IWW organisation. Locals were formed but soon disbanded; the paid organisers who might have sustained them through a difficult period were unavailable because of financial stringency. It was a vicious circle. By late 1908 all that remained was a handful of locals in the East, catering for foreign workers; a few hundred migrants in the Far West.[16]

It was amidst these difficulties that the IWW amended its position on the relationship between political and industrial action. Connolly's view on this was clear. Industrial organisation and action should be supplemented with political work, even if the thrust of the latter was propagandist:

to repudiate political action or to shelve it indefinitely would be to lose the value of the propaganda made by the volunteer force.[17]

The direction of his ideas was highlighted in a letter to Matheson. Earlier condemnation of Keir Hardie's 'Labour Alliance' strategy had been succeeded by the view that despite all the debilitating compromises, such a coalition between political and industrial organisations furnished a significant exemplar. The vital distinction would be that in Connolly's envisaged structure the industrial component would have revolutionary consequences. The defect of the British Labour Party lay in the type of alliance involved:

If that body was dominated by Industrial Unionists, instead of by pure and simplers, if it was elected by the Industrial Unions and controlled entirely by them, and capable *at any moment* of having its delegates recalled by the unions, and had also its mandate directly from the rank and file organised in the workshops, it would be just the party we want.[18]

The belief that the envisaged solidarity of Industrial Unionism could generate a firmly socialist commitment was a revolutionary version of the hope that Connolly had expressed a decade earlier. Then he had been optimistic about the political implications of trade union intervention in Dublin municipal politics. That earlier expectation had been betrayed rapidly by events; whether the IWW could provide a basis for an effective Socialist Party remained, in the most immediate sense, an open question.

The forces within the IWW antipathetic to any political activity were gathering strength. The Socialist Party presence had diminished and the style of De Leon and his committed supporters was likely to produce an anti-political reaction. By the Spring of 1908 as Connolly was developing his ideas on the appropriate political–industrial relationship, others were expressing strongly anti-political views. Sometimes this reflected distaste for the SLP but it could extend to the assertion that any political activity would be a worthless diversion. Frank Little, later a 'Wobbly' martyr, expressed this viewpoint:

I do not believe that you can get the ends we are fighting for through a pure and simple political ballot party ... We can never do it as long as we depend upon going out and sticking a piece of white paper into a capitalist ballot box.[19]

For Connolly, the achievement of political power required the conquest of economic power, but this in turn could be facilitated by political propaganda; for the anti-political section, the political future could take care of itself. At the moment all energies should be committed to the IWW. Ben Williams, a 'Wobbly' with a SLP past epitomised this approach:

The IWW is a way out of which everything else will develop. Let us 'make straight the way'.[20]

During the Winter of 1907–8, Williams had allied with Connolly against De Leon; he then became a significant figure in the moves that culminated during September 1908 in De Leon's expulsion by that year's 'Wobbly' Convention.[21]

This meeting was more homogeneously working-class than its predecessors, with a distinctive contribution coming from workers who had ridden freight trains from the West Coast. De Leon was excluded from the Convention by a vote of forty to twenty-one, and then after a confused debate the political clause was dropped from the 'Wobblies' preamble by thirty-five to thirty-two.[22] Following the 1907 Convention, Connolly had welcomed 'the squelching of the anti-political crowd',[23] but now with their apparent success, he was philosophical. He conceded that the previous position had been confusing; he considered that the change reflected majority opinion in the IWW and he did not wish the shift to be an obstacle to cooperation with 'fellow revolutionists'.[24] In retrospect the change seems not so clear cut as it might have appeared at the time. Connolly was not alone amongst IWW members in continuing his political activities. Rather the significance of the decision was that any political loyalties should be kept outside the IWW in order to preserve industrial unity.

Connolly's firm attachment to political action necessarily raised the question of the most appropriate instrument, now that he had rejected the SLP, with no immediate prospect that the 'Wobblies' would develop a political dimension. Connolly took a more sanguine view of the Socialist Party of America, the organisation that he had rejected so emphatically five years before. In fact, he joined the Party before the Chicago decisions; the strength of his belief in political action necessitated an outlet. His adherence was accompanied by abundant reservations about the SPA's position and with a limited expectation of its likely contribution to the abolition of capitalism:

I believe in the necessity of an uncompromising political party of Socialists, and I do not believe that the Socialist Party of which I am a member is yet such a body. But I believe that the conduct of De Leon has rendered impossible any clear cut movement in *America* except as an evolution out of the SP for agitation purposes, *and for the final revolutionary act out of the IWW.*

The factionalism of the SPA was attractive, especially to someone who had bleak memories of De Leonite discipline. Revolutionaries were under no compulsion to accept the compromising policies of the Party's Right Wing. The left were in a minority; at the 1908 Convention, an attempt to commit the Party to Industrial Unionism had been defeated by 138 votes to 48, but Connolly was optimistic that this would change:

... at last I made up my mind to join because I felt that it was better to be one of the revolutionary minority inside the party than a mere discontented grumbler out of political life entirely.[25]

Connolly's relationship with his new party was not always an easy one in New York City where the lines between the SPA and the SLP had been tightly drawn. Further West the division had been more blurred and it was there that from June 1909 he spent eleven relatively prosperous months as a Socialist Party organiser.[26] Such work meant that his involvement with the IWW was limited, but in May 1910 he took a significant part in a tin plate strike at New Castle Pennsylvania, where the 'Wobblies' were heavily involved.

These were his last activities in the American Labour Movement, and demonstrated his dual commitments to political activity and to Industrial Unionism. He returned to Ireland in July 1910 with a view of Socialist strategy that owed much to his American experiences. It was expressed in a series of writings produced between his departure from the SLP and his return across the Atlantic. Most significant were the later chapters of his 1909 pamphlet *Socialism Made Easy*. These carried a title appropriate for their syndicalist message: *The Axe to the Root*.[26]

Connolly emphasised that the working class would not be united politically until it had achieved industrial unity. He was essentially optimistic about the prospect for achieving such solidarity as workers extended their sympathies from their craft, to their industry and then to their class. The AFL strategy urged political unity whilst sticking to a craft basis for trade union organisation; this was self-contradictory. Instead effective political action necessitated industrial organisation that embraced the entire working class. Within such a development, disputes between industrial unionists about the proper place of political action were irrelevant:

Everyone who has the interests of the working class at heart should strive to realise industrial unity as the solid foundation upon which alone the political unity of the workers can be built up and directed towards a revolutionary end. To this end all those who work for industrial unionism are truly cooperating even when they care least for political activities.[27]

Beyond such formulations, Connolly attempted a more precise presentation of the relationship between industrial and political activities. On the one side, he saw industrial struggle as the key to working class emancipation:

the fight for the conquest of the political state is not the battle, it is only the echo of the battle. *The real battle is the battle being fought out every day for the power to control industry*.[28]

Despite this juxtaposition, Connolly saw political organisations as making a vital contribution towards the development of class consciousness. Industrial battles had their limitations as well as their strengths, and these had to be transcended. The most effective way was through the ballot box:

Such action strips the working-class movement of all traces of such sectionalism as may, and indeed must, cling to strikes and lock outs, and emphasises the class character of the Labour Movement. IT IS, THEREFORE, ABSOLUTELY INDISPENSABLE FOR THE EFFICIENT TRAINING OF THE WORKING CLASS ALONG CORRECT LINES THAT ACTION AT THE BALLOT BOX SHOULD ACCOMPANY ACTION IN THE WORKSHOP.[29]

Yet ultimately for Connolly, it was economic power that was decisive. In part this claim came out of his general view of revolutionary transformation:

... the proletarian revolution will in that respect most likely follow the lines of the capitalist revolutions in the past.

In Cromwellian England, in Colonial America, in Revolutionary France, the real political battle did not begin until after the bourgeoisie, the capitalist class had become the dominant class in the nation. Then they sought to conquer political power in order to allow their economic power to function freely.[30]

But his judgement had a justification other than this deterministic and historically-inaccurate view. For Connolly, Industrial Unionism, understood as a response to the development of Trusts,[31] should be seen as a prefiguration of how a Socialist society should be administered. The portrait had strong similarities with that developed by De Leon shortly after the foundation of the IWW. Industrial unions would control each industry, electing supervisory staff and administering each industry according to an assessment of social needs. Such a framework would replace the old territorial form of government:

representatives elected from these various departments of industry will meet and form the industrial administration or national government of the country.[32]

Hopefully such a view of Socialism would exorcise fear of bureaucratic authoritarianism – instead, there would be a blending of thorough democracy with 'expert supervision'. This strategy for Socialism was clearly in opposition to those who argued that Socialist objectives could be advanced through assiduous work on national and municipal bodies. In Connolly's view such activities could have a propaganda value, but they could not produce any substantive Socialist achievements:

the political state of capitalism has no place under Socialism, therefore measures which aim to place industries in the hands or under the control of such a political state are in no sense steps towards that ideal; they are but useful measures to restrict the greed of capitalism and to familiarise workers with the conception of common ownership. This latter is indeed their chief function.[33]

Of itself, the 'Constructive Socialist' strategy backed by the SPA Right Wing and identified particularly with Victor Berger of Milwaukee was a blind alley.[34] But Industrial Unionism could provide the vital connection between trade union routines and socialist transformation:

it invests the sordid details of the class struggle with a new and beautiful meaning.[35]

To organise a workplace under the banner of Industrial Unionism was to form a basis for a Socialist alternative – 'a fort wrenched from the control of the capitalist class'.[36] Such an organisation would prefigure what was to come – it could also serve as an alternative source of power against the capitalist state:

On the day that the political and economic forces of labour finally break with capitalist society and proclaim the Workers' Republic these shops and factories so manned by Industrial Unionists will be taken charge of by the workers there employed and force and effectiveness thus given to that proclamation. Then and thus the new society will spring into existence ready equipped to perform all the useful functions of its predecessor.[37]

At the most general level, Connolly's critical analyses of existing Socialist and trade union organisations fit easily into debates amongst his contemporaries in a variety of societies. Much discussion grew out of a concern that current Socialist policies were too cautious and constituted a betrayal of working-class interests. Diagnoses focused frequently on the development of extensive bureaucracies that gave those involved a commitment to continuity, and partly as a consequence of the need for appropriate managerial skills, on the growth of bourgeois leaderships within socialist parties. Such leaderships enjoyed differential resources and could insulate themselves to some degree from rank and file pressures. Essentially such processes could be seen as involving the displacement of publicly-proclaimed goals. What had once been means to the achievement of Socialism became objectives in themselves. The maintenance of an efficient organisation could have corrosive effect upon radical commitments.[38]

Connolly's analyses of the shortcomings of Labour and Socialist organisations clearly belong within this broad response. His criticisms of Hyndman and of De Leon emphasise the extent to which bourgeois leaders equipped with rhetorical and forensic skills could dominate and ultimately help to deradicalise socialist parties.[39] Even at this elementary level, problems arise. Why should it be accepted that middle-class leaders shift such bodies in a conservative direction? Such a claim often incorporates the image of an inherently radical rank and file persistently thwarted, at least within conventional organisations by a talented and more easily satisfied leadership. It is not easy to demonstrate such repeated frustration. A more plausible justification would be one based on the prefiguration principle. Connolly had emphasised the damaging effect that De Leon's dominance had had on the initiatives of SLP members. Arguably, an organisation in which elitism was so well established could be considered an inappropriate vehicle for working-class emancipation since its own procedures still embodied the submissiveness of workers to conventional middle-class definitions of competence. This claim fits closely with the emphasis made by Connolly and others on the way in which Industrial Unionism could provide a basis for the construction of a new social order. It has an immediate plausibility and serves as a sharp reminder that organisations, directed supposedly to radical transformation may embody some of the most negative features of existing society. Even so, the connection between means and ends has to be argued in specific cases not simply assumed as a general principle. It is untrue that there have been no examples of elitist, closed – even conspiratorial and violent – groups acting in ways that enjoyed subsequent popular approval. Connolly's own actions in 1916 can be characterised in such terms. The complex argument about the relationship between means and ends is affected significantly by the availability of choices. Socialists may have to face the decision of what they should do, if the freedom to develop open democratic organisations is circumscribed or prohibited by the State.

What is striking about the perspective developed by Connolly during his later American years is that it seems to assume a degree of space within capitalist society, wherein the Socialist alternative can begin to develop. Even when this space diminishes there is optimism that workers' power at the point of production will be an effective counterweight:

in case of a Supreme Court decision rendering illegal the political activities of the socialist party, or instructing the capitalist officials to refuse to vacate their offices after a national victory by that party, the industrially organised workers would give the usurping government a Roland for its Oliver by refusing to recognise its officers, to transport or feed its troops, to transmit its messages, to print its notices, or to chronicle its doings by working in any newspaper which upheld it.[40]

It was an expectation that made optimistic claims about workers' solidarity and rulers' liberalism. Above all it made the assumption that workers could be radicalised at a time of low unemployment; otherwise the vital sanction of workplace power would be ineffective.

This optimism extended to the claims made about the feasibility of a democratic socialist society. A diagnosis that the roots·of socialist degeneration lay in organisational factors could lead to Michels's conclusion that there was no hope of an effective, durable, democratic organisation. Choices could be made only between competing elites. Michels's claim for an iron law of oligarchy rests on conceptual incoherence and unsystematic and partial citing of evidence. But he does demonstrate to an extreme degree the claim made by so many of his contemporaries: that existing socialist and trade union organisations contained strong oligarchic tendencies. Optimists, observing such tendencies, had to demonstrate how they could be overcome. Thus, the young South Wales miners who wrote *The Miners' Next Step* as a positive response to this problem, developed plans for trade union organisation that could combine a vigorous, decentralised participatory democracy with the possibility of solidaristic and radical action.[41] Like Connolly, they saw such an organisation as anticipating the future structures of a socialist society. Their prospectus has never been tested against the harsh limits of experience, but at least it provides a reasonably coherent organisational proposal. In contrast, Connolly reflecting on his American experiences offered only very general formulations.[42] Socialist organisation would combine democratic procedures with the effective use of expertise. Difficulties, such as conflicts of interest between producers and consumers, were not really examined.

Connolly's optimism was only one element in any effective response to the increasingly complex and sometimes discouraging experiences of Socialists during the years of the Second International. He diagnosed a problem of deradicalisation often in narrowly organisational terms;

he asserted that it could be solved but provided little detailed guidance as to method. Some who developed similar responses went further towards the offering of organisational solutions. But these did not develop very far. August 1914 meant not just the collapse of orthodox Second International Social Democracy but also the end of a relatively brief period in which to be on the left within the Socialist movement was to share views similar to those developed by Connolly during his American years.[43] Whether the hope of a route to Socialism based largely on workplace power and Industrial Unionism wa a chimera or a viable strategy which was deflected by events at Sarajevo is in one sense an open question. But there remains the possibility of measuring Connolly's expectations about American developments against the subsequent record. Does such an exercise highlight significant weaknesses within his perspective, or can any failure of his prognostications be accounted for by contingent factors?

The raising of such a question can appear misguided. After all, it was during Connolly's sojourn across the Atlantic that the German sociologist, Werner Sombart posed his question: 'Why is there no Socialism in the United States?' The question has continued to fascinate and for many the broad contours of Sombart's answer have remained credible.[44] In fact, discussion of several of the claims advanced by him already had a lengthy history. Many nineteenth century writers had demonstrated some awareness of 'American exceptionalism'.[45] Marx and Engels, for example, had paid attention to the prospects for Socialism in this most purely capitalist society. Frequent claims had been made about the relative affluence of sections of the American working class. Sombart's aphorism: 'All Socialist utopias come to nothing on roast beef and apple pie',[46] was a more colourful expression of a commonly held view. Commentators had focused with varying degrees of sophistication on the opportunities available for social and geographical mobility. Attention had been paid to the political realm. Many American male workers had acquired formal political rights without the struggles encountered by many Europeans. The character of the American party system inhibited the development of effective third parties. In several respects, it was argued that the purity of American capitalism limited the growth of Socialist politics – the economic system operated more effectively in the absence of feudal residues, and the framework of a liberal politics had been established without the dispute being widened to cover the legitimacy of capitalism. Yet almost paradoxically some analyses of the lack of Socialist commitment within the American working class emphasised the continuing strength of ethnic loyalites, generated either in Europe or in the 'ante-bellum' South. Such a divided proletariat, it was argued, had no hope of mounting an effective Socialist challenge, yet the sources of working-class division in this purest of capitalist societies typically included the legacy of pre-capitalist conflicts.

This last problem was one that preoccupied Connolly in his activities amongst Irish–American workers. The question of ethnic solidarities should lead to the reflection that the American situation was more complex than the common image of an increasingly bourgeois proletariat might imply. Connolly, like several of his contemporaries spent much time arguing that the material condition of American workers was not one of affluence, rather the breadline was a 'great American institution'.[47] Equally, the liberal political system was inaccessible to the vast majority of Negroes and to many immigrants and migrant workers. It is possible to excavate an alternative history of some sectors of the American working class, emphasising the centrality of poverty, exploitation and repression. More fundamentally, doubts can be raised about some assumptions on which analyses pessimistic of Socialist potential in the USA have founded their case. It is far from clear that relative affluence need have a deradicalising impact on workers; it may lead to rising and perhaps unfulfilled expectations, backed by increasing self-confidence and organisational competence. Similarly, ethnic solidarities need not produce impossible obstacles to working-class unity. Such older cultural patterns may provide the bases out of which an effective class strategy can develop.[48] Claims about the political system need careful scrutiny. Why should the ballot – however restricted in fact if not in theory – limit socialist politics? Can it not be seen as an essential prerequisite for a mass socialist party? Any assertion that the American party system inexorably squeezed out any Socialist challenge requires detailed justification. That a first-past-the-post system firmly protected incumbent parties is a claim queried by the British case. Arguably, the 'winner-take-all' characteristic of American Presidential elections counts as a crucial factor; but against this, there stands the decentralised character of American politics. This allowed for the possibility of significant Socialist growth at municipal or state level. By 1910, there seemed signs that this was happening.

This last reflection leads to perhaps the most sceptical comment. In one sense, Sombart's question was misleading. If it is understood as referring to the prospects for a significant Socialist presence in American politics, then between 1900 and 1912, the future looked in some ways encouraging.[49] In November 1904, Debs had polled 402,000 votes in the Presidential election; four years later with a more effective campaign, the Socialist vote increased by less than 20,000. This was a severe disappointment, although in 1908, the Democrats running Bryan for the third time had arguably checked the drain of voters to the Left. Yet despite this discouraging result, Socialist enthusiasm seemed to grow. Party membership increased; municipal successes offered the chance to hold

office in a few cities. In 1910 Victor Berger was elected to the Federal
Congress and in the complex Presidential contest of 1912 Debs raised
his vote to almost 900,000 – an all-time high of 6%. This political
growth was accompanied by increasing prominence for the IWW as it
sought to organise immigrant workers in Eastern textile centres and steel
mills, and primary producers farther West.[50] This pinnacle of a Socialist
presence in the American Labour movement seemed to several contemporaries more a springboard for future growth. Indeed some years
earlier Sombart after portraying the pressures that pushed American
Socialism to the margins had concluded with a curiously discordant
verdict:

all the factors that till now have prevented the development of Socialism in the
United States are about to disappear or to be converted into their opposite, with
the result that in the next generation Socialism in America will very probably
experience the greatest possible expansion of its appeal.[51]

This expectation perhaps adds weight to the view that the measuring of
Connolly's strategy against the United States experience should not be
vetoed by the claim of American exceptionalism.

The core of his case lay in his hopes for the Industrial Workers of the
World. Thus in advocating his strategy to Irish workers, he emphasised:

the system of organisation ... which has enabled the Industrial Workers of the
World ... to defeat the Steel Trust, the most powerful Trust in the World – to
defeat it in the very hour of its victory over the old-style trade unions.[52]

This is a very sanguine characterisation of the dispute at McKees Rocks,
Pennsylvania in the summer of 1909.[53] This exploded in the shops of
the Pressed Steel Car Company, a firm notable for its zealous pursuit of
scientific management techniques, a strategy that generated high profits
and employees' hostility. As Connolly noted, the AFL-based affiliates
were already ineffective in the steel industry and were anyway limited
to American-born craftsmen. The dispute at McKees Rocks began with
unskilled and unorganised immigrant workers, largely from Eastern
Europe. Able to build on communal solidarity and fortified by some who
had radical European pasts, they faced severe difficulties due to their
dependence on company housing, the partiality of the State authorities
and perhaps most damaging, the – at best – ambivalence and – at worst
– hostility of skilled American workers. Violence followed the use of
strike breakers and provided an occasion for the skilled sector to seek
a settlement. This met with rejection by the unskilled men and brought
in the IWW. The 'Wobblies' worked together easily with the immigrant
strikers. Employment of blacklegs produced further violence, escalating
into a confrontation between strikers and the authorities. Twelve
people died. The violence seems to have been simply the response of
embattled strikers to blacklegging and evictions, but it conjured up for

the respectable, the spectre of an alliance between revolutionary trade unionists and disaffected immigrants. Faced with this fear, employers, skilled workers and concerned citizens came together to produce a settlement. This was greeted by 'Wobblies' as a victory. Vincent St John was euphoric:

Company beat on all points. Strikers all members of IWW and in control.[54]

This verdict was echoed by Connolly in his advocacy of 'Wobbly' strategy.

The judgement could not be maintained by the unskilled strikers. They soon discovered that the 'victory' was illusory. They found their situation at work no better than that which had produced the strike. When they walked out again, the company used their skilled American colleagues to break the strike. They did so in a heavily symbolic manner, walking through a picket line behind an American flag. The dispute benefited neither the unskilled workers nor the IWW. Pressed Steel learnt their lesson and played effectively on ethnic and skill divisions within the workforce. By 1912, the 'Wobbly' presence in the plant was minimal.[55]

Connolly subsequently discovered at first hand the limitations of 'Wobbly' influence in the Pennsylvania steel towns. In the Spring of 1910 he went to New Castle, to participate in a protracted and ultimately defeated tin-plate strike.[56] His presence was itself a symptom of Socialist vulnerability. He became briefly the editor of the local Socialist newspaper. The local leaders had been gaoled. Strategies based in the workplace seemed highly vulnerable to the coercive power of the State. It was hardly the balance of forces prognosticated by advocates of Industrial Unionism.

These specific events perhaps permit some general comments. On the positive side, unskilled immigrant workers at McKees Rocks were able to organise a strike. The IWW's role in this was significant but contributions were made also by the strikers' communal solidarities and by some individuals' experiences in radical European politics. Such militant organisation was vital if Connolly's – and others' – hopes of effective action by the American working class were to be realised. But the gains proved transitory; a persistent feature of 'Wobbly' activities. One crucial aspect of this decline was clearly the existence of established trade unions organising mostly skilled American born males and affiliated to the American Federation of Labor. Such organisations were both product and exacerbator of working-class divisions. They could be used by employers to reward some workers at the expense of others. In his support for the 'Wobblies' Connolly was effectively committed to a strategy of Dual Unionism. Was this an avoidable weakness in his strategy?

The craft-based trade unionism, typical of the AFL was dismissed by Connolly as offering no basis for a Socialist politics. Rather it was 'the most dispersive and isolating force at work in the labour movement'.[57] Yet, however bleak his verdict, it was directed at the dominant pattern of American trade unionism. Part of Connolly's optimism rested on his belief that industrial developments would generate a more inclusive and revolutionary trade unionism, but his case also rested on the view that the dominance of the AFL need not be seen as inevitable. Rather it had emerged in part as the result of contingent factors.

This argument involved Connolly in making a positive assessment of the Knights of Labor as they existed at their zenith in the mid 1880s:

a mass organisation that ... aimed to organise all toilers into one union and made no distinction of craft, *nor of industry*, and that ... cherished revolutionary aims.[58]

He acknowledged that the Knights were in one sense utopian since their organisational structure paid no heed to the contemporary preoccupation of workers with immediate craft interests. Equally he suggested that modifications to incorporate craft and industry-wide interests could have been made whilst retaining the essential character of the Knights. Such a reform needed only the contribution of an effective and creative organiser, but this absence, plus the anti-radical panic generated by the Haymarket bombings facilitated the growth of the rival AFL.[59]

Such an analysis allowed Connolly to present the Federation as a 'usurper'. Organisational failings and reactionary hysteria had:

destroyed the growing unity of the working class for the time being.[60]

A natural line of development had been broken:

The industrial union, as typified to-day in the Industrial Workers of the World, could have ... developed out of the Knights of Labour as logically and perfectly as the adult develops from the child. No new organisation would have been necessary and hence we may conclude that the Industrial Workers of the World is the legitimate heir of the native American labour movement, the inheritor of its principles, and the ripened fruit of its experiences.[61]

This interpretation raises complex historiographical questions. Undoubtedly the Knights contained pre-industrial ideological legacies and these can be used to argue that the natural development was from such utopianism to the more pragmatic and more effective AFL. In contrast there was Engels' contemporary judgement, absorbed by some later historians, that the Knights represented an intial move by the American working class towards a more united form of class action.[62] But acceptance of this characterisation of the Knights' complexities is insufficient to demonstrate that such radical potential stood a good chance of realisation. Later accounts have claimed that the demise of the Knights was less accidental than Connolly suggests. Already managements operated to split their employees by offering favourable treatment to craftsmen in separate organisations. Moreover the relative permeability of political machines – at least at their lower levels – arguably diluted the political implications of militant industrial action and also provided a further basis for working-class divisions. The dispersion of the Knights' radical promise may indicate more durable constraints than any indicated in Connolly's account.

Yet it is also necessary to consider the view that socialists should be dismissive of the AFL. Several shared Connolly's opinion. Debs discounted attempts to win over the AFL. They were 'as wasteful of time as to spray a cesspool with attar of roses'.[63] In contrast, figures on the Socialist Right worked assiduously to expand their influence within the Federation, braving attacks from both Gompers and their own left wing, and arguing the Socialists must seek alliance with existing trade unions. If that meant compromising with organisations that were less progressive than Socialists would wish, then so be it. Socialist success within the AFL was always very limited.[64] In the early 1890s, the political personality of the Federation was not firmly established and Socialists had hopes that a progressive political programme might be adopted. These were squashed at the 1894 Convention and from then on in the aftermath of industrial defeats and with a rising tide of nativism, the position of the AFL on both industrial and wider political issues became conservative. When members of the newly formed Socialist Party began working in the Federation in the early 1900s, they faced a daunting prospect. Gompers and his allies were dominant, Socialists made little impact, and when faced with legal attacks, the AFL turned in 1908 not to the Socialist Party, but to the Democrats. Max Hayes, a leading Socialist at AFL Conventions, wrote disconsolately from the 1911 meeting:

The Socialists are simply up against a blank wall, and can't get a thing through no matter what its merit may be. All argument might as well be bottled up. The machine is in absolute control ...[65]

Given the policies of the Federation, the industrial strategy championed in their various ways by Socialists such as Connolly and Debs was not simply a dual unionist one, if this is understood as the offering of revolutionary alternatives to established trade union organisations. Most unskilled recently arrived immigrants had no such choice. The AFL offered protection to skilled established American born male workers, a partiality highlighted in its support for immigration restrictions. If attention is focussed on set-piece debates and on the positions of leading AFL personalities then the view of left-wing Socialists that boring from within was a blind alley, seems justified. But such a bleak assessment of the prospects for Socialists inside the AFL did not mean that the organisation could be ignored. It may have been racist, sectionalist and unavailable, but contrary to Connolly's dismissal of it as 'an usurper on the throne of labour',[66] it had established a reasonably firm presence amongst some of the most secure sections of the American working class.

In such circumstances, one route lay through the individual unions. The consequences of Socialist successes could be diluted or deflected within the AFL but arguably over the long haul such victories could make some difference. American unions could be won for Socialism or for political independence in the same fashion as their British counterparts. It was a strategy that Connolly explicitly rejected. He advocated a socialism based on revolutionary trade unionism and denied the political relevance of Socialist advances within old-style unions. Yet especially given the limited achievements of the IWW it is important to emphasise that Socialists achieved some advances in AFL affiliates such as the United Mine Workers and the tailoring trades unions.[67] The significance of such advances was frequently ambiguous, but certainly in British counterparts, some links between union victories for socialist activists and the political behaviour of members can be detected.

The trade union picture was more complex than Connolly suggested. His portrait of American labour developments was provocative but partial. A valid refusal to dismiss the radical facets of the Knights of Labor meant a playing down of their limitations. His explanation of AFL expansion failed to do justice to its strength in some sections of the American working class. By viewing such craft-based organisations as transitory, he absolved himself from any consideration of an appropriate strategy for Socialists within this sector. Work within AFL affiliates was often unrewarding. The immediate impact on the specific union was often unclear; any significance on the wider stage of the AFL was typically invisible. For Connolly such activities were open to the same objections as those he had made about British Labour developments. But the alternative was to ignore a bloc of trade union organisations that showed no sign of disappearing. Indeed it was the 'Wobblies' that demonstrated repeated evidence of fragility. Local organisation was often transitory, and even when it proved more durable, a preoccupation with immediate benefits meant that for most participants, the transition to a revolutionary commitment was never made. Contrary to Connolly's expectations, except for the minority, the IWW strategy did *not* 'invest the sordid details of the daily incidents of the class struggle with a new and beautiful meaning'.[68]

This persistent hiatus raises the question of the political significance of 'Wobbly' activities. One theme has emerged already in the reference to the New Castle dispute and highlights a perennial difficulty for the IWW. The central claim that workers' industrial power could offset coercive state institutions was falsified painfully for 'Wobblies' in successive industrial disputes and free-speech fights. Political authorities responded myopically to complaints about employer or vigilante violence or engaged in repressive measures of their own. In the context of war and the Russian Revolution, coercion by the State would become much more thorough culminating in the wholesale arrest of 'Wobblies', the Show Trials of 1918, and draconian sentences. The Red Scare of 1919–20 was a final act in an illiberal onslaught that did much to destroy revolutionary trade unionism in the United States. The deported miners of Bisbee Arizona, the bodies of 'Wobbly' martyrs, the political prisoners sentenced by Judge Landis at the Chicago Trial – all were tragic reminders of the hollowness of the 'Wobblies' fundamental strategic premise.[69] In such a crisis, there was no space for such a revolutionary alternative to develop. It was a realisation that Connolly would come to terms with after his return to Ireland.

If the liberalism of the authorities could not be assumed, this signposted the need for revolutionary trade unionists to be active in the political arena. Such involvement arguably could limit the repressive activities of governments, and also help to establish connections between militant industrial activities and wider political initiatives. This was an emphasis that Connolly had made repeatedly. In his view, the 'Wobblies' should – and would – develop a political presence. Their failure to do so arguably increased their vulnerability to State repression. Could the type of link that Connolly envisaged have been made?

At one level this raises a very general issue. The problem of American Socialist weakness is sometimes approached through the lack of durable connections between industrial struggle and class-based politics. In this broad context the 'Wobblies' predicament and the failure of Connolly's expectation seem an exemplification of a recurrent phenomenon. Although this is a valid emphasis, some qualifications are appropriate. The strength of the connection elsewhere should not be exaggerated. Where it appears significant, it may owe much to other factors, especially communal ones capable of including people not directly involved through the workplace. Moreover within the United States, at the height of Socialist influence, there were locations where such connections began to develop.

Such an admonition against excessive generalisation leads to a consideration of Connolly's precise hope that, in the absence of a specifically 'Wobbly' political presence, the Socialist Party could be won for a strategy of revolutionary Industrial Unionism. Acknowledging that advocates of this position were in a minority, he hoped that the Party's tolerance of factional debate would aid a shift to the position that he expected to be validated by industrial developments.[70]

Connolly left the United States just as the argument within the Socialist Party intensified. Some on the Party's Right saw attractions in the strategy of British Labour and hoped for a 'Labour Party' that would involve a close relationship with the AFL. Such an expectation was impracticable nationally, but added to internal wranglings. On a local level, some Socialist electoral breakthroughs most notably in Milwaukee, had depended on the support of skilled trade unionists. Even if a national deal was impossible, leaders such as Victor Berger were keen to maintain harmonious relationships with local AFL affiliates. This, plus a broader view of electoral prudence, led to increasing concern lest the Socialist Party be associated with 'Wobbly' 'anarchism' and 'violence'. Yet there were developments that seemed to favour the Left. Local Socialist organisations often worked easily with the IWW in strikes and free speech campaigns. Most notably, early in 1912, Party and revolutionary union came together in the famous Lawrence textile strike. The collaboration culminated in the strikers achieving their original demands.[71]

On this occasion, the alliance incorporated even the normally hostile Berger, but such harmony was transitory. Beneath the surface, differences of principle and tensions between personalities combined to make a denouement almost inevitable. The explosion came as the result of a speech made in New York by the 'Wobbly' and Socialist Party member, 'Big Bill' Haywood. He derided the effectiveness of political action, and argued that Socialists could not be hamstrung by considerations of legality. It was not just a clash of strategies but also of experiences within the diversity that was the United States – the organiser of miners in an often violent Far West against the assiduous municipal Socialists of Eastern cities. The latter seized their opportunity. At the Socialist Party convention in May 1912, the delegates supported by 191 votes to 90 a constitutional amendment that would expel 'any member of the party who opposes political action or advocates sabotage or other methods of violence as a weapon of the working class'. This was followed by a national referendum to recall Haywood from the Party's National Executive. It succeeded easily; Haywood received less than one-third of the votes cast. These defeats for the 'Direct Action' section were followed by a sizeable exodus; nearly 23,000 members left in 1912–13.[72]

The question remains: how inevitable was this destruction of Connolly's hopes? Contingent factors can be highlighted. Debs agreed with the Industrial Unionist critics of the AFL but opposed Haywood's rhetoric. He seemed to desire a compromise but showed an unwillingness to confront the implacable Berger with his commitment to total victory. In the absence of an effective reconciliatory group, the conflicting tendencies ripped the Party into two discordant sections. It was a polarisation to be found in varying forms in other national Labour movements in the years before 1914; within the American Party, the sheer diversity of experiences made any compromise even less likely. Victory for the Right in an open conflict was predictable – and for reasons that Connolly had himself outlined. Party decisions were dominated by cautious municipal politicians and bureaucrats. The SPA demonstrated precisely those traits that had led Michels towards his iron law of oligarchy and syndicalists towards denunciations of established forms of labour organisation. 'Direct actionists' within the Party demonstrated by their failure that they had no effective solution to this predicament.

This analysis has an impact that is inevitably deflationary. Critiques of Socialist strategy are all too easily destructive of a thinker's value. Any claims for originality are diluted through an emphasis on the extent to which problems and responses were shared with contemporaries. More drastically, any belief that strategic arguments are valid is destroyed by measuring them against recalcitrant circumstances. What then was the value of the strategic position that Connolly took back with him to Ireland?

Clearly his hopes for the American Left were to be buried beneath the accumulated failures of Socialist politics and revolutionary trade unionism. The simple judgement that this highlights the exceptionalism of the United States is untenable. The years that Connolly spent there were notable for the relative strength of American Socialism, and any demonstration of inevitable failure requires an argument, not just an assertion.

European Socialists might join their American comrades in expressing long-term optimism, but they could find little that offered immediate encouragement. This was particularly true for those who like Connolly placed themselves on the left of the Socialist movement. Their organisations were affected by controversies similar to those that divided the American Socialist Party, and European Left-Socialists generally achieved no more success in winning control of their parties and trade unions. There were moments when Connolly, confronting the problems of Socialist propaganda, denied this. Indeed he portrayed an American working class corrupted by capitalist values, whilst its European counterpart achieved an evermore developed class consciousness:

Whilst in Europe, the toiler has risen to a conception of the dignity and mission of his class, in America the ambition of the toiler is to be a slave driver instead of a slave ... this applies not only to the native-born American but to the working class of America as a whole, Irish as much as any other. The spirit of America is on them – the spirit of grab.[73]

Yet it was not the case that when Connolly left the United States, he quit a bastion of capitalism for a continent in which revolutionary Socialists – or indeed Socialists of any variety – were close to effective power. The American/European dichotomy is inappropriate, not just because it implies a misleading contrast, but also because it rests on an unacceptable level of generalisation. On both sides of the Atlantic, the prospects for socialist growth varied between regions and industries. Did the Irish situation offer any distinctive promise for the application of

Connolly's strategy? Inevitably the increasing emphasis on the National Question would be a major obstacle. By the time Connolly returned to Ireland, the British Liberal Government was facing a new parliamentary situation in which Irish MPs held the balance of power. The introduction of a Home Rule Bill seemed inevitable with all the consequential deepening of divisions within the Ulster working class. The complex relationship between competing definitions of nationality, the alliances generated by these, and militant class-based action would be fundamental for the remainder of Connolly's career.

If this was a powerful obstacle to the development of a revolutionary strategy, there was an important sense in which the IWW exemplar could seem relevant to the Irish situation. Whatever the claims made about revolutionary Industrial Unionism as an appropriate form of workers' organisation in the age of the Trust, the principal appeal of the 'Wobblies' was to impoverished workers, unskilled in terms of conventional definitions. Often they had an agrarian past possibly as recently arrived immigrants suffering from the elitism of native Americans. Perhaps they lived in a rural present as lumberjacks or itinerant farmworkers. Either way, they were not so much a population integrated into the routines of industrial capitalism, as people who had made the long journey from peasant traditions to American urban uncertainty, or who experienced the tightening grip of capitalist priorities in the Far West. Here was a potential constituency, previously unorganised and largely disparaged by existing unions, composed of groups who were in the process of radicalisation through the uneven and sometimes brutal impact of American capitalism. Similarly, large sections of the Irish working class were impoverished, often casually employed, unorganised and largely ignored by British trade unions. As with some of the 'Wobblies', experiences in rural Ireland could lead many to take a hostile view of government. Moreover, any potential working class radicalism did not face two obstacles that limited the impact of such strategies in the United States, and in several of the more developed European economies. Outside Belfast, conventional trade unions were weak; there was no significant parallel to the AFL which could blunt any radical challenge. Socialist political organisation was very limited, and could not claim to be a credible alternative to a militant industrial policy. The limitations of Irish industrialisation arguably helped to produce a radical potential amongst an impoverished working class; perhaps they also helped to ensure that some of the conventional obstacles to its institutional expression had a relatively slight presence. Could such a diagnosis demonstrate that in much of Ireland, there existed the experiences and the organisational space for a revolutionary policy of Industrial Unionism? This question would provide a second theme for Connolly's last years in Ireland – a question posed as the result of American experiences and now to be answered in an Irish context.

Chapter 5

Socialism and the *Gael*

When Connolly returned to Ireland, he brought not just a socialist strategy based on Industrial Unionism, but also a more thorough perception of the need to relate Socialist politics to the specific traditions and experiences of the Irish working class. Several basic claims had been developed in his earlier ISRP propaganda: the linking of socialist and national causes; the antipathy to pro-capitalist nationalists; the belief that the working class would be the agent of national emancipation; the insistence that such an achievement would be invalid, if capitalism was not ended. The continuities are important. Nevertheless, it is important to remember that two of his most reflective works: *Labour in Irish History* and *Labour, Nationality and Religion* were published in 1910. His history project had been several years in the making. Early drafts of some chapters had been published in *The Workers' Republic*. Similarly, his concern with the relationship between socialism and ethical issues was longstanding. It had surfaced in his Edinburgh years and his 1904 polemic with De Leon had included disagreements on marriage and religion. Yet these two published works were both written in America, and were influenced by his experiences with Irish American workers.

In the United States, Connolly encountered the first significant urban Irish working class.[1] Although the zenith of Irish immigration had occurred in the post-Famine years, the Irish continued to arrive in significant numbers until well after 1900. The move typically involved far more than a geographical shift. Migrants moved from a highly traditional peasant world to a sophisticated urban one. New arrivals from the West of Ireland confronted the vastness of New York City. Moreover, the 'New World' was not just one of skyscrapers and metropolitan promise and frustration: it was also one of wage-labour, often a novelty in itself. In such circumstances, it is hardly surprising that the Irish in America not only sought to maintain many of their old communal loyalties, but also brought traditional systems of authority into their new workplaces.

Connolly had a sharp perception of the way in which European rural decay and American capitalist growth were compelling a mass transfer of people. When he saw a newly-arrived Italian peasant woman and her children changing trains at Youngstown, Ohio, the vignette generated a reflection on how often such a migration involved clear losses, but only dubious gains:

think ... of the thousands of instances in which all that martyrdom, all that travail of emigration and breaking of home ties brought no relief to the sufferers, brought them only from the companionship and human sympathy of the old world to the cruel unfeeling environment of a new world, mad for gold, of a world basing all its activities and relations upon a 'cash nexus' upon a calculation centering around the dollar.[2]

Such experiences could be seen as producing a heavy resistence to socialist arguments. Immigrants could secure support from their own communal networks. These involved cross-class alliances and could become linked to established political organisations. Such investments of energy and time were diversions from any commitment to trade union, let alone socialist activities. Their consequence – the institutionalisation of ethnic differences within political structures – limited the chance of achieving workers' solidarity when confronted by a crisis.[3]

Such claims secure abundant support from American experiences but they do not have universal validity. Some trade unions transcended ethnic divisions; linguistic, communal and class solidarities could operate in the same direction; the arrival of new groups could erode traditional expectations. Specificity is essential in looking at this issue.[4] What points can be made about Irish–American workers and their receptivity to Socialist arguments?

There exists a stereotype captured in the comment of George B McClennan, Mayor of New York City in 1907:

There are Russian Socialists and Jewish Socialists and German Socialists! But thank God! There are no Irish Socialists![5]

In part, such hostility or at best apathy has been explained through the influence of Irish Catholicism with its antipathy to projects of political and social change. The continuing relevance of such religious precepts rested on the maintenance of an ethnic identity after arrival in the United States. Indeed such precepts were ambiguous. As Connolly would argue the actual position of Catholic leaders on such controversies could be remarkably at odds with what their fundamental religious principles permitted or implied. Religious influences and interpretations should be understood therefore not as adequate explanations but in the context of political and trade union attachments.

When faced with the Presidential contest of 1908, Connolly strongly commended the Socialist Party candidate to Irish workers. This was accompanied by a dismissal of their traditional choice, the Democrats. He presented them as a party of small businessmen, declining as the Trusts squeezed this class base. The characterisation was dubious, and in 1908 the Democrats' Presidential poll rose whilst the Socialist Party showed only a slight advance. Yet Connolly also acknowledged that the Democrats retained a significant presence in many communities:

the political party of the Democracy may hang on to a sordid existence in local affairs by means of its control of graft, whilst entirely eliminated as a serious aspirant to national power.[6]

It was precisely through such local fiefdoms that Irish electors were organised for the Democrats. As the Presidential campaign developed, Connolly had to acknowledge the strength of such machines. Against the graft, the immediate benefits and the ethnic identity represented in a traditional Party attachment, he proclaimed a class solidarity that would cut across older loyalties whether based on sentiment or pragmatism:

we must let the capitalist parties know that Irish workers are not married to the Democratic party, and that if we were we would soon secure a divorce on the grounds of 'incompatibility of interests' and set up our housekeeping alone, or rather in company with all the workers of every other race and nationality who understand their class interests.[7]

It was a forlorn hope.

If older political loyalties cemented together with a communal identity proved largely resistant to Socialist arguments, this of itself could be viewed as underlining Connolly's basic case that a strong Socialist movement depended on an effective Industrial Unionism. Perhaps the role of such an economic organisation was of particular importance given the facility with which Catholic anti-Socialists could connect the Socialist cause, with what were, for Connolly, irrelevant issues:

I am wearied unto death listening to Socialist speeches, and reading Socialist literature about materialism and philosophy and ethics and sex and embryology and monogamy and physiology and morism and platonism and determinism from men to whom the more immediate question of unionism is a sealed book ...

Industrial Unionism offered an effective route through such a maze of distractions:

... it will bring the Irish into the Socialist movement through the only gateway the Socialist philosophers have left unencumbered by their speculations and the only gateway by which a political party of the working class can make its demands effective ...[8]

Once again it was a hope that ran up against a stereotype. Irish–Americans were very visible in the trade union sphere, but to a very large degree, their activities were within AFL affiliates. They could be industrially militant. Henry George commented that 'the Irish burn like chips; the English like logs'.[9] But it was all usually within strict limits. Such union officials often played a significant part in setting the style of such organisations – the preoccupation with economic issues, a high level of organisational consciousness, a desire to protect hard-won benefits against the demands of more recent arrivals from Southern and Eastern Europe, and of Negroes. The image emerges of cautious, socially-conservative trade unions officials influenced perhaps by religious leaders or by the requirements of the Democratic machines, at any rate a bulwark against Socialist growth. The Irish brought with them neither experience of socialist politics nor often of industrial employment. They were available for integration into a-political trade unionism and Democratic politics. Yet there were exceptions. The Molly Maguires in the Pennsylvania coalfields of the 1870s − radical in tactics if ambiguous in ideology − were Irish-dominated: there were prominent Irish figures in the Knights of Labor; second generation Irish trade unionists played significant roles as Socialist advocates in some trade unions, most notably the Shoeworkers.[10] Irish Americans clearly could be won for Socialism, although the prospect was generally discouraging.

Faced with these difficulties, Connolly played a leading part in forming the Irish Socialist Federation.[11] From January 1908, he edited *The Harp* to propagate his developing views on the relationship between nationalism and socialism. The ISF had a stall at the Socialist Party's 1908 Convention. Its speakers propagandised in New York City streets. Its influence was limited.[12] *The Harp* had chronic financial problems. Late in 1909, Connolly claimed that it had only 800 subscribers and was difficult to maintain.[13] Elizabeth Gurley Flynn recalled the limited response that he achieved to his propaganda:

It was a pathetic sight to see him standing, poorly clad, at the door of Cooper Union or some other East Side hall, selling his little paper. None of the prosperous professional Irish, who shouted their admiration for him after his death lent him a helping hand at that time. Jim Connolly was anathema to them because he was a Socialist.[14]

The significance of *The Harp* lies much more in the evidence it furnishes of Connolly's ideas at the time that he was working on *Labour in Irish History*, and giving thought to the question of the relationship between Socialism and Catholicism.

One basis for Connolly's commitment to this strategy lay in his realisation that a particular image of what was involved in an Irish identity was utilised for anti-socialist purposes. There was a need for a:

proletarian organisation to combat the evil teaching and practices of the capitalist politicians and schemers who prey upon the workers of our race in America.[15]

The effectiveness of such politicians' strategy came in part from their ability to utilise the concern about Ireland's oppression by Britain:

The Irish are the only race in America among whom are organised associations for the express purpose of assisting capitalist parties in the old country. The United Irish League of America is a case in point. Its one end and aim is to boost the reputation of the representatives in Parliament of the Irish capitalist class, to popularise their propaganda and finance their organisations. As it claims to speak in the name of Ireland it holds the attention and wins the sympathy of the Irish in America, and working on this basis, it succeeds in delivering the Irish vote to the political parties of the American capitalist class and the Irish dollars to the Irish capitalist.[16]

The proper response for Irish Socialists required them to resist a superficial interpretation of Socialist internationalism. Such a limited view had destroyed Socialist credibility within Irish communities; a destruction made the more complete on account of the Irish feeling that they were an oppressed nationality:

the man or woman who broke away from and kept aloof from contact with things Irish and with an Irish environment became, in the eyes of their fellow-countrymen and women, deserters from the weaker side in a fight, and therefore objects of opprobium and hatred. In the case of those who became Socialists, this was invariably the course of events; the dislike and hatred did not precede, but followed from the breaking away from Irish associations.

The proper response for Irish Socialists was not the maintenance of isolation but a demonstration:

that Socialism made its devotees better equipped mentally and morally to combat oppression than any scheme evolved by the invertebrate Irish middle class politicians.

This involved working with other Irish organisations in the literary, educational and revolutionary fields even if these had no specifically Socialist commitment. Through the columns of *The Harp*, Connolly expressed some support for the language enthusiasts of the Gaelic Revival. Central to his project of an Irish Socialism, there stood the writing of a history of Ireland:

we propose to make a campaign amongst our countrymen and to rely for our method mainly upon an imparting to them a correct interpretation of the facts of Irish history.[17]

During the Summer of 1908, *The Harp* began to publish some chapters of Connolly's work on Irish history; by the beginning of 1909, he offered a twofold justification of his project – Socialists could find their arguments strengthened by an awareness of the Irish past; but perhaps more crucially non-Socialists could be persuaded that the most compelling interpretation of 'all the welter and chaos of our national struggle' had a Socialist content, 'a steady social evolution'. Its course lay:

from the *common ownership of the clan* through the forcing house of capitalist property onto the higher ground of the *common ownership of all the workers* in each free nation, in a world knowing no master.[18]

This argument provided a central thread to *Labour in Irish History*.

In one significant sense, this text belongs to a genus that has become familiar much more recently. It is an attempt to correct the limitations and the distortions of conventional historiography, to bring into the spotlight, those 'hidden from history'. Such an exercise can produce a more accurate historical account, but it can also serve as a means of legitimising a Socialist project. In part this comes from the deflationary impact that such an exercise can have on the apologies offered by ruling groups; but also a rediscovery of the histories of radical Irish movements can offer ethical and intellectual continuities with modern Socialists. One element within Connolly's approach was expressed sharply in a *Harp* comment of September 1908:

What would we think of the historian who would picture the life of the daughter of an Irish aristocrat of today, and then tell us that this was a picture of the life of a typical Irish girl of the twentieth century? We would laugh him to scorn. Yet that is the manner in which history is written.[19]

If one rediscovery was that of the experiences and initiatives of sub-ordinate classes, another placed Connolly's work within the broad current of the Gaelic Revival. He related his work to the recent book by Alice Stopford Green, *The Making of Ireland and Its Undoing*. Published in 1908 and reviewed in *The Harp*,[20] this focused on the destruction of Gaelic culture following the Conquest of the sixteenth and seventeenth centuries. This was presented as a 'rupture' which rendered subsequent developments in a basic sense abnormal. The liberation of Ireland required a reconnection with the older traditions. A first step was the exorcism of more recent images of Irish history:

the whole concept of orthodox Irish history for the last 200 years was a betrayal and abandonment of the best traditions of the Irish race.

For Connolly, the loss was not just of a national culture, but also of a communal society:

the new Irish educated in foreign standards ... adopted as their own the feudal–capitalist system of which England was the exponent in Ireland, and urged it on the Gaelic Irish.[21]

As analysed later, this location was symptomatic of a growing difficulty for Connolly. His Socialism was attached increasingly to a divisive con-ception of the Irish nation.[22] In immediate terms, the context provided its quota of romanticism; Connolly was heavily idealistic about the social structure of the old Ireland based on the clan system. He simply neglected to discuss the place of slavery within that society.

More significantly, this socialist interpretation within the broad current of the Gaelic Revival analysed a variety of historical episodes and individuals to make a basic political point. The strategy of the Home Rulers and the history that they utilised in order to strengthen their case should be rejected. The argument necessitated the elucidation of funda-mental assumptions that can organise and characterise the historical material. An attempt to develop a productive rather than a destructive relationship between socialist and nationalist perspectives can be found at the beginning of *Labour in Irish History*:

In the evolution of civilisation the progress of the fight for national liberty of any subject nation must, perforce, keep pace with the progress of the struggle for liberty of the most subject class in that nation ... the shifting of economic and political forces which accompanies the development of the system of capitalist society leads inevitably to the increasing conservatism of the non-working class element and to the revolutionary vigour and power of the working class.[23]

This primary proposition contains its ambiguities. In what sense *'must'* the progress of the fight for national liberty 'keep pace' with the struggle for working-class emancipation? It could be interpreted as a sociological claim derivable from Connolly's basically materialist position. As Irish capitalism develops so the economic and the political significance of the working class increases. It expands in numbers and in awareness; its perceptions are sharpened by the absence of economic ties such as those cementing other classes to some form of Union with Britain.

Such an interpretation can be measured against subsequent Irish developments. Some sections of the Irish bourgeoisie were prepared to support some degree of political separation; some important sections of the Irish working class were not. Such problems raise doubts about Connolly's assumptions which will be considered in detail later. Nevertheless his proposition is capable of a second interpretation flowing out of the ambiguity of that crucial word, 'must'.

This second characterisation is an ethical one that appears frequently in Connolly's writings. National and class emancipations must keep pace with one another since national independence, without the destruction of capitalism, would be worthless. He had expressed this view in the late 1890s; he would express it after his return to Ireland in a later pamphlet, *The Reconquest of Ireland*:

the Labour Movement of Ireland must set itself the Reconquest of Ireland as its final aim ... the reconquest involves taking possession of the entire country, all its power of wealth-production and all its natural resources, and organising these on a cooperative basis for the good of all ... this and this alone would be a reconquest.[24]

In proclaiming this ambitious role for Irish Labour, Connolly was nevertheless realistic enough to acknowledge that the likely course of events would be more tortuous. The achievement of a Home Rule Parliament could normalise political divisions along class lines. In such a situation the demythologising impact of *Labour in Irish History* would be significant.

Optimism about such a scenario was heightened by Connolly's largely orthodox historical materialism. Any understanding of Irish history must utilise a method that could penetrate beneath the superficial evidence of institutional forms and political rhetoric. Thus, in attacking the conventional Nationalist claim that the Act of Union had had a destructive effect on the Irish economy, he spelt out his methodological position:

... the socialist philosophy of history provides the key to the problem – points to the economic development as the true solution.[25]

The early forms of mechanised industry were applicable in Ireland but soon British coal supplies fatally handicapped Irish competitors:

A native Parliament might have hindered the subsequent decay, as an alien Parliament may have hastened it; but in either case, under capitalistic conditions, the process itself was as inevitable as the economic evolution of which it was one of the most significant signs.[26]

Similarly, Connolly opposed the conventional Nationalist image of the Famine. Culpability was not simply a matter of national oppression; it came from the English commitment to capitalism:

No man who accepts capitalist society and the laws thereof can logically find fault with the statesmen of England for their acts in that awful period. They stood for the rights of property and free competition, and philosophically accepted their consequences upon Ireland; the leaders of the Irish people also stood for the rights of property and refused to abandon them ...[27]

Connolly's ripostes to conventional Nationalist historiography clearly owed much to the application of conventional emphases within Second International Marxism – the concentration on economic constraints; the emphasis on capitalism as a concept that can be applied scientifically to demonstrate the shortcomings within the perceptions of both agents and commentators. Yet Connolly was also typical in his acceptance of an evolutionary perspective that owed something to claims which were not specifically Marxist. Like several of his contemporaries he was attracted by the findings of the American, Lewis Morgan, as presented in his book, *Ancient Society*. This source had a particular legitimacy for Marxists.[28] Engels in his *Origins of the Family* had relied strongly on Morgan for his discussion of Primitive Communism. In fact the type of claim advanced by Morgan typified the direction taken by several writers in the 1870s. Perceptions of historical time were extended drastically. The possibility of an evolutionary social science emerged. Engels claimed that Morgan had provided independent support for a Marxist view of history. In fact many Marxists came to amalgamate their original perceptions with elements of an evolutionary sociology. They did so without worrying too much about theoretical incompatibilities. Thus, for Connolly, the methods employed by Morgan could be utilised to clarify the remote Irish past. He had provided 'the key' for studying the American Indians. Hopefully:

the same key will yet unlock the doors which guard the secrets of our native Celtic civilisation.[29]

It would reveal that Socialist values had a venerable Irish pedigree.

A more immediate and more feasible task concerned the discrediting of commonly held views about Irish society and politics since the late seventeenth century. One essential thrust concerned the view that much of Ireland's troubles stemmed from the Union. The way in which Connolly employed his historical method to attack conventional views about the economic consequences of the Irish Parliament's abolition, has been noted. Equally, he was concerned to devalue the significance of those Irish leaders who had been dedicated to pragmatic negotiations with Britain. His attack on O'Connell paralleled claims commonly advanced by him against the Home Rule politicians of his own day. Whatever his initial sympathies with labour demands, the 'Liberator' was gradually drawn into a more hostile relationship. As he:

grew in strength in the country, and attracted to himself more and more of the capitalist and professional classes in Ireland, and as he became more necessary to the schemes of the Whig politicians in England, and thought these latter more necessary to his success, he ceased to play for the favour of organised labour, and gradually developed into the most bitter and unscrupulous enemy of trade unionism Ireland has yet produced ...[30]

The basing of a Nationalist strategy on the priorities of Irish capitalists; the impact of deals with London politicians – the reactionary significance was, for Connolly, obvious. O'Connell's political path was paralleled by that of the post-Parnell Parliamentary Party. Their lack of sympathy for labour's demands would become apparent in the Dublin Lock Out of 1913.

If Connolly's history had its demonology extending from Grattan through O'Connell to Redmond, it also claimed a positive Nationalist tradition. This was summarised by the dates, 1798, 1848 (with qualifications) and 1867. On one level, it could be viewed as a tradition of Physical Force Republicanism that culminated in 1916, and was always available as a counterpoint to the varied pragmatisms of the constitutionalists. But Connolly viewed this alternative strand as possessing a popular social content or at least a potential that could culminate in a viable Irish Socialist movement.

His analysis of the radical alternative generated a powerful criticism of dominant views, although at the same time it produced its quota of unresolved issues. One of his earliest involvements in Nationalist politics had been in the Wolfe Tone centenary celebrations of 1898. He expressed a consistent criticism of orthodox Nationalists. They offered an expurgated account of Tone and his associates:

The middle-class 'patriotic' historians, orators and journalists of Ireland have ever vied with one another in enthusiastic descriptions of their military exploits on land and sea, their hairbreadth escapes and heroic martyrdom, but have resolutely suppressed or distorted their writings, songs and manifestoes.[31]

In contrast, Connolly emphasised their radical–democratic credentials: a strategy centered around an appeal to the mass of the people, a willingness to prosecute a class war, a vigorous anti-sectarianism, an internationalist outlook. It was emphatically not the style of later constitutional Nationalists. Irish Socialists could claim to be their only valid heir.

One problematic aspect of Connolly's presentation concerns its historical adequacy. Whatever the non-sectarianism of leading figures, this was not always matched by the intentions and actions of nominal followers. The Wexford Rising of 1798 strongly Roman Catholic in membership and style, involved attacks on local Protestants, and seemed much more fuelled by local grievances than by the wider visions of the United Irishmen.[32] In the North East, where support had involved sympathy for the values of revolutionary France, this was diminishing by 1798, in part perhaps because of revived religious tensions. Any interpretation that suggested '1798' as a demonstration of the appeal of non-sectarian Republicanism carried dangers, if this promise was absorbed by later Socialists without an accompanying awareness of the strategy's difficulties.

This raises the narrower but complex issue of the significance of this episode for Connolly's overall view of Irish history. There are passages where he suggests that contingent factors prevented a radically different outcome. French intervention could have happened in the 1790s and would probably have been decisive. The lack of vigour shown by the French commander of the Bantry Bay expedition is specifically cited:

Had he been a man equal to the occasion and landed his expedition, Ireland would almost undoubtedly have been separated from England and become mistress of her own national destinies.[33]

For hypothetical purposes, let it be assumed that these contingent factors had been different and also that the sectarian obstacle had been overcome; so had the coercive capacity of the British State a constraint to which Connolly devotes no attention. Instead there is the highly unlikely event of a Radical Republican regime in Ireland.

The significance for Socialists would be obscure. Connolly had previously devoted some attention to the argument that in the 1780s a bourgeois revolution had failed to materialise:

Had a strong enterprising and successful Irish capitalist class been in existence in Ireland, a Parliamentary reform investing the Irish masses with the suffrage would have been won under the guns of the Volunteers without a drop of blood being shed; and with a Parliament elected under such conditions the Act of Union would have been impossible.[34]

The comment is reminiscent of Marxist judgements on the failure of liberal bourgeois revolutions in nineteenth century Germany. In each case, it remains debatable how much should be explained by compelling material factors and how much by strategic failures and successes. But Connolly does seem to suggest a very restricted material base for a republican success in Ireland. If such a regime had been instituted, backed perhaps by French bayonets, it would have been a radical bourgeois one. Its potential from a Socialist viewpoint could be only that it indicated a sizeable stride forward towards the Socialist goal. Even this would be true only within a uniform evolutionary perspective. Recalling that Connolly had already made some comments suggesting that Irish lack of development could provide advantages for Socialists, such a radical capitalist breakthrough could be characterised as on balance damaging for Socialist fortunes.

Ultimately, Connolly's case for the United Irishmen was not entangled in this complex thicket of 'might have beens'. Rather the organisation was a relevant exemplar for Socialists:

a plan of campaign ... on the lines of those afterwards followed so successfully by the Socialists of Europe – a revolutionary party openly declaring their revolutionary sympathies, but limiting their first demand to a popular measure such as would enfranchise the masses, upon whose support their ultimate success must rest.

But once again, the question of such a revolution's content arises. Clearly, Connolly did not see this as socialist:

these men aimed at nothing less than a social and political revolution such as had been accomplished in France, or even greater, because the French Revolution did not enfranchise all the people ...[35]

Moreover, Connolly had made some sharp comments in the past about the tendency of Socialists to view the French case as a valid model. He had noted the 'baneful inheritance' for Socialists of that image of revolution. The need then had been to destroy the constraints of feudalism; now it was to construct institutions based on the productive achievements of capitalism. Constructive, not iconoclastic, communal not individualist, Connolly had placed the impending Socialist revolution in a very different category from that of 1789:

We have to remember that the French Revolution was an uprising of the capitalist class, that their tactics may not be our tactics, and that their victory added another to the list of our enemies in power.[36]

Connolly was clearly successful in establishing the radical Republicanism of the United Irishmen; their significance for Socialists, even by his own tenets remained less obvious.

His analysis of the Irish contribution to the year of revolutions, 1848, is hedged with more qualifications. Once again the essential failure is presented as avoidable. He notes the few leaders who saw the need to link broader national demands to the immediate plight of the people. Their remedies were to withhold rents, to retain crops and to block roads and railways to prevent food being taken from the country. If this strategy had been followed widely, the results would have been, in Connolly's view, dramatic:

Had such advice been followed by the Young Irelanders as a body it would, as events showed, have been enthusiastically adopted by the people at large, in which event no force in the power of England could have saved landlordism or the British Empire in Ireland.[37]

His analysis demonstrates a characteristic concern of Connolly that a radical rank and file could always be frustrated by cautious or corrupted leaders:

The simple fact is that the Irish workers in town and country were ready and willing to revolt, and that the English Government of the time was saved from serious danger only by the fact that Smith O'Brien and those who patterned after him, dreaded to trust the nation to the passion of the so-called lower classes.[38]

Once again the question of the feasibility and significance of such an alternative should be separated from Connolly's attempt to discover elements relevant to an Irish Socialist strategy. An option may have been unlikely; and even if achieved still limited in its social significance. Instead attention can be devoted to the analysis of individual radicals. Connolly devotes some consideration to John Mitchel citing passages that in their denunciation of the destructive impact of a Free Trade system, show strong affinities with the contemporary writings of Thomas Carlyle. As with his Scottish counterpart, Mitchel could mount scathing attacks on popular movements. He welcomed the February 1848 Revolution in France for its overthrow of:

the enlightened pedantic political economy (what we know in Ireland as the English political economy or the famine political economy).[39]

Yet he then denounced the June insurrection of Parisian workers; a shift explained by Connolly as the product of a lack of information following his imprisonment.[40] The reponse is inadequate. Elitism and racism continually appear in Mitchel's writings along with his denunciations of capitalist individualism and British rule in Ireland. During his American exile he emerged as a supporter of slavery and of the Confederacy. He belongs within the tradition of the Romantic critique of capitalism, essentially anti-liberal and productive of both radical and reactionary implications.

Connolly's most positive analysis of any figure in the 1848 Movement came in his discussion of James Fintan Lalor. This reflected a longstanding view. One of his earliest publications during the ISRP years had been a pamphlet of Lalor's writings.[41] His interpretation led him to view Lalor as an 'Irish apostle of revolutionary Socialism'.[42] One significant basis for this assessment lay in Lalor's concern that the struggles of Irish radicals formed part of a wider conflict that incorporated popular movements in other societies. Most crucially however, it rested on Lalor's insistence that national and economic demands must be synthesised. The claim that popular sovereignty was the foundation of nationality was tied to the critical issue of land:

The principle I state and mean to stand upon is this, that the entire ownership of Ireland, moral and material, up to the sun and down to the centre, is vested of right in the people of Ireland; that they, and none but they, are the land-owners and law-makers of this island; that all laws are null and void not made by them; and all titles to land invalid not conferred and confirmed by them; and that this full right of ownership may and ought to be asserted and enforced by any and all means which God has put into the power of man.[43]

The similarities with Connolly's claim that the national revolution must be also a socialist one are obvious. But there is a clear divergence over the content of desirable economic changes. Lalor's concern centered around the plight of the small agricultural tenants. Their continual reduction to the state of landless labourers was deplorable. He offered nothing to the bulk of the propertyless; instead he sought to revive a stable and viable class of tenant farmers. This was to be a central theme in radical Irish agitations but it hardly constituted a suppressed Socialist alternative.

A similar point can be made about Connolly's discussion of Fenianism. While it is easy to show that the movement's support came from urban workers, rural labourers, poor farmers plus some who had risen into the lower middle class, it does not follow that their support was based on more than a desire for national independence. Opponents might have condemned Fenianism as 'communist'; a few revolutionary socialists might have hoped that such a condemnation was valid. But such a claim reflected neuroses, unsubstantiated optimism or rhetorical exaggeration. The Fenian orthodoxy was clear:

Irishmen begin to feel that we must regain our lost independence 'at all hazards' ... Any plan short of this for bettering the condition of Ireland commences work at the wrong end ...[44]

Besides such an assertion, Connolly's attempts to relate Fenianism to expanding working class organisation, both within Ireland and internationally, provide only suggestive but misleading signposts.[45]

Assessment of *Labour in Irish History* must begin by emphasising the qualities of a work written often under conditions of personal hardship: unemployment, poverty, the carving out of periods for research and writing from the demands of more immediate political activities. Unlike many of the popular histories produced by Connolly's Socialist contemporaries, it is of more than antiquarian interest. Issues are raised which remain central to historical debate. They emerge in a sharp if sometimes simplified fashion that demonstrates Connolly's stylistic commitment:

the teaching of social science does not mean the juggling with a vocabulary of scientific phrases and with a difficult technical terminology.[46]

Within the present analysis three significant questions emerge which connect with Connolly's subsequent political strategy.

Constitutional Nationalists with a stake in the existing order might fight to define the history of the National Question and its current significance in narrowly political terms, yet Connolly showed easily that economic and social arguments had always played a central role. For the Socialist, this offered the comfort that concern with such questions was compatible with a firm position on issues of nationality. Nevertheless, a problem arose when Connolly attempted to show that earlier figures – most notably Tone and Lalor – made claims that had substantive significance for Socialists. It might well be the case that they provided impressive examples of revolutionary commitment, and of the synthesis of economic, social and national claims. But Connolly's interpretations tended to play down the bourgeois–radical limits of the United Irishmen and to offer a partial portrait of Lalor. As a demonstration of a Socialist pedigree the argument had its difficulties. It also suggested a practical problem for Connolly's own strategy in that it could lead to an exaggerated estimate of how far this radical tradition contained a potential for socialist development.

Another related question about the potential for Irish Socialist development recurred during Connolly's analysis. His conventional historical materialism plus his evolutionary socialism would suggest that capitalist developments would need to mature in Ireland before a transition to Socialism could be feasible. Yet sometimes his argument suggests the significance of 'might have beens'. The earlier analysis of '1798' suggests that his considered alternative might have been a dubious prospect for Socialists. His treatment of the 1840s was at one point more explicit on this theme:

Had Socialist principles been applied to Ireland in those days, not one person need have died of hunger ...[47]

Assuming this is not a fragment of utopianism, it counts as a clear suggestion that some sort of Socialist development was feasible in a predominantly rural society with a largely traditional agriculture, and only a small urban working class. Certainly in some of Connolly's earlier writings, there had been hints that societies need not move to socialism along a uniform road. The claim that capitalism was an English import, the radical facets of Irish Nationalism, the pressures that were increasing on Irish agriculture and the strategic role of Ireland vis à vis the British Empire – all or some could be used to justify a specifically Irish route. Such claims left their mark on Connolly's view of Irish history and lived uneasily alongside his expressions of support for the orthodoxies of historical materialism and evolutionary socialism.

The feasibility of an Irish path to Socialism remained as a problem to be explored through fundamental political choices that would include a search for any Socialist potential contained within the more radical variants of Irish Nationalism. Such a development included an acceptance of a particular notion of what it was to be Irish. Connolly's commitment comes through clearly in *Labour in Irish History*. Its status as a Socialist variant within Gaelic historiography, and its support for the tradition of Direct Action Republicanism show how far Connolly, despite his anti-sectarian principles, had come to accept a view of Irish nationality that was Gaelic and Catholic. This was demonstrated further by a significant silence. Catholic–Protestant tensions are examined down to the defeat of the United Irishmen which was presented with some degree of ideal-isation as a movement capable of bridging the sectarian divide. But after that Connolly's account became essentially an analysis of Catholic Nationalism. There was no discussion of the development of working-class Unionism in the North-East, and no suggestion that Ulster's agitations against the Gladstonian Home Rule proposals indicated a substantial difficulty for any Irish route to Socialism.

Within the Nationalist tradition as defined by Connolly, his claims about the socialist and national causes developing together faced obstacles on account of the attitudes of official Catholicism. He had experienced this hostility both in Ireland and in the United States. Any response required an acceptance of one fundamental fact. Ireland and Poland were distinctive amongst communities aspiring to national independence in pre-1914 Europe. In both cases, the Catholic Church was perceived widely as the symbol of a people's struggle against foreign domination. So neither society experienced the nineteenth century battle to settle the boundary between Church and State that was elsewhere so characteristic of Catholic Europe. Accordingly, it was difficult for either Radical–Liberal or Socialist movements to emerge, hostile or indifferent to a Church so central to the national struggle.[48]

Eventually, Connolly would claim somewhat idealistically that the oppression of Catholics had made them a significant revolutionary force in the Irish context – their emancipation would mean the emancipation of all:

the Irish Catholic has realised instinctively that he, being the most oppressed and disfranchised, could not win any modicum of political freedom or social recognition for himself without winning it for all others in Ireland. Every upward step of the Catholic peasant has emancipated some one of the smaller Protestant sects; every successful revolt of the Catholic has given some added security even to those Protestant farmers who were most zealously defending the landlord. And out of this struggle the Catholic has perforce learned toleration.[49]

It was an optimism belied by the cultural claims of some leading advocates of 'Irish Ireland', and experienced as false by those such as the playwright J. M. Synge whose work was felt to be at odds with the idealised stereotypes of an often puritanical nationalism.[50]

This claim was supplemented by a more pragmatic one. Connolly claimed that the Catholic experience could add something worthwhile to the Socialist cause. Tom Bell, a Scottish comrade and founder-member of the SLP, recalled his early surprise at Connolly's emphasis on his Catholic background – and also his response to Bell's questioning:

> Well, it is like this. In Ireland all the Protestants are Orangemen and howling Jingoes. If the children go to the Protestant schools, they get taught to wave the Union Jack and worship the English king. If they go to the Catholic Church they become rebels. Which would you sooner have?[51]

The optimism reflected the distinctive position of the Catholic Church as a symbol of an oppressed nationality, but it left unresolved the issue of what in Socialist terms was the consequence of such rebelliousness. Any attempt to resolve this led Connolly into a consideration of the degree of compatibility between Socialist and Catholic claims.

One frequent response was that the question did not have much importance. The SPD's Erfurt Programme of 1891 had declared that Socialist Parties should not be concerned with questions of religious belief and this had been accepted as authoritative by the Socialist International. Nevertheless, there were pressures within Socialist organisations to take a firmly anti-religious line. Sometimes these reflected the conservatism of religious organisations; sometimes they could be viewed as a manifestation of the reductionism inherent in a strongly determinist approach to beliefs. Even many Socialists who were prepared to take a tolerant view nevertheless believed that eventually religious commitments would be discarded as so many illusions. These were emphases that Connolly never made. Arguably this distinctiveness was not just attributable to his Catholic background, but also reflected the quality of his Edinburgh Socialist apprenticeship. As noted in an earlier chapter, this had included the example of former members of the Socialist League with their insistence on the centrality of a moral dimension to Socialist growth.[52]

Connolly's central argument on the question of Socialist–Catholic compatability was based on his repeated assertion that Socialism was only concerned with economic issues. All else was not an integral part of a Socialist position. This view, he articulated as early as January 1896 when criticising an Edinburgh clergyman for his attacks on Socialism as anti-marriage.[53] More significantly, he followed this with an attack on the socialist–feminist Edith Lanchester. Whilst chairing a meeting for her during a Scottish tour, he warned the audience of his difference with the speaker:

> Socialism had no connection with speculations on family life and was nowise responsible for the opinions of individual socialists on that subject.[54]

Most dramatically, his views on marriage and on religion provided a significant element in his 1904 polemic with De Leon:

The abolition of the capitalist system will undoubtedly solve the economic side of the Woman Question, but it will solve that alone. The question of marriage, of divorce, of paternity, of the equality of woman with man are physical and sexual questions, or questions of temperamental affiliation as in marriage, and were we living in a Socialist Republic would still be hotly contested as they are today.[55]

This avoidance of any simplistic reduction of all conflicts to the economic is characteristic. The emphasis on the survival of personal dilemmas under Socialism shares something with the view of William Morris.[56] Yet, Connolly's approach can be contrasted with that of another Socialist weaned in a Catholic culture, Antonio Gramsci:

It seems clear that the new industrialism wants monogamy; it wants the man as worker not to squander his nervous energies in the disorderly and stimulating pursuit of occasional sexual satisfaction. The exaltation of passion cannot be reconciled with the timed movements of productive motions connected with the most perfected automatism.[57]

Sociologically, perhaps, the contrast can be related to the divergent places of the Catholic Church in Irish and Italian societies; conceptually, it is important to see what Connolly's approach emphasised and what it omitted. One response would be that despite his organisational work with women in the Belfast textile industry, and despite his firm support for womens' suffrage, Connolly held conventionally patriarchal views on personal relationships. These were reflected in the imagery which he characteristically used to discuss womens' virtues;[58] his position on marriage can be seen as one facet of this. Two comments seem in order. One is simply that many of his Socialist contemporaries who held much more reductionist ideas expressed views at least as patriarchal as those of Connolly. More fundamentally, any perspective that places significant weight on the influence of economic factors runs the risk of marginalising ethical debate. Connolly, whatever the inadequacies of his specific claims, at least attempted to sketch out some territory for ethical argument. In contrast, Gramsci's presentation shows a sharp sense of the way in which social institutions and practices might develop, often without deliberate social engineering, as bulwarks of a particular economic order. Such an emphasis did not prohibit the debating of moral claims, although insensitive or authoritarian adherents might act as though it did.

These considerations provide much of the intellectual background to the 1910 pamphlet, *Labour, Nationality and Religion*.[59] Connolly also utilised a claim that he had discussed earlier in *The Harp*: the Catholic bureaucracy was extremely adaptable and would accept the advent of socialism as it had done earlier radical changes.[60] Such a shift could be legitimised through a selective presentation of its previous doctrines.

The clear implication is that Connolly expected Catholicism to survive under Socialism. Much of the pamphlet was a vigorous and effective demonstration of the discrepancies between the contemporary claims of the Church and its fundamental principles. On questions such as the rights of private property, the Church acted as an apologist for the values of capitalism and in so doing abandoned its own older principles.[61] Connolly had no illusions about the traditional social function of the Catholic Church:

Ever counselling humility, but sitting in the seats of the mighty; ever patching up the diseased and broken wrecks of an unjust social system, but blessing the system which made the wrecks and spread the disease; ever running divine discontent and pity into the ground as the lightning rod runs and dissipates lightning, instead of gathering it and directing it for social righteousness ...[62]

Yet such thorough criticism of the Church as an institution, backed by the claim that Catholic doctrines had been perverted to serve the interests of dominant classes, did not lead to a wholesale rejection of such fundamental religious claims. Indeed his argument suggested that only within a Socialist society was there hope for the realisation of such values.

Connolly was however selective about the religious precepts that would be realised. He accepted an orthodox materialist view of the Reformation and turned this against Catholic apologists for capitalism:

... as capitalism taught the doctrine of every man for himself and by its growing power forced such doctrines upon the ruling class it created its reflex in the religious world, and that reflex, proclaiming that individual belief was the sole necessity of salvation appears in history as the Protestant Reformation. Now the Church curses the Protestant Reformation – the child – and blesses capitalism, its parent.[63]

Prepared to explain away Protestantism in economic terms, he did not acknowledge the acceptability of such a reduction in the case of Catholicism. The demarcation of a territory wherein Socialists could debate ethical claims was important; the dimensions of the territory raised serious difficulties. On the one side, Connolly's claims had some affinity with those who criticised liberal-individualism as destructive of pre-capitalist, perhaps medieval virtues. Socialism could resurrect such values, but in an egalitarian context. But in contrast, his presentation diverged sharply from those writers – often English – who would link Socialist politics to a radical–democratic tradition that was essentially Protestant. Their Socialist legitimation looked back not to a Gaelic culture and communal ownership, but to the Seventeenth Century Radicals and their legacy expressed often in the language and practices of Old Dissent.[64]

After his return to Ireland, he employed the insights developed in his American years. He argued for a distinctively Irish Socialist movement that would relate positively to a national culture:

the phrases and catchwords which might serve to express the soul of the movement in one country may possibly stifle it in another.[65]

This commitment had produced a Socialist approach to Irish history and it had begun an analysis of how historical materialism could connect with ethical arguments. Such developments were tributes both to Connolly's creativity and to the complexity of pre-1914 Marxism. But his responses also suggested immediate problems. His conception of Irish nationality was divisive inside Ireland; outside Ireland, it could produce hostility, indifference or misunderstanding amongst Socialists. Moreover, his attempted synthesis of Socialism and Nationalism raised one fundamental difficulty: what if 'the phrases and catchwords' inhibited or even mutilated the Socialist message? When Connolly landed in Derry in July 1910, he hoped to work as organiser for the reformed Socialist Party of Ireland. He brought with him a perspective developed through the tough years in the United States; now the theory had to meet the realities of Ireland in the Age of Carson and Larkin.

Chapter 6

Unionism and the working class

Connolly's mature position on the relationship between Nationalism and Socialism in Ireland encountered a forbidding reality. Prior to 1910, the Belfast working class and popular Unionism were barely present in his writings. As the city's organiser of the Irish Transport and General Workers' Union he experienced directly Unionist opposition to Home Rule.[1] British political conflicts had forced the Irish issue to the top of the political agenda, since the re-election of a Liberal Government newly dependent on Nationalist and Labour support, ensured that a Home Rule Bill would be introduced. Destruction of the Lords' permanent veto seemed to guarantee that eventually it would become law. The only alternative seemed to involve the Government's early defeat in a general election. This was unlikely. No election need be held before the end of 1915 – and by then, a parliament would have been established in Dublin. For Connolly, this would be a limited but significant step. Although it would fall far short of Irish independence, the provision of such an assembly would help to normalise political alignments in class terms. It would mean 'the entrance of Ireland upon the normal level of civilised self-governing nations'.[2]

These liberal and socialist expectations were confronted by the escalating response of the Unionists.[3] Initially, Irish opponents of Home Rule and their British Conservative allies tended to see Ulster as the sharp end of a wedge that might hack Home Rule to pieces. But gradually the emphasis shifted to the possibility of separate treatment for the North. The popular basis of Ulster Protestant resistance became clear. Thousands signed the Ulster Covenant of September 1912. Plans were developed for a Provisional Government in the event of Home Rule becoming law; soon the Ulster Volunteer Force could count 100,000 members under the command of an experienced army officer. Ulster Unionists and British Conservatives claimed fidelity to Constitution and Empire whilst advocating Direct Action to protect them. Faced by these pressures the Asquith Government began to temporise. In March 1914 a scheme was announced for the 'temporary' exclusion of Ulster. Scornfully rejected by Unionists, it spread panic amongst Nationalists who saw the spectre of permanent partition in the wake of any Conservative victory at the polls. A few days later the Curragh Mutiny revealed the strength of Unionist sentiments in the upper echelons of the Army. Late in April, successful gun-running at Larne and other Northern ports opened the Government to charges of at best weakness and incompetence and, at worse, partiality to Unionist claims. The Government's Irish policy was a shambles; optimistic expectations of a smooth transition to Home Rule in which all parties accepted the rules of an overtly liberal political order had been destroyed. Connolly, notwithstanding his Socialism, had shared something of this optimism. Its destruction, before the outbreak of the War, left its mark on his judgements about Socialist strategy.

His expectations were bruised further by the actions of the Protestant working class. In July 1912, Protestant workers expelled not just Roman Catholics from the shipyards, but also those who would not back militant Unionism. This included any who supported Independent Labour. Connolly's own attempts to build effective trade union organisation were hampered severely by the Home Rule furore, by his own clear position on the National Question, and by the fact that the ITGWU was an Irish and not a British organisation. Protestant sectarianism was a crippling handicap:

Our fight is a fight not only against the bosses but against the political and religious bigotry which destroys all feeling of loyalty to a trade union ... the feeling of the city is so violently Orange and anti-Home Rule at present that our task has been a hard one all along.[4]

The formal institutions of the Belfast Labour Movement declined in their representativeness. Socialist influence grew on the Trades Council, but this both produced and was assisted by the withdrawal of trade union branches dominated by Unionists.[5] In the Spring of 1914 the Trades Council's claim to speak for Belfast's workers against Partition showed how insulated its debates had become.[6] Similarly, Connolly's view at the 1914 Irish Trades Union Congress that Partition might be stopped by industrial action demonstrated an incredible myopia about the Belfast situation:

... were the Labour movement able to call out the textile operatives of Belfast or even its spinners, and to keep them out until Ulster threw in her lot with Ireland, the paralysis of industry and loss of profit to Belfast capitalists would frighten the guns out of the hands of the Carsonite army without the shedding of a single drop of blood.[7]

Although Connolly did not claim that this strategy was instantly applicable he clearly saw it as worth consideration. Moreover his diagnosis suggests a repeated theme in his analysis of Ulster: that economic self-interest would dissolve sectarian loyalties. Before looking in more detail at Connolly's argument, it is important to emphasise how far removed his scenario was from the Belfast of 1914. Few textile workers were organised – those that were belonged often to a union dominated by Unionist organisers. Connolly's own union, despite its non-sectarian position had only minimal success outside the Catholic working class. Even if it could have mobilised its members against Partition – and its organisational weakness made this doubtful – such action could be characterised as essentially Nationalist.

Eventually, at the end of July 1914, Connolly acknowledged that Protestant workers were fervent supporters of the Unionist cause:

We here in Belfast are just in the grip of a group of reactionaries who for their base class purpose have turned the attention of all away from all questions of social regeneration and plunged us into a maelstrom of evil passions where all have lost the power of self-control. The workers of the North-East corner are abandoning themselves body and soul to the leadership of the Orange ascendancy.[8]

Gone was his earlier optimism that Unionist opposition was temporary, that the Orange ascendancy was 'in the paroxysms of its death-struggle' and that once Home Rule had been established 'the old relations of Protestant and Catholic (would) begin to melt and dissolve'.[9]

Working Class Unionism raised fundamental problems for Connolly both as a Nationalist and as a Socialist. Earlier analysis showed how he became committed to a Gaelic interpretation of Irish identity. He was aware that this carried difficulties for him as a union organiser in Belfast, but he was prepared to accept the risk. Late in 1911, he lectured to some Belfast Socialists on Irish subjects:

it does not do me much good from the point of view of the Union in this Orange hole, but we must chance that ...[10]

Beneath this attachment to a specific and controversial characterisation of Irish identity, there was an assumption about the natural indivisibility of Ireland. Wartime controversies would produce a contrast with a nation that he viewed as an artificial construct:

Belgium as a nation is, so to speak, but a creation of yesterday – an artificial product of the schemes of statesmen. Whereas, the frontiers of Ireland, the ineffaceable marks of the separate existence of Ireland, are as old as Europe itself, the handiwork of the Almighty, not of politicians. And as the marks of Ireland's separate nationality were not made by politicians, so they cannot be unmade by them.[11]

The assertion ignored – or was intended perhaps to foreclose – controversy over competing definitions of Irish identity: the Anglo–Irish, the cross-class Unionism of the North, Home Rulers who visualised an Irish future as part of the British Empire, Sinn Feiners and Gaelic League enthusiasts who sought an 'Irish Ireland'. The geophysical basis could be employed to argue that any characterisation of Irish identity should incorporate the varied experiences of those who inhabited the island. But any such general claim left open the issue of its feasibility. The growth of Unionist opposition to Home Rule demonstrated the limitations of

Connolly's emphasis on Gaelic tradition, but more fundamentally it raised doubts about the feasibility of any synthesis.

Northern developments also raised difficulties for Connolly the Socialist. These can be approached through his belief – shared by many of his Socialist contemporaries – that there was a normal pattern of development for working-class politics: the more advanced the capitalism, the more radical the working class. But this was clearly not so in Belfast:

According to all Socialist theories North-East Ulster, being the most developed industrially, ought to be the quarter in which class lines of cleavage, politically and industrially, should be the most pronounced and class rebellion the most common.

As a cold matter of fact, it is the happy hunting ground of the slave driver and the home of the least rebellious slaves in the industrial world.[12]

A dominant feature of Connolly's explanation was the emphasis on ruling-class manipulation. Sectarian emotions were heightened as an efficient means of preventing the formation of an economically and politically united working class. Unionist aristocrats and capitalists could be presented as one side of a manipulative ritual which was completed by the obfuscatory practices of reactionary Nationalists:

The question of Home Government, the professional advocacy of it, and the professional opposition to it, is the greatest asset in the hands of reaction in Ireland, the never-failing decoy to lure the workers into the bogs of religious hatred and social stagnation.[13]

This presentation of Unionist/Nationalist conflict as a diversion from the 'real' class struggle suggested there were grounds for optimism. Settlement of the Home Rule controversy would kill the plausibility of such a distinction and permit the emergence of a politically unified working class. Socialist propagandists could prepare for this by informing Protestant workers of their real class interests and exposing the mythical quality and damaging consequences of cherished historical beliefs. Connolly's underlying optimism could be based on conventional Socialist grounds, but the emphasis on manipulation was also made by orthodox Nationalists who saw Protestant activities as deviant and requiring special explanation. This commonly held view would be expressed clearly by Roger Casement at his Old Bailey Trial in the Summer of 1916:

We aimed at uniting all Irishmen in a natural and national bond of cohesion based on mutual self-respect. Our hope was a natural one, and if left to ourselves, not hard to accomplish. If external forces of disintegration would but leave us alone we were sure that Nature itself would bring us together.[14]

Occasionally Connolly suggested that the bases for working-class Unionism were more complex, and thus implied that the commitment was likely to be more enduring than the manipulation emphasis suggested. In one comment written in the Spring of 1913, he suggested that the historical development of the Protestant community helped to explain the continuing strength of cross-class coalitions:

… the Protestant always saw that the kings and aristocrats of England were opposed by the people whom he most feared; and from recognising that it was but an easy step to regard his cause as identical with theirs.

This is the reason – their unfortunate isolation as strangers holding a conquered land in fee for rulers alien to its people – that the so-called Scotch of Ulster have fallen away from and developed antagonism to political reform and mental freedom.[15]

Subsequently, Connolly noted that Presbyterians had once been discriminated against, alongside Catholics, but following their own emancipation, they had become part of a Protestant bloc. He subsumed this phenomenon under a general claim:

There is no use blaming them. It is common experience in history that as each order fought its way upward into the circle of governing classes, it joined with its former tyrants in an endeavour to curb the aspirations of these orders still unfree.[16]

Hence the Catholic working class, the most oppressed of all, would be the agent of final emancipation.

This argument at least had the merit of extending beyond a simple claim of ideological manipulation and thereby indicating some of the historical roots of sectarianism. Nevertheless it also implied that this history was one in which many Protestants had subordinated their essential interests to those of their rulers. Moreover, its historical status was used by Connolly to suggest that Protestant opposition to Home Rule was anachronistic:

there is no economic class in Ireland today whose interests as a class are bound up with the Union. The Irish landlords who had indeed something to fear from a Home Rule Parliament elected largely by tenant farmers, as would have been the case in the past, have now made their bargain under the various Land Purchase Acts, and being economically secured are now politically indifferent. Only the face of religious bigotry remains as an asset to Unionism.[17]

This dismissal licensed Connolly's derisive response to the Unionist campaign against Home Rule. Since he saw no significant economic interests at stake, he characterised the demonstrations of Unionist opposition as insignificant. The Home Rule issue had its value as a manipulatory tactic but since nothing crucial was at risk, it could eventually be abandoned as a source of political division. The Orange ascendancy was:

a dying cause … even although in the paroxysms of its death struggle it assumes the appearance of an energy like unto that of health.[18]

Unionist threats could be dismissed as theatrical:

the gun today is a wooden gun and the threats today can only terrify those who
see things with the eyes of children ...[19]

Yet Connolly's analysis of class interests raised serious problems.
Certainly the Irish landlords were a dying class, in the process of being
abandoned by their British cousins, but the vehemence of Conservative
and Southern Unionist opposition to Home Rule demonstrated clearly
that the abandonment was far from straightforward. More seriously there
was the question of the Northern capitalists. Connolly said very little
about the attitude of this class towards the Union, and only considered
its relationship to Protestant workers through the persistent emphasis
on manipulation. At this point, faced with such absences, it is necessary
to stand back from the limitations of Connolly's analysis.

An exploration of the bases of Ulster Unionism raises complex
problems which have been examined in a valuable fashion in some recent
studies.[20] Connolly's assessment obviously ignored the question of how
Northern capitalists perceived their interests. Typically, these were
viewed as dependent on the continuing integrity of the Empire. Home
Rule and its alleged consequences could damage imperial credibility.
Thus a picture emerges of Belfast as part of a developed industrial
capitalism, one apex in a 'golden triangle' completed by Liverpool and
Glasgow. The contrast with the remainder of the Irish economy was
acute, and leads back to Connolly's paradox – a developed capitalism
with a working class little interested in Independent Labour, let alone
Socialist, politics. Instead it was willing to accept landed or capitalist
leadership and to absorb and employ sectarian arguments. Indeed,
Unionist politicians could be pressurised into more sectarian paths by
the demands of working-class supporters.

The impact of the paradox rests of course on the pervasiveness of a
simple model of working-class radicalisation under capitalism. Disputes
about the legitimacy of political institutions, divergent characterisations
of national identity, incompatible religious claims – all in the last
analysis should be seen as diversionary and temporary. Eventually, 'real'
economic conflicts would come to dominate and would remould political
alignments. Such a reductionist optimism left its mark on many Second
International Socialists. Faced with recalcitrant facts they sought explanations that protected the integrity of the overall framework. In this
context, Connolly's assessment of working-class Unionism was typical.
From August 1914, such accommodations had far less credibility. The
mobilisation of working classes behind national claims and symbols was
too great a series of anomalies. Similarly the emergence of mass Fascisms
and the lengthy post-1945 stabilisation of capitalism highlighted the need
to abandon any such simple perspective on working-class radicalisation.

Yet Connolly's analyses of working-class Unionism are cited frequently. Much Socialist discussion of the issue has taken his claims as a valuable starting point.[21] But subsequent argument is limited by the terms of his argument and more fundamentally by a set of expectations that stand at variance with seven decades of working-class history. Rather assessments of Connolly's diagnosis should begin with the recognition that class conflict, omnipresent under capitalism, has demonstrated almost infinite varieties of extent and expression. Faced with such complexities, attempts to understand a particular development through employing an image of the 'normal' which has been attained only rarely is to court analytical sterility.

One route to a more thorough appreciation of the complexities of Protestant working-class politics in Belfast is to start with an awareness of the extent to which developments paralleled those in British industrial centres.[22] In 1885, Alexander Bowman, Secretary of the Belfast Trades Council, and essentially a Liberal stood as an Independent Labour candidate in North Belfast. It was a development familiar in several towns and cities over the next decade as respectable trade unionists encountered the limitations of bourgeois-dominated political organisations, and moved slowly and perhaps reluctantly to a more independent position. Similarly, the formation of the Independent Labour Party in January 1893 was matched by the inauguration of a Belfast ILP. The city was not exempt from the politically significant industrial experiences of the 1890s. In October 1895, many of Belfast's engineering workers became involved in a lengthy strike that was a significant milestone on the road to the Engineers' lockout of 1897–8.[23] By the middle of the decade, the previously cautious Trades Council included a minority of Socialist delegates. This history can be presented in terms applicable to far more than one city: sporadic political interventions with some claims to independence, the initiation of Socialist propaganda, an industrial dispute with radicalising potential, the winning-over of some trade-union activists to a Socialist politics. Even some of the limits to the Belfast development can be presented in a fashion that inhibits any claims to singularity. Belfast ILP propagandists encountered verbal and physical attacks – some fuelled by religious emotions – made little progress and eventually seemed to lose heart. Yet such obstacles, frustrations and disillusion were encountered often by their British counterparts. The engineering dispute left little legacy in terms of working-class radicalisation, yet the political consequences of contemporary British industrial disputes were often ambiguous. In particular, perhaps, any political legacy of the Engineers' struggles was very limited. Many craftsmen remained ready to seek benefits through conventional industrial practices rather than through new political loyalties. Similarly, the growth of a Socialist group on the Trades Council might have been slow, but it could suggest that Belfast working-class politics were developing along lines shared with many British cities.

Such an expectation appeared to be borne out by the response to the formation of the Labour Representation Committee. In June 1903, Keir Hardie and Ramsay MacDonald addressed the inaugural meeting of the Belfast LRC. Subsequently, preparations were made to contest North Belfast with William Walker, City Councillor and Carpenters' official as the candidate.[24] Deaths of two sitting Members meant that Walker fought the seat three times in less than two years. The margin of defeat was narrow in September 1905, and even closer in the General Election four months later.[25] In this context of growing self-confidence it was perhaps appropriate that early in 1907 the city was the venue for the Labour Party Conference, the only occasion that that body has met outside Britain.

Yet Labour's position was arguably in decline – shortly afterwards, a third contest in North Belfast saw a heavy defeat for Walker.[26] Labour never again reached the electoral heights of 1905 and 1906. It is time to turn to the question of Belfast's distinctive features. In doing so, it should be emphasised that a decline in electoral popularity from the level of 1906 was not unique to Belfast Labour. In Britain, the losses were recouped; in Belfast they were not. Precision about why and how Belfast was different is essential.

Attention has been drawn earlier to the limited political legacy of the 1895 engineering dispute. Employment in the shipyards subsequently expanded through to 1914 with brief interruptions for the depressions of 1904–5 and 1908–9. In this environment traditional craft unionism could operate effectively. Shipyard workers did not need help from the Trades Council, nor were they led to query existing economic and political arrangements. Similarly effective craft practices existed in some British centres at that time. The typical consequences were a vigorous sectionalism, the inhibition of any wider consciousness and the maintenance of traditional political loyalties. Within the Belfast context, the effectiveness of craft organisations in the economically vital shipyards provided conditions conducive to sectarian growth.[27] One legacy of such trade practices was the domination of skilled trades by Protestants.[28] Effective job control typically served to demarcate in terms of skill, industry and respectability and provided that the craftsmen's world remained stable, it served as a bulwark against radical politics. In Belfast it also helped to demarcate in terms of religion. The qualities often presented as characteristic of the skilled worker could be presented as the monopoly of one religious community.

Economic and trade union developments provided a basis for sectarianism, but assessment of its complexities requires an examination of the relevant ideologies. Typically, emphasis has been placed on the role of

Orange culture with its celebrations of Protestant virtues and supremacy. Working-class political organisations frequently bear the marks of the ideological preoccupations of their formative periods. Initial moves towards political action by the Belfast Trades Council were swamped by the first explosion of opposition to Home Rule in 1886. Some leading figures on the Trades Council were prominent in the Orange Order. Such connections should be placed in the context of the growing involvement of Conservative leaders in this hitherto largely working-class body. The strengthening of one more weapon against Home Rule involved cross-class alliances under landed and bourgeois leadership. The negative implications for the development of an effective working class politics are obvious. The Orange phenomenon can be viewed as an exceptionally effective strategy for integrating an industrial working class into a capitalist society. The argument slides back towards Connolly's claim about manipulation.[29]

The question – how can workers be integrated into a capitalist system – provides a productive basis for investigating much working-class politics. Even the most efficient solutions can carry complex consequences. Orange ideology was not simply a manipulative device that could be employed or suspended at the behest of Unionist leaders. Rather some of its manifestations could be unwelcome. Orange enthusiasm could lead to conflict between Protestant workers and the authorities. Its language could serve as a currency for expressing grievances internal to the Protestant community and in doing so, class antagonism could be articulated.

This possibility was demonstrated at a by-election in South Belfast during 1902.[30] The official Unionist machine nominated a Fellow of All Souls'. He was opposed by an Orange shipyard worker Tom Sloan, claiming to stand as a representative of the Protestant working class. Such workers were characterised as exponents of a vigorous unblemished Protestantism, in contrast to Unionist MPs who were effete, readily absorbed into the Conservative's parliamentary majority and thus were poor defenders of Protestant interests. Sloan won, provoking the question in Keir Hardie's *Labour Leader*, 'Is Belfast Awakening?'[31] This optimism built on Sloan's proletarian roots and expressed labour sympathies; it ignored his sectarianism. As an MP he was sympathetic to labour demands, but his support remained within a sectarian framework. When the Independent Orange Order developed in the aftermath of Sloan's victory, this could not be characterised as a revolt of Protestant proletarians against the domination of Orange affairs by landlords and capitalists, but was much more a localised response to the disciplining of working class zealots. Orange radicalism could be blocked easily if Unionist leaders took a tougher line against the Balfour Government's alleged partiality towards Nationalist and clerical demands. When

Unionist MPs did precisely this in 1904–5, the disruptive impact of the critics was contained. The Orange community was far from monolithic; its relationships could not be appreciated through a concentration on the manipulatory aspects. There was some scope for the articulation of grievances that blended class and sectarian loyalties. Yet such conflicts remained almost wholly within a Protestant framework and provided no basis for a belief that Orange radicalism could help to produce a working-class consciousness that could transcend religious divisions. The Orange component was both more complex and more resistant than Connolly's analysis suggested.

At least, his discussion of the Protestant working class considered, albeit inadequately, the Orange dimension. More seriously, he paid practically no attention to a second ideological component with wider and graver implications for a revolutionary socialist.[32] This was expressed in the perspective of the Belfast LRC during its peak years of 1903–7. Leading trade unionists in the city viewed British developments as offering appropriate standards. They argued that Belfast wage levels should be comparable with those of British industrial cities and not those of less developed Irish centres. They affiliated their own LRC to the British counterpart. Such comparisons and initiatives were essentially Unionist, as the Trades Council's newspaper, the *Belfast Labour Chronicle* made clear:

we stand forth to-day for independence, the most hopeful and virile party in British politics.[33]

The difficulty in combining Unionist and Labour allegiances soon became clear. Walker in his first North Belfast campaign not only acknowledged his personal opposition to Home Rule, but under pressure from the Belfast Protestant Association responded positively to a sectarian questionnaire.[34] His tactics produced protests from British Labour leaders. In theory they had no agreed position on Home Rule, but most significant members of the organisation remained true to their Liberal origins and supported the policy.[35] Here was a fundamental problem for Protestant trade unionists wishing to argue a Labour case in Belfast. For the moment Walker could claim that British Labour tended to favour Home Rule since reactionary Ulster MPs had been consistent opponents of progressive labour reforms.[36] Such a rationalisation was a brittle basis for a Labour Unionism. As the Home Rule issue became more urgent and the pressures for Protestant solidarity intensified so the viability of such a Labour presence diminished within the Protestant community.

The problem is not grasped adequately however, if it is characterised as a situation in which Walker and his associates combined Unionist and Labour commitments with the former being the stronger and in a crisis proving to be decisive. Rather the Labour Unionist position claimed to be a genuinely Progressive politics. The underlying justification shared some features with other Labour and Socialist arguments including that of Connolly. Traditional sources of conflict would give way to a pre-occupation with economic and social questions,[37] but for Belfast Labour leaders, this prognostication could be employed to stigmatise many priorities of Nationalist Ireland as reactionary and undeserving of Socialist sympathy. Home Rule was a regressive proposal; so was the recent enthusiasm for the revival of the Irish language. The argument was basically the same:

anything which tends to divide the people into separate and opposing factors is evil, and all which tends to unification is useful and desirable.[38]

The harmful consequences of Home Rule would flow in part from the consequential growth of clerical influence:

there is no victory in changing lay for clerical tyranny in any country.[39]

The stagnation of much of the Irish economy had led to Nationalist trade unionists favouring Protection to support inefficient industries:

The Irish trade unionists outside Belfast are protectionists of the most extreme type. Mere tinkering with tariffs is not enough for them. They want men and goods from other countries kept out of this country at all costs. The dislike of men and things English is astonishing and ought to be a revelation to those good people who believe the nationalist party to be a wing of the party of progress.[40]

This identification of Protectionism with backwardness and reaction was common in British Labour circles before 1914. In contrast the Belfast Labour leadership appeared to proclaim that outward-looking optimism that would be destroyed so thoroughly in August 1914:

Class ties are stronger than those of race and the workers of all lands and climes have a common class interest.[41]

But an elaboration of this sentiment injected a complexity:

Nationalism is dead or dying and Imperialism is the transition stage to inter-national union of the proletariat all the world over..[42]

At one level this reflected the insensitive and crude Progressivism of much Second International thinking. Modernisation in large units was a prerequisite for Socialist development. Industrial workers were a progressive force; peasants were not. Thus the interests of Belfast workers could be safeguarded only within the United Kingdom where they could be forwarded by an expanding labour movement; under Home Rule they would be swamped by backward rural elements under clerical influence. Thus this 'progressive' labour position shared much with other Unionist diagnoses that explained Northern growth and Southern backwardness in terms of the interaction between individual character and religious belief.[43] Moreover, the claimed dichotomy between nationalism and internationalism was superficial. This Labour Unionism aimed at a better deal for workers within the context of a democratised United Kingdom and a flourishing British Empire.

In 1911, Connolly entered into an ill-tempered and discursive polemic with William Walker on whether Irish Labour should develop its own party or should work through the British Labour Movement.[44] Amongst the recriminations Connolly sought to expose the hollowness of Walker's claim that he was the true internationalist. Rather such a claim failed to disguise the underlying dependence on British imperialism:

the conception of Internationalism accepted by our Comrades of the ILP in Belfast required for its spread the flash of the sword of militarism and the roar of a British eighty-ton gun.[45]

This indictment was not relevant simply to Walker and his Belfast colleagues. It applied also to several representatives of British Labour who combined such democratic and social imperialism with support for Home Rule. Arthur Henderson once gained applause from a Belfast audience for a concise presentation of this Labour perspective:

They could not have a sound empire without a sound heart, and they could only have that by having in the heart of the empire a people that were contented and prosperous.[46]

Once again, analysis of the Protestant working class uncovers elements that were not unique to Belfast. In that specific context, the combination of effective craft unionism, democratic and social imperialism, and militant Protestantism led in the context of Home Rule crisis to developments that eroded the optimism of both liberals and socialist. But the underlying problem for a revolutionary socialist such as Connolly obviously went beyond the distinctiveness of Orange rhetoric and a working-class split along sectarian lines. The analysis of Labour Unionism demonstrates a working-class movement attached materially and ideologically to an imperialist state. It was a problem whose ramifications extended far beyond Ulster. The question soon to be posed by Lenin begins to emerge. The peculiarities of Ulster merge into the general question of the deradicalisation of Labour and Socialist organisations.

Connolly's American experiences had led him to propose Industrial Unionism as a response to the problem of organisational conservatism. His continuing commitment to this strategy after 1910 remained largely in isolation from his analysis of working-class Unionism except insofar as he suggested militant industrial action as a force that could disperse sectarian illusions. It took the events of the Dublin Lock Out and the outbreak of War to lead him towards a more radical and inclusive consideration of these issues. Only in his polemic with Walker is there some sort of hint that complex questions of Socialist strategy could be encapsulated in what could appear to be just a Nationalist–Unionist argument. The controversy should be placed in the context of an Irish Labour Movement whose factional alignments were experiencing a transformation. The old division between Belfast Labour leaders with their 'progressive' doctrines and more socially conservative trade unionists from the South had ensured normally the dominance of 'advanced' Belfast. But as Northern self-confidence waned, a new strategic option emerged in the form of the Irish Transport and General Workers' Union – inclusive organisation, militant action, its symbol the fiery rhetoric of Jim Larkin. Now it was plausible if simplistic to link working-class Nationalism and syndicalism in contrast to the discreet reformism of Belfast Labour Unionism.

Such was the choice that might appear to confront Irish Socialists in the Summer of 1911. Yet one significant counterfactual argument must be considered. Larkin's industrial debut in Ireland had been made in the Belfast dock and transport disputes of 1907.[47] As an official of the British-based National Union of Dock Labourers he mobilised workers with little tradition of trade union organisation, in militant action. 'Belfast 1907' in its tactics, its violence, its ethos of workers' revolt provided a foretaste of what was to happen across sizeable sections of British industry from 1910 onwards. In terms of the city's politics the disputes have been interpreted as a glimpse of the feasibility of united working class political action. Larkin was a Home Ruler; he spoke alongside Unionist trade union officials. The strikers were supported by the Independent Orange Order and eventually by the political leader of Catholic West Belfast, Joe Devlin. Eventually workers' solidarity gave way to more traditional confrontation beween police and Nationalists, but some commentators have seen this fragile and transient unity as a vital lost opportunity. Thus Emmet Larkin, having noted the union of the I.O.O. the Nationalists and the local LRC, comments how:

This ... did not survive the ending of the labour troubles. This breakup of an alliance so pregnant with possibilities was the real tragedy and lesson of Belfast in 1907.[48]

This verdict should be regarded with scepticism. Previous analysis has noted how the effective operation of craft unionism limited the possibilities for political radicalisation amongst skilled workers and provided scope for sectarian developments. The events of 1907, relevant only to semi- and unskilled workers would not change this situation. Moreover the dispute offered no challenge to the views of those such as Walker with their synthesis of 'Progressive' social views and opposition to Home Rule. Indeed, the eventual erosion of workers' unity could strengthen their assessment that Home Rule was a divisive and anachronistic irrelevance. Most fundamentally, the counterfactual case depends heavily on the claim that industrial solidarity and militancy were likely to promote political harmony of a labour or socialist kind. In fact a tough response to the intransigence of the employers was compatible with any position on the National Question. Involvement in a strike did not solve such divisions but pigeon-holed them. Once the disputes had ended then they reappeared.[49]

Connolly's Belfast years saw the destruction of any hopes of an effective non-sectarian working class political movement within the city. Whilst it is difficult to believe that the complexity of local politics ever permitted much space for such a development, it is important to remember that in several respects the politics of working-class Belfast were not unique. The pattern of trade union development and the support given by prominent Labour leaders to social imperialism had their British equivalents. The difference came in that within the Belfast context, the limited attempts to build a labour presence withered in the face of the Home Rule crisis. Confronted with such a discouraging prospect, Connolly faced the possibility that the underdeveloped South might offer a better prospect for revolutionary socialists. This implied a more complex assessment of the potential for working class radicalism than that implied by the 'normal' model of working class development. Yet the impact of the Home Rule crisis had not just been to destroy whatever Socialist potential remained within the Protestant working class. Orange reaction provoked its Nationalist counterpart – and for the Labour Movement this could be even more dangerous:

Labour is ever encouraged to revolt against the Orange sweaters of the North, but nothing must be done to encourage any such revolt against the Nationalist sweaters of the South ... The revolt of Labour when it can be manipulated as an asset of the Home Rule movement is all right, but the revolt of Labour against the slum landlords, grabbers and sweating employers who control that movement is a very naughty, unpatriotic, anti-Irish, irreligious, blasphemous, immoral, factionist, traitorous, cloven-hoof sort of iniquity that ought to be suppressed.[50]

Connolly's attempt to synthesise the claims of Nationality and Socialism was not just threatened by the actions of the Protestant working class. Further south, his position would be tested by the Dublin Lock Out of 1913.

Chapter 7

Lock Out

During the Autumn of 1913, Sir George Askwith, Chief Labour Adviser at the Board of Trade travelled to Dublin in an attempt to resolve a dispute that had locked out 25,000 of the city's workers. He was no stranger to seemingly intractable industrial conflicts. His autobiography presents him struggling in those immediate pre-war years with the complexities of the first national strikes on the railways and in the mines, and with the vehement resentments of workers in a bewildering variety of more localised disputes. Sometimes, Askwith played some part in the achievement of a settlement; in Dublin he failed. The locked-out workers and their dependents, perhaps 100,000 people in all, struggled on through the remainder of the year before gradually returning to work in the early months of 1914. In its longevity and in its demonstrations of class-based hostility, the Dublin Lock Out is prominent, even in the industrial climate of 1910–14. Askwith's characterisation of its distinctiveness went beyond an appreciation of the worker's determination:

It was a very different disturbance ... If the disputes in the ports and inland cities of Great Britain had been chiefly based upon economic causes, the serious riots in Dublin, although founded on poverty, low wages and bad conditions included determination to establish the transport workers' union as the 'one big union' in Ireland, and to put into practice the doctrines of syndicalism.[1]

This verdict raises the question of how far 'Dublin 1913' should be seen as an attempt to apply Connolly's doctrine of Industrial Unionism with its anticipated radical potential.

The grievances that fuelled the anger of the locked-out workers and their families were long-standing. Attention has been paid already to the appalling experiences of large numbers of the Dublin working class: low wages, irregular work, obscene housing, high death rates. An effective collective resistance had begun only with the arrival of James Larkin's Irish Transport and General Workers' Union. Its significant impact on Dublin began in 1911 and attention soon focused on its determined use of the 'sympathetic strike'.[2] Connolly saw the tactic as a recognition of the indivisibility of working-class interests, but in Dublin its popularity was a consequence of the city's employment structure:

... it was not mere cold reasoning that gave it birth in Dublin. In that city it was born out of desperate necessity .. what is known as general or unskilled labour bears a greater proportion to the whole body of workers than elsewhere. And hence the workers are a more movable, fluctuating body, are more often as individuals, engaged in totally dissimilar industries than in the English cities, where skilled trades absorb so great a proportion and keep them so long in the one class of industry.[3]

The union achieved some success and its membership increased. In 1911, its affiliation to the ITUC was for 4,000 members; a year later this had risen to 8,000 and by 1913 to 14,000.[4] The expansion of the Transport Workers' significantly changed the style of Irish Trade Unionism and in Dublin it established a significant presence amongst the unskilled workers.

Yet the growth of the ITGWU must be kept in proportion. Its rising membership was encouraging, but hardly demonstrated a hegemony over the Irish working class. Its increasing prominence within the ITUC owed something to factional manoeuvring.[5] On the Dublin Trades Council, its delegates needed the support of radical Nationalists.[6] Outside the principal centres of population it counted for little and in Belfast its prospects were cramped by its reputation as a Nationalist Union. Whatever distinctive qualities it injected into Irish industrial life came essentially from its Dublin activities. Yet the union was not an organisation brought to beleaguered Dubliners from outside. Its priorities, its strategy and its culture were informed by the experiences and demands of many of the city's workers.

Perceptions of its distinctiveness were moulded inevitably by the personality of James Larkin. Even many sympathetic to the struggles of the Dublin workers expressed their reservations about his lack of tact. His style posed obstacles for both conventional trade unionists and middle class sympathisers. A *New Statesman* portrait in the dispute's early days epitomised this distancing:

He is one of those born revolutionaries who know not diplomacy, but who believe that the Kingdom of Heaven must be taken by violence today and tomorrow and the day after ... His utopia, we feel, would be a world where a general strike was going on all the time. Big and black and fierce, he is a Syndicalist of the street corners ... He calls to the surface the very depth of unrest. His theory seems to be that a city should never be allowed a moment's peace so long as there remains a single poor man whose wrongs have not been righted. His genius ... is inflamatory. He preaches turmoil.[7]

Reservations about Larkin were not restricted to the unpredictable consequences of his fiery radicalism. Connolly's revolutionary credentials were unassailable, yet he had severe misgivings about Larkin's autocratic tendencies:

I begin to fear that our friend Jim has arrived at his highest elevation, and that he will pull us all down with him in his fall ... He must rule or will not work, and in the present stage of the Labour Movement he has us at his mercy.

And he knows it, and is using his power unscrupulously I regret to say ... I am sick of all this playing to one man ...[8]

The revolt of the Dublin workers was based on harsh material factors, yet discussion of the dispute, its origins and possible solutions centred around Larkin's volcanic personality.

Such a dominant image is significant, it helped to mould the responses of contemporaries, but it was a caricature. Larkin, like A. J. Cook and Arthur Scargill, spoke for workers in revolt, not just against employers, but also against cautious trade union officials. He envisaged the union, not simply as an industrial instrument, but as the basis for the flowering of a socialist culture.

But by the Summer of 1913, industrial conflict in Dublin had become symbolised in the clash of two individuals. William Martin Murphy was the dominant figure in the city's business community. A living refutation of the Unionist claim that the Nationalist tradition did not produce efficient entrepreneurs, his austere style was a universe removed from Larkin's rumbustious agitation. His business interests were diverse: railway contractor, hotel and department store owner, proprietor of the *Irish Independent*, a director of the city's United Tramway Company. A firm disciplinarian, he might acknowledge the existence of old-style conservative trade unions, but his antipathy towards the Transport Workers' was total. In particular, the doctrine of the 'sympathetic strike' challenged Murphy's perception of managerial prcrogatives. Larkin's weekly the *Irish Worker* lampooned Murphy as the quintessential ruthless capitalist: the latter was determined to resist the union's incursions into his businesses.[9]

Throughout August 1913 the tension increased as Larkin's attempts to organise workers in the *Independent* and the tramway company were met by Murphy's dismissals of union members. In response, the doctrine of sympathetic action was employed against a leading wholesaler who refused to boycott Murphy's newspapers. Eventually, on 26 August, the organised section of the tramwaymen struck for better wages, shorter hours and an end to the most onerous management practices. The dispute had begun.

Some respectable trade union leaders were concerned about the risk of violent confrontation and over the weekend of 30–31 August this occurred in a dramatic form. Police, already overworked and underpaid, took out their frustrations against pickets and uninvolved bystanders. Connolly and another trade unionist, William Partridge were arrested on incitement charges; Larkin, sought by the police, appeared dramatically in disguise at a banned meeting in Sackville Street. The result was further police violence against a crowd composed of the committed and the curious. Subsequently, the police encountered angry demonstrations in some working-class districts, truncheons were used vigorously, houses entered, furniture smashed, the occupants assaulted. The weekend's riots produced two deaths. They also transformed the dispute into something much more fundamental.[10]

The police action raised questions of civil liberties. A Liberal MP observing the violence in Sackville Street saw no provocation. Rather, he had witnessed 'the most brutal constabulary in the world ... the police baton and kick men prostrate on the ground'.[11] The British TUC already in session at Manchester, heard an emissary from Dublin and passed a resolution condemning the police. Keir Hardie travelled to Dublin, attended the funeral of one of the victims and spoke at a mass meeting. A combination of liberal principles and trade union solidarity was forging a vital yet ultimately ambiguous link between the British and Irish labour movements.[12]

The weekend's fury helped to ensure in Dublin that any hope of conciliation was destroyed. Trade union officials of all persuasions had to acknowledge that any chance of an easy settlement was dead. The police action heightened the determination of strikers and intensified class consciousness on both sides. Working-class neighbourhoods responded predictably to their weekend's experiences; 'respectable' Dublin found its voice in the leader-columns of most of the City's press where middle-class neuroses about 'mob' violence were given uninhibited expression.[13] Most crucially, many of Dublin's employers, encouraged by Murphy, concluded that here was a valuable opportunity to destroy Larkin's union. Employees were presented with a stark choice – the union, or a job.

Connolly was involved in the dispute throughout. He travelled to Dublin following the tramwaymen's walk out and was arrested rapidly on a charge of incitement. Sentenced to three months, he went on hunger strike and was soon released. During Larkin's subsequent absences – either in jail or on British speaking tours – he led the embattled union. He played a significant and judicious part in the attempts to gain more support from British unions. When the dispute was over, he pondered its significance for his view of socialist strategy.[14]

One useful starting point is a consideration of the degree to which the ITGWU could be seen as embodying distinctive strategic principles and objectives. Did it come anywhere near to Connolly's ideal of Industrial Unionism, vital to the overthrow of capitalism and the inauguration of a Socialist Commonwealth? If it had any distinctive qualities should these be explained in terms of its specifically Irish – or perhaps Dublin – environment?[15] Attention has been drawn to the need not to exaggerate the union's influence by 1913. If the analysis is extended from a consideration of the degree of support to an estimation of its significance, then once again caution is needed. Certainly, there were radical facets: the syndicalist proclivities of leaders, Larkin's based on emotion, Connolly's on theoretical argument and American experience, the tactical use of the sympathetic strike, the commitment of the membership, once impoverished and unorganised, and now growing in self-confidence. Yet the union's programme was conventional enough. The objective might be a Socialist society but the more immediate goals – a legal Eight Hour Day, work for the unemployed, pensions at sixty, adult suffrage, nationalisation of transport and land – would not have raised eyebrows in the most respectable British trade union circles. They even included Compulsory Arbitration Courts – an enthusiasm of Larkin that found little support amongst his British counterparts.[16]

Moreover, throughout the dispute, Connolly combined industrial and political toughness with a readiness to negotiate. But the 'all or nothing' style of many Dublin employers helped to promote the view that this was a clash of irreconcilable interests. They thereby gave credence to their own claim that the union's leaders were thoroughgoing revolutionaries. Certainly Connolly drew political conclusions from the dispute, but neither he nor Larkin saw the conflict as a decisive step towards an easily attainable political objective. In fact, Connolly, in one article, saw the formation of a Conciliation Board as a solution to the immediate issue. The result would be a much more ordered system of industrial relations:

let the Union proceed to organise all the workers possible, place all disputes as to wages before the Board, and only resort to a strike when agreement cannot be reached by the Board ... strikes would be rare.

A more co-operative system of bargaining would provide one basis for a wider transformation:

Thus we will develop a social conscience, and lay the foundation for an orderly transformation of society ... into a more perfect and juster (sic) social order.[17]

This outlook contrasted sharply with the views of some radical contemporaries within the British trade union movement. Those responsible for *The Miners' Next Step* indicted the South Wales' Miners' Federation's attachment to conciliation. It had helped to depress real wages, it had lent credence to the coalowners' arguments; it had facilitated the rise of trade union oligarchs.[18] More generally, the syndicalist sentiments of the young Welsh radicals had much in common with Connolly's views but on this issue the discrepancy highlights the degree to which Connolly remained attached to an evolutionary view of Socialist growth. The Lock Out was certainly not seen by him as signposting a feasible short-cut to political power.

One plausible interpretation of the dispute would be that Dublin was experiencing a significant growth of 'New Unionism' almost a quarter of a century after this had occurred in several British centres, and Irish industrialists and publicists were reacting with a hostility similar to that once demonstrated by their British counterparts. Yet in Britain, those 'New Unions' that had survived had become accepted elements within the industrial scene. Was it not reasonable to believe that Ireland would develop along similarly reformist lines? The British 'New Unions' like the ITGWU had often been founded and led by Socialists. They thus acquired a Socialist commitment but this was not complemented readily by a Socialist rank and file. Their membership could be attracted by immediate material benefits without consenting to the union's official political stance.[19] Was it not likely that a similar anti-climax awaited Larkin and Connolly?

Against this expectation, arguments can be adduced suggesting that the Transport Workers' need not become domesticated in the same fashion. Possibly in Nationalist Ireland the growth of militant trade unionism could be viewed as a threat to the economic order since industrial workers, along with many others, were predisposed to question the legitimacy of the British State. Once an industrial dispute raised questions of public order then such scepticism could be significant. But such a political argument meets with complex cross-currents. The Government enquiry into the police produced a conclusion calculated to boost the profits of whitewash manufacturers. The view that the police generally acted 'with conspicuous courage and patience' could be viewed as one more example of British insensitivity.[20] But the police concerned were Irishmen and were supported by a wide spectrum of 'decent' and visible Irish opinion. Nationalist traditions of hostility to the British State might affect Labour's style, but so might Nationalist reluctance to support a specifically class-based radicalism.

Perhaps a putative distinctiveness can be investigated more profitably through an emphasis on the under-development of much of the Irish economy, thereby providing a radical answer to Connolly's Belfast paradox. Arguably, many Dublin workers were integrated only marginally into the dominant institutions and mores of urban capitalism. They had entered a satiated labour market, propelled there by rural deprivation, often carrying memories of agrarian exploitation and possibly the belief that 'Direct Action' was an appropriate response to economic grievances. Unskilled, poorly paid, appallingly housed, they perhaps provided a potentially radical basis for Larkin's union. Once again, this characterisation raises the general issue of appropriate bases for working class radicalism. In some ways Dublin with its largely unskilled, underemployed, impoverished and traditionally unorganised working class was different from most British urban centres. The contrast perhaps indicates the extent to which such workers needed a separate Irish organisation. Within a broader British union, their distinctive needs could be all too readily marginalised. More elusively there arises the question of whether such needs were likely to lead to a more radical industrial or political strategy. Did the divergence secrete a revolutionary opportunity or did it offer only the possibility of an aggressive trade unionism?

This raises a fundamental question: what political initiatives were available to this working class? In Britain, 'New Unionism', at least at the levels of officials, activists and programmes had made a substantial contribution to the emergence of the Labour Party. Arguably the scope for a comparable Irish development was restricted. At the 1912 ITUC Connolly had successfully moved a resolution for the formation of an Irish Labour Party but progress was extremely slow.[21] Connolly argued that Larkin evinced no enthusiasm for the project, but perhaps there was a more substantial difficulty than the mercurial quality of Larkin's interests.[22] The growth of the British LRC down to 1906 can be attributed in part to the political opportunities provided by an often old-fashioned and ineffective Liberalism. In contrast the Parliamentary Party and its constituency machinery still dominated the Nationalist political scene. Despite the problems posed for its strategy by Unionist mobilisation in the North, and by Liberal pusillanimity in London, it seemed likely to do so until Home Rule had been achieved. If the early prospects for a strong Labour Party along British lines were so unpromising, then it could seem that working-class interests would be served better by a campaign of aggressive industrial action.[23]

Yet Connolly had never accepted such a concentration of working class energies into the industrial arena. Throughout his 'Wobbly' period, and later he argued for a dual strategy of industrial organisation and political education. Hopefully, the consequences would be revolutionary, but his desire to avoid sectarian isolation had led to his involvement in the formation of the Irish Labour Party. For him in the Dublin of 1913, growing self-confidence and unity in the industrial sphere would be combined with a developing class solidarity at the ballot box. Supportive evidence that this happened as the result of the Lock Out is very limited. Labour already had a modest presence in the Dublin City Council: six members out of eighty in 1912 rising to eight the following year.[24] Any expectation that the Lock Out would produce a significant working class shift to Labour voting proved to be mistaken. In the elections of January 1914 only one Labour candidate was successful. Connolly still viewed such an electoral confrontation as the model for future growth. It:

can in the future alone make labour politics a reality. It was the fight on the industrial battlefield being transferred and fought out by the same contestants on the political battlefield.[25]

Consolation could be sought in the overall vote; excuses could be found in the alleged malpractices of opponents; but one contributor to the Trades Council's post-mortem was more pessimistic:

there must be something wrong in the labour movement when only one of the Candidates was returned.[26]

These results can be employed to argue that the militancy of the Lock Out was extremely limited in its political consequences, and that the Irish Labour Movement contained no more radical potential than its British equivalent. Yet by the time the municipal contests were held, the Lock Out was crumbling. These contests did not offer a test of the claim that Dublin workers would move from militant and effective industrial solidarity to a more class-based politics. Rather, if there had been a dramatic shift to Labour in January 1914, this would have been much more a desperate search for a political alternative to a failing industrial strategy and far removed from Connolly's hope for a working class growing in unity and effectiveness on both fronts. The Dublin Lock Out reinforced the harsh experiences of Connolly's American years and worked against the optimistic style of his basic theorising.

The collapse of the Dublin workers' resistance cannot be separated from the complexities of Anglo–Irish trade union relationships. This essential connection led Connolly to ponder some central issues of socialist strategy. Many British trade union officials had grave reservations about Larkin's tactics and style. Even when the British TUC responded immediately to the reports of the Dublin riots, the mover of the resolution, James Sexton, offered his support in a back-handed fashion. Clearly unhappy about the ITGWU's aggressive tactics, he consoled his audience with a topical comparison:

however black Larkin or Connolly may be, it was white compared with the black of Sir Edward Carson.[27]

In Sexton's case, the animosity could be seen as personal since he and Larkin had quarrelled over the ITGWU's secession from the National Union of Dock Labourers. More fundamentally however, it quickly became clear that several trade union officials opposed any involvement of their organisations in sympathetic action for the Dublin workers. They were prepared to give financial support and to provide negotiators to facilitate a settlement, but for many officials, that was where support should end. For Larkin it could not be enough:

although money was a very useful thing, it had never won a strike.[28]

The reluctance of many British leaders must be placed in the context of their own preoccupations since 1910. Often they had experienced tough battles with advocates of militant rank and file action inside their own unions. Now the Dublin dispute seemed likely to increase such pressures with Larkin as the hero of such radicals. Quite apart from the Irish dimension, the late months of 1913 saw a rash of railway disputes, often generated by unhappiness at the consequences of the 1911 National

Settlement.[29] In this climate, officials such as Jimmy Thomas and J. E. Williams of the NUR looked with hostility on demands that railwaymen should 'black' Dublin traffic. The pressures increased as some railwaymen took matters into their own hands, and were suspended; the consequence was predictably a walk out by their colleagues. In mid-September there were stoppages in Liverpool and Birmingham; at the beginning of December there was a much more extensive strike in South Wales, following the dismissal of two Llanelli drivers.[30] Although several NUR branches supported sympathetic action, the disputes were settled by national officials; in the South Wales case the settlement did not include the reinstatement of the two drivers. A more crucial intervention came from Havelock Wilson the maverick anti-Socialist Seamen's leader, when he ordered his members to resume work as the Dublin port strike faltered.[31]

Given such actions, it was predictable that someone of Larkin's temperament would denounce such leaders. By mid-October he was denouncing some officials for their 'flagrant treachery ... industrial and political blackguardism'.[32] Connolly's response was more measured; he welcomed the involvement of British officials as negotiators but only so long as they acted as allies. He was uneasy about their apparent susceptibility to 'the blarney of soft-spoken Dublin employers'.[33] A sympathetic journalist noted the contrasting combination of 'lucid Connolly and red-hot Larkin';[34] when the TUC finally met on 9 December to consider the dispute, Larkin's rhetorical prelude helped to turn the meeting into a shambles. Thomas and Havelock Wilson personalised the dispute; Larkin repaid their attacks with interest. Connolly attempted to rescue something from the wreckage, but requests for sympathetic action secured little support.[35]

A reasoned case against such requests came from the Miners' President, Bob Smillie. Such a strategy could not be employed on demand:

The next step they took for a national stoppage would have to be seriously thought out, as the fight once undertaken would have to be fought and won. The rank and file must be consulted before they took that step ... He had no mandate from the miners to support a national strike.[36]

Smillie suggested that if members were ballotted, they would possibly reject sympathetic action, and this would be the final blow to the Dublin worker's cause. For him, the Triple Alliance with its ambiguous promise of workers' power still lay in the future.

Enthusiasm for the Dublin cause came not just from some rank and file trade unionists but also from many Socialists within the ILP and the BSP. Yet even within the political side of the Labour Movement, the ITGWU's strategy had its critics. Philip Snowden used the columns of the Conservative *Morning Post* to attack 'wild and revolutionary appeals'. Ramsay MacDonald employed those of the Liberal *Daily News* to denounce the union's key strategy:

The sympathetic strike is poor fighting. It demoralises Trade Unionism, weakens collective action and produces reactionary prejudice in the public mind.[37]

The contrast with Connolly's principled defence was sharp; for the latter such action:

means the practice of what Christians have been preaching without practising for the past 2,000 years.[38]

The attacks of Snowden and MacDonald are dismissed too lightly if they are seen as early demonstrations of the priorities that would lead them out of the Labour Party eighteen years later. Rather, the view that they articulated in 1913 was characteristic of one strand in ILP thought. Socialism would come through sagacious political action based on communal consent, not through emotional sectional responses that were essentially oppositional and destructive.

The difficulties of Dublin workers in securing more support within the British Labour Movement were not limited to the unsympathetic priorities of cautious trade union leaders and respectable ILP MPs. Crucially, trade union leaders showed themselves able to limit and terminate unofficial action and to withstand pressures for a change in policy. National officials settled such disputes through negotiations with employers and then pressurised those involved into acceptance; branch resolutions in favour of sympathetic action were uncoordinated and in- effective. The vital Special TUC was insulated carefully against too much radicalism. A resolution on 'personal attacks' preceded a debate on the question of support for Dublin. The swapping of insults came before any discussion of the principle of 'sympathetic action'. Connolly's immediate reaction was that a disastrous ordering of the agenda had produced a damaging result:

the men who drew up the agenda for the Conference, and who put a lengthy discussion of personalities before the question of helping Dublin had given the whole Labour Movement a set-back.[39]

Whether this ordering was achieved innocently is debatable. What is not open to question is that the critics of the ITGWU had no need to employ a loaded agenda to secure an acceptable outcome. The composition of the Congress ensured that. The meeting had been deferred for three weeks, ostensibly to permit consultation with the rank and file. This did not happen. Smillie acknowledged that the MFGB had not discussed the question of support for Dublin. Delegations were typically selected from within a tight circle. Whatever radical sentiments on this issue existed amongst union members would not percolate through to many of the delegates.[40] In common with other syndicalists, Connolly had discussed frequently the need for the accountability of trade union officials. The events of 9 December 1913 showed that this aspiration remained far from realisation.

Even the quality of some of the Transport Workers' support was ambiguous. Some leading advocates of 'Direct Action' were unreliable. Thus Tillett, closely associated with the *Daily Herald*'s strong demands for sympathetic action, moved the resolution opposing attacks on trade union leaders at the special TUC.[41] More significantly the sympathetic action that did develop on the railways requires more precise analysis than a simple claim that this demonstrated rank and file support for the Dublin workers. The context was one where groups of railwaymen were stopping work for a variety of reasons. The South Wales dispute occurred in sympathy with the sacking of two drivers who had refused to handle Dublin traffic; but their colleagues struck to reverse the dismissals, not specifically over the Irish question. Moreover many South Wales footplate staff were aggrieved over the Eight Hours Question and a strike over this had been deferred just a few days before.[42] The Irish dimension provided just one strand in a skein of grievances and principles. Similarly the earlier stoppages in Liverpool and Birmingham grew out of the suspensions of just a few, and once again in the latter case, there were reports of disquiet at bonus payments in some of the goods yards.[43] Even the *Daily Herald*, always keen to discover cases of solidaristic class action, suggested that more traditional loyalties could have been significant:

in those districts where there are railwaymen bound by religious and political ties to the Irish transport workers, there is evidence of a determination to refuse to handle blackleg goods emanating from Dublin.[44]

Such bases for rank and file action were too ambiguous or too limited to be effective counterweights to the determination of national officials. Connolly and Larkin spent much time trying to mobilise British support; ultimately they failed. The outcome left its mark in Connolly's subsequent writings.

His journalism during the dispute was produced for propaganda purposes in Ireland and in Britain and was largely factual and agitational in content. As the extent of the workers' isolation became evident, he made two observations of wider significance. The financial support, the food ships, the sympathetic strikes, the vast and enthusiastic crowds that had attended his and Larkin's meetings – all enabled him to maintain his faith in the essential radicalism of the working-class:

To the idea of working class unity, to the seed of industrial solidarity, Dublin was the great event that enabled it to seize the mind of the masses, the germination force that gave power to the seed to fructify and cover these islands.

I say in all solemnity and seriousness that in its attitude towards Dublin the Working-Class Movement of Great Britain reached its highest point of moral grandeur – attained for a moment to a realisation of that sublime unity towards which the best in us must continually aspire.[45]

Clearly, this idealised the rank and file response, although the degree of support was impressive. It contrasted with the actions of many British trade union officials:

We asked for the isolation of the capitalists of Dublin, and for answer the Leaders of the British labour movement proceeded calmly to isolate the working classes of Dublin.[46]

This dichotomy between radical rank and file and reformist leaders had been central to his earlier syndicalist writings. Now he utilised these recent experiences to assess and adapt his views on trade union organisation and strategy. Whilst the fragmentation of traditional craft organisations clearly militated against effective class action and pointed towards the development of Industrial Unionism, Connolly accepted that events demonstrated the need for further refinement of this conception.[47] In Britain there had been a number of trade union amalgamations inspired to some degree by the ideal of Industrial Unionism. Yet subsequent performance did not demonstrate the radicalism that some protagonists of the ideal anticipated. Connolly might have focussed attention on the National Union of Railwaymen and its leaders' negative role in the Dublin dispute. He devoted more space however to a discussion of the Transport Workers' Federation. Its leading figure Robert Williams had been much more sympathetic towards the ITGWU, and had been barred from the Special Congress on a technicality.[48] Yet, Connolly claimed that despite Williams' radicalism, the development of the Federation had reduced the industrial effectiveness of the workers concerned. Although the organisation dated from September 1910, Connolly credibly saw the successful port stoppages of the following summer as victories for militant local action:

It was its very sporadic nature, its swiftness and unexpectedness that won.

But subsequently such initiatives had been cramped. Amalgamations had been carried out 'in the main by officials absolutely destitute of revolutionary spirit', a reasonable verdict on the place of such officials as Havelock Wilson and James Sexton within the TWF. Only the outward form altered:

Into the new bottles of industrial organisation is being poured the old, cold wine of Craft Unionism.

The old sectional unions at least allowed for close links between officials and rank and file. Now in the new complex organisations there was scope for procrastination and the shifting of responsibilities:

The local official can conscientiously order the local member to remain at work with the scab, or to handle tainted goods, 'pending action by the General Executives' ... the chances are a million to one that the body of workers in distress will be starved into subjection, bankrupted, or disrupted, before the leviathan organisation will allow their brothers on the spot to lift a finger or drop a tool in their aid.[49]

Such an assessment was a response to the arguments of Bob Smillie against immediate sympathetic action. The procrastination approach was employed also by Jimmy Thomas who advised his members to wait for one 'great united effort'.[50]

Connolly's analysis growing out of his frustrations as a leader of the beleaguered Dublin workers highlighted a significant problem about decision making and democratic accountability within large complex trade unions. Whether it provided an adequate explanation of say, the failure of London port workers in 1912 compared with their successes twelve months earlier is doubtful. Although the TWF appeared more in control of the later dispute, the appearance was perhaps misleading. The 1912 dispute grew out of rank and file actions which led the officials to call a port-wide stoppage. The problem arose when the Federation failed to secure effective support from its members in other centres. The London workers were defeated more by lack of sympathetic action elsewhere than by the caution of their leaders. It was an explanation that did not fit Connolly's characterisation of radical rank and file and reformist leaders.[51]

His initial remedy was to emphasise the continuing value of the local strike even if this might destabilise the organisation. For him, the alternative risked eroding working class militancy through inaction, an outcome that should be avoided. He suggested that some of the perils could be circumvented through selecting responsive leaders and retaining them only so long as they remained close to their members.[52] This was naive. It ignored the organisational complexities of large unions that Connolly himself had outlined and also the powerful oligarchic tendencies that had helped to blunt the Dublin workers' appeal within Britain. Moreover he soon acknowledged that with the development of Industrial Unionism, a thorough adherence to democratic precepts could undermine industrial effectiveness. Recalling that capitalist Cabinets declared war and informed parliament afterwards, Connolly asked rhetorically:

Can we not evolve a system of organisation which will leave to the unions the full local administration, but invest in a Cabinet the power to call out the members of any union when such action is desirable, and explain their reasons for it afterwards?[53]

The desire to combine accountability with industrial effectivenes was characteristic of his syndicalist contemporaries. The authors of *The*

Miners' Next Step had recently proclaimed the ideal: 'Decentralisation for Negotiating ... Centralisation for Fighting'. Its elusiveness and its importance would be revealed in the complex history of sympathetic action through to the failures of 1921 and 1926.

The Lock Out not only led Connolly to reconsider the adequacy of Industrial Unionism as a revolutionary strategy; it also helped to shift his perception of relationships between British and Irish workers. His distinction between sympathetic rank and file and unsympathetic leaders has already been examined within his syndicalist framework. Inevitably with his commitment on the National Question, consideration of the relationship between the two Labour Movements raised the question of the relationship between their respective nations. During the Lock Out, Connolly argued against any simple identification of England as the oppressor. Government should be distinguished from the working class and moreover he suggested a more complex relationship:

We are told that the English people contributed their help to our enslavement. It is true. It is also true that the Irish people duly contributed soldiers to crush every democratic movement of the English people.[54]

This verdict was offered with Connolly still optimistic about the growth of rebellion amongst both working classes. Wtih the isolation and defeat of Dublin's workers, this judgement became much more difficult. The actions of British trade union officials could revive old animosities. Connolly abandoned platitudes for May Day 1914. He told the predominantly Scottish readership of *Forward*:

I cannot this May Day felicitate you or the working class of the world in general on the spread of working class solidarity. Instead of it I see much mouthing of phrases, much sordid betrayal of our holiest hopes.[55]

Alienation had been deepened by the reopening of a longstanding dispute between Connolly and the British Labour Party. As the crisis over the Home Rule Bill intensified, the Nationalist MPs began to look for compromises, and British Labour MPs faithful to their traditional policy went along with this. Connolly opposed this response, partly on substantive grounds – any hint of Partition should be opposed – and also because it ignored the claims of Irish Labour organisations.[56] British Labour's continuing connection with the Parliamentary Party could be viewed charitably as evincing a wish to settle the Home Rule controversy and move on to more important business.[57] Yet it could be utilised also to demonstrate the relatively conservative quality of the British Labour Party. Such a conclusion would strengthen the case for Irish Labour to go its own way; it could suggest also that British shortcomings were based on more than leaders' conservatism and organisational constraints. Rather the continuing British domination of Ireland could affect the outlook of the British working class. The ground was being prepared for Connolly's response to August 1914, a development accompanied by and probably affected by shifting attitudes to a range of Nationalist organisations and individuals.

The polarisation of classes during the Lock Out destroyed any illusion that Ireland was a harmonious community in which class conflict had no place. Connolly had invested much time in attempts to synthesise national and socialist commitments. The events of 1913 underwrote his earlier rejections of some forms of Nationalist politics, but they also provided new starting points for thoughts on this complex relationship – and ultimately for action.

His longstanding criticism of the Parliamentary Party appeared to be corroborated firmly by its lack of response to the dispute. He had ridiculed Nationalist MPs consistently as a clique of socially-reactionary politicians who engaged in radical rhetoric simply in order to deceive progressives in both Ireland and Britain. Connolly's verdict was predictable:

The semi-radical phrases with which the middle-class Home Rule Press and politicians so often duped the public (and sometimes themselves) were seen to have no radical feeling behind them. Sham battle-cries of a sham struggle, they were hurriedly put out of sight the moment the war-cries of a real conflict rose upon the air.[58]

The claim that such Nationalists were pro-capitalist and anti-worker could be supported by pointing to Murphy, once an Irish MP, still a self-proclaimed Home Ruler, but the epitome of the tough, anti-trade union employer. The judgement could be amplified by noting the almost universal lack of comment on the dispute from the Nationalist MPs.[59] Preoccupied with Home Rule, they saw the Lock Out as an unwelcome and destructive diversion. Connolly's dismissal of the Parliamentarians would have been strengthened still further, had he known of the privately-expressed views of John Dillon. When confronting rural exploitation, Dillon had revealed himself as one of the more socially aware of his political generation, but faced with the anger of Dublin workers, his sensitivity failed him. Aware of Murphy's inflexibility, he nevertheless attacked Larkin in unrestrained terms and largely ignored the economic basis of urban discontent:

Larkin is a malignant enemy and an impossible man. He seems to be a wild international syndicalist and anarchist and for a long time he has been doing his best to burst up the party and the national movement.[60]

He saw the confrontation as wrecking the social cohesion of Dublin at precisely the moment when Home Rule seemed available. In part, Dillon's hostility to Larkin could be regarded as a reflection of the prejudices and ignorance of a middle-class politician deeply knowledgeable about rural society, but uninformed about and probably fearful of urban unrest. Nationalist images of Ireland often left little room for the harsh realities of city life. Larkinism also challenged the political near-monopoly of the Parliamentary Party. Most obviously it did so through the insistence that Labour had distinctive political interests that necessitated a separate organisation, although as yet the Irish Labour Party offered the most minimal electoral threat. More fundamentally the Transport Workers' use of sympathetic action was backed by Connolly's frequent claim that this was none other than the old Land League tactic of the boycott employed in an industrial setting. This could strike a chord with those Nationalists who sought inspiration in the old physical force tradition and dismissed the Parliamentary Party as unambitious and ineffective.

In their opposition to aggressive trade unionism, the MPs could rely on resources much more extensive than those available through what was already perhaps a decaying political machine. Larkin's union was confronted by 'respectable' Dublin opinion, most significantly perhaps by several representatives of the Catholic Church.[61] This became most apparent late in October when the ITGWU acting in concert with some British sympathisers decided to send some children of the locked-out workers for holidays in Britain. The result was a hysterical onslaught from several Catholic organisations, that this would endanger the children's faith. Boats and railway stations were picketed by zealous priests and their supporters. Some arrests were made on charges of abduction. For Connolly this typified the misuse of religious sentiments that he had attacked in *Labour, Nationality and Religion*. Yet the emotions engendered proved powerful. The scheme was largely blocked. When some Dublin employers brought in English strike breakers, his bitterness towards those who manipulated religious and thereby national sentiments was deep. They assessed the English connection as good or bad, depending on their class interests:

A crime to deport Dublin children in order to feed, clothe, and house them better than they ever were before. All the newspapers are against it. It is not a crime to import English scabs to take the bread out of the mouths of Dublin men, women and children and to reduce them to slavery. The newspapers are over-joyed at it ...[62]

Connolly's response had a parallel with his treatment of Orange politics. He hoped that a demonstration of partiality and myopia would be sufficient antidote. Yet Connolly in accepting a definition of Irish nationality that emphasised its Gaelic roots, faced a difficulty with Catholic and other propagandists who presented Socialism as English and therefore anti-national. Sometimes the language was grotesque, but the challenge was a crucial one for those wishing to construct an Irish Socialist movement. This aspiration could be denounced as the most damaging instalment of a process of national and religious demoralisation:

the immoral literature, the smutty postcards, the lewd plays, and the suggestive songs were bad, yet they were merely puffs from the foul breath of a paganised society. The full sewerage from the 'cloaca maxima' of Anglicanisation is now discharged upon us. The black devil of Socialism, hoof and horns, is amongst us.[63]

This identification of Socialism and labour agitation with damaging foreign influences was to be found also in the writings of Arthur Griffith, the dominant figure of Sinn Fein.[64] At this point though, the relationship between Socialism and conceptions of Nationality becomes much more complex.

Griffith was identified particularly with the position that the route forward for Ireland was through self-sufficiency, not just in economic terms but also intellectually. He was an effective propagandist and during his American years Connolly had discussed Sinn Fein's doctrines.[65] He welcomed the emphasis on self-reliance reflecting that the working class needed this in order to achieve its emancipation. Yet he totally rejected Griffith's economic outlook. This was based on the Protectionist doctrines of the German economist Friedrich List and proclaimed the need for an Irish manufacturing sector. The implication was that the initial investment would only be attracted if wages were relatively low. Connolly's Socialist response was dismissive – the prospectus:

appeals only to those who measure a nation's prosperity by the volume of wealth produced in a country, instead of by that distribution of wealth amongst the inhabitants ... (it) rests upon a capitalist conception of progress.[66]

It seems predictable that Griffith should ignore the strongly Irish emphasis of Larkin's Union and attack its leader as an English agitator,[67] and its tactics and Socialist objective as an alien and damaging import. Yet simply to focus on this aspect of Griffith's response is to ignore the complexity of the Sinn Fein position.

The organisation was small and largely dominated by Griffith but other members felt more positively towards the locked-out workers. This helped to lead Griffith to a considered presentation of his views on the labour question. In contrast to the 'Know-Nothing' response of almost all of the Parliamentary Party, Griffith at least acknowledged that the plight of the Dublin workers was appalling. He struck a note reminiscent of Connolly in his claim that:

Irish Labour deserves well of the Irish nation for it was more faithful to it in the past than Irish Capital.

Equally, his denunciation of liberal economics recalled some attacks by Socialists, as well as that of the 1848 polemicist John Mitchel:

my affirmations and beliefs are fundamentally at variance with the blessed system of Free Trade and Open Competition.

Like Mitchel he presented this economic system as quintessentially English. Moreover, he went on to make a point heavy with implications for the future of the British Left. This economic order was supported by the 'English' Labour Party:

who, while clamouring against Capital maintain in being the most iniquitous abuse of the power of Capital the modern world records.[68]

But he viewed the relationship between capital and labour as essentially harmonious. Antagonisms were produced by the competitive economy, and could be removed, given Protection and State intervention. The character of Griffith's proposed system remains elusive; should it be seen simply as an anticipation of a managed capitalism, or more sharply as carrying quasi-fascist overtones? Certainly, it was anti-liberal and at least for Griffith, it ruled out any solution that was socialist and class-based. This rejection was vital, yet it is equally important to emphasise the degree to which the growth of new Nationalist groups, offering alternatives to the Parliamentary Party raised novel questions for Connolly.[69]

The Lock Out clearly put Griffith under pressure to clarify his views, not simply because of disagreement within his own organisation, but also because some other Dublin intellectuals took a more positive attitude towards the locked-out workers. Their motivations were diverse. Francis Sheehy-Skeffington, socialist, pacifist, feminist, supported the workers throughout and found himself roughly handled by Catholic demonstrators during the confrontations over the 'deported' children.[70] This issue brought W. B. Yeats into the columns of the *Irish Worker* with an indictment paralleling Connolly's condemnations of the abuse of religious enthusiasm for political purposes:

I charge the Dublin Nationalist newspapers with deliberately arousing religious passion to break up the organisation of the working man ...[71]

Arguably for Yeats, the issue was more general than this industrial conflict. He had been a member of that beleaguered group that had defended the plays of J. M. Synge against the powerful vulgarities of Murphy-style nationalism.

A more sustained commitment to the workers' cause came from Yeats's old college friend, the Co-operator, journalist and creative thinker George Russell ('AE'). He exploded into the argument with his 'Open Letter' published in the *Irish Times* on 8 October 1913. The issue was presented as one of autocracy versus democracy. In the past, some Dublin capitalists had backed popular agitations that had destroyed landlordism. It had been obvious for a long time, that as a class the city's capitalists were incompetent philistines with less to recommend them than the landed elite they had helped remove. Now their collective action had focussed public attention on their failings. Even a victory would prove hollow:

You may succeed in your policy and ensure your own damnation by your victory. The men whose manhood you have broken will loathe you, and will be always brooding and scheming to strike a fresh blow ... You are sounding the death-knell of autocracy in industry ...[72]

This response led 'AE' to a *Daily Herald* Rally in the Albert Hall where he denounced the Parliamentary Party and proclaimed an intellectual's support for the Dublin workers:

I am a literary man, a lover of ideas, but I have found few people in my life who would sacrifice anything for a principle ... For all their tattered garments, I recognise in these obscure men a majesty of spirit. It is in these men in the towns and in these men in the cabins in the country that the hope of Ireland lies.[73]

This sentiment was one emphasised by Connolly ever since the start of his Dublin propaganda in 1896. Perhaps appropriately at this meeting they spoke from the same platform.[74]

This intransigence of the employers and the obvious hardship of a large section of the Dublin working class mobilised many of those who made pre-1914 Dublin such an intellectually vital place. It could appear as a simple matter of proclaiming a common humanity against hard-faced employers and compliant authorities. As 'AE' emphasised in Swiftian vein:

James Larkin deserved to go to jail. He was preventing a socialogical (sic) experiment of great importance to Ireland from being carried out. We have never accurately determined how little human beings can live on, and how little air space is necessary for families ...[75]

This humanitarian response brought out a further figure on the side of the workers, one who would form eventually the most significant relationship with Connolly.

Patrick Pearse, mystic and poet, Head of St Enda's School, was in 1913, essentially a cultural Nationalist. Increasingly close to the Irish Republican Brotherhood, it was natural that he should speak at the inaugural public meeting of the Irish Volunteers on 25 November.[76] Yet by then Pearse's compassion had been stirred by the sufferings of the locked-out workers. The previous month he too had written sardonically about a possible experiment:

I would like to put some of our well-fed citizens in the shoes of our hungry citizens ... I would ask those who know that a man can live and thrive, can house, feed, clothe and educate a large family on a pound a week to try the experiment themselves ... I am quite certain that they will enjoy their poverty and their hunger ... they will write books on 'How to be Happy though Hungry'; when their children cry for more food they will smile; when the landlord calls for the rent they will embrace him; when their house falls upon them they will thank God; when policemen smash in their skulls they will kiss the chastening baton ... in the alternative they may come to see that there is something to be said for the hungry man's hazy idea that there is something wrong somewhere.[77]

As yet, Pearse could offer little as a remedy. He was 'old-fashioned enough to be both a Catholic and a Nationalist'.[78] Yet whatever his hope of national harmony the harsh reality of 'Dublin 1913' rendered neutrality impossible. Sympathy for the workers did not lead however to support for any Socialist proposals – like Griffith he regarded foreign domination as the core of the problem; an end to British rule was therefore the 'sine qua non' of any solution. He offered little that was precise on the Irish way forward, claiming only that Ireland once free could support four times its present population.[79] This dream of Gaelic self-sufficiency clearly involved a significant extension of State activity, although this could not be characterised as distinctively Socialist. For the moment, Pearse's response to the plight of the Dublin workers was little more than the instinctive sympathy of an outraged humanitarian.

Eventually Pearse and Connolly would influence each other far more; the Socialist would awaken the Nationalist to some of the sufferings of the Irish working class; the Nationalist would help to persuade the Socialist to participate in a rising that lacked a specifically socialist content. Although their names would become indissolubly linked through the events of 1916, it would be a profound mistake to focus on the 1913 Lock Out as the episode that initiated the collaboration of Pearse and Connolly. The conflict carried a variety of implications for Connolly; not the least significant is the revelation of a variety of Nationalist viewpoints expressing a complex assortment of responses to the emergence of a militant Labour movement – the xenophobic name-calling of Griffith fitting uncomfortably amongst the variety of Sinn Fein responses, not least the more considered statement of his own position; Yeats's anti-philistine sentiment; 'AE's co-operative commitment; his and Pearse's humanitarian passion; Sheehy-Skeffington's Socialist idealism. These were not the sum. Thomas MacDonagh spoke out against the brutality of the Dublin police; so did Countess Markiewicz.[80] Padraic Colum, appalled at the insensitivity of the employers suggested that the dispute was popularising alternative methods of production:

Socialism and cooperation used to be ideas that were quite remote from us. Now they have become actual, and every day that the industrial struggle continues they will become more actual. Usual methods of production and distribution are being hampered, and we are becoming interested in alternative methods.[81]

Together these responses recall the vivacity of Dublin's intellectual life at this critical moment as capital and labour confronted one another, and the Home Rule Bill plodded over the parliamentary obstacle course. This vivacity by-passed the politicking of the Parliamentary Party, an organisation whose historic task seemed on the verge of fulfilment and whose rituals seemed increasingly passé to some radicals. Here was a series of challenges for a Socialist such as Connolly – points of growth for a reconciliation between Socialist and Nationalist ideals but also the risk that a seductive variant on a Nationalist theme could deaden a Socialist commitment. If 'Dublin 1913' reveals the variegated geography of radical Ireland, it also leaves a significant problem. Why did the crucial alliance become that between Pearse and Connolly? To answer this is to move forward from the complex legacy of the Lock Out to the challenges of wartime. But in so doing it is essential to note one institutional legacy of 1913. When the struggle was at its most intense, on 13 November, with pickets under pressure from police, Connolly addressed a Dublin meeting:

I am going to talk sedition. The next time we are out for a march I want to be accompanied by four battalions of trained men with their corporals and sergeants. Why should we not drill and train men as they are doing in Ulster?[82]

Here was the proposal for an Irish Citizen Army: after many vicissitudes it would provide a link through to Easter 1916.

Chapter 8
The choice

The events of August 1914 came for Connolly as the culmination of a melancholy sequence. The shadow of Partition threatened the development of class politics in Ireland, the effectiveness of Carson's tactics and the weak reaction of the Government suggested a growing illiberality that threatened hopes of Socialist development, the Lock Out had demonstrated that if trade unionism were to serve as a vital element in a Socialist advance, then organisational problems must be solved. Both the Home Rule crisis and the arguments over sympathetic action during the Lock Out showed that understanding between Irish and British Labour Movements was far from perfect. Then came the War.

The collapse of all hopes of Socialist Internationalism in August 1914 was, for Connolly, both decisive and traumatic. In all belligerent countries, the vast majority of Socialists and trade unionists supported their respective national governments. The patriotic road was taken in Britain, not just by the more cautious and self-consciously respectable Labour leaders, but by several who had proclaimed a more radical commitment. Ben Tillett, the ambiguous ally of the locked-out Dubliners, and C. B. Stanton the radical Miners' Agent from Aberdare moved from violent declarations of class war to unrestrained jingoism.[1] Only their vehemence of expression was constant. In contrast some who had characterised pre-war industrial militancy as divisive and destructive, condemned the duplicity of pre-war diplomacy and the escalating authoritarianism of the wartime state. Thus, MacDonald and Snowden who had attacked Syndicalism as a corrosive alternative to constructive Socialism distanced themselves from the patriotic wing of the Labour Movement.[2] For a Socialist such as Connolly who continued to express an unqualified opposition to the War, old expectations were transformed. Bleak images were dominant. Most Labour MPs backed the British wareffort. More seriously for the hopes of Second International Socialism, the German Social Democrats, the party that had dominated international Socialist debates for a quarter of a century, came in from the cold and supported the Imperial Government. Perhaps the former Socialist, John Burns, almost isolated in his resignation from the Liberal Government provided an appropriate epitaph for a generation of Socialist hopes: 'National blood is thicker than Socialist water'.[3]

The dichotomy might be appropriate for Britain, France and Germany.

Within Ireland, there were obvious complexities. These centred in part around the question 'which nation' but even amongst those who saw themselves as Irish Nationalists, the challenge of 'August 1914' was divisive. The Parliamentary Party, for so long one of Connolly's principal targets came out firmly in support of the War. For many of them, the prospects of the Irish nation were bound up with those of the British Empire. Inevitably, this decision produced scathing comments from Connolly, but the implications went much wider.[4]

The controversies surrounding the Lock Out had highlighted a gulf between the conventional political world of the MPs and the priorities and style of several of the younger creative Nationalists. For several years the Parliamentary Party had coped easily with its critics. Those within the apparently ritualistic Fenian tradition seemed few and ineffective; whatever potential Sinn Fein had once had seemed by 1913 to have been largely spent. But the Home Rule crisis could pose a more fundamental threat to the paramountcy of the Parliamentary Party. The Irish Volunteers founded in November 1913, could propel any Nationalist response to Unionist intransigence, far beyond the rule-governed civilities of parliamentary politics. Intemperate action could upset the strategy of the MPs as their moment of triumph approached. Not surprisingly, Redmond and his allies worked assiduously to expand their influence within the Volunteers. By June 1914, it seemed that the organisation could be constrained by the priorities of the Parliamentarians.[5]

Whether such a limitation would have survived a continuing deadlock over Home Rule is questionable; what soon became apparent was that it could not survive the outbreak of war. Redmond's immediate pledging of the Volunteers to the defence of Ireland and his support for the War were divisive enough, but he was soon encouraging the Volunteers to go 'wherever the firing-line extends, in defence of right, of freedom and of religion in this war'.[6] When he appeared alongside Asquith at a mass recruiting meeting in Dublin's Mansion House in late September, the Volunteers were already in the process of splitting. The numerical dimensions of the split seemed heavily in Redmond's favour. One estimate suggests that he retained the support of 150,000 Volunteers; 16,500 of these had enlisted by November 1914 and 30,000 by the following Autumn. In contrast, only between two- and three-thousand followed Eoin MacNeill behind a policy of refusing to support the War in the absence of Irish self-government.[7]

Although a numerical comparison provides some sense of proportion, it does not indicate the whole truth. During the early stages of the War the authority of Redmond and the Parliamentary Party remained strong over the wider Nationalist population. The critics' priorities and condemnations did not seem to be shared widely. The Irish recruiting figures were perhaps the sharpest testimony to their isolation. Nevertheless the

Parliamentarians' position involved significant weaknesses. A lengthy war could erode its credibility as the demand for recruits continued and the threat of conscription emerged. Tensions would be heightened as a political crisis produced the death of the Liberal Government and the formation of a Coalition in which Liberal Home Rulers sat alongside Carson and Bonar Law. Commitment to the War led Redmond and his colleagues into concessions and compromises that demanded tortuous reconciliation with the sentiments of their Irish supporters.[8]

Against such uncertainty and vacillation, the anti-Redmond Volunteers seemed to represent something definite. Relatively few, they appeared committed against Partition and for 'Home Rule Now' as a precondition for any involvement of Irishmen in a British war. But, as Easter 1916 would reveal, fundamental divergences lay beneath this facade. Some represented by MacNeil and Bulmer Hobson viewed the Volunteer's role in essentially defensive terms. Their armed strength could force concessions from the British Government; violence should be used only if an attempt was made to disarm the Volunteers. In contrast, Pearse, MacDermott, Plunkett, MacDonagh and Ceannt, all active within the organisation, would provide much of the nucleus for the Easter Rising.[9] The relationship between such Nationalists and the radical wing of the Labour movement was complex. Certainly it could be argued that at least these tendencies were united by their distaste for the Parliamentary Party's manoeuvrings and priorities, and more positively the Lock Out had produced some hints of agreement on specific issues. But the dispute had deepened hostility between members of Larkin's union and middle-class Nationalists. This had surfaced at the inaugural meeting of the Volunteers when Labour activists had heckled one of the speakers.[10] At one level the Irish Citizen Army could be characterised as a manifestation of this sense of a separate identity but with the end of the Lock Out, its role as a workers' defence force was redundant. Eventually in October 1914, the ICA came under Connolly's control. It was a very small organisation but under his leadership it became a group with an insurrectionary commitment.[11] Faced with the destruction of Socialist internationalism and Redmondite support for Britain's war, Connolly attempted to synthesise the priorities of revolutionary Socialists and radical Nationalists.

His immediate response emphasised the destructive impact of the conflict on Socialist expectations. He sketched features of pre-war Socialist growth – rising electoral support, an expanding press, a strong trade unionism, the growth of anti-militarist sentiments – in a fashion characteristic of Second International Socialists. But:

now like the proverbial bolt from the blue, war is upon us, and war between the most important, because the most socialist, nations of the earth. And we are helpless!!

He hoped vainly for some act of revolt by Continental workers. Any such response, he viewed as morally justified:

> no general uprising of the forces of Labour in Europe could possibly carry with it, or entail a greater slaughter of socialists than will their participation as soldiers in the campaigns of the armies of their respective countries ...

Such a revolt could be significant even if unsuccessful. At least, Socialist credibility would be preserved:

> Even an unsuccessful attempt at social revolution by force of arms following the paralysis of the economic life of militarism, would be less disastrous to the socialist cause than the act of socialists allowing themselves to be used in the slaughter of their brothers in the cause.[12]

Such an inspirational justification of a Socialist revolt foreshadowed that provided in a Nationalist context in 1916.

Such Socialist hopes were unfulfilled of course. Connolly felt his isolation keenly: 'I may be only a voice crying in the wilderness, a crank amongst a community of the wise'.[13] Soon he ceased to contribute regularly to *Forward* and by the end of 1914, the *Irish Worker* had been suppressed. Attempts to have a replacement – the *Worker* – printed in Glasgow were thwarted rapidly by the authorities.[14] Only in May 1915, did he succeed in bringing out the Dublin-based *Workers' Republic*. By then, he had already offered a diagnosis of the Socialist debacle to the American readership of the *International Socialist Review*. Proper Socialist organisation, in his opinion, could have prevented the War. Although many of the belligerent nations had sizeable Socialist Parties backed by significant votes, these were divorced from any effective industrial presence. For Connolly, effectiveness required of course, revolutionary trade unionism organised after the principles of the IWW:

> The Socialist voters having cast their ballots were helpless as voters until the next election; as workers they were indeed in control of the forces of production and distribution; and by exercising that control over the transport service could have made the war impossible. But the idea of thus coordinating their two spheres of activity had not gained sufficient lodgement to be effective in the emergency.[15]

Thus, Socialist claims to be internationalist were simply rhetorical.

The Socialist collapse of 1914 did highlight the extent to which earlier rhetoric had made a naive assumption about effective coordination between political and industrial organisations. Obviously, Connolly's analysis ignored many factors. Like many within his Socialist generation, he tended to ignore the degree to which reactionary ideologies had permeated Labour movements; when he did focus on ideological aspects, he tended to respond in an optimistic and mechanistic fashion. Even within the organisational field, his focus on this particular absence

begged the question of whether such a revolutionary industrial organisation was feasible. Earlier discussion has indicated how limited such
developments had been within the United States, and how sceptical
Connolly had been about the organisational forms adopted by British
industrial unions. But his negative and justified reactions to such trade
union developments offered little comfort to any hope of an effective
partnership between militant trade unionism and a Socialist political
organisation.

Once the War seemed established as a way of life, then Connolly had
little hope of working-class revolt in the belligerent nations. Nevertheless, he emphasised any hostile reaction by workers against employers'
and politicians' pressures. Such battles typically centered around living
standards and working conditions but they were also influenced by the
expansion of State involvement in industry. Thus he welcomed the
successful strike of South Wales miners in July 1915. Although this was
concerned with wages and devoid of political intentions, for Connolly
it nevertheless had political significance:

had the Government succeeded in terrorising them, we might all have bidden
a long farewell to our industrial liberties. Successful in Wales, the capitalist class
that runs these islands would have been ruthless in Ireland.[16]

The miners' success was due in part to the indispensability of their work.
They were able to make significant economic gains under wartime state
control. Much more protracted and less successful battles developed in the
munitions industries where workers faced an alliance of employers and
the state. In Connolly's view the liberal decencies were under attack:

All trade union rights are assailed, all trade-union liberties are denied, the working
class is everywhere menaced by an unscrupulous master-class in alliance with
a military power in the hands of men who have grown up in hatred of democracy,
and with a contempt for the class from which private soldiers are drawn.[17]

The power of the State backed by the plea that the War required special
concessions from labour gave engineering employers the opportunity to
pursue changes that they had long desired. As yet, wartime demands
would disguise their full significance, but once these abated Connolly
predicted a bleak future for once-proud artisans:

The end of the War will find the British worker utterly demoralised by the advent
of new conditions in the workshop. The apprenticeship system smashed, the Division or Dilution of Labour everywhere introduced, women and girls thoroughly
expert in the work of performing certain processes hitherto part of the work of
men, new machines installed ... All the old safeguards will be broken down.[18]

This assessment with its underpinnings of sectionalism and sexism
shared much with those made by Clydeside Socialist contemporaries.
Like some of them Connolly hoped that this challenge would lead to a

less sectional trade unionism but in the British context he viewed such a possibility with scepticism. Trade union officials had conceded too much and demobilisation would lead to mass unemployment. The combination would place post-war trade unionism in a very vulnerable position. The gloomy prognostication oversimplified subsequent British development. Initially in the brief post-war boom the Labour challenge would be deflected by adroit Government tactics, but Connolly offered a relevant if exaggerated anticipation of developments in long-established British industries, once the boom had collapsed. Unlike many trade union leaders, he expected nothing from any collaboration between labour organisations and the Wartime State.

If his alternative was to protect and extend centres of working-class power, he has no illusions about the difficulties. He saw these as com-pounded in the British context. At this point, his concern with the development of a Socialist resistance to the War came into contact with his preoccupations as an Irish Nationalist. Already critical of the response by some British Labour leaders to the Dublin Lock Out, his tone hardened appreciably after August 1914. Despite his sympathy for the South Wales and Clydeside workers, he reacted vehemently to the Bristol TUC of September 1915. The patriotic wing of the Labour Movement had a field day, and Lloyd George, speaking as Minister of Munitions, campaigned for trade union co-operation in the war effort. Connolly saw no socialist potential in this gathering:

We have ere now looked hopefully to the British Trade Union Congress, but our hopes are gone. The British Empire is ruled by the most astute ruling-class in the world; the British working-class is the most easily fooled working-class in the world.
God help the poor Irish as long as they remain yoked to such a combination.[19]

Thus, analysing of the bases for an effective opposition to the War led to a consideration of the relationship between Britain and Ireland. If the working class in the metropolitan centre was hopelessly corrupted, how about the possibility of a revolt in Ireland?

Despite his view that the challenge of the War necessitated a decisive and thorough response from Socialists, Connolly remained assiduous in his conduct of routine union business. As 'de facto' leader of the ITGWU, following Larkin's journey to the United States late in 1914, he negotiated wage settlements and attempted to rectify the financial weakness of the union.[20] Politically, he attempted to give more substance to the formal commitment to an Irish Labour Party. As yet, such an initiative lacked any effective institutional form and faced fundamental problems in mobilising rank and file support. This deficiency was demonstrated clearly in June 1915, when a by-election occurred in Dublin's College Green constituency. The Dublin Trades Council decided to run its

President, Thomas Farren against the Redmondite nominee. The latter was attacked as both anti-working class, and a weak Nationalist but the criticisms developed in the brief Labour campaign were limited.[21] In no sense was there a presentation of an anti-war case, nor were there any arguments supporting Republican Nationalism. Farren's poll was a small one; his opponent triumphed easily on a low turnout. Connolly's post-mortem acknowledged the ideological and organisational weaknesses of Labour, even in such an urban working-class constituency:

It is an object lesson in the value of organisation ... The Labour candidate did not win because the electors were not sufficiently imbued with labour principles to rally to his aid ...[22]

Subsequently, he developed a much more far-reaching and pessimistic analysis of the degree to which Irish workers had been corrupted in both Socialist and Nationalist terms by the British connection.

He had argued consistently that this relationship had absorbed the loyalties of Irish landlords and capitalists. Typically, he had maintained that the working class had not been so deluded. This statement of faith had always been myopic about the strength of working-class Unionism; faced with the impact of Government propaganda Connolly was forced to revise his previous estimate of the Nationalist working class:

the evil influence upon large sections of the Irish Working Class of the bribes and promises of the enemy cannot be denied.[23]

Only 'the militant Labour Leaders' were exempt from the entangling web of the British connection. He saw the root of the corruption as economic. Recruitment figures were raised by the attraction of regular wages and separation allowances. Characteristically for a Socialist trained in the Marxism of the Second International, there was only a slight emphasis on the ideological roots of support for the British war effort. Yet whatever the inadequacies of Connolly's analysis, as a thorough examination of the deradicalisation of labour movements in wartime, the implication was clear. In Britain, the institutions of the Labour Movement were dominated by supporters of the War, but at least they provided space for some action by anti-war elements or by those unhappy about particular industrial policies. Some actions by trade unionists could carry political implications, although typically their significance was ambiguous. But in Ireland unionisation was weaker and outside Belfast its industrial bases did not include sectors of military significance. Within the political sector Labour's presence was slight. The Irish Labour Movement did not offer even the few narrow footholds available to British anti-war Socialists as bases for any attempt to radicalise a largely unsympathetic population. Any attempt at an effective intervention in Ireland had to employ other resources, whatever the implications for Socialist orthodoxy and priorities.

Any understanding of how Connolly viewed such an intervention should begin with an awareness that, faced with the devastation of Socialist hopes, he believed that Ireland could make a distinctive and significant contribution to the destruction of capitalism:

Ireland may yet set the torch to a European conflagration that will not burn out until the last throne and the last capitalist bond and debenture will be shrivelled on the funeral pyre of the last warlord.[24]

This expectation rested on a claim that the British Empire played a central role within world capitalism. Ireland's special relationship with Britain would allow any Irish radical movement to play an effective part in the weakening of both the Empire and the wider economic system. The claim was a Socialist–Nationalist counterpart to one of the fears that had fuelled British opposition to Home Rule. Early in 1916, Connolly elaborated on this theme. Ireland, in a wartime situation, could be a weak link in the chain of British Imperialism:

We shall continue in season and out of season, to teach that the 'far flung battle line' of England is weakest at the point nearest its heart, that Ireland is in that position of tactical advantage, that a defeat of England in India, Egypt, the Balkans or Flanders would not be so dangerous to the British Empire as any conflict of armed forces in Ireland ... That a strong man may deal lusty blows with his fists against a host of surrounding foes and conquer, but will succumb if a child sticks a pin in his heart.[25]

Although at one level Connolly's Socialism led him to identify capitalist rivalries as the fundamental cause of the War, he also wished to claim that the British contribution to the disaster was especially significant. A longstanding industrial dominance was under threat:

... since Germany could not be beaten in fair competition industrially, it must be beaten unfairly in organising a military and naval conspiracy against her.[26]

The British working class had been deluded by their rulers' imperialist pretensions:

Enslaved socially at home, the British people have been taught that what little political liberty they do enjoy can only be bought at the price of the national destruction of every people rising into social or economic rivalry with the British master class.

Perhaps a change in consciousness needed the sufferings of war:

– if it requires war to free the minds of the British working class from that debasing superstition, then war we shall have.[27]

The argument could be seen as a courageous encounter with what was, for a revolutionary Socialist, a harsh prospect. The response could be characterised as a combination of revolutionary defeatism, and a claim that a colonised society could help to emancipate the working class of the metropolitan power.

This portrait only offers a partial understanding of Connolly's position on the Anglo–German conflict. Soon after the War began, Sir Matthew Nathan took up his appointment in Dublin as Under-Secretary. He gave himself a rapid course in Irish political opinions. The fruits were listed in a notebook. They included a list of radicals accompanied by succinct appraisals. Against Connolly's name, Nathan added the comment, 'Socialist and pro-German'.[28] This should not be dismissed as the simplistic prejudice of an inadequately informed administrator. Although Connolly decorated Liberty Hall – the Transport Workers' headquarters – with the slogan, 'Neither King nor Kaiser, but Ireland', much of his early wartime propaganda gave credibility to the characterisation.

Admittedly his first treatment of a German theme – a tribute to Karl Liebknecht following an unfounded rumour of his death – was impeccably internationalist,[29] but this was succeeded by arguments presenting the War as a British conspiracy against Germany. These were supported by an image of industrial harmony that would have gratified German industrialists:

Basing its industrial effort upon an educated working class, it accomplished in the workshop results that this half-educated working class of England could only wonder at. That English working-class trained to a slavish subservience to rule-of-thumb methods, and under-managers wedded to traditional processes saw themselves gradually outclassed by a new rival in whose service were enrolled the most learned scientists cooperating with the most educated workers in mastering each new problem as it arose, and unhampered by old traditions, old processes, or old equipments.

He also presented a sentiment that had played its part in ensuring Social Democratic support for the German Government. British policy would help to produce:

the spectacle of the savage Cossacks ravishing the daughters of a race at the head of Christian civilisation.[30]

Whilst such positive presentations of the German position were most apparent in his writings during late 1914, even in March 1916, he presented a comparison that bore no relationship to the realities of German imperialism:

The German Empire is a homogeneous Empire of self-governing peoples; the British Empire is a heterogeneous collection in which a very small number of self-governing communities connive at the subjugation, by force, of a vast number of despotically-ruled subject populations.[31]

The simplifications, the distortions and the omissions within Connolly's characterisations of Germany are obvious. Thus he often ignored the significance of autocratic elements within both the political and the industrial systems. Perhaps most fundamentally, given his view of socialist strategy, he failed to consider the barriers to trade union growth and the divisions within the trade union movement.

The motivations for such passages can be only surmised. Arguably there was an element of reaction against the tone of British propaganda: the attacks on 'militarism' as if it were a peculiarly German trait, and the insistence that liberal Britain was well suited to be the friend of small nationalities.[32] In seeking perhaps to puncture such claims, Connolly unnecessarily painted a relatively positive portrait of the German alternative. Such tactical responses were perhaps complemented by more substantive claims. Arguably the illiberality of German political institutions mattered less, given that recent events seemed to have exposed British liberal pretensions as a hollow sham. Perhaps the evolutionary perspective that Connolly had espoused over so many years left its marks. His portrait of German industry suggested that it was a more advanced form of capitalism than its British counterpart and therefore provided a better basis for Socialist growth. This led to the crucial point that Germany had the most mature Socialist movement:

the best educated working class in the world, the greatest number of labour papers ... the greatest number of Socialist votes in proportion to the entire population. All this was an index to the high level of intelligence of the German working class as well as to their strong industrial and political position.[33]

It required only Connolly's characteristic equation of working-class interests with those of the nation for him to claim that such developments provided 'an infallible index to the high civilisation of the whole German nation'. He maintained this perspective in the face of evidence that most members of the SPD supported the War, and despite the awareness that he would participate in an essentially nationalist revolt that would stand out against the tenets of this evolutionary perspective.

Obviously Connolly's appraisal of Germany was influenced also by his Nationalist priorities. Yet the old dictum that Britain's enemy was Ireland's ally left untouched the problem of how far Imperial Germany could be a sympathetic supporter. The parallels drawn at least implicitly in Nationalist arguments – between Germany and Republican France in the 1790s – failed to answer fundamental questions. Presumably status as an enemy of Britain did not entail a commitment to the claims of small nationalities. But the problem was not subject to critical discussion – and the Proclamation of Easter 1916 duly made reference to 'gallant allies in Europe'.[34]

Connolly's pro-German arguments clearly owed much to Nationalist sentiments. They offered one indice of the degree to which his choices were influenced by such priorities. Nevertheless, he came to the military collaboration of April 1916 through a complex route. As early as September 1914 he had worked with some revolutionary Nationalists in a short-lived Irish Neutrality League.[35]

Connolly seems to have been unaware of the existence of a Republican conspiracy. Instead he invested his hopes in the small ICA, and by the Summer of 1915 the *Workers' Republic* contained articles on street fighting.[36] Any possibility of a significant revolt depended on the achievement of some arrangement between the Citizen Army and the revolutionary Nationalists operating inside the Volunteers' organisation. Gradually, suspicion gave way to understanding. The ICA and the Volunteers marched together in August 1915 at the set-piece funeral of O'Donovan Rossa.[37] Connolly's articles focussed increasingly on national themes. They eulogised the pantheon of Irish heroes – Tone, Emmet, Davis, Lalor, Mitchel, and the Fenians – that had long been espoused by Connolly and which was subscribed to by the revolutionary Nationalists.[38]

Connolly employed examples from this tradition to argue the case for audacity. Past revolts had lacked this quality:

In 1848, as later, the real revolutionary sentiment was in the hearts of the people, but for the most part they who undertook to give it articulate expression were wanting in the essential ability to translate sentiment into action. They would have been good historians of a revolutionary movement, but were unable to take that leap in the dark which all men must take who plunge into insurrection.[39]

The justification for such actions should not be sought solely – or even principally – in their likelihood of success. He commended the example of the Manchester Martyrs because they had acted despite a discouraging situation:

Let us remember that by every test by which parties in Ireland today measure political wisdom, or personal prudence, the act of these men ought to be condemned.[40]

But such an act helped to maintain the credibility of Nationalist politics. Such an inspiration was imperative in the context of Redmondite perfidy. Connolly's insistence on the need for some demonstration of Nationalist resolve left open the possibility that the Citizen Army would act alone if circumstances seemed to rule out other options. By late 1915, the threat of conscription suggested that unilateral action might occur. Connolly voiced impatience with revolutionary rhetoric:

we are not revolutionists. Not by a thousand miles ... We strictly confine ourselves to killing John Bull with our mouths.[41]

Pessimism alternated with moments of optimism. In December 1915, he welcomed a growing identity between 'the forces of real nationalism and labour'.[42] But a month later urgency was again the keynote:

The time for Ireland's battle is NOW.
The place for Ireland's battle is HERE.[43]

This insistence led to Connolly's introduction to the IRB's Military Council. After a long discussion he agreed to desist from independent action, and instead to participate in the Rising planned for Easter 1916. As he elliptically informed readers of the *Workers' Republic*:

The issue is clear and we have done our best to clear it ... (for) that fruitful blessed day of days, we are ready. Will it find you ready too?[44]

Chapter 9

Might-have-beens

1916, that critical year for Irish Nationalism was arguably decisive for Irish Socialism. One assessment of Connolly's decision to participate in the Rising would be that he thereby committed himself, and significantly through his participation, the small Irish Socialist movement, to support an insurrection that could have no socialist legacy. Thus, instead of socialist involvement transforming Irish Nationalism, it was Irish Socialism that found itself absorbed and marginalised. This negative verdict has been pronounced by, amongst others, Eric Hobsbawm:

So far from transforming it, the Marxist element in Irish nationalism has produced little more than another nationalist saint and martyr, and a social revolutionary tinge on the radical fringes of the IRA ... in its own Marxist terms, the Connolly–Marxist–Nationalist policy must be regarded as a failure.[1]

This bleak assessment fits a conventional interpretation of 1916 and its legacy: the post-Rising reprisals; the identification of the rebels with Sinn Fein; the latter's supersession of the Parliamentary Party, the War of Independence and the Civil War. The cumulative political legacy with alignments determined by postures adopted between 1916 and 1923 included the political marginality of Labour. Since the twenties Irish Socialists have confronted the consequences of an incomplete national revolution and of a social revolution that did not happen. The interpretation is at least a salutary warning for those who view uncritically Connolly's legacy as a viable synthesis of socialist and nationalist ideas.

Such thoughts are significant, but they do not provide an adequate response. If one comment of Lenin warns against a simplistic focusing of Socialist hopes on Nationalist movements, this must be supplemented by his verdict on the Easter Rising:

Whoever calls *such* an uprising a 'putsch' is either a hardened reactionary or a doctrinaire hopelessly incapable of picturing a social revolution as a living thing.

For to imagine that social revolution is *conceivable* without revolts by small nations in the colonies and in Europe, without the revolutionary outbursts of a section of the petty bourgeoisie *with all its prejudices*, without a movement of politically non-conscious proletarian masses against landlord, church, monarchical, national and other oppression – to imagine that means *repudiating social revolution* ...

Whoever expects a 'pure' social revolution will *never* live to see it. Such a person pays lip service to revolution without understanding what revolution really is.[2]

As with Connolly, there is an insistence that revolts of oppressed peoples be placed in the context of Great Power rivalries. There is a hint that the revolutionary merits of any action should not be identified with its immediate consequences. A revolt may be inspired by ambiguous motives and generate diverse consequences; but internationally its revolutionary impact may be significant. This argument is close to Connolly's metaphor of a boy with a pin. Above all Lenin's argument insists that realistic standards should be employed in any assessment of revolutionary opportunities.

One response to these general reflections would be that by 1916, Connolly had ceased effectively to be a Socialist, and therefore analysis of a Socialist's decision to participate in the Rising is beside the point. This interpretation was presented forcefully by Sean O'Casey:

Jim Connolly had stepped from the narrow byway of Irish Socialism onto the broad and crowded highway of Irish Nationalism ... The high creed of Irish Nationalism became his daily rosary, while the higher creed of international humanity that had so long bubbled from his eloquent lips was silent forever, and Irish Labour lost a leader.[3]

The verdict was supported by passages within Connolly's wartime writings. He condemned Irish MPs' support for the War not from the standpoint of Socialist principle but from that of national tradition:

Ireland was attacked by every poisonous agency ever brought to bear upon the mind and soul of the people. Her religion, her love of nationality, her strict sexual morality, her natural affection for the weak, her sympathy for suffering and distress – every high and noble instinct implanted in her by ages of suffering was appealed to that her children might deny the past of their country.[4]

Following his commitment to action at Easter, he proclaimed the need to preserve national identity, even if this task recruited only a small minority:

It is not the will of the majority which ultimately prevails; that which ultimately prevails is the ideal of the noblest of each generation ...[5]

Under the pressures of war, the Irish working class seemed to have been deposed by Cathleen ni Houlihan; the hope that choices be made democratically was superseded by the judgement of the principled few.

Such emphases do not give the complete story. Connolly faced with the near-disintegration of effective socialist politics placed a heightened emphasis on Nationalist themes, but the historical exemplars that he employed had long been present in his writings. He continued to emphasise the centrality of socialist and labour questions. Thus, in January 1916, he acknowledged that the failure to develop the One Big Union in Ireland had damaged the prospects for the kind of national emancipation that he wished to see:

Had we been able to carry out all our plans, as such an Irish organisation of Labour alone could carry them out, we could at a word have created all the conditions necessary to the striking of a successful blow, whenever the military arm of Ireland wished to move.[6]

Although Connolly still emphasised that working class and national interests should not be separated, his appraisal of trade union weaknesses showed how far the situation fell short of his ideal. Yet he saw action as essential.

With this diagnosis and this priority, collaboration with people who were neither socialist nor working class was inevitable. Some Nationalists had expressed support late in 1913 for the locked-out Dublin workers. Arguably Connolly subsequently had some influence on Pearse. The latter's late writings reveal not only that the two men agreed on the basic components of the Nationalist tradition, but that Pearse's concern with social questions did not die with the conclusion of the Lock Out. Although he remained sceptical about class-based politics, he acknowledged in his final pamphlet that private property should not be a fetish. It should be held 'subject to the national sanction'.[7] The facts of a specific case could license its limitation or even its abolition. Moreover, Pearse emphasised that without popular consent, a Government of capitalists had no legitimacy. Indeed such a qualification for office should not be attractive:

the people, if wise, will not choose the makers and administrators of their laws on such arbitrary and fantastic grounds as the possession of capital, or the possession of redheads, or the having been born on a Tuesday ...[8]

The point should not be exaggerated. Pearse did not enter the General Post Office on Easter Monday 1916 as a Socialist; but equally Connolly did not simply abandon his longstanding Socialism for an uncomplicated Nationalism.

Behind the issue of ideological compromises, there stands the question: what did Connolly hope to achieve through an insurrection? Pearse's commitment to the idea of a blood-sacrifice as a remedy for Irish passivity is well known. One of his most outspoken comments in this vein would be employed by O'Casey in his anti-Rising masterpiece, *The Plough and the Stars*. The heroism of the European War and the consequential sacrifices should be welcomed:

it is good for the world that such things should be done. The old heart of the earth needed to be warmed with the red wine of the battlefield. Such august homage was never before offered to God as this, the homage of millions of lives given gladly for love of country.[9]

The sentiment was shared by some of Pearse's closest collaborators, most notably Joseph Plunkett, but Connolly reacted vehemently:

No, we do not think that the old heart of the earth needs to be warmed with the red wine of millions of lives. We think anyone who does is a blithering idiot. We are sick of such teaching and the world is sick of such teaching.[10]

The rejection was at one with many of Connolly's earlier writings which had demonstrated both awareness and abhorrence of the impact of modern military technology. When he initially argued for insurrection to halt the war, he claimed that this would reduce casualties.[11] Yet he was not exempt from the sacrificial religious imagery employed by some radical Nationalists. His analysis of the corruption of the Irish working class by the British connection led to a proposal that must have won Pearse's approval:

no agency less potent than the red-tide of war on Irish soil will ever be able to enable the Irish race to recover its self-respect or establish its national dignity in the face of a world horrified and scandalised by what must seem to them our national apostasy.

The argument focused on the recovery of credibility rather than on any substantive outcome. It fitted in with Connolly's repeated claim that the Irish in the wartime crisis had to keep faith with their most vital Nationalist traditions. The argument was buttressed by redemptionist imagery:

Without the slightest trace of irreverence, but in all due humility and awe, we recognise that of us as of mankind before Calvary, it may truly be said
   'Without the Shedding of Blood there is no Redemption'.[12]

Such a passage indicated the degree to which a Socialist operating within a Catholic Nationalist culture could absorb dominant imagery, especially at a critical moment.

   Such passages should not be taken as conclusive evidence that Connolly capitulated to a redemptionist mysticism. Characterisation of the Rising is a complex matter. The most credible analysis would appear to be one which focuses on the symbolic aspects with the ceremonial proclamation of the Republic, ensuring that an idealised tradition of thorough opposition to British rule remained unbroken.[13] Too much attention should not be given to the strategic planning and the prelude of orders and counterorders that produced such a tangle of misunderstandings. A heavy concentration on such incidents as the voyage of the 'Aud' and the conflicts within the Volunteers tends to imply that with better fortune, the rebels could have made a military showing that would of itself, have transformed the situation. That military matters could have gone better is obvious; that the outcome could have been radically different seems implausible. An emphasis on the Rising as a symbolic event does not mean that justifications must be sought in the realm of mysticism. Attention has been paid already to one argument for insurrection: 'the child and the pin' argument. Its potency did not depend on metaphysical claims about blood sacrifice. Rather it is a specific example of a more general contention that an insurrection's value lay not in the immediate victory of those involved but in the radicalising impact of their action. Yeats' poem *The Rose Tree* can be seen as a presentation of the blood-sacrifice doctrine, but it also made a pragmatic political case. The paralysis that resulted from Redmondite domination could be ended by an act of heroism:

> 'O words are lightly spoken'
> said Pearse to Connolly.
> 'Maybe a breath of politic words
> Has withered our Rose Tree;
> Or maybe but a wind that blows
> Across the bitter sea.'

> 'It needs but to be watered,'
> James Connolly replied,
> 'To make the green come out again
> And spread on every side,
> And shake the blossom from the bud
> To be the garden's pride.'

> 'But where can we draw water,'
> said Pearse to Connolly.
> 'When all the wells are parched away?
> O plain as plain can be
> There's nothing but our own red blood
> Can make a right Rose Tree.'[14]

Connolly had used more austere language to make the same point late in 1914.

If the British Government once more throws off the mask of constitutionalism and launches its weapons of repression against those who dare to differ from it, if once more it sets in motion its jails, its courts martial, its scaffolds, then the last tie that binds these men to the official Home Rule gang will snap.[15]

The analysis was prescient as a prognostication of the Rising's ability to generate the symbolism for a new mass Nationalist movement. The implications for Socialism were another matter, but Connolly's underlying optimism did not seem to desert him. Writing at the end of January 1916 to the Glasgow Socialist, Arthur MacManus, he claimed that Government repression of civil liberties and the brooding threat of conscription had implications that went beyond the specifically Nationalist:

the outstanding fact ... which stood out in the Government's policy of persecution was the potentialities of Social Revolution which their action developed.[16]

Such optimism appears to have informed his arguments with those Volunteers opposed to an early insurrection. Bulmer Hobson, outside of and opposed to the conspiracy recalled one exchange with Connolly in a Dublin restaurant:

His conversation was full of cliches derived from the earlier days of the Socialist movement in Europe. He told me that the working class was always revolutionary, that Ireland was a powder magazine, and that what was necessary was for someone to apply the match. I replied that if he must talk in metaphors, Ireland was a wet bog and that the match would fall into a puddle.[17]

Connolly's fundamental assumptions remained those that had moulded his activities as a Socialist. The innate radicalism of the working class was stifled and betrayed by cautious Labour leaders whose dominance was facilitated by undemocratic organisations. The radicalism could be realised through democratic structures and bold initiatives. In 1916, organisational footholds were sparse. All that remained were bold initiatives.

At this point, two voices demand attention: one Socialist, the other Nationalist. The former belonged to Francis Sheehy-Skeffington, perhaps the Rising's most tragic victim. Feminist, pacifist and vegetarian, he did not participate in the insurrection. Instead, he attempted to organise groups to prevent looting. This did not reflect any attachment to private property, but rather a desire to protect the rebels from dismissal as a pillaging mob. Seized as a hostage by British troops and shot on the instructions of Captain Bowen-Colthurst, his murder became one of the earliest causes of post-Rising antagonism to the British Government.[18] His unique role in Irish politics was portrayed eloquently by the poet, James Stephens:

the most absurdly courageous man I have ever met with or heard of. He has been in every trouble that has touched Ireland these ten years back, and he has always been in on the generous side, therefore and naturally on the side that was unpopular and weak ...

Like Connolly he paraded his principles to an often unresponsive city undeterred by threats and bearing no malice against any violent response:

he accepted blows and indignities and ridicule with the pathetic candour of a child who is disguised as a man, and whose disguise cannot come off.[19]

Sheehy-Skeffington's pacifism seemed far removed from Connolly's ultimate response; yet they shared much. It was not just that they had a common attachment to Socialism. Sheehy-Skeffington also had a firm commitment to the Nationalist cause. Indeed in January 1916, Connolly praised him for his support for an elusive synthesis:

He had shown ... that it was possible to be an advocate of advanced social reform, and at the same time to be intensely national.[20]

Significantly, it was to Sheehy-Skeffington that Connolly turned for a literary executor prior to Easter 1916. He could ensure that the Socialist message would not be condemned to trivialisation or distortion.[21] It was a crowning irony that one of the Rising's most barbarous episodes destroyed any such hope.

This substantial area of agreement renders more urgent the question of why Sheehy-Skeffington dissented fundamentally from any proposal for an armed insurrection. One simple answer would be his pacificism, but he was too reasoned a thinker to be content with such a terse rejection. A more thorough explanation can be found in 'An Open Letter to Thomas MacDonagh'.[22] The recipient had been a teaching colleague; by May 1915 he was committed clearly to the more militant section of the Volunteers. Significantly, Sheehy-Skeffington emphasised their common ground, as well as their differences. He too had been attracted by the Volunteers, once they had shaken off 'the Redmondite incubus'; but crucially, he rejected the organisation's militarisation. Certainly a vigorous Volunteer movement could heighten Irish people's self-respect, but this promise was flawed fatally by the emphasis on military credibility. Those who were less scrupulous about the use of violence would come to dominate:

True, Ireland's militarism can never be on so great a scale as that of Germany or England; but it may be equally fatal to the best interests of Ireland. European militarism has drenched Europe in blood; Irish militarism may only crimson the fields of Ireland. For us that would be disaster enough.[23]

His accusation was not just that military methods would pervert the organisation, its ideals and the society whose interests it claimed to advance. He further argued that such a method for achieving political change was anachronistic. This claim involved a very modern emphasis. One limitation on Volunteer membership was significant:

women are left out ... Consider carefully why: and when you have found and clearly expressed the reason why women cannot be asked to enrol in this movement, you will be close to the reactionary element in the movement itself.[24]

Instead he envisaged an organisation of men and women committed to national objectives, but only through reasoned argument; ready to be martyrs but not prepared to kill. For Sheehy-Skeffington this offered:

the only way out of the tangle ... the only way in which we, the oppressed and exploited, can reconcile our hatred of the oligarchies and our hatred of organised bloodshed.[25]

Addressed to Thomas MacDonagh, the argument could have been addressed even more pertinently to Connolly who shared many of Sheehy-Skeffington's fundamental principles.

Its bleak prognostications acquired significant support from subsequent events. Dedication to military objectives marginalised social priorities. The exclusion of women from the Volunteers reinforced the traditional stereotypes of Irish society. Over time the drive for national independence through a combination of military and political methods produced an insensitivity towards violence that culminated in the barbarities of the Civil War. Yet it would be unreasonable to condemn Connolly as lacking sensitivity towards the brutal consequences of any military action. Rather, he considered the options of accepting the continuing mass slaughter of the War, or of acting in a fashion that would produce its own casualties, but which might shorten the larger conflict. For him such a choice might justify insurrection, especially if it also might loosen the grip of capitalism. The issue is fundamental and complex. One question is how much credibility should be attached to Sheehy-Skeffington's alternative.

Socialists who adopted this position could be found in several European societies. Thus many members of the British ILP condemned the War, expressed pacifist principles and resisted conscription often at great personal cost, including in several cases death in prison. Connolly admired such Socialists but their divergence from his position in 1916 was often acute. The ILP's official newspaper, the *Labour Leader*, condemned the Rising as 'a crime'. The use of violence was decisive:

We are opposed to armed force whether it be under the control of the Government or under the control of a labour organisation.[26]

Such a condemnation raises the problem of the pacifist position's viability. It furnished moving examples of individual heroism, but it was unclear whether anything else was on offer as an immediate strategy. Its advocates hoped that such actions could help the construction of a Socialist movement that could be a significant force once the War had ended. This contrasted sharply with the claim made by Connolly, Maclean and Lenin that the War provided both the need and the opportunity for a revolutionary breakthrough. Those who looked forward to Socialist growth, once the War had ended, were often unable to make a distinctive impact after 1918. By then, the political world had been revolutionised, not least because of interventions by Socialists who saw the War as opportunity rather than obstacle. Such evidence does not of itself destroy the credibility of the pacifist option. The Socialist interventions did not have the consequences anticipated by their proponents; indeed those who advocated Socialist-pacifism, whether in Ireland or elsewhere could maintain that such violent and early interventions blighted hopes of significant socialist growth. Yet pacifists rarely made specific recommendations about how such growth could be achieved. Sheehy-Skeffington's precise claims on this point were obscure. To a Socialist such as Connolly, oppressed by the illiberality of the State and by the need to halt mass slaughter, but believing that wartime chaos offered some scope for radical change, Sheehy-Skeffington's principled option had little immediate relevance.

The second significant voice was informed by very different preoccupations. Eoin MacNeill was neither Socialist nor pacifist.[27] A Gaelic scholar and head of the Volunteers, he offered thorough opposition to the strategy of armed insurrection and played a significant part in ensuring that most Volunteers did not participate. His political reputation suffered as a result. He has been dismissed too readily as a cloistered academic swamped by the demands of revolutionary nationalism. In fact the truth was very different. In February 1916 he offered a detailed moral and strategic critique of the insurrectionary option.[28] Unlike Sheehy-Skeffington's case, this was a response by someone who acknowledged the validity of military action.

His argument began with a moral claim that military initiatives could be justified only if these were backed by a good prospect of success. Moreover, this should be immediate, and not some vague long-term possibility. Otherwise, those responsible for an insurrection would be responsible for any deaths. The decisive assessment of likely consequences should be based on a thorough scrutiny of the evidence, not on individual intuition nor 'a priori' maxims. A reliance on premonition meant an abandonment of reason in favour of individual psychology as the vital determinant. Maxims if applied uncritically could be treacherous guides. Thus MacNeill submitted several such formulae, employed by Revolutionary Nationalists to a sceptical investigation. Whether the War offered a crucial opportunity to advance Irish interests was a a matter for reasoned judgement, not one of faith. The claim that Irish Nationalists had acted too slowly in past crises was historically false. Even if it were valid, this need offer no guidance for the present. The incantation that Ireland should take the initiative was at one level empty. It was also misleading. Any initiative in Ireland lay with the British forces; Hallowed formulae were dealt with dismissively:

I do not care and will not care a rap for maxims or formulae or catchwords or feelings or forebodings, or for the reproaches either of our own time or later times. Organisation, preparation, calculation are the necessary preliminaries to any decision ...[29]

MacNeill acknowledged that a sacrificial strategy could be acceptable but only given the imminent destruction of Irish nationality. He did not see this condition as near to fulfilment. Essentially his assessment was relatively optimistic. Those who favoured a grand gesture:

are really impelled by a sense of feebleness or despondency or fatalism or by an instinct of satisfying their own emotions or escaping from a difficult and complex or trying situation.[30]

Indeed, a revolt would make matters worse. It would provide a credible justification for repression of the Volunteers. His preferred alternative began from the claim that if Irish rights could be secured without military conflict, then this would be preferable. He acknowledged that this would be a difficult strategy for a force undergoing military training.

Nevertheless he considered that the Volunteers had established themselves as a significant element in Irish politics and were invulnerable to
government repression unless an insurrectionary adventure provided an
excuse. The wise strategy was to increase the Volunteers' strength.
Military action should come only if an attempt was made to disarm the
organisation.

This tactic offered the hope of securing mass support. MacNeill
insisted against some of the poets that:

> our country is not a poetical abstraction ... There is no such person as Caitlin
> Ni Uallachain or Roisin Dubh or the Sean bhean Bhoct who is calling upon us
> to serve her. What we call our country is the Irish nation, which is a concrete
> and visible reality.[31]

He claimed that radicals were often blind to the need to win support,
not just because they dealt in poetic abstractions but more mundanely
because they generalised from their own emotions to those of the wider
population. This could produce a disastrous miscalculation:

> ... the only possible basis for successful revolutionary action is deep and wide-
> spread popular discontent. We have only to look around us in the streets to realise
> that no such condition exists in Ireland. A few of us, a small proportion, who
> think about the evils of English government in Ireland are always discontented.
> We should be downright fools if we were to measure many others by the standards
> of our own thoughts.[32]

This thorough and reasoned response to the insurrectionary case grew
immediately out of MacNeill's justifiable anxiety about the intentions
of some of his colleagues within the Volunteers. Equally, its principal
thrusts were directed at the repeated demands for early action made by
Connolly.[33] A strength of the argument lies in the thorough emphasis
on the need to justify actions through a reasoned presentation of the
evidence. If this criticism is applied to Connolly's advocacy of military
action, certainly it is the case that he emphasised such propositions as
'Ireland has always struck too late'. Yet it would be misleading to suggest that in his case such claims were simply acts of faith. Typically, they
were based on historical arguments, often controversial and sometimes
implausible, but as such Connolly's maxims were not open usually to
MacNeill's most fundamental objection.[34] Equally, despite his growing
support for traditional Nationalist sentiments, Connolly could be accused
only rarely of personifying 'Ireland' in a fashion that ignored or distorted
the sentiments of the country's inhabitants. Throughout his career he
polemicised against Nationalists who dealt in such mystifications. One
such comment from the period when he had committed himself to an
insurrection makes the point:

> We are out for Ireland for the Irish. But who are the Irish? Not the rack-renting,
> slum-owning landlord; not the sweating, profit-grinding capitalists; not the sleek

and oily lawyer; not the prostitute pressman – the hired liars of the enemy ...
Not these but the Irish working class, the only secure foundation upon which
a free nation can be reared.[35]

Greater complexities are raised by the moral position taken by
MacNeill. The assertion that military means should be employed
normally only if there is a reasonable prospect of success led to two
difficulties. The first centres around the fact that despite the Easter
Rising's military defeat, it could be regarded in a longer perspective as
relatively successful in Nationalist as opposed to Socialist terms.

Yet the path from the reprisals through to the War of Independence
and the formation of the Free State was complex. Easter 1916 did not lead
directly to the guerrilla campaign of 1919–21. During the intervening
three years, the tactical options were complex, and the military campaign
that emerged eventually was fundamentally different from the symbolic
set piece of 1916.[36] That the rebels gambled on some such chain of
events is clear; that it was a reasonable gamble was much less obvious.
The emphasis on what was a reasonable choice raises the second issue,
that of available options. Repeatedly, Connolly argued that the costs of
passivity were likely to be devastating; an increasingly illiberal State
would not permit the development of a credible opposition and the
prospects for labour and nationalist organisations would be grim. Against
this assessment, MacNeill argued for the development of support and
influence; constraints were not that tight.[37]

Assessment of this alternative is complicated by the fact of the Rising.
This radically affected subsequent developments and thus these offer an
inadequate guide to the validity of MacNeill's strategy in a hypothetical
situation where no insurrection had taken place. But one sombre fact
provides a backcloth to any consideration. Political organisations that
have concentrated on building up their forces in anticipation of a supreme
opportunity when these could be employed decisively have rarely been
able to consummate their strategy. Two decades later, the shattered
organisations of German and Austrian Socialists would offer bleak
monuments to the problem of ascertaining the opportune moment. The
cultivation of organisational maturity could become all too easily a goal
in itself.

One justification relevant for Connolly but not for MacNeill concerned
the likely impact of a Rising upon international Socialist opinion. The
actual impact was minimal. Only Lenin took a favourable view of its
possible significance:

A blow delivered against the British imperialist bourgeoisie in Ireland has a
hundred times more political significance than a blow of equal weight would have
in Asia or Africa ... The dialectics of history are such that small nations powerless
as an independent factor in the struggle against imperialism, play a part as one
of the ferments, one of the bacilli, which facilitate the entry into the arena of

the *real* power against imperialism, namely the socialist proletariat ... The misfortune of the Irish is that they rose prematurely, when the European revolt of the proletariat had not yet matured.[38]

How far sections of the European working class could be characterised as revolutionary during the immediately succeeding years is a difficult and debatable question. What is not contentious is that from the Autumn of 1917, events in Russia transformed the tempo of Socialist politics. Revolution was on the political agenda. The transformation has a significant implication for Irish political developments.

If an Irish Rising had occurred not in April 1916 but in the Spring or Summer of 1918, then the context would have been dramatically different.[39] Ireland faced the threat of conscription, the Parliamentary Party withdrew from Westminster to campaign against its introduction, the MPs did so in collaboration with Sinn Fein and Labour organisations. Resistance to the Government's proposal had clerical support. The most dramatic evidence of labour involvement was an effective general strike on 23 April. Throughout the Summer, the Government engaged in widespread and radicalising repression. Coercive legislation was employed; several Sinn Fein leaders were arrested amidst allegations of a German plot; Sinn Fein, the Volunteers and the Gaelic League were all suppressed as 'dangerous associations'. Arguably, a military rising in this context would have had substantial popular support; the context would have meant that several of the criteria stressed by MacNeill in his memorandum would have been satisfied.

Certainly the international implications could have been very different from the indifference and misunderstanding that had greeted the 1916 initiative. War weariness was corroding the will to fight of soldiers on both Western and Italian Fronts. It had done so already in the East. A significant revolt in Ireland would have required the transfer of British troops and any consequential repression might have provoked an angry response from Irish soldiers within the British Army. This is a tantalising 'might have been'. Possibly a 'premature' rising in 1916 stripped the boy's pin of much of its power.

A putative Irish revolt in 1918 would have had its Socialist facets. Indeed what is striking about actual Irish developments after 1916 is the extent to which images derived from the Russian Revolution left their mark on the rhetoric and the expectations of Irish labour. Its distinctive voice was not muffled immediately by the tricolour. One legacy of 1916 was the weakening of deferential routines in the countryside. Labour organisations expanded dramatically and even the cautious post-Rising leadership felt this radical tide and made concessions. The ITGWU grew significantly in rural and small town Ireland.[40] Many of its activists were determined not to be absorbed by Sinn Fein. Whilst the latter sought to emulate the hegemony of the Parliamentary Party, labour activists prized their independence; not least because of Sinn Fein's willingness to consort with conservative Nationalists. Ironically this concern for independence was heightened by returning soldiers, keen like their counterparts elsewhere to secure economic improvements, but with little incentive to join Sinn Fein. Thus Nationalist Ireland shared in the post-1917 radicalisation of labour that characterised much of Europe. It shared also in the subsequent containment and defeat of labour hopes.

The Irish experience of this declension was shaped inevitably by the national struggle. Labour's optimism was crushed between two mill-stones. On the one side, the beleaguered British administration was unwilling or unable to distinguish between Nationalist and labour agitations; on the other, Sinn Feinn tended to use the developing alter-native administrative structures to impose the priorities of landlords, employers and farmers.

Perhaps it was predictable that as the conflict with the British forces became more ruthless, Labour activists came to co-operate with Nation-alists whom they opposed on economic questions. During a battle for political independence, the National Question was likely to have a heavy impact on immediate political allegiances. But such pressures did not result in the automatic suppression of a class dimension within Irish politics. Socialists and trade union leaders often made a distinction between a temporary alliance with conservative elements on the National Question and the underlying divergence on economic issues. Following the inauguration of the Free State, class tensions could still find expression in prolonged industrial battles. Thus in 1922 and 1923 the Transport Workers fought with some initial success, but later unavailingly against a concerted attempt to cut farmworkers' wages in County Waterford.[41]

Already one Irish Labour voice had attacked any hope that the nation-alist struggle could generate a socialist revolution. In March 1922, a correspondent to the newspaper *Voice of Labour* had dismissed as 'romantic' any expectation of an IRA–worker alliance. The 'realism' was founded on a pessimistic view of the bases for economic radicalism. Both pro- and anti-Treaty factions of the IRA were dominated by farmers and shopkeepers whose outlooks were confined to narrowly capitalist priorities. Even the rural landless labourers were motivated only by land-hunger. Such industrial workers as there were within the Free State would accept the Treaty and attempt to use the resulting institutions to their advantage. But their endeavours would be cramped by unavoidable constraints. The British connection was still decisive; Ireland's economy depended on essential imports. There seemed no chance of any revol-utionary breakthrough across the water. So long as this was the case, any radical Irish initiative would face the threat of British intervention. Such speculation was unrealistic anyway, since the Irish Labour movement was in no sense revolutionary. As the analysis concluded:

There are no Lenins, Trotskys, Krassins, Radeks or Litvinoffs in the Irish Labour movement.[42]

The writer was probably Thomas Johnson; the argument was explicitly against the expectations of some British Communists.[43] It certainly reflected Johnson's own cautious style. More broadly it provided a deflating argument against anyone inclined to take a simplistic view of Nationalist mobilisation as a springboard for socialist growth. Indeed, a sceptic might have added that some observers exaggerated the degree to which there had been mass involvement in the War of Independence as opposed to mass acceptance of many of its consequences.[44]

Nevertheless, Socialist pessimism in 1922 involved considerations that extended beyond specifically Irish features. Working-class initiatives had been defeated throughout much of Europe. Recession had blunted workers' power; the political authority of capital had been re-established; the Soviet Union had been isolated. The future of Socialism within Nationalist Ireland could not be separated from this wider development. Moreover, the *Voice of Labour* argument focussed specifically on the bleak prospects for revolutionary socialists. It failed to deal, except implicitly, with the scope for a moderate Labour Party in Ireland. This tendency remained weak under the Free State. The evidence suggests that Labour's decision to stand aside in the 1918 General Election in order to permit a clear vote on the National issue was not decisive. Rather, after 1918 the Party lost out over a lengthy period. Moments of relative success were subordinated to what in retrospect were decisive setbacks. The continuing centrality of unfinished National business was clearly significant; but so too were industrial defeats which stripped political Labour of an important trade union resource.[45]

A harshly realistic analysis of 1916 and of its actual historical consequences is necessary. For Socialists, the outcome was depressing; a verdict that needs to be placed against naive claims that Connolly in theory and in practice offered a viable synthesis of nationalist and socialist politics. No such synthesis ever existed to be deflected from a triumph by contingent circumstances. Equally, it would be misleading to characterise Connolly's actions as one vital contribution to the marginalisation of Labour and Socialist politics after the formation of the Free State. The fate of Irish Labour with all its distinctive features cannot be separated from the more general defeat of European Labour. On both the narrower and broader stages there are intriguing and complex 'might have beens'. Connolly's action in 1916 and the debate over the consequences should not be the subject of an historical idealisation, nor of an understandable but misleading presentation as socialist apostasy. Rather it was a choice made in what seemed to a long-standing Socialist, an increasingly bleak situation. As such, it raised for Socialists the perennial question of the baffling interplay between creative initiative, and firm, perhaps, dimly perceived constraints. Pearse had believed that faith could combat the problem. His poem 'The Fool' gave this answer to those who counseled prudence and realism:

> O Wise men, riddle me this: what if the dream come true?
> What if the dream come true? and if millions unborn shall dwell
> In the house that I shaped in my heart, the noble house of my thought?[46]

Such millions have not lived in Pearse's dream of a Gaelic Ireland; nor have they lived in a realisation of the ideals that inspired the Bolsheviks. Yet both actions demonstrate not simply the unpredictable consequences of radical political initiatives; they also show a willingness to strike out against the tyranny of normality. Their complex legacies have shaped respectively the subsequent histories of Ireland and of the Socialist Movement. The Irish Socialist Movement has been shaped by both. The problems of the twenties and of later were obviously connected closely to the developments that had led from GPO to the Free State. Less apparent, but still significant, there were the consequences of the Bolshevik Revolution – the rising tide of radical expectations, its containment – and then ebb. This was a European phenomenon manifest in a divergent form in each society. In Free State Ireland, it was affected radically by the prevalence of the National Struggle and by the relative weakness of Labour, both industrially and politically.

1916 and 1917 were vital but they have all too easily become prisms through which we are presented with distorted images of the past. Thus any recovery of Connolly's politics requires an act of historical imagination.

Part II

John Maclean

A disputed legacy

Simply as a name, he claims our acquaintance. John Maclean qualifies for a footnote in the consciousness of many English Socialists. But such 'honourable mentions' leave unanswered some vital questions. One route into the complexities is provided by a comparison with Connolly. Both were political martyrs; Connolly at the hands of a British Army firing squad, Maclean through loss of employment, the harshness of the Scottish prison system, illness and early death. Such martyrdoms can improve the chances of posthumous political influence, but its direction depends heavily on who establishes control over the legacy.[1]

Problems in understanding Connolly's politics have been compounded because of his sanctification either as a member of the Nationalist pantheon, or as a Socialist with a sensitive feel for the revolutionary potential of Irish politics. In Maclean's case, the initial difficulty arose not from the dominance of a misleading characterisation, but from the near-oblivion that enveloped his reputation after his premature death in November 1923. This bleak outcome was predictable. With Scotland firmly part of the United Kingdom, and demonstrating relatively strong support for both Labour and Communist Parties, there seemed little reason to honour Maclean. His emphasis on revolution dismayed many Labour partisans, whilst Communists rejected his case for a separate Scottish Party, and were antagonised by his refusal to join the British alternative. Socialists within both parties could unite in rejecting Maclean's commitment to Scottish independence and his inauguration of a Scottish Workers' Republican Party.

Subsequent characterisations of Clydeside politics owed much to the accounts of committed Communists such as Willie Gallacher and Tom Bell.[2] The image of a 'Red' — potentially revolutionary Clydeside in- evitably provoked the question of Maclean's contribution. These writers were keen to acknowledge the value of his wartime agitations. He had been prominent in the anti-war section of the British Socialist Party and had worked alongside future Communist stalwarts. His sufferings as a political prisoner had made him a symbol of principled opposition to the War far beyond the Clyde. Briefly he had served as Soviet Consul in Glasgow.

Such writings drew a sharp distinction between this Maclean and the Maclean who denounced the formation of the British Communist Party, and espoused Scottish independence. This contrast was frequently justified through claims about Maclean's mental condition following his release from prison in December 1918. Growing political isolation was presented as a consequence of paranoia.[3] The impact of prison upon Maclean's health remains a question with an elusive answer, not least because of the continuing unavailability of some Government documents. Yet the weight of the evidence militates against such a simplistic dismissal of Maclean's later political choices. Certainly his prison experiences had a damaging impact on his health; his subsequent polemics intertwined political claims and sometimes violent rejections of former allies. Maclean's increasing isolation produced, and was intensified by personal grievances. But this marginalisation raises important issues about revolutionary socialist strategy and prospects, and about the relationship of socialist objectives to nationalist ones. These questions should not be reduced to a psychological case-history.

Radical revisions of such images and verdicts have been fuelled not simply by further historical research, but also by more immediate political concerns. Within Scotland, there had always been a few, most notably Hugh MacDiarmid, who had insisted on Maclean's significance as a principled Scottish Socialist. In particular MacDiarmid emphasised Maclean's eventual linking of socialist prospects with political independence.[4] The failures of Labour Governments in the sixties, the decay of Labour's Scottish organisation, the growth of the Scottish National Party; together these could facilitate a growing belief within some sections of the Scottish Left that a concern with national independence was relevant to socialist strategy. Such an emphasis inevitably generated interest in possible precursors. Maclean was an obvious candidate.[5]

The British context provided another inducement to reconsider Maclean. Disillusion with both Labourism and orthodox Communism provoked quests for suppressed options free from the stultifying compromises of one, and the moral degeneration of the other. Once again Maclean could be presented as a significant figure, marginalised in those vital post-1918 years when arguably the basic structures and strategies of the modern British Left had been established.[6] Now that the failures of these dominant strategies were apparent, why not return to the politics of someone who had stood out against such developments?

Such responses, whilst understandable, produce their own difficulties. Silence or distortion is answered with presentations of Maclean as principled Socialist, committed Nationalist, Marxist unpolluted by the chicanery of the Third International; someone who might have affected radically the development of the Scottish – or perhaps the British – Left. But this possibility was blocked by State oppression, sectarian conspiracy and death. The older distortion readily feeds a contrasting hagiography. In turn, this can invite a further revision in which Maclean is marginalised once again as an unworldly figure preoccupied by issues remote from the concerns of the Scottish working class.[7]

The images mount: the products of memory, myth and research, of historical controversies and political pressures. There is the principled Socialist broken by Government persecution and consigned to self-destructive isolation. Against this, stands the revolutionary – nationalist, proclaiming a Scottish road to Socialism, but beset by enemies on the Left as much as by servants of the State. From outside the revolutionary camp, there emerges the far-Left eccentric, heroic, honest but isolated and therefore futile, a tragic demonstration of the sterility of such a commitment. Inevitably this complex and controversial legacy is a daunting obstacle to any attempt at the elucidation of Maclean's significance as a Socialist – Nationalist.

Perhaps some progress can be made by presenting some basic propositions. The sources seem to agree at least on one point. Maclean was an honest, principled Marxist Socialist whose political quarrels stemmed in part from an unwillingness to compromise basic values when faced with an inhospitable environment. In particular, his response to the War, a policy of using the conflict as a springboard for revolution made him almost unique amongst prominent British Socialists.

Connolly made a similar assessment and then carried through a complex response which linked his commitment to revolutionary socialism with the priorities of the 'Direct Action' Republicans. For Maclean, whose prominence until August 1914 had been essentially as an educator and a propagandist, there existed no equivalent option. Yet this absence should not be employed to dismiss his later emphasis on Scottish independence as an incidental or an eccentricity. Such dismissals perhaps reveal more about the preferences of Socialists – especially English ones – than they do about Maclean's politics. An emphasis on his eventual Nationalism need not imply that there was any significant chance of Scottish independence, but it can place Maclean's position in a wider context. International developments could appear encouraging; the Bolsheviks' expressions of support for national self-determination were balanced by the professed attachment of the Allies to the same principle. Within Scotland many sections of the Labour Movement during and after the War expressed support for Home Rule; some individuals seemed ready to go further. In part, this reflected Labour self-confidence about Scotland's economic future, and concern that 'progressive' Scotland could be held back by conservative England. Irish developments had also had an impact on sections of the Scottish Labour Movement. Some immediate reactions to the Easter Rising evinced a hostility or a lack of understanding, but the gradual shift of Labour towards sympathy to the Republicans was given a sharper edge in Scotland by the presence of many Irish people in Scottish Labour organisations. Maclean was certainly not idiosyncratic in his developing support for Nationalism – both Scottish and Irish. The distinctiveness comes, as with Connolly, in the claim that the goals of socialism and national independence could be synthesised fruitfully within a revolutionary strategy.

Any analysis of Maclean must face a further problem stemming from the character of his writings.[8] These were written largely under pressure for journalistic deadlines and are typically agitational in purpose, and in style. There is no equivalent to Connolly's work on Irish History nor to his polemic on Socialism and Religion. Nevertheless, significant claims about Maclean's politics can be extracted from his writings, although it is vital not to become imprisoned within his assumptions and arguments. Such a limitation would risk accepting his beliefs about what was feasible. Equally, a resolute focus on what actually happened coupled with a failure to listen seriously to what Maclean was saying, leads all too readily to an acceptance that events could not have been otherwise, and that Maclean was a utopian. Disputes over what was possible are central to the debates over Maclean's significance. This presentation will attempt to locate his activities within the context of Scottish politics, and to do so with an eye for suppressed alternatives in the crucial areas of socialism and nationalism.

Chapter 1

A model Social Democrat

John Maclean's early politics epitomised the assumptions and objectives of Social Democratic orthodoxy during the quarter-century of the Second International. He came to Socialist politics from Calvinism and through Secularism. Despite his claim that Blatchford's 'Merrie England' was the text that precipitated his move to Socialism, his style always demonstrated the high-minded seriousness that characterised these earlier attachments. His Socialist activities were centred in the Pollokshaws Branch of the Social Democratic Federation.[1] He seems never to have been attracted to the Independent Labour Party; nor unlike Connolly and several Scottish Socialists did he join the De-Leonite Socialist Labour Party. Instead he gave his loyalty to an organisation that claimed to be a paragon of Marxist orthodoxy, but which was relatively unimportant within the Scottish Left. The Social Democrats could point subsequently to some growth in Glasgow. By 1911 the Party claimed six branches within the city. Nevertheless, the ILP dominated the city's Left. It could utilise Radical–Liberal sentiments in a fashion that was often unavailable to self-consciously marxist groups.[2]

The strategy embraced by Maclean as a member of the SDF was unexceptional. Socialism could and should be pursued through an organisation that proclaimed the objective openly. Socialists who allied with trade unionists inside the Labour Party and failed to secure such a commitment, were diluting the prospects for socialism. The pre-1914 Labour Party was not an effective instrument for Socialist growth; rather it was a means whereby working-class interests could be subordinated to the priorities of the Liberal Party.[3] This assessment did not lead Maclean into sectarianism. He co-operated regularly with ILP members on propaganda work and he strongly supported any Labour candidate who emphasised his attachment to Socialism.[4] In his view the failure to achieve the unity of ILP and SDF organisations in the late 1890s had been damaging as it had left the stage clear for a non-socialist Labour Alliance.[5] The lost ground had to be regained. In the end the characteristic expression of working class politics would be an explicitly Socialist organisation which individual trade unionists would join. Late in 1911, Maclean could welcome the formation of the British Socialist Party as a limited step in that direction.[6]

His attitude towards industrial struggles was informed by a similar perspective. He chronicled for readers of *Justice* the involvements of groups of Scottish workers in the conflicts of 1910–14.[7] Often these disputes involved unskilled workers. After 1909, Scottish craftsmen were able frequently to exploit their scarcity in the labour market without resort to strike action. Sometimes militancy could appear as a contrast with the flaccidity of Labour's political leadership. Involvement in an industrial confrontation could be a powerful educational force:

Never were the masses so pugnacious ... never before were they so class-conscious ... No doubt we would like to see them fight for something substantial; but to get them to fight the masters at all is a God's blessing in this realm.

Once action was taken, then the experiences of those involved would be:

more effective than all the theory we might fire at our benighted class from this till doomsday. Fighting leads to new facts, these to our new theory, and thence to revolution.[8]

Yet such optimism seemed to be belied by events. There remained a tantalising gap between industrial responses and political consequences. Thus, for May Day 1913 Maclean characterised Scottish workers as:

still seething with revolt industrially, but lying like lambs politically.

Nevertheless, the fundamental hope remained:

It is a pleasure to see them revolt in any shape or fashion, however. And they are winning all over, even though the gains be microscopic.[9]

Essentially Maclean was firmly orthodox in his insistence that industrial discontent must be channelled through an effective socialist party.[10]

This prescription meant that he opposed syndicalist doctrines that seemed to ignore or marginalise the contribution of political organisation. He expressed satisfaction that in Scotland there was little evidence of 'that parasitical and new phased Anarchism entitled Syndicalism'.[11] This opposition was based partly on syndicalists' alleged lack of political strategy and also on the belief that the desired form of social organisation denied majority rights in favour of sectional claims:

the majority has the primary right. If I did not believe that, I would not be a Social Democrat. If I believed that the employees ... had the supreme claim, I would be an out-and-out Syndicalist.[12]

Maclean's position – and by implication the underlying strategic problem – came out clearly in his discussion of the Clydebank strike of Singer workers in the Spring of 1911. Industrial Unionism was the way forward; it would emerge out of the amalgamation of existing unions. This development needed to be linked with a political organisation able to express this growing unity. This dimension was vital since:

the socialisation of industry cannot be accomplished by the direct seizure of the factories and the land by the unions.

Such an assertion denied 'the naturalness of the state and politics'.[13]

It was to the task of building such a party that Maclean dedicated his energies: educational work through Marxist economic classes, propaganda meetings, election campaigns, work in the Co-operative Movement, attempts to achieve a more militant and more self-consciously Socialist strategy for trade unions. Progress was slender. By January 1913, he was querying the 'wastefulness and the spasmodic nature of lecture work'. Considerable expenditure had not had 'the direct results we should desire'.[14] In 1914, the BSP could look forward to contesting only a handful of Scottish seats at the next General Election. Any hope that Scotland would move towards Socialism along the route favoured by the optimists of the Second International did not seem very plausible.[15]

The BSP's Scottish weakness was just one facet of that Party's failure to realise the hopes that had attended its formation in 1911. Originally an amalgamation of Social Democrats, dissident ILP members and unattached Socialists, it was by 1914, little more than the old Social Democratic organisation under a new title and with the old weaknesses: a limited membership, electoral failure and the dubious benefit of a continuing association with the idiosyncratic H.M. Hyndman.[16] Already Maclean was demonstrating political disagreements with the Hyndmanites, but as yet he typically channelled his concern into proposals for improving party organisation.[17] Fundamentally however, the BSP confronted a crippling difficulty because of the existence of the Labour Party. Whatever its incoherences and its electoral failures, the latter had far more credibility as an articulator of working-class demands. Socialists to the left of the Labour Party faced a crucial problem of political space; already the thoughts of some within the BSP were turning towards the possibility of affiliation to the larger body.

Even within the wider Labour context, Scotland was not an area of relative strength. Only three Scottish constituencies returned Labour members in December 1910. In several cases, Scottish Labour candidates fared worse in their 1910 contests than they had done in 1906.[18] Scottish by-elections between 1911 and 1914 showed little evidence that Labour's position was improving. Scotland might have produced several significant individuals within the Labour Movement, and provided some organisational innovations, but in 1914, the prospects of mass support for Labour or Socialist candidates remained dubious. Some reasons were obvious. Scotland, like the rest of the United Kingdom, still contained many working-class males, let alone women, who lacked the vote. This limitation would disappear at some point, but whether it would benefit Labour and Socialist candidates remained an open question. Clearly many

Scottish workers were still happy to vote for a Liberal or a Unionist, even when a Labour alternative was available. Arguably recent events in Ireland had exacerbated sectarian tensions in Scotland and thereby strengthened, perhaps temporarily, workers' identifications with the older parties. Certainly Scotland in 1914 did not seem likely to provide a basis for a mass Socialist movement in the immediate future. On occasions Maclean acknowledged this pessimistic prospect; he presented Scotland as 'a political puzzle ... instinctively conservative and proverbially cautious', these traits were expressed in continuing support for Liberalism.[19]

This cautious assessment of the prospects for Socialism in Scotland was complemented by several of his judgements on the quality of Scottish trade unionism. His admiration for Bob Smillie was obvious and occasionally he expressed optimism about the political implications of events in the coalfields. More often he commented on the limited ambitions of the Miners; he claimed that railway trade unionism was more backward in Scotland than further south and he attacked the passivity of the Scottish Trades Union Congress.[20] Both politically and industrially the picture of the Scottish working class that emerged from Maclean's pre-war writings was unlikely to encourage Socialists. He suggested rather that hopes should be pinned on a wider movement for Socialism within the British working class. This early assessment needs to be placed against subsequent claims by Maclean and others that Home Rule or separatism was an appropriate strategy for Socialists, because of the relatively advanced nature of Scottish workers' politics.

Appraisal of this question also requires some evaluation of whether the condition of Scottish workers in 1914 contained a potential for significant radicalisation. During the pre-war years Scottish industry seemed superficially strong, and this apparent security arguably affected not only workers' conditions but also their perceptions.[21] In 1913 the level of unemployment amongst the insured population stood at $3 \cdot 8$ per cent for the United Kingdom as a whole, but in Scotland the figure was only $2 \cdot 1$ per cent. The Scottish working class included a relatively high proportion of skilled men. Glasgow, which would contribute so much to the development of Maclean's politics, was particularly notable for its concentrations of heavy industry and of skilled craftsmen. In no way before 1914 could the city be characterised as locked into a peripheral sector of the British economy. Rather its shipyards and engineering shops, its self-confident bourgeoisie and skilled workers could give credibility to the accolade: Second City of the Empire.[22]

This façade of success hid the potential for decline and thereby arguably a basis for working-class radicalisation. Major Scottish industries depended heavily on exports. Already the low-paid jute workers of Dundee faced Indian competition and had helped to elect an admittedly conservative craftsman as a Labour Member against both Liberal and Conservative opposition. Although the Western coalfields still dominated Scottish coal production, these were declining. The emphasis was shifting to Fife with its reliance on exports to Europe. This growing tendency for Scottish coal to be used outside Scotland was reflected in the decline of the steel industry. Although such symptoms of decay seemed to be balanced by the buoyancy of engineering and shipbuilding, a narrow focus on levels of output could be misleading. Beneath the pre-1914 revival of Clydeside shipbuilding lay a tardy utilisation of new technology. Engineering was reliant heavily on exports; it faced the challenge of cheaper competition and the threat of saturated markets.

These potential difficulties paralleled those looming for other well-established sections of British capitalism. Scottish employers, like their counterparts elsewhere, were keen to reduce costs and to implement technical innovations. The consequences in the near full employment conditions of the immediate pre-war years were the discontents and disputes chronicled by Maclean for readers of *Justice*. As he sometimes acknowledged, their immediate political significance seemed obscure. However, the fact that such challenges were similar to those facing workers elsewhere in Britain seemed to support Maclean's calls for a solidarity wider than any specifically Scottish initiative.

Only outside the workplace did many members of the Scottish working class share an experience that was distinctive. Housing was often appalling. The reasons for the dominant role of tenements in urban areas may be debatable; the consequences by 1914 in terms of overcrowding and lack of basic amenities were not. Some areas on Clydeside were increasingly subject to housing shortages, as the demand for labour outran the supply of accommodation.[23] Maclean had been interested in the housing issue from his earliest days in the Pollokshaws SDF.[24] Significantly, this was a basis for a distinctively Scottish radicalisation based on the local community rather than the workplace and thus utilising the enthusiasm of both women and men.

This movement would become significant under the intensified pressure of wartime, but until then, industrial disputes seemed much more significant as indices of working-class radicalisation. In his responses, Maclean, like other Socialists, focussed on what should unite workers rather than what divided them. This came through when he considered cases where national or religious loyalties could militate against the creation of a wider class solidarity. A visit to Belfast during the dock strike of 1907 produced an orthodox and erroneous assessment of that dispute's political impact:

The strikers and thousands of workers knew that they must cease quarrelling about Catholicism and Protestantism because ... they would be playing the game of the capitalists. I believe religious riots are a thing of the past.[25]

The prognostication that class or occupational claims would become dominant seemed more plausible in the context of the labour disputes of 1910–14. During the Summer of 1911 Maclean propagandised in the Rhondda Valley as the strike of the Cambrian Combine miners moved towards its bleak conclusion. Whilst admitting that support from the South Wales Miners' Federation had been limited, he argued that ultimately the clash should provoke a much wider demand for a minimum wage in the coal industry. This could be effective only if miners in all British coalfields stopped work. Maclean was appalled at the recent attitude of Scottish miners' representatives:

To the disgust of the strikers, they have learned that the Scottish delegates to the last conference of the MFGB have been their worst enemies.

The issue was very simple:

it is purely one of class combination and solidarity for a specific purpose.

Such a strategy offered some hope as against the capitulations of Labour leaders. Maclean's advocacy was fuelled by his identity as a Scot, but it urged a strategy of class – or in this case occupational – solidarity:

Now as a Scot, I have felt the disgrace here in Wales as keenly as if I were a miner ... It is my fervent wish that at least Scotland will not distinguish itself as a blackleg country in mining affairs ...[26]

His hopes were realised to a significant degree early in 1912 when Scottish miners participated in the first all-British coal strike, and secured some legislative recognition of their claim to a minimum wage. Despite the very limited immediate benefits, Maclean looked forward to the achievement of a national miners' union 'ready to strike a blow at any time, and with paralysing suddenness'.[27] Anything approaching this organisational goal was remote, but the achievement of a wider solidarity was a significant development. In terms of support for the strike, miners had exceeded the achievement of railwaymen the previous summer. When the dispute was labelled the first 'national' coal strike, the nation was of course Britain. The objective was to secure the intervention of the British State against recalcitrant employers. The strategy had achieved enough to suggest the possibility of greater benefits in future. Scottish particularism could seem an obstacle to industrial solidarity, and thereby to political radicalisation.

   This position emerged strongly when Maclean discussed some Liberal proposals for Scottish Home Rule. His only positive comment was pragmatic. If a Scottish Parliament was inaugurated:

we ought to be ready to make of it a democratic machine, and to use it for all it may produce.

But his basic attitude was dismissive. Such a legislature would be one more instrument of capitalist rule:

a buffer betwixt us and our goal, or a brake to curb our revolutionary fervour.

There was no hint of Connolly's claim that a settlement of the National Question would clear the decks for a class-based politics. In part, this perhaps reflected Maclean's view that, for most Scots, Home Rule was not a significant issue. More fundamentally his position rested on an argument about economic standardisation. National particularisms would wither in the face of technical change and the rise of trusts. Capitalist concentration would be matched by the expansion of the Labour Movement; the vital clash would be between big battalions. The growth of a centralised state was presented as a precondition for socialism; decentralisation, whether inspired by Home Rule or by syndicalist sentiments, was a mistaken strategy:

The establishment of a Scottish Babel would ... be a retrograde step and should meet with our opposition and ridicule. What is good or bad for England is good or bad for Scotland.[28]

Despite such a thorough dismissal of this institutional proposal, some of Maclean's pre-war comments did suggest that Scottish developments afforded some unique opportunities for Socialist activities. These centred around the land question.[29] The plight of the crofters had long been a rural tragedy in which Maclean's parents had shared as childhood victims of the Highland economic crisis. The continuing grievances of the crofters and memories of oppression brought by Highlanders into industrial communities raised the possibility of an aggressive radicalism linking rural and urban discontents in a distinctively Scottish synthesis.

The Irish parallel was a compelling one for some activists. John Murdoch, the crofter's champion of the 1870s and 1880s had linked in his own activities, not only the agrarian struggles but also the national claims of the two societies. Certainly in Ireland, the land question had provided an economic kernel to the Nationalist movement. Although the resulting protests could take radical forms, the legacy from a Socialist viewpoint proved disappointing. Although Government schemes for peasant proprietorship did not smother opposition to British rule, they helped to produce a peasantry that was economically and socially conservative. Yet it was still possible to look at the Irish experience and see how a fusion of economic and national grievances could promote a deep antagonism to government authority.

Yet attempts to find similarities in Scotland encountered significant obstacles. There was no direct parallel to the displacement of the traditional Irish landed elite. Instead the Highland Clan Chiefs typically served as the modernising allies of the British Government.[30] The objectives of the latter were strongly political, concerned from the mid-eighteenth century with the subordination and radical remoulding of Highland society. Their success would destroy the basis for revolts, not just against the British State, but also against a developing capitalism within which some sections of Scottish society played a leading role. The destruction was thorough. One legacy was radical. The impoverishment and depopulation of the Highlands left a continuing basis for unrest. But the enormity of the change drastically limited the potential impact of Highland radicalism.[31] On their own the people were too few. The economic and cultural gulf between the North and industrial Scotland was huge. There was no significant scope in the nineteenth century for that synthesis of rural radicalism and Nationalism that first transformed Irish politics and then as a consequence remoulded those of Scotland and England.

Despite these tight constraints, Highland discontents made a significant mark on the development of the Scottish Left. The crofters' predicament: impoverished and congested holdings next to vast, empty spaces was a perennial spur to radical politics. In the 1880s, agricultural depression turned radicalism into revolt; land occupations led to confrontations with the military. The agitation also provided an alternative strategy to direct action. Expansion of the rural franchise produced in December 1885 a bloc of Crofters' MPs at first Independent, but absorbed rapidly into Gladstonian Liberalism. They were too few to act as a long-term independent group, and on most issues, including significant religious controversies, they were Radical Liberals anyway. They could point to the Gladstonian legislation of 1886 which improved the crofters' legal position, but did little to alleviate the fundamental problem of land shortage.[32] Despite the limited response, the Liberalism of the former Crofters' Members provoked little criticism in the Highlands where the Liberals retained their electoral dominance until well after 1918.

This contrast between impoverishment and normally conventional politics frustrated Maclean. At the beginning of 1914, he celebrated the land raids of some Lewis crofters, but saw little political consequence:

In spite of all, the Highlanders still vote Liberal or Tory. Marvellous men have we in Scotland.[33]

He attacked Government land policies as inadequate. Quiescence did not indicate that an answer had been found:

there undoubtedly is peace in the crofting area. But it is not the peace of contentment. Rather it is the peace of desolation.[34]

His own prescription hardly accorded with the crofters' objectives. Although they could act collectively against perceived injustices, their objective was the highly individualistic one of securing more land for each family. In contrast, Maclean advocated a Government takeover of the land which would be cultivated on a co-operative basis.[35] This paralleled Connolly's response to the Irish agrarian problem. Both remedies could be linked back to beliefs about a communal past in the optimistic hope that such sentiments remained relevant to the contemporary preferences of Irish peasants or Scottish crofters.

Such an attempt to develop a Socialist response to the Highland land question was symptomatic of wider developments. The Highland Land League of the 1880s had been a broadly-based Radical group. When it was revived in 1909, its position was much closer to labour or indeed to socialist sentiments. It had a limited membership, and was attractive especially to some with Highland connections who had moved south and had made links between rural grievances and the politics of the labour movement.[36] This shift was reflected in the history of Maclean's own family, and it is therefore not surprising that he proclaimed the need for such an alliance:

The peasants, like the farm servants, must be taught that their only friends are the toiling industrial slaves.[37]

Even this hope presented the peasantry as recipients of a wisdom developed elsewhere. Maclean seems to have shared many conventional Second International assumptions about the frequently reactionary political role of peasants.[38]

The revival of the Highland Land League was fortified also by Irish developments. The Gaelic Revival and later the political strategy of Sinn Fein could seem significant exemplars to some Scots. Irish and Scottish peasants could be portrayed as victims of English domination; so could Gaelic culture. Since the adversary had the same national basis, the economic and cultural struggles should be combined. Several years earlier, John Murdoch had emphasised both agrarian and cultural dimensions; in contrast, the Crofters' MPs had been absorbed all too readily into a British party system and the London-based parliamentary system. In the early 1900s those who argued for a Scottish variant on Sinn Fein were isolated figures. Insofar as Scottish Nationalism had any political significance, this was on account of the Home Rule enthusiasm of some Liberals. Yet against this background of general indifference the land question provided a meeting ground for some socialists and nationalists.

Within those dedicated to Scotland's Gaelic revival, one individual was to have a significant future relationship with Maclean. The Hon Stuart Erskine had been born in Brighton in 1869. The second son of the fifth Lord Erskine, he had learnt Gaelic from his nurse, and had become active in the Scottish Home Rule Association. From there he became strongly committed to the Gaelic revival and began to style himself the Hon Ruaraidh Erskine of Mar. In 1904, he began publication of a nationalist journal: *Guth na Bliadhna (the Voice of the Year)*. It was committed firmly to the restoration of Gaelic. Patrick Pearse was an early contributor.[39]

This world and that of the BSP internationalist seemed a universe apart, but Maclean's concern with the land question was leading him to make some statements whose emphases converged with those of some Nationalists. In a reference to the Clearances, he noted that the beneficiaries were not only rich but foreign:

The beautiful glens and islands were depopulated to make way for sheep and deer, and English and American plutocrats.

Despite the continuing Liberal domination of Highland politics he still advocated his orthodox socialist solution and was heartened by the sight of a Hebridean school teacher reading Kautsky's *The Social Revolution*.[40] But the Irish parallel was already influencing his thoughts. A land raid on the Isle of Lewis provoked an unfavourable comparison that nevertheless hinted at some grounds for optimism:

It is a pity that the Gaels of Scotland have not the fire and go of the Celts of Ireland whose dare-devil determination has gained holdings and housings for them ... We trust that this raid will be the precursor of a Gaelic movement to clear all landlords out of the Highlands.[41]

Maclean normally so insistent on the internationalist class-based Socialist standpoint was prepared to advocate an agitation defined partially in national – cultural terms. In this context his positive reference to the Irish land agitation suggested that he might regard peasant proprietorship as an advance. Arguably, this could be justified in terms of a growth of self-respect. Perhaps this was implicit in Maclean's argument, but the Irish case demonstrated persuasively the pitfalls in any attempt to discover a socialist potential within the replacement of landlords by owner-occupiers.

These emphases remained peripheral to Maclean's view of Scottish political prospects. Essentially he remained until the outbreak of war, an orthodox Second International Socialist. He was keen to campaign openly on the pure doctrine, concerned to develop the widest-possible class-based solidarity, prepared usually to dismiss other controversies as diversionary or translatable into the language of class and socialism. Although he was aware of the obstacles to effective propaganda and to the achievement of solidarity, he seems to have viewed the battle as winnable. Capitalism, whatever its horrors, would allow Socialists space and time to make their case. If it were made with enthusiasm, clarity and relevance then it would persuade.[42]

At the start of August 1914, Maclean was optimistic that the struggles impending in the coal industry would bring the newly-developed machinery of the Triple Alliance into operation:

If the miners come out, I can see no escape for the railwaymen and the transport workers, who are practically pledged to support one another.[43]

But in August 1914, as other alliances were mobilised, the old socialist certainties collapsed.

Chapter 2

Internationalism

The collapse of a familiar world fragmented the Socialist movement. Many members proclaimed or assumed the compatability of nationalist and socialist principles, and supported their own governments. Others said little about the War and devoted themselves to protecting working-class living standards. Open opponents of the War were divided. Some emphasised their principled pacifism; others viewed the conflict as an interruption in the evolution of society towards Socialism. They argued for a negotiated peace in order to resume this progressive path. A few argued not just against the War, but also for action to subvert support for the conflict. At first, such claims stood out against the bleak pessimism that followed the collapse of the International. Eventually such demands for action based on internationalist principles would be transformed into the claim that the War was not an obstacle to Socialist growth, but an opportunity for revolution.

In their distinctive ways, Maclean and Connolly provide the two most significant members of this last tendency within the British Left. Yet there is an obvious divergence. Both were clearly strengthened in their revolutionary commitments by the crisis. Maclean however focussed on the necessarily international quality of any socialist strategy, whilst Connolly was prepared to link the prospects for Irish Socialism to a Nationalist revolt. But such a simple dichotomy fails to do justice to the positions of both men. The nuances of Connolly's response have been examined. Similarly Maclean's principled internationalism was proclaimed amidst developments that led him – and others – to revise their judgements about the Scottish working class. Its pre-war stigmatisation as backward gave way to the view that, at least on Clydeside, workers were demonstrating a radicalism that could have far-reaching consequences. Such a revision could influence evaluations about the Socialist significance of specifically Scottish initiatives. Eventually such a corollary would be influenced by the increasing salience of Irish developments. The Easter Rising and the consequential political developments meant that the Irish connection would become more relevant for some Scottish Socialists.

These elements were significant wartime legacies for Maclean but they should not lead to any neglect of his principal contention. His opposition to the War, and his responses to particular issues were based on an unqualified commitment to internationalism as an essential element in any socialist position. Yet this cannot be regarded as the response of an idealist amazed at the fallibility of erstwhile comrades. He could not have been wholly surprised by the events of August 1914. He had encountered the zeal with which Hyndman and his associates had advocated a policy of national defence within the BSP. The impact of recruiting propaganda seems to have been clear to him. After Lord Roberts had spoken in Glasgow in the Spring of 1913 Maclean acknowledged that militaristic propaganda had made some advance:

some of us who have addressed meetings know that it has had tremendous influence in awakening the murder-passion, ironically dubbed 'patriotism'.[1]

The war's immediate impact on Glaswegian politics is unclear. Maclean claimed, in the early weeks that there was 'no enthusiasm whatever' for the War, and that he was holding 'fine meetings'.[2] At least he seems to have been able to speak in public relatively free from disruption by hostile audiences. Such tolerance did not necessarily indicate that the War was unpopular amongst the city's working class. The level of recruitment was high; many workers readily made weapons to kill other workers. Relatively few prominent Socialists came out thoroughly against the War.

Those who did, often worked together despite old organisational rivalries. Individual members of the ILP spoke alongside Maclean; so did members of the SLP. Each organisation had its internal divisions.[3] The columns of *Forward* reflected the diversity of views inside the ILP; Maclean's problems within the BSP were acute. Hyndman's faction dominated decision-making within the national Party during the early stages of the War, and thereby denied Maclean his customary outlet in the columns of *Justice*. He protested vigorously against the support given to recruiting campaigns by the BSP's Executive. He at least would not be deflected from the struggle against capitalism. This had to be resolved within each society:

The only real enemy to Kaiserism and Prussian militarism ... was and is, German social democracy.

Similarly:

Our first business is to hate the British capitalist system, that with 'business as usual' means the continued robbery of the workers.[4]

This was almost his last contribution to *Justice*.

Maclean's local position within the BSP was stronger. In the Spring of 1915, he argued that whereas Scotland as a whole was 'about evenly divided', 'Glasgow is practically solid' against Hyndman.[5] The Party's Glasgow District Committee briefly solved the problem of a journalistic outlet for Maclean. In September 1915, it began publication of *The Vanguard*. This promised to be a reliable forum for his views, but in January 1916, it was suppressed.[6]

This action was symptomatic of the increasing difficulties encountered by Glasgow's anti-war Socialists. Already in November 1915, Maclean had been gaoled for five days under the Defence of the Realm Act;[7] concurrently he was dismissed from his teaching post by the Govan School Board.[8] These events were contemporary with the culmination of the Glasgow rent strikes. The Government responded with legislation to hold down rents.[9] The Winter of 1915–16 saw further conflicts, this time between Clydeside munitions workers and the Government. The workers' instrument was the Clyde Workers' Committee: an independent organisation of the rank and file, it reflected both the militancy of some Glasgow workers, and the failure of trade union officials to respond to wartime grievances.[10] The battles centred initially around dilution and later around conscription. The Government gained decisive victories. Its policies were implemented; some trade unionists were deported away from Glasgow; some Socialists and trade unionists were imprisoned. Maclean was found guilty of sedition in April 1916. He was sentenced to three years' penal servitude. These defeats marked the end of the most significant period of wartime conflict on Clydeside.

Maclean's political position, as these battles reached their decisive stage, can be approached through his writings in *The Vanguard*. His internationalism was unqualified. He had no reservations about the decisions of the Zimmerwald Conference. A supportive article concluded with the emphatic declaration: 'we in Glasgow are internationalists, first, last, and all the time'.[11] This enthusiasm was supplemented by the contributions of Maclean's Russian associate, Peter Petroff. He argued that the collapse of the Second International was attributable in part to the limited impact that its declarations had had upon the vast majority of the organised working class. Petroff dismissed any proposal for a rebuilding of this discredited organisation. Instead:

We must ... purify our parties, and immediately proceed to gather our forces, participate in all the chance encounters between the workers and the capitalists, sharpen the class struggle and make ourselves ready for drastic revolutionary action.[12]

It was an argument that would soon be heard much more frequently.

The challenge posed by the collapse of Socialist credibility was paralleled by one precipitated by the collapse of liberal civilities. The pre-war political system has allowed some space for Socialists to develop their case; now the scope seemed to be narrowing drastically. Like Connolly, Maclean was keenly aware of the State's increasing intolerance of dissent. He saw employers and Government acting together to erode trade union rights through the Munitions Act; he claimed that the right of public meeting was threatened by hostile crowds supported by sympathetic police; above all there was the threat of conscription.[13] These developments belied the claim that for workers there could be a decisive difference between liberal Britain and Germany dominated by Junkers. Faced with such challenges, Maclean claimed that workers could respond only through strike action as a hopefully united class:

The only way to retain our freedom − the small shred of it we now possess − is by solid combination as a class. The only weapon we can use today is the strike.[14]

He dismissed the purist view that such a strategy should be used only to achieve socialism. Rather it could be employed as a vital stage in the development of a more radical outlook:

... the only way to fight the class war is by accepting every challenge of the master class and throwing down more challenges ourselves. Every determined fight binds the workers together more and more, clears the heads of our class to their robbed and enslaved conditions, and so prepares them for the acceptance of our full gospel of socialism, and the full development of the class war to the end of establishing socialism.[15]

This was the framework within which Maclean appraised Clydeside developments. The rent strike could be the beginning of a much more radical action: 'the political strike, so frequently resorted to on the Continent in times past'.[16] The Clyde Workers' Committee might mobilise discontents in a way that by-passed conservative trade union officials. The specific issues − rents, dilution, conscription − were important for Maclean not simply on account of their immediate consequences, but because the support, the self-confidence and the perceptions developed in these battles could serve as a durable basis for Socialist initiatives.

These expectations were not fulfilled. He was certainly prominent in the later stages of the rent campaign and was one of the speakers at the celebrated demonstration in George Square on 17 November 1915. But he became involved only after the direction and the style of the movement had been established. The campaign owed much to an ILP centred policy on housing that had developed before the War. Several of the leading figures in the rents agitation were ILP women. They were supported by some trade unionists from the same Party especially in the shipbuilding districts of Govan and Partick. Thus, the campaign could bring together communal solidarity, industrial strength and a political programme.[17] Within this development, Maclean's distinctive proposals met with little support. The Glasgow Trades Council did not discuss a suggestion by him that a general strike should be called to force the pace on the rents' issue.[18] His hope that the agitation could lead to a more fundamental challenge was not fulfilled. The rents' campaign remained precisely that, although the issue could serve as a focus for working-class discontents over a wider range of issues. The ILP element within the movement was happy to focus on a specific problem where they could offer a plausible short-term programme to aggrieved tenants. The legislative response by the Government was sufficient to take the edge off the agitation, but it left the Glasgow ILP with a credible record on which to build further support. In contrast, Maclean, much more an individual than a member of a locally effective party, could offer no plausible strategy for widening the campaign. Indeed his hope that this might happen was expressed alongside his claim that the Government's response represented a significant victory for working-class pressure. But this victory was simply a culmination to a specific campaign not a springboard for more success.

Maclean warned that such a victory was likely to produce a Government counter-stroke.[19] This came when the Clyde Workers' Committee attempted to confront Government demands over dilution and conscription. Once again Maclean was involved, although as with rents his role was not a central one. The CWC was dominated by shop stewards from some of the large engineering plants. Their political affiliations varied. David Kirkwood was a member of the ILP; Willie Gallacher, the Chairman, although a member of the BSP had been influenced heavily by the doctrines of the SLP and worked closely with members of the latter Party such as John Muir and Arthur MacManus. Some members had been influenced by Maclean's propaganda. Although the membership of the Committee was centred on the engineering plants, both Maclean and his political colleague, the former bank-clerk James MacDougall, attended CWC meetings.[20]

Whatever their political differences, it was perhaps inevitable that the immediate challenge of dilution would unite the shop stewards together in an attempt to protect their workmates' industrial interests. Muir formulated a response which presented a dilution as inevitable and essentially progressive, and demanded nationalisation and workers' participation as a *quid pro quo*. This was an attempt to secure some reforms, arguably with a socialist potential, but which was mindful of immediate constraints. These socialist shop stewards effectively acknowledged that their organisational strength rested on the privileges of craft unionism. Any hope of a broader solidarity remained an ideal.[21]

Already Maclean had expressed some scepticism about the radical potential of the CWC; it was addicted 'to academic discussions and futile proposals'.[22] Along with his associates he attacked Muir's strategy. In part their criticism focused on its sectional limitations. Benefits would accrue to the relatively privileged craft workers in munitions plants. The CWC leaders denied this and claimed:

Our demand is 'That the Government must take over all industries and national resources, and vest Organised Labour with direct share in the Management'.[23]

As a statement of principle this was unobjectionable, but the CWC made their demands as part of a negotiating strategy for the munitions plants. Any success would be limited therefore to this sector:

The Clyde Workers had discussed the question and came to the conclusion that no proposals from Lloyd George be entertained unless the Government took over all munition works and gave the workers part control of the works management.[24]

Maclean thus implied the probability that, despite the Socialist pedigree of the CWC leadership, its reliance on craft workers' grievances would damage the prospect of any broader opposition to government policy.[25] Yet his was merely a dissenting voice. To point to the dangers inherent in sectionalism was much easier than to suggest a credible alternative.

A similar assessment can be made about a much more basic dispute. Maclean attacked the CWC for failing to connect the dilution controversy to the question of the War. Most of the leading shop stewards said little about this fundamental issue. They regarded it as divisive, and like many other trade unionists, preferred to concentrate on immediate objectives. Maclean emphasised that any success for Muir's strategy would improve armaments production. Workers would be implicated even more in the military conflict:

If the Clyde Workers took part control of the munitions work, they would thus accept part responsibility for the War.[26]

Maclean saw the professed relationship between such a strategy and Socialism as a dangerous illusion. He compared it with Lloyd George's claim that Government shell factories had a Socialist content:

This kind of Socialism is as much of a tragedy as Lloyd George's at Christmas was considered a joke.[27]

This prophecy would be fulfilled. Later in the War, Kirkwood, Gallacher and MacManus helped to organise production in Beardmore's Mile End Shell Factory. Kirkwood looked back on their achievement with pride:

What a team! There was never anything like it in Great Britain. We organised a bonus system in which everyone benefitted by high production ... The factory, built for a 12,000 output, produced 24,000. In six weeks, we held the record for output in Great Britain, and we never lost our premier position.[28]

Maclean's position can stand as a paradigm of incorruptible Socialist principles against the tangled web woven by the CWC leaders. At the heart of his case was the argument that dilution was intended – and would serve – as a fundamental attack on trade union strength:

Lloyd George's purpose is to coax you to relax your Trade Union rules about non-union workers. The dangers ... are the weakening of your unions and the lowering of your wages'.

The culmination could be industrial conscription 'to break Trade Unionism'.[29] Yet once again he failed to offer any strategy for confronting the immediate challenge of dilution. There was no hope of persuading a majority on the CWC to oppose munitions production. Even if such a decision had been taken, there is no evidence to indicate that it would have secured support in the workshops. Clearly the Shop Stewards had never attempted to link immediate grievances to the question of the War, but to suggest that this failure was decisive is to substitute a formula for an investigation. Once again the credibility of Maclean's strategic arguments becomes a crucial question. Did the failure to marry Socialist principle with a feasible strategy represent a missed political opportunity or, in that 1915–16 winter, was such a synthesis unavailable?

The distinction between observation and hope was blurred frequently by Maclean. His *Vanguard* writings presented an optimistic assessment of working-class radicalisation.[30] A similar judgement emerges in Gallacher's recollections with images not just of revolt, but of working-class solidarity, as munitions workers marched in protest against the prosecution of rent-strikers:

From far away Dalmuir in the West, from Parkhead in the East, from Cathcart in the South and Hyde Park in the North, the dungareed army of the proletariat invaded the centre of the city.[31]

Against such expectations of revolt and celebrations of unity, there stand other images. Harry McShane shared Maclean's reservations about the Clyde Workers' Committee's silence on the War but he was aware of the social conservatism of many engineering workers:

It wasn't easy to rouse up engineers; they were very respectable with their blue suits and bowler hats, and used to come to mass meetings with their umbrellas. Gallacher dressed like that as well.[32]

The contrasting memories of participants have their more polarised counterparts in the analyses of historians. Walter Kendall's quest for an indigenous revolutionary movement has involved an emphasis on the potential significance of the Clydeside struggles, and of Maclean's principled stand. He suggests that the possibility of further growth was aborted by the 'artificial' formation of the Communist Party. In contrast both Christopher Harvie and Iain McLean have expressed scepticism about any image of 'Red Clydeside'. The former's dismissal summarises this characterisation:

Forget the Red Clyde: throughout World War I, Scotland was overwhelmingly patriotic. Tactless enforcement of the Munitions Acts admittedly caused episodes of industrial discontent ... but after the spring of 1916 ... tranquillity reigned.[33]

The complexities of the wartime situation have been emphasised by Joseph Melling.[34] The confrontations should be located in a wider framework of shifting relations, not just between capital and labour, but also between each of these elements and the State. Moreover, he emphasises the degree to which bases for working-class initiatives should be sought not just in the changing experiences of the workplace, but also in community-centred grievances such as the housing crisis.

The industrial strand within the wartime unrest can be sketched quickly. Employers in engineering and shipbuilding were already eager to rationalise production pre-1914; the War provided both incentive and justification. Craftworkers faced a heightened threat to their status in a situation of labour scarcity. It was an intensified variant on the type of situation that had fuelled several workers' revolts in the immediate pre-war years. The Clydeside craftsmen were led frequently by committed Socialists, some of whom claimed to favour a revolutionary assault on capitalism. Any significant wartime dispute necessarily involved the State. For the class-conscious Socialist, developments such as the Treasury Agreement, the Munitions Act, and the dilution campaign, all promised a widening of the struggle beyond the narrowly industrial to an overtly political confrontation.

This had been Maclean's hope at the end of 1915. A comparison with the reality can lead to a sharp puncturing of expectations. A negative verdict would emphasise that these militant workers were typically concerned to defend their privileges against unskilled men and women. The number of plants that could be relied on to take effective action was small, essentially those where socialist leaders of the rank and file had developed a firm basis of support. Even then, such backing did not entail any acceptance of their shop stewards' socialism. This limitation was acknowledged by the CWC's Socialist Labour Party faction, although like Maclean, they hoped that such industrial struggles might have political implications:

It must not be thought that the rank and file are Socialists. The committee was formed to stem the onslaught on the privileges won by organised labour in the past ... insofar as the Clyde Workers' Committee is the rallying point of these workers attempting to form a resistance to the *immediate encroachments* of Capital upon Labour, it was up to the local SLPers to lend their help.[35]

Yet several self-proclaimed revolutionaries met the dilution challenge by attempting to negotiate a deal that would have involved more efficient munitions production. This deflationary judgement harmonises readily wtih the eventual failure to prevent dilution on the Government's terms.

There was little solidarity amongst munitions workers, let alone the wider working class. Agreement was reached on a plant by plant basis with little opposition.

The collapse of the campaign against dilution highlights another significant factor. The authorities lost neither the capacity nor the determination to govern. There were significant tensions between Government Departments and between industrialists and the State; there were fiascos such as Lloyd George's Glasgow visit in December 1915. But at critical moments Ministers and civil servants acted decisively. They responded to the rents campaign by legislation that rejected traditional economic prescriptions and to the dilution struggle through a combination of lengthy negotiations and effective coercion.[36]

These arguments come often as a self-consciously realistic riposte to more traditional claims. Within the history of British Socialism, it can seem one more example of a familiar litany: an occupational solidarity that militates against a wider class-based movement, a State controlling affairs at critical moments, Socialists able to obtain audiences and workshop followings but seemingly unable to mobilise this support for specifically Socialist purposes. These emphases can appear particularly damning in the case of Maclean. He was a teacher, not an industrial worker, a member of a party deeply divided over the War, a critic of the CWC leadership's silence on the political and military aspects of the War. He can appear the very model of a middle-class sectarian. This judgement is echoed in the contemporary verdict of a Government official. Early in 1916, the Ministry of Munitions' Labour Officer for Clydeside considered how to deal with the Governments' opponents. He made a distinction:

I am afraid that the removal of almost any one of these men, (with the possible exception of MacLean or Petroff who are not working men or officials of societies here) would at once cause a big strike.[37]

A sharp response to this dismissal, is available. Whatever the claims made about Maclean's marginality, from April 1916, he spent more than three of his remaining seven and a half years in gaol. This could indicate the tendency of governments to panic, but it could suggest perhaps that at particular moments, the possibility of a significant radical initiative should not be discounted.

This last possibility raises an important problem for the revised assessments of Clydeside politics. Some of these interpretations' strengths come from the limited range of options on offer. Once simplistic expectations of revolution have been put to the historian's sword, there remains only working-class sectionalism, craft-based elitism, socialist isolation and ineffectiveness. The heroic images of the rhetoricians are stripped away to reveal the mundane actuality. But it is not the case that defences of sectional privileges, and of lost or vanishing worlds, never contain a potential for socialist growth. Although such a development would have many problems, the emergence of significant centres of Socialist sentiment amongst such threatened groups has been a relatively frequent occurrence. At the very least, the Clydeside agitations gave a prominence to a group of articulate Socialists. Many had significant roots in industry; several had some grasp of Marxian economics, either through Maclean's classes or the educational courses of the SLP. There could not be revolution at the drop of a hat, but there could be the growth of a significant Socialist current based in part on workplace organisation.

From this angle the Clydeside events of 1915–16 have a wider significance. Although the local movement was damaged by the deportations and gaolings of early 1916, the organisational model could be emulated by workers elsewhere. It would be naive to present such rank and file movements as always articulating the radical and democratic sentiments of the workplace as against the bureaucratic caution of union officials. Often this was so; sometimes officials or shop stewards could be more radical than a traditionalist sectionalist workforce. Yet even with its many difficulties, this was a Left-movement in a line of descent from the industrial militancy of 1910–14 which retained a significance through until 1926.[38] Often self-consciously Marxist, proclaiming itself as a democratic manifestation of workers' power, it was a challenge to the politics of the Labour Party. Many of its emphases and expectations were shared by Maclean, although his pre-war distaste for syndicalism must be remembered. Nevertheless his already shifting views on the place of industrial struggle and organisation were affected further by wartime developments. Essentially an appraisal of the political significance of the Clydeside industrial battles requires this wider context. Dismissal as craft-based and elitist is then much more difficult.

In contrast, the rent agitation strengthened the position of the Labour Party, and especially of the ILP. Yet it would be mistaken to see this dispute as occupying a sphere separate from the specifically industrial battles. Arguments over rents served as a focus for a variety of working-class discontents about welfare services and the escalating price of necessities. Several of those active on the rents issue also had roles in the industrial movement; Socialists, including Maclean argued at factory-gate meetings, for industrial action to aid the housing agitation. The network of Clydeside Socialists was such as to prevent any sharp demarcation between campaigns.[39] Nevertheless, the CWC was reluctant to become closely involved in the rents struggle but some links between workplace and communal mobilisations were achieved. The 17 November demonstration displayed a readiness not just by shipyard workers, but also by those in engineering to strike in support of defaulting tenants. The links however were brittle. The CWC made no attempt to connect the arguments within the workshops with the housing campaign.[40] Whether such a synthesis would have combined industrial resources and a wide political appeal in a way that would have generated a more radical challenge to the government remains a speculative matter. What is clear is that the possibility was never tested.

Once again the rent agitation had its shortcomings from the standpoint of a Socialist such as Maclean. Militancy on rents could be combined with firm support for the war. As the placard carried by one child on a demonstration proclaimed:

My father is fighting in France; we are fighting the Huns at home.[41]

Landlords and factors could be stigmatised as 'unpatriotic'. The limitations should be noted, but as with the emphasis on craft unionism, they should not monopolise analysis. More crucially, the rent campaign involved impressive mobilisations of working-class communities; it brought together men and women, the political and the a-political, Orange and Green. It was a solidarity that went beyond that available to the munition workers. Arguably the failure of the two agitations to combine on a more durable basis represents a significant 'might have been'.

Any suggestion of a missed revolutionary opportunity on Clydeside in the Winter of 1915–16 is absurd, but there were arguably significant opportunities for growth on the Left; Shop Stewards' organisations bore the marks both of craft conservatism and revolutionary hopes; the ILP formally so cautious, was deeply involved in communal agitations. Within a wider perspective it is possible to argue that some of the parameters of the inter-war British Left were emerging: a sizeable Labour Party flanked on its Left by a critical Marxist element. But much remained open in 1916. The character of a future Labour Party was obscure; its Glasgow presence was significantly to the left of much of the British leadership. The absorption of many syndicalist sentiments and many syndicalists into the Communist Party was not a development that could have been predicted.

Whatever the assessment of political options, it is at least clear that Clydeside at the end of 1915 was not a deferential society. Rent strikes, workers' demonstrations, discontent in workshops, the hostility at Lloyd George's Christmas Day meeting; all underlined the inadequacy of old methods of control both in the workplace and in the community. The State responded by becoming more involved in crucial areas: pegging rents, deporting shop stewards, gaoling Socialists. When Maclean was sentenced at Edinburgh, he left behind a relatively open political prospect. The Glasgow Labour Movement had been defeated over dilution, but bases for future growth had been provided through both the rent and the industrial struggles. Moreover, Maclean held a secure position within this Left. Although his emphasis on opposition to the War could be a basis of controversy, he had worked with members of the ILP and SLP and non-socialist trade unionists in the rent and dilution campaigns. He had a high reputation as a Marxist educationalist; he remained in the BSP, an organisation recently affiliated to the Labour Party. With future prospects appearing relatively open, Maclean seemed likely to play a central role for several years; it all seemed far removed from the image of the suspicious, eccentric, even unbalanced, isolate portrayed by later detractors.

Chapter 3

Revolution?

Maclean was released from prison on a ticket of leave at the end of June 1917. The political landscape had changed radically since his conviction. The Easter 1916 Conference of the BSP had witnessed the defeat and secession of the Hyndmanites.[1] The events in Salford meant that Maclean's Party became far more homogeneously anti-war, and that Easter's events in Dublin were to have a far reaching impact on his political ideas. By June 1917 the political consequences of the Easter Rising were becoming clearer. The severity of the immediate British response, the lengthy and abortive negotiations over a political settlement, the brooding threat of Irish conscription – all were weakening the credibility of the old Nationalist Party and strengthening support for Sinn Fein. Shifts in Irish allegiances inevitably affected the politics of the Irish in Britain. Links with the Liberals were weakened; hope was offered to Socialists. Some viewed this essentially as an electoral opportunity; for Maclean, it became much more. The Irish crisis would become fundamental to his developing ideas on the connections between nationalist and socialist movements.

If Maclean was unusual in the extent to which he came to emphasise the Irish dimension, his response to developments in Russia was more typical. When he was released, the Tsar had been deposed, the Kerensky Government ruled uneasily, Russia remained in the War. By the time of his re-arrest in April 1918, the Bolsheviks had taken power; Russia was no longer at war; the British Labour Movement was beginning to divide over its attitude towards a regime about which relatively little was known. Maclean was sentenced to five years' penal servitude but was released shortly after the Armistice. This time there had been even more dramatic political changes. The Bolsheviks remained in power, although under growing pressure from the now victorious Allies; the Hohenzollern and Habsburg dynasties had collapsed. Some hoped and others dreaded that Bolshevism would move westwards. In Britain, the immediate context of Maclean's release seemed much more familiar, as the Government capitalised on patriotic sentiments and Opposition confusions to win an overwhelming electoral victory. Even here, apparent continuity could not hide some significant changes. The Liberal Party was disabled as a coherent force, and a reformed Labour Party moved into the space, encouraged by a widening of the franchise. In Ireland, Sinn Fein supplanted the old Nationalists and initiated a policy of abstention from Westminster.

An assessment of Maclean's relationship to these changes must begin with an awareness of the extent to which he became a 'cause célèbre' on account of his imprisonments. Questions were asked in Parliament; petitions drawn up; meetings held; resolutions passed. Campaigners for his release came not only from the Labour Movement, but included some Radical Liberal MPs who turned libertarian principles against Ministers who had once claimed to hold them.[2] The protests gave Maclean prominence as a symbol of Socialist opposition to the War. The considerable sympathy for Maclean's sufferings in prison, often did not imply acceptance of his politics. The distinction must be borne in mind during any attempt to assess his importance.

Such agitation could lead Government Ministers to suggest late in 1918 that an amnesty would be the more prudent course. George Barnes facing an electoral challenge from Maclean circulated his Ministerial colleagues:

> The continued agitation about John Maclean constitutes a serious danger for the Government. Mass meetings have been held in many places ... and resolutions continue to pour in demanding his release.
>
> I think that no good purpose is being served by keeping him in prison and that a favourable opportunity presents itself for his release.

After pointing out that only Maclean and 'a tram conductor named Milne' could qualify as Scottish political prisoners, the Minister concluded:

> it would be an act of grace ... to release both of them before the agitation assumes larger and more dangerous dimensions.[3]

The weekly reports compiled by the Ministry of Labour placed a similar conclusion within a broader framework – what the writer of one report characterised as 'the spread of the bacillus of Bolshevism in Central Europe'. In Britain an effective liberal response should be feasible:

> It is desirable and should be possible to maintain that essential national unity without which effective reconstruction would be impossible. This result will most probably be obtained if restrictions on personal liberty of speech and action are reduced to a minimum, and such restrictions as are inevitable tactfully administered.[4]

Maclean's allegations about his prison treatment complicate any assessment of his political significance. At his later trial in May 1918, he accused the prison authorities of attempts to drug his food.[5] He made similar allegations throughout the rest of his life. Any verdict on this aspect must be tentative due to the continuing non-availability of some Government papers.[6] Sources agree that he was in a very weak condition following his release late in 1918. He had been on hunger strike and had

then been forcibly fed. MacShane, whilst rejecting the wider claims about
the impact of prison on Maclean's mental state, has acknowledged that
at that stage 'he was erratic, and it was obvious that he was not yet
well'.[7] This consensus does not license subsequent arguments about
Maclean's mental deterioration after 1918 – nor can it cope with his
own claims about drugging during his earlier imprisonment.

Perhaps most fundamentally, two issues have to be distinguished.
One is the unresolved empirical matter of whether either Maclean's
allegations about his prison experiences or detractors' claims about his
mental state have any validity. More important, there is the issue of
Maclean's continuing political credibility. Can his opinions and actions
be relegated to a museum of political idiosyncracies where they are
catalogued as the passions of an honest but unbalanced idealist; Yet his
political statements are as coherent after 1916, as they had been earlier.
The changes in his political strategy, the shifting emphases, the spectacular miscalculations and the penetrating insights – these should not
be reduced to an explanation in terms of personal eccentricity. Rather
they should be viewed as responses by a hitherto largely orthodox Social
Democrat to a dramatically changing political environment.

Educational work occupied much of Maclean's time in the months
between his two imprisonments. From December 1917, he spoke
regularly in Glasgow, and he also propagandised amongst the miners in
Lanarkshire and Fife.[8] The significance of this campaigning is hard to
assess. Gallacher painted a positive retrospective portrait:

The work done by Maclean during this period of 1917–18 has never been equalled
by anyone. His educational work would have been sufficient for half a dozen
ordinary men, but on top of this he was carrying on a truly terrific propaganda
and agitational campaign.[9]

The BSP press conveyed a similar message:

Maclean's popularity in Scotland is rising like a flood tide. Meeting after meeting
demonstrates conclusively that the principles of Revolutionary Socialism which
Maclean stands for are captivating the minds of the workers.[10]

One official assessment expressed concern about the increasing prominence of revolutionary sentiments at meetings on Clydeside and in Fife
and Lanark. Particular emphasis was given to the role of Maclean:

– a man of considerable influence among the malcontent population of Glasgow
and ... in the mining districts of Lanarkshire and Fifeshire.

He had acquired more significance with his appointment as Russian
Consul General in Glasgow:

– he utilises this new found position to expound to his hearers his Bolshevik
ideas.[11]

In contrast, Tom Johnston offered a very different verdict at the time of the 1918 trial. He saw Maclean as paying a price for his lack of understanding about working-class priorities and sentiments:

He advocated a Social Revolution by Bolshevist methods, and alas, the bulk of the workers do not want a Social Revolution by any method, but go on rivet hammering competitions and scrambling for overtime and regard the John Macleans as 'decent enough but a bit off'.[12]

Whilst Johnston's comment could provoke equivalent questions about how close he and other ILPers were to many working-class sentiments, his claim was delivered from a position of relative strength. In the two years following the imprisonments and deportations of 1916, the ILP came to dominate the Glasgow Left to an even greater degree than previously. It built on the support engendered by the rents campaign; it achieved unity in opposition to conscription; the ILP kept the city's Left together. Inevitably, the Marxist organisations – both BSP and SLP – had smaller roles. Whatever the enthusiasm engendered by Maclean's meetings, it is important to locate this in the context of the ILP's local hegemony.[13]

This characterisation of the situation in Glasgow has to be placed alongside the awareness that when Maclean left gaol in June 1917 the options for the Left seemed to be changing rapidly. Earlier that month the ambiguous Leeds Convention had welcomed recent events in Russia, and had called for the development in Britain of Councils of Workers and Soldiers.[14] In part, the proposal was smothered by vagueness about its political purpose; for many, any commitment seemed to end with rhetoric. It was also crushed by the tough response of the authorities.[15]

Generalised enthusiasm about Russian developments ended with the Bolshevik success. The implications for practice elsewhere were absorbed slowly by the European Left. Despite the initial lack of information, Maclean's response was unequivocal. The Bolshevik model – whatever that involved – was something to admire and to emulate. The response fitted in with his earlier hope that the pressures of a capitalist war could provide revolutionary opportunities for Socialists. From 1 February 1918, his commitment received official backing with his appointment as Soviet Consul in Glasgow.

Verbal support was one thing: translating this into a politically effective form was another. Although Maclean had argued for Socialist Unity on his release in June 1917, his energies were devoted to the arguments inside the BSP. He had been elected to the Party's Executive soon after his 1916 conviction; he was elected once again at the 1918 Conference. Yet his eminence within the Party's Scottish section did not mean that the BSP would move readily to back his ideas on war and revolution.

When the 1918 Conference debated the question of 'Socialists and Peace', most contributors expressed the view that had been the Party orthodoxy since the 1916 split. Socialists should oppose the War and work for an international Socialist Conference. This could press for an early peace and discuss plans for Socialist activity after an Armistice. Although there was abundant rhetorical backing for the Bolsheviks, Maclean was the first speaker to question this strategy:

the British Government would not allow Socialists to go to the International. They were going to finish the war ... the passing of resolutions in the present circumstances was merely a pious joke ... the Capitalists made their move but we came to our Annual Conference to 'resolute' – and then went away and waited another year before we met to 'resolute' again.[16]

Maclean's judgement on how this might be achieved came in other contributions to the Conference. The key lay in an alliance between Socialists and trade unionists – especially the Shop Stewards' Committees in engineering and the Reform Committees that were developing in some coalfields:

There was a spirit of revolution developing inside the workshop ... We should get our comrades to carry on the discussion here, to talk and think revolution.[17]

His optimism was not restricted to Clydeside; at this stage he believed that revolutionary sentiment might grow widely. The military stalemate could provide a Socialist opportunity:

Our unified purpose should be to seize the chance when our enemy at home was weak, to sweep the capitalist class out of the way and bring about peace. We were in the rapids of revolution.[18]

Wartime experiences had modified his former concern with the growth of a Socialist Party. He was prepared now to place a major emphasis on organisational forms and tactics that owed much to those syndicalist tendencies that he had once execrated.

This shift did not mean that Maclean ceased to regard a Socialist Party as significant. He continued to emphasise the interdependence of industrial and political battles; his plans for a Scottish Labour College showed the priority that he gave to Socialist education.[19] Clearly a Party committed to what he viewed as an effective strategy could make a decisive contribution. Yet his problem went deeper than a disagreement with a significant element within the BSP. That Party was affiliated to the Labour Party and the larger organisation was itself undergoing major reforms. By the Spring of 1918, it had a new structure and a formal Socialist objective. The significance of such changes was as yet unclear.[20] Labour support for those of its MPs who remained in the Government was declining, but however far the Labour Party distanced itself from the Government, the BSP's affiliation inevitably produced scepticism from revolutionary socialists. The issue was debated at the BSP's 1918 Conference. Maclean was optimistic about the prospects that a mass Socialist movement might emerge to the Left of Labour:

The Labour Party at present was bound up with capitalism and fighting Socialism. The whole of Society was in the melting pot; we had a chance of developing a force and organisation that would sweep the Labour Party on one side, and develop the workers' class consciousness industrially and politically. In this country, the working class put up the best fight in South Wales and on the Clyde where it did not care for the Labour Party. With proportional representation and payment of election expenses, we could and should run our own candidates.[21]

This scenario provokes the complex issue of feasibility. The argument is myopic or dismissive about ILP strength in Glasgow, but equally, it is perhaps only in retrospect that so much seems preordained: the restructuring of the Labour Party, its elevation to the status of major Opposition party, the progress to Government, and alongside this, the marginalisation of revolutionary movements. But these developments took place in a changing environment. Clearly by the early twenties, Britain, like most other capitalist societies in Europe, had achieved a significant level of stability. No revolutionary organisation was likely to achieve mass support in the foreseeable future. Yet the verdict on 1918 and 1919 might be more complex. The War had shattered expectations of normality. Some regimes had collapsed; others seemed threatened. Once again the question emerges – more fundamentally perhaps than for the Winter of 1915 – 16 – was there in Britain a missed opportunity for a significant growth of revolutionary organisations?

One analysis can be dismissed as placing incredible weight on Maclean's hypothetical contribution. Kendall, as part of his rehabilitation, lays extraordinary weight on Maclean's arrest in 1918:

Maclean's imprisonment shut down the dynamo which powered the revolutionary movement on the Clyde and eliminated the only man with the revolutionary will to power which might have turned growing discontent towards open insurrection ...[22]

One response could be that this exaggerates Maclean's capacities as a revolutionary leader as opposed to an educator and propagandist. The validity of this judgement remains unclear as Maclean's talents in this direction were never tested. More crucially, the claim implies that his imprisonment was vital since other relevant conditions had been met.

Instead of such an unsupported contention, it is important to examine some of these other requirements. Attention has been paid to Maclean's belief in the need for a socialist party with mass support. Even if the BSP were won for a revolutionary policy could it be a credible instrument? The organisation remained small. It affiliated to the Labour Party on a membership of 10,000; possibly this was an exaggeration. At the 1918

Conference, 59 branches were represented including ten from Scotland and twenty from London.[23] It was hardly a party with a mass membership; in some localities including Glasgow the ILP was an obstacle to growth. A reconstituted Labour Party would furnish a greater one. At the level of political activism, there was little to suggest any mass radicalisation of the working class, but there were centres, and perhaps moments that seemed to offer some hope to the left. Could these have been utilised by perceptive revolutionaries in order to make a significant impact? This was a possibility that concerned some on the Right of the Labour Movement; it was one of the motivations behind Henderson's efforts to reform the Labour Party.

Such a radical development depended on events beyond the ambit of formal political organisations; in particular, as Maclean made clear, it rested on workplace antagonisms. Yet the channelling of industrial discontents into radical political channels was a task that lay far beyond the resources of the relatively few revolutionary Socialists who hoped for such a development.

During 1917–18 Maclean devoted considerable attention to the Scottish coalfields.[24] He spoke at meetings in Fife, but more significantly he propagandised in Lanarkshire. In this Western coalfield he supplemented the work of his close colleague James MacDougall who had gone to work at a Blantyre pit, after his release from prison. The latter's propaganda had helped towards the formation of a Lanarkshire Miners' Reform Committee in the summer of 1917, and this was followed by a similar development in Fife.[25] These events were seen by Maclean as encouraging. The Reform Committees were modelled on the pre-war South Wales organisation and campaigned for a more democratic union structure and a more aggressive industrial policy. They emphasised the need for a specifically working-class education and rejected nationalisation in favour of workers' control.

The political optimism expressed by Maclean frequently emphasised developments in the coalfields. Thus he welcomed a one-day stoppage by Lanarkshire miners in August 1917 as evidence of their changing political perceptions.[26] There is no doubt that there were several bases for discontent amongst miners: the 'comb-out' of men for the services, the discontent with high prices and claims that union procedures often worked in an undemocratic fashion. Such grievances could produce strikes and criticism of officials, but these should be distinguished clearly from questions of opposition to the War or of revolutionary politics. Even in South Wales, support for these radical positions was limited, and normally debates within the Miners' Federation occurred within a framework of support for the War.[27] Arguments were not about this general principle but about terms on which support should be given. Yet whilst there was no prospect of industrial action in the coalfield having an immediate wider political relevance, the activities of the Reform Committees alongside the bureaucratic conservatism of older officials could mean that many younger miners would be attracted to more radical politics.

Similar distinctions can be made in the engineering industry.[28] The CWC was reformed when the deportees returned, and in some places, the rank and file movement extended well beyond its traditional craft base. The Shop Stewards' Movement established a national leadership in August 1917. Five months later, a crisis developed over a Government decision to remove skilled young men from munitions works into the army. The initial resistance seemed not only solid but potentially radical. Although fuelled by the concern of a craft-based elite, strike action had implications for the war effort. But appearances were misleading. Where spokesmen seemed keenest for national action, as in London and on Clydeside, there had been no ballots in the workshops; in Manchester and in Sheffield opposition had been expressed to any strikes against the War. Such uncertainties meant the collapse of any semblance of a national movement; soon it was reduced to unofficial stoppages that were little more than belated defences of craft status. Even these were swamped in the patriotic response to the German offensive of March 1918. Arguably this was the one occasion when shop-floor activities came anywhere near a connection with the anti-War movement. The collapse of the resistance came shortly before Maclean's expression of revolutionary optimism at the BSP Conference.

His months in gaol during 1918 covered the time of the Allied counter-attack and the end of German and Austrian resistance. As a military victory became increasingly likely, so opposition to the War became limited to those inspired by Socialist or pacifist principles. When Maclean was released from prison at the beginning of December, he found himself in the midst of the General Election campaign. Lloyd George led a combination of Conservatives, some Liberals and a handful of patriotic Labour candidates. The principal opposition was provided by the Labour Party attacking on a much wider front than in pre-War elections. It too was a broad coalition, extending from aggressively pro-War trade union candidates to anti-War Socialists sponsored by the BSP and the ILP. The distinctive electoral presence of the Revolutionary Left was slight.[29]

Maclean stood in the Gorbals Constituency as a BSP – and therefore a Labour-candidate. He had announced his intention to contest the seat during the previous Winter.[30] His opponent was George Barnes, once General Secretary of the ASE and the city's first Labour MP. He had served in the Lloyd George Coalition as Minister of Labour and had forfeited the support of several local activists. The BSP's affiliation to the Labour Party meant that Maclean's putative candidacy came before the latter's National Executive. This body had been very reluctant to grant endorsement and had justified this by pointing to the uncertainty produced by Maclean's return to prison. Belatedly the NEC acquiesced – in part because of the continuing pressure from local activists, but more crucially because Barnes remained in the Lloyd George Coalition despite Labour's decision to sever all connections with it.[31]

Most Labour candidates faced severe problems in 1918. The euphoria and relief engendered by victory aided the Government. The defective electoral register and low turnout arguably handicapped Labour. Maclean's difficulties were particularly acute – a prisoner at the start of his campaign, his health allowed him only to appear at eve of poll meetings.[32] His performance was not such as to raise his supporters' confidence. Tom Bell, later President of the Communist Party recalled:

Persecution obsessions and questions irrelevant to the Election made up the subject-matter of his speeches. The wild enthusiasm with which he was received at each of his meetings evaporated in murmurs of sympathetic concern ...[33]

A local Labour Party activist went so far as to claim:

We had Barnes defeated ... only for John MacLean's wild outburst the night before the poll.[34]

Such appraisals may well have been influenced by subsequent political differences, and there is little credibility to any claim that Maclean's platform deficiencies lost the election. Nevertheless it is clear that he was hardly an ideal candidate.

Barnes's position exacerbated this weakness. He presented himself as a Labour candidate, despite the support given to him by Lloyd George and local Conservatives. *Forward* accepted that there would be habitual Labour voters who had previously backed Barnes and who would be unwilling to support Maclean.[35] Predictably, the Coalition candidate campaigned vociferously on the issue of Bolshevism and sought to draw the perennial line between 'respectable' Labour and extremism.

What is striking is how far Maclean's campaign, under the guidance of Gallacher, emphasised short-term issues such as housing, temperance and education. His supporters recalled Maclean's involvement in the rent agitation. These demands were placed in a class-conscious context:

The real issue is the struggle between the employing class and the worker[36]

but, in many ways, Maclean's programme was an orthodox Labour one. Nevertheless, he symbolised a principled revolutionary socialism. His return to Glasgow with the mass procession through the city, the waving of the Red Flag, the cheers for the German Revolution – all were dramatic statements of his distinctive position. For some nervous onlookers, the demonstration might have had overtones of recent events in Berlin.[37]

It was not just European revolutionary developments that made their mark on Maclean's campaign. The legacy of the Easter Rising was also offered some promise. The Irish vote had been a significant factor in Barnes's earlier victories; but now, the official Irish organisations decided to back Maclean. Barnes was presented as a member of an administration responsible for continuing repression in Ireland; the initiative within many Irish organisations in Britain was shifting away from old Nationalists towards supporters of Sinn Fein. Whether this organisational decision was effective at the ballot box is unclear. The BSP press claimed an enthusiastic Irish meeting for Maclean.[38] 'Catholic Socialist's' postmortem in *Forward* denied that the Irish were responsible for Labour defeats:

If all sections of the working-class had worked as dourly and voted as solidly as the Irish section, Capitalism in Scotland would have received its death blow on Saturday. They were excellently disciplined and worked equally for extreme men like John Maclean and for the most Conservative Trade Unionist.[39]

This seems exaggerated. The *Glasgow Observer* – Catholic and often sympathetic to Labour – admitted that the recommendation in favour of Maclean had received only limited support from Irish electors.[40] Yet the backing of Irish activists for Maclean was important; it focussed attention on an important shift in Scottish politics as Irish organisations moved increasingly to a pro-Labour position.[41] Ultimately Maclean did not benefit politically from this shift, but the formal alliance of December 1918 was a harbinger of a significant development in his ideas.

For the moment, the most obvious feature of the contest was Maclean's defeat – 7,436 votes against 14,247 for Barnes. Interpretation is difficult. Labour's Glasgow performances fell well below the expectations of both supporters and opponents. Only one seat was won with a near-miss in a second. Disillusionment was sharp:

We picked ourselves up from the dust ... to find disappointment and chagrin and disgust in every ILP room. So much had been expected and so little had been gained. The meetings had been wonderful, the reports and prospects so encouraging; but there were the cold, hard figures that could not be explained, and there were the capitalists dancing with delight at the overthrow of Labour.[42]

This chagrin is important in any assessment of Clydeside radicalism. The difficult circumstances of the election must be acknowledged, but any characterisation of Glasgow as a potential 'Red Base' must come to terms with the fact that less than one in five of the Glasgow electorate met even the undemanding requirement of a vote for Labour. Maclean had the specific handicap of an opponent who could still claim some Labour credentials, but it would be simplistic to interpret his vote as one cast for revolutionary socialism. At most, these voters were undeterred by Barnes's emphasis on Bolshevism, and Maclean's political record.[43] There were some conventional grounds for supporting Maclean: the decision of the Irish organisation; the emphasis by his supporters on immediate issues; the fact that he could be presented as a Labour candidate. *Forward* emphasised this last point. The choice in Gorbals was the same as elsewhere:

Labour versus the Coalition – and John Maclean, being the Labour candidate must receive the support of every citizen who desires to stand by Labour.[44]

December 1918 was one of the last occasions when Maclean acted as an integral part of a broad Labour Movement. During the next two years alignments would change and harden as Labour established itself as a significant force in industrial Scotland. Maclean was amongst those Socialists who continued to reject Labour's cautious politics; they faced the challenge of constructing an alternative party.

Chapter 4

Retrenchment

The election results dampened Socialist enthusiasm only briefly. 1919 was the year when the Labour Movement debated the efficiency and the morality of 'Direct Action' as an addition, or even an alternative to an electoral road on which Labour had been robbed, and would be so again. Some sceptics regarded enthusiasm for 'Direct Action' as corrosive of Labour prospects. *Forward's* response to the 1918 Election results, indicated how far an influential section of the Glasgow ILP was attached to the pursuit of constructive socialism through conventional channels:

And straightway working men said that political action was of no use, that it was hopeless to expect ever to usher in a Cooperative Commonwealth by political action, that we must look to the mass strike, or the Soviet, or seizure of workshops, or some other sudden and catastrophic method of displacing capitalism. *But it is precisely this oscillation from political to industrial action and from industrial to political action that has destroyed Labour as a fighting force for the past hundred years.*[1]

Yet less than a month after this admonition had been published, Glasgow's engineering workers struck for a forty-hour week.[2] The events of this stoppage soon came to occupy a vital place in evocations of Red Clydeside. The Scottish Secretary, Robert Munro, wrote agitatedly of a 'Bolshevist rising'. Strikers attempted to halt tram services and power supplies.[3] Escalation culminated in the George Square riot on 31 January 1919 when police attacked sections of a mass demonstration. Several strike leaders were arrested. Already a decision had been taken to shift troops to Scotland; by the following morning, the military presence was highly visible within the city.

In retrospect, Gallacher characterised the conflict as a missed opportunity when a radical rank and file were stymied by an inadequate leadership:

A rising was expected. A rising should have taken place. The workers were ready and able to effect it; *the Leadership had never thought of it.*[4]

The reality was much more mundane. Certainly the objective of shorter hours to combat unemployment was one much favoured in radical trade union circles; similarly the strategy of mass picketing to spread the stoppage had much in common with some pre-1914 confrontations. But attempts to secure wider occupational and geographical support were largely unsuccessful. After a fortnight, the action ended in defeat.

Maclean spent the most dramatic days of the stoppage on a speaking tour of England for the BSP.[5] Shortly before, he had presented his assessment of the immediate political prospects. Certainly it was crucial to defend the Russian Revolution, but it would be naive to consider that a strike could be achieved in Britain, specifically on this issue:

... the workers are not generally of our way of thinking, and so are unable to see that their material interests are bound up with Bolshevist stability in Russia.[6]

Nevertheless, Maclean considered that revolution was very much on the agenda. Russia could be saved 'by developing a revolution in Britain no later than this year'.[7]

The working class could be mobilised around a campaign for reductions in hours. This would attract both those in jobs, and those returning from the War, fearful of unemployment. Maclean placed particular emphasis on the demands of the Miners' Federation, and especially on the role of the Miners' Reform Movement. Already the Federation under pressure from its left wing had agreed to a demand for a six-hour day. The self-confidence of the Miners could provide a kernel for a wider class campaign. The development of workplace committees modelled on the Miners' Reform Groups could be the start of a strategy with revolutionary implications:

Once we get the mass on the move on this issue, we shall be able to take control of the country and the means of production at once, and hold them tight through disciplined production under the workshop committees and the district and national councils.[8]

The contrast with Maclean's pre-War denunciations of syndicalism was sharp.

From this perspective, the Forty Hours' Strike could appear as premature – but Maclean argued that such a reservation should be discounted:

historical events never start and shape themselves as we plan them.[9]

Moreover, he was sanguine about the readiness to strike of the Fife and Lanarkshire miners. But strike action in the Scottish coalfields was contained. The Scottish Miners' Executive dominated by older officials, was unsympathetic. It decided to disassociate itself:

from the present erratic strike movement and recommend the miners of Scotland to continue at work pending the reply of the Government to the miners' demands ... so that in the event of an unfavourable reply being received from the Government, a common course of action may be decided upon by the miners all over the British coalfields.

Miners should disregard any pickets and not be deflected into 'unconstitutional stoppages ... engineered by irresponsible persons'.[10] This declaration highlights some significant aspects of trade-union responses to the issues of 1919–21. Union officials saw occupational solidarity as a recent – and perhaps brittle – achievement. It had to be protected. This desire militated against allegedly quixotic alliances with other groups, and thereby strengthened trade union sectionalism. The focus of the MFGB's campaign was the British State. They – and to a lesser degree some other groups of workers – had secured benefits from wartime Governments.[11] They hoped that such a relationship would continue; if not, they had much to defend. Moreover, the development of bargaining with a centralised British State meant that solidarity amongst all British miners seemed much more relevant than any alliance between Scottish miners and other Scottish workers.

Such priorities were opposed by the radicalism of some younger miners, hostile to the oligarchic practices and cautious policies of established leaders. But the achievements of the radicals were limited. Most progress had been made in parts of South Wales, but the Reform Movement had left little mark on many English coalfields. Further north, the activities of Maclean and MacDougall had made some contribution to the development of radical movements, especially in Fife and Lanark. In these coalfields, the Reform Committees had some influence on events early in 1919. The Fife coalfield was already affected by a stoppage over surface workers' hours. The Reform Committee attempted to transform this into a wider campaign on wages and hours but the officials managed to secure a ballot vote narrowly in favour of a return to work. It was a verdict responded to with reluctance in some of the pits. Events in Lanarkshire were more dramatic. Many miners had stopped work, and thousands demonstrated in front of the Union headquarters in Hamilton. As a result, the Lanarkshire Executive met members of the Reform Committee, and agreed to a one-day stoppage. Such a gesture contained the immediate anger; in the absence of wider support, it had no other significance. Within a few days, all Scottish miners were back at work.[12]

In retrospect, the bureaucratic caution of most trade union leaders and the continuing divisions between unions seem the dominant features of the industrial challenges of 1919. Yet such emphases must be placed against the volatile atmosphere of the immediate post-armistice months – unrest amongst the police and amongst soldiers anxious for demobilisation; fears that the collapse of the regimes in Germany and Austria–Hungary were instances of a far wider threat to established institutions. Anxious Ministers saw the red flags and heard the denunciations of capitalism; street demonstrations in Glasgow could appear to reflect recent events in Berlin. The events and legends of the Forty Hours' Strike helped to produce an anti-Bolshevik panic amongst Glasgow's middle class.[13] The hysteria could grip Ministers at critical moments.

Sometimes their pronouncements were clearly intended for political effect; others such as Munro's response to the George Square riot seem to have been based on genuine apprehension. Both Cabinet Ministers and panicky suburbanites showed a bleak and unwarranted pessimism about the underlying durability of capitalism in Western Europe.

The year certainly provided occasions for panic. The Miners, self-confident following their wartime gains, demanded wage increases, a six-hour day and public ownership. Initially their campaign was deflected by the appointment of the Sankey Commission. This arraigned the coal-owners and provided some spectacular political theatre, but more fundamentally it helped to blunt the Miners' challenge and left a mountain of mistrust between the MFGB and the Government. By the Autumn, the possibility of a concerted trade union attack carrying radical political implications had receded. Paradoxically this was demonstrated by the national rail strike in September. The Government might mark its advent with the rhetoric of class warfare, but a settlement was achieved by those two pragmatists, Lloyd George and Jimmy Thomas. Some Ministers and union leaders considered the agreement to be a model of how to defuse radicalism by meeting immediate demands. Similar tactics were pursued elsewhere, although mining remained a harsh exception.[14]

Throughout much of 1919, Maclean continued to write as if revolution remained feasible. He saw the advent of the Sankey Commission as an indication of some Miners' officials' fear of radical change. As a counter-weight, he hoped that Reform Movements could be effective. Once again, he exaggerated the ease with which radical rank and file initiatives could replace or by-pass conservative leaders.[15] Moreover, he had a naive assessment of the radicalism of some trade union officials. In particular, his judgements about Robert Smillie ignored the Miners' President's commitments to the ILP and to parliamentarianism.[16]

His associate, James MacDougall, had no illusions about the conse-quence of the Sankey proceedings. Whatever radicalism there had been in the coalfields had been contained and diminished:

Only a small minority of the miners have been able to withstand the influence of this soporific.[17]

Yet, in the Autumn, Maclean still saw the Miners' role as crucial. The MFGB were embarking on their campaign for public ownership following the Government's refusal to act on this matter. He saw such an agitation as facilitating the growth of the Reform Movement, and raising the con-sciousness of workers inside and outside the industry.[18] On occasions he still spoke as if revolution were imminent, but sometimes he suggested that the initiative had perhaps been lost. Thus the railway dispute had shown a willingness to resist the Government, but that was an insuffi-cient basis for a more radical strategy:

If a General Strike can be avoided at this juncture, I think it advisable; for the Government has shown its preparations and its control of food and vehicles. A General Strike should have behind it the impetus for a Labour attack, whereas the impetus is on the side of the capitalist Government.[19]

At this juncture, Maclean's strategy was in part, as ever, educational. He looked forward to the inauguration of the Scottish Labour College; he welcomed the MFGB agitation for public ownership. On the organisational level, he anticipated an extension of workplace movements. Firmly rejecting any suggestion that capitalism would collapse of its own contradictions, he emphasised the need for a massive creative effort by the working class.[20] As 1919 drew to a close, this seemed increasingly unlikely. The Miners' campaign produced little response. Workshop organisation was already under pressure as activists were victimised. The slackening of the industrial struggle helped preoccupations to shift towards the question of party organisation.

Throughout 1919, Maclean's involvement with industrial issues and his emphasis on workshop organisation as a basis for Socialist development did not mean that his commitment to the BSP diminished. He served on its National Executive, he wrote regularly for its newspaper, he spoke at major rallies and propagandised around the branches. In October, he still saw the party's role as crucial:

Events this year have proved that no organisation in Britain has a greater influence than the British Socialist Party on the policy of the working class. We in the end are going to triumph because we apply the materialist interpretation of history to events as they occur, and use it to find out what next great events are liable to take place, so that we may suggest to our class the tactics to be pursued.[21]

Impeccably orthodox, this testimonial might have been, but the BSP in fact did not benefit from that year's industrial climate. Electoral trends suggested a significant shift in working-class opinion compared with the previous December, but this change offered slight encouragement to revolutionaries. The Labour Party had an encouraging year at the polls; a series of impressive by-election votes culminated in sweeping gains in the November municipal contests. In Scotland a Labour candidate sponsored by the Scottish Miners captured Bothwell in July. A 1918 deficit of 332 became a majority of 7168, as voters reacted to rising coal prices, and celebrated the humiliation of the coalowners before the Sankey Commission.[22] Revolutionaries might hope that such a change would be a prelude to further radicalisation. They would be disappointed. Bothwell represented a strengthening of an already existing connection between Labour and sections of the Scottish working class. In particular, the miners in whom Maclean had invested so much hope were moving to a firm identification with Labour. In future, their self-confidence would be eroded by Government antagonism and economic disaster, but the link between occupation and Party would endure. In fact, industrial defeat perhaps strengthened it. Such a development presented a major hurdle for those seeking to build a significant revolutionary party. The strengthening of Labour left them a very limited space.

The inauguration of the Communist International in March 1919 had meant that the formation of a Communist Party presumably involving the BSP became an issue of immediate concern.[23] Subsequently, the BSP held a referendum on affiliation to the new International. The result was favourable by 98 branches to 4. An ideological debate within the Party was won by those who favoured what had become understood as the Bolshevik model. As Theodore Rothstein expressed it:

... the Revolution will not come about through the instrumentality, either of Parliament or of the trade unions, but by the direct-action, political and economic, of the rank and file through their politico-economical organisations of the Soviet type.[24]

In contrast to E. C. Fairchild's insistence that the variety of conditions across Europe required divergent strategies.[25] Rothstein proclaimed the universalisability of his case:

... every country can claim exemption from the operation of social and historical forces on the plea of 'peculiarities', since every country is 'peculiar', but under-lying all peculiarities are the same social factors: modern industry, capitalism, proletariat – and now the world war – which are bound to produce the same effects.[26]

Obviously the Russian influence was highly significant, in mobilising support for the Soviet as an instrument for Socialist strategy; but so too was the legacy of the Shop Stewards' Movement.[27] Guided by such maxims, the BSP entered into protracted Unity negotiations in June 1919, with the SLP, the Workers' Socialist Federation, and the South Wales Socialist Society. As the lines began to be drawn more tightly between parliamentary and Bolshevik roads to Socialism, Maclean was committed unequivocally to the latter. When Fairchild presented his case at the Party's 1919 Conference, Maclean condemned him as having 'gone over to the enemy'.[28] But this fundamental agreement on doctrine did not keep Maclean within the BSP. He attended his last Executive meeting in February 1920;[29] he was not a delegate at the Annual Conference that April.

Much about this rift remains obscure. Subsequent recriminations have ensured that differences became highly personalised. Maclean seems to have quarrelled with Theodore Rothstein who was increasingly influential within the BSP on account of his Russian connections and his rigorous polemics. Apparently the latter had suggested that Maclean devote himself full-time to the 'Hands Off Russia' Campaign. Presum-ably any abandonment of his educational work for a specific political agitation, no matter how important, was unattractive. Harry McShane has suggested that this lay at the heart of Maclean's disenchantment:

They were asking him to drop all the educational and agitational work that he had done for years. John refused to do that; he and the executive of the BSP fell out, and finally he left. Like us, he objected to their lack of an industrial and political perspective for Britain: 'Hands off Russia' was the only policy they had.[30]

This is a more significant claim than anything based on personalities. After all, Maclean had argued that the most effective way to protect the Russian Revolution lay in the development of militant and potentially revolutionary industrial activity. It had seemed a dubious thesis at the start of 1919; by the end of the year it was apparent that such a campaign was not a plausible strategy. Instead, support for Russia could be mobilised perhaps by more conventional political methods that could produce a response from those sections of liberal opinion that objected to Allied Intervention.

This option ran the risk of involving the supposedly revolutionary BSP in some politically questionable associations. In Maclean's view, this was already happening. Cecil L'Estrange Malone had been elected to Parliament as a Coalition Liberal in 1918. He had also been active in an anti-Socialist organisation, the Reconstruction Society. A visit to Russia in the Autumn of 1919, shifted him to support of Non-Intervention. By February 1920, he was speaking in the 'Hands Off Russia' Campaign, and contributing to *The Call*.[31] Five months later, he formally joined the BSP. Maclean saw Malone's involvement as clear evidence of the Party's degeneration:

To allow Malone to lead a Revolutionary Party after a record such as his is high treason to Communism. You might as well appoint Churchill 'honorary' President of the Russian Republic.[32]

Arguably, Maclean saw a discouraging parallel with pre-war Social Democracy when organisations claiming a commitment to Marxism had disintegrated at the hands of leaders who had other priorities. In a more charitable mood, he saw the Party as one victim of a general attack that had blunted the industrial challenge and isolated the miners from other trade unions. The BSP had been 'maimed by the years's onslaught of capitalism'.[33]

Negative appraisal of the BSP's final year was not simply an idiosyncrasy of Maclean, Harry McShane has recalled the disillusion within the Glasgow BSP as activists awaited the conclusion of the protracted Unity discussions:

a lot of resentment built up. Most of it centered on the attitude of the BSP leadership. The BSP became more and more inefficient with no clear policy, but the people at the top were bureaucratic and authoritarian ... Although we were one of the most active branches in Scotland, with forty members, we finally broke with the BSP in January 1920.[34]

On May Day 1920 MacShane discovered that Maclean too was outside the BSP.[35] His support for the Russian Revolution and for revolutionary socialism remained unadulterated. But these commitments were becoming linked to a particular organisational development that would terminate shortly in the emergence of a British Communist Party. It was this pairing that Maclean rejected.

Chapter 5

Isolation

At last, Maclean was on the political margin. He had broken with the BSP, the organisation to which, along with its precursor, he had given his loyalty throughout his Socialist career. The breach occurred just as that Party was moving into membership of a movement that claimed to be both international and revolutionary. His isolation was punctuated by two terms of imprisonment, from May to August 1921, and for a further twelve months from the following October. At the end of November 1923 he died. This time of isolation involved a little over two years of political activity. Quite apart from the fundamental question of feasibility, there was little opportunity to develop a coherent or durable political alternative.[1]

Dismissal of this phase is a temptation. Much of Maclean's energy was spent in bitter polemic against other left organisations. In particular, he attacked Gallacher and the leaders of the Glasgow ILP.[2] He can appear readily as isolated, suspicious, and irascible; it is easy to characterise these last years as the decline of a principled socialist into sickness and paranoia. His health was certainly deteriorating: prison and poverty ensured that. Eventually his energies were exhausted. A continuing preoccupation with his prison treatment is clear, yet his political comments, when free from sectarianism, were frequently perceptive. In one sense, he had always been a purist, committed thoroughly to what he regarded as socialist principles. But he had never been an incorrigible isolate. Attention should be given to his claim that none of the existing organisations on the left seemed an appropriate vehicle for his aspirations.

His criticisms of the British Communist Party incorporated his earlier judgements about the degeneration of the BSP. The new organisation was dominated by a clique which included not only some who were ill-acquainted with Marxism, but at least one, Malone, whose past record was one of hostility. Moreover the Party was an ideological mongrel:

a heterogeneous mixture of anarchists, sentimentalists, syndicalists, with a sprinkling of Marxists. Unity in such a camp is likely to be impossible.[3]

This at least pinpointed the heterogeneity of political positions within the pre-1920 revolutionary left. Eventually some clarity would emerge with a developing agreement on the content and relevance of the Bolshevik model. Yet Maclean, long before this development, expressed doubt about inappropriate Russian influence:

We stand for the Marxian method applied to British conditions. The less the Russians interfere in the internal affairs of other countries at this juncture, the better for the cause of revolution in those countries.[4]

Whilst Maclean's strictures merit serious scrutiny, they clearly did not plumb the depths of the difficulties facing the new organisation. Its failure to achieve a strong membership cannot be attributed solely to the circumstances of its conception. Any overtly Socialist Party faced peculiar difficulties in Britain, in part on account of the restricted space left by the Labour Party. The problem was exacerbated by the working-class defeats of 1921–22.

In the Spring of 1920, Maclean seemed to have absorbed the setbacks of the previous year, without abandoning the judgement that a significant revolutionary advance remained feasible. In part, this rested on a belief that kindred developments were likely in Europe. Allied involvement in Germany had blocked revolutionary growth there, but a breakthrough could occur elsewhere:

The collapse of Italy or France will push to the top, the representatives of the workers, the right-wing first and then inevitably, the left-wing ... This summer or autumn may see Europe going 'red' with necessary reaction in Britain.[5]

Radicalisation in Britain did not depend on fidelity to any existing organisation. Instead agitation for an appropriate programme – something that the Government could not concede – would produce the necessary organisational innovations. The need was to find an equivalent to the Bolshevik emphasis on 'Peace, Bread, Land'. The counterpart recommended by Maclean was for a six-hour day, £1 a day minimum, a fifty per cent reduction in the price level and full wages or national work for the unemployed.[6]

The demands were formulated as a means to working-class unity; but this prospectus depended on a judgement that the initiative still rested with the trade unions. Looking back from the vantage point of Communist Party orthodoxy, Tom Bell subsequently claimed:

The call for a six-hour day would hardly be likely to bring about immediate united action. Here, it would appear, Maclean's idealism outstripped his sense of reality.[7]

Yet such a judgement about what was feasible was not limited to Maclean. Some of the planks within his programme were advocated by Rank and File organisations. But the containment of 1919 marked not a stopping-point on a march towards socialism but the death of effective industrial radicalism. It was an assessment that Maclean and others were reluctant to make. Nevertheless, he soon acknowledged that the Programme had not dispelled working-class pessimism. The response must be to intensify educational work:

we revolutionists must buckle to more strenuously than ever in the work of widening the concepts and outlook of our class.[8]

Unusually, this was coupled with an admission that the lot of the Socialist propagandist could be unrewarding:

Untrained and particularly exhausted workers must seek pleasure in all forms of relaxation – they cannot be bothered about theory. Many have declared that 'The Vanguard' was dull, too heavy for them. Consequently, concrete proposals must be used to rouse our class.[9]

This campaign was carried on by a small team of propagandists who held factory-gate meetings and produced pamphlets. McShane has claimed that the meetings produced a keen response.[10] The immediate hope was that the propaganda would affect trade-union policy. The tactics of the Miners' Unofficial Reform Committees and the Shop Stewards Movement would be expanded:

Surely it is possible for Socialists of the left-wing to work through their unions as do our comrades in South Wales.[1]

The goal should be the 'One Big Union' organised from the workshop upwards. It was a scenario that had much in common with Connolly's Industrial Unionist writings. The national committee:

must be a permanent one, linking up all industries and organising the production and distribution of wealth, and in conjunction with political representatives will do the work that ought at present to be done by the Capitalists' Parliament. Parliament must fade away when Labour unites scientifically and commands control of the land and workshops of the country.[12]

Yet as Maclean projected such a development, the beginnings of depression and the victimisation that followed the Forty Hours' strike were combining to destroy any effective organisation in the workshops. In his 'Open Letter to Lenin' written at the start of 1921, he criticised those who continued to claim that such initiatives could provide the basis for a revolutionary movement:

I have been at work gates all summer and autumn up and down the Clyde valley ... victimisation after the premature Forty Hours strike crushed the workshop movement ... No industrial movement of a radical character is possible outside the ranks of the miners ...[13]

Soon the miners would be defeated; the staple industries of Central Scotland entered a depression which would be lifted only by another war. Effective trade union organisation was eroded and sometimes broken. Unemployment and the organisation of the unemployed became major preoccupations for Socialists.

Maclean had been active in the Glasgow unemployed movement of 1908.[14] In the Autumn of 1920, he began attempts to develop a similar

campaign. Throughout the Winter of 1920–1 he led unemployed
demonstrations, attacked the inadequacy of official Labour responses and
lobbied City Councillors.[15] These initiatives generated some response
from the unemployed. McShane claimed that in October 1920, Maclean
had the active support of about 200 of the unemployed, but that in the
following February he could attract a meeting of about 3500. Yet his
associate's optimism was qualified:

The unemployed are beginning to see clearer every day. If only the workers in the
workshops kept pace with them all would be well.[16]

The contrast indicated a recurrent cleavage within the inter-war working
class; it was one more obstacle to the Socialist dream of effective working-
class unity. Moreover, only a minority of the unemployed participated
in organisations and demonstrations. They provided only a limited basis
for a durable political movement.

As unemployment mounted and short-time working and the fear of
redundancy blighted the conditions of those in work, Maclean showed
an awareness of the deradicalising, numbing consequences. He understood how poverty and insecurity devastated working-class resources and
shattered self-confidence. Early in 1921, he emphasised how recession
was affecting not only the unemployed but also those who retained jobs:

Unemployment today has struck terror into the hearts of those at work, as
starvation is meant to tame the workless.[17]

Yet he still evinced the optimism of the revolutionary. Previously he
had placed his faith in a working class strong in the workplace expressing
its demands in factory-based organisations which could campaign on
issues that could vanquish sectionalism. Now in the bleaker environment of a depressed Scotland, poverty would generate a radicalisation,
borne out of suffering not success. His propaganda for the Immediate
Programme might have persuaded him of the demise of workshop
organisation but it left him with a belief that economic circumstances
would exorcise illusions:

Unemployment and the fear of it is dropping the last scales from the eyes of the
working class worshippers of Capitalist patriotism.[18]

This claim was made specifically in the context of an analysis of the
Scottish situation. It culminated in an appeal for a Scottish Communist
Party. Along with Maclean's insistence that a deteriorating industrial
situation still contained revolutionary opportunities, there went an increasing emphasis on a distinctively Scottish dimension to his political
arguments.

This development could be characterised as a decline from a class-
based Socialist internationalism into an obscurantist escapism, a

withering vision at the moment when prospects for a genuinely revolutionary growth on an international scale seemed encouraging. Alternatively, Maclean's concern with the specifically Scottish situation could be presented as an attempt to relate socialist priorities to the opportunities and limitations presented by a national culture. A distinctive history had produced a working class with its particular strengths and weaknesses. Down to 1914, Maclean had tended to present Scottish workers as backwards. The events of the War and its immediate aftermath encouraged a different estimation.

Although Maclean's pre-war writings had expressed the orthodox internationalism of Second International Social Democracy, his comments on the Highland land question had given an occasional Scottish twist to his argument. Throughout the War, his concern to present an untarnished internationalism had dominated his politics, but in 1919, before he parted from the BSP, his interest in Scottish issues became much more visible.

When Ruaraidh Erskine organised a memorial on Scottish independence for presentation to the Paris Peace Conference. Maclean was approached for his signature.[19] His response had similarities with the position previously held by Connolly. He favoured 'a Parliament or Soviet of workers for Scotland' but the road to this did not lie through negotiations with the Paris Peace Conference. Rather it would involve 'the revolutionary efforts of the Scottish working class'. Connolly had argued that genuine Irish independence required a Socialist Ireland; in the aftermath of 1917 Maclean argued that Lenin and Trotsky were the best allies of those who desired Scottish independence. Woodrow Wilson's expressed enthusiasm for self-determination should be discounted:

he is but the representative of brutally blatant capitalism in America, a capitalism that means to crush Mexico under its 'heel of steel' as it already has the Philippine Islands and Cuba.

The goal had to be 'the Socialist Republic in which alone can we have real Home Rule'.[20]

Maclean's response to Erskine's initiative might be classifiable as Socialist internationalism contrasted with narrow nationalism. Yet as his expectations of any revolutionary breakthrough remained unfulfilled and perhaps as his concern grew about the development of the BSP, so he shifted ground. By the end of 1919, he had joined Erskine's National Committee.[21] One possible explanation could place emphasis on Maclean's growing belief that a more advanced Scottish working class was hampered by its more conservative English counterpart. Such a note of impatience can be found perhaps in his response to the Forty Hours' Strike:

I know that socialists in the Scottish industrial belt can be relied upon. Are our brothers across the border going to funk it or fight as the Yorkshire miners have done ...?[22]

Alongside the concern that unrest would not spread, there remained a belief in the revolutionary potential of English workers, and most firmly of socialists in the South Wales coalfield. Maclean spent much time in 1919 propagandising in England.[23] He did not make as yet a dichotomy between revolutionary Scottish workers and quiescent English ones.

The developing Scottish emphasis within Maclean's politics must be placed in the wider context of the Scottish Labour Movement. It then loses some of its distinctiveness. Sympathy for Home Rule had been expressed by Scottish Labour organisations for several years, but during the War, the commitment became much more serious. From its foundation in 1915, the Scottish Council of the Labour Party passed a Home Rule resolution at each year's conference. The Scottish TUC passed similar resolutions starting in 1914. Four years later, the Scottish Home Rule Association was re-established and by the early twenties had achieved considerable prominence. Moreover, Labour and Socialist organisations provided its dominant components.[24]

This involvement was symptomatic of the increasing emphasis placed on specifically Scottish issues by the Labour Party. Its Scottish Programme for the 1918 Election included two proposals with a distinctively National flavour: 'The Self-Determination of the Scottish People' and 'Complete Restoration of the Land of Scotland to the Scottish People'.[25] The style of such proposals highlighted the centrality of the Radical–Liberal legacy for the Scottish Labour Movement. The land proposal also indicated the desire of some Labour politicians to develop support in the Highlands. The Party's Scottish Council fought the election in alliance with the Highland Land League.[26] The organisational connection was an attempt to link urban and rural radicalisms. Moreover, specifically Scottish cultural themes could be important for some Scottish Labour Leaders. Smillie might have been President of the MFGB and committed to the view that Scottish miners should seek economic advances in alliance with their English and Welsh counterparts. Yet he also declared:

I am with you heart and soul for the revival of the Gaelic language.[27]

When the HLL and Labour's Scottish Council issued a joint appeal, the emphasis on national distinctiveness was paramount:

The English people show a mark disposition to conservatism, while the Scottish people on the other hand, are undoubtedly progressive in political thought and action. The result of the Union has been that Celtic culture and Scottish ideals are discouraged, while the tendency is for the ideals and culture of England to be thrust on our country. Large areas of Scottish land have been denuded of people, in order to provide sporting grounds for the idle rich.[28]

The final sentence expressed a sentiment voiced by Maclean in his pre-War writings. Awareness of national distinctiveness as a politically relevant factor had been given a greater edge by wartime developments. Scotland's heavy industries prospered and continued to do so throughout 1919. A sanguine appraisal of the Scottish economy heightened Scottish Labour's confidence about its own political prospects. This optimism seemed threatened by too much dependence on British institutions. Sometimes trade union leaders from the South seemed unsympathetic to Scottish initiatives. Wartime difficulties had exacerbated longstanding impatience with the inadequacy of Whitehall responses to Scottish Labour issues.

These emphases had their critics within the Labour Movement. Joseph Duncan, an official of the Scottish Farm Servants' opposed the arrangement with the Highland Land League. He argued that Labour should develop a trade-union based Party for the Highlands, and should avoid deals with those whose attachment to the Party was dubious. In contrast, Smillie argued that he was:

in favour of uniting all the forces which were opposed to the present system and the Highland Land League seemed to him unanimous in their desire to wipe out the existing system and replace it with a better order.[29]

Shortly after the 1918 Election, confronted with evidence of the Land League's electoral weakness, Scottish Labour moved towards Duncan's strategy.[30] At one level the debate could be regarded as one more round in the perennial controversy about appropriate alliances for a Labour Party. More specifically, it indicated a tendency for Scottish Labour to become preoccupied with economic matters. National questions would be assessed increasingly in economic terms; cultural or specifically political justifications would be less important. If this were the case, any Labour commitment to Home Rule would be very dependent on the continuing buoyancy of the Scottish economy. Such an initiative for an impoverished society would be much less attractive.

Maclean's interest in Scottish independence must be regarded as a variation on a much wider development within the left. The differences are obvious. The Labour objective was Home Rule; Maclean eventually argued for independence. His position looked forward to the revolutionary overthrow of capitalism; the Labour position was at most evolutionary, and based its political hopes on the continuing strength of Scottish industry.[31] Yet, these divergences were within a broader view that the appropriate political structures for Scotland should be a matter of concern for the left. Maclean's interest in the question should be placed in that context.

The development of his views obviously owed something to his revolutionary interests and the awareness of Scottish identity that can be found in some of his pre-War writings. However, attention should be also given to a complementary change that affected a small but intellectually significant section of Nationalist opinion. The Russian Revolution had a profound impact – not just on several Scottish Socialists, but on Ruaraidh Erskine. The influence can be traced in his journal the *Scottish Review*.[32] He expressed support for the Bolsheviks, not primarily as revolutionary socialists, but because of their challenge to established political structures. Yet if Erskine's principal argument was centred around the prospect for national self-determination, it was coupled with a claim that had a socialist potential:

It is principally through their efforts that the notion of National Self-Determination enjoys its present world-wide vogue, and however selfish and hypocritical may appear the lip-service which the Feudal and Imperial governments of Europe have conspired to do to that principal, yet emphatically is it one that has come to stay. Again, in making war upon the Bourgeois or Capitalist State, the Russian Revolutionists have deserved more than passing well of humanity at large ... the continued existence of the subsisting Capitalist System is obviously incompatible with true democratic rule.[33]

The War moved some Scottish Socialists towards a keener appreciation of National issues. Erskine shifted, if not to Socialism, then at least to an acknowledgement that working-class participation was vital for an effective democratic nationalist movement:

Until the people reign – until the Proletariat is everywhere in undisputed power – it were folly to expect enduring Peace, drastic Retrenchment, or honest and searching Reform.[34]

During the War and its immediate aftermath, the *Scottish Review* gave increasing coverage to labour issues. William Diack, an Aberdeen trade unionist used its columns to emphasise the progressive quality of Scottish Labour politics. Thus he claimed that Scottish Trades Councils were more likely than their English counterparts to favour Peace by Negotiation.[35] Perhaps the Labour Party could be an appropriate instrument for Progressive Nationalists. Such emphases could be stifled easily. Trade union bureaucracy, based often in England, could be a deadweight. The NUR Executive had blocked a proposal favouring Scottish representation at the Peace Conference, although the Scottish Executive members favoured this.[36] Nationalists' distaste for 'English Government' could fuse with union activists' antagonism towards bureaucratic officialdom.

These convergences help to illuminate Maclean's developing blend of nationalism and socialism, yet even he could lag behind the hopes of Erskine and Diack. When Maclean began to give a more specific content to his plans for a Scottish Labour College, he was criticised for failing to provide 'a definite place for the study of Scottish history from the national and democratic point of view'. This omission was contrasted unfavourably with Connolly's approach to history – undeniably the work of a socialist yet indicating that he was 'heart and soul with the Gaelic revival in Ireland'.[37]

This comparison was illuminating. The Easter Rising had been viewed unsympathetically by many Scottish Socialists and Home Rulers, but Erskine had given the rebels coded support in the *Scottish Review*.[38] The following year, H.C. MacNeacaill proposed the withdrawl of Scottish MPs from Westminster.[39] The tactic had an eighteenth-century Scottish precedent, but a contemporary Irish one. The terms were similar to those later employed by Maclean. He too saw the Irish conflict as crucial, although his response was more complex. Gaoled immediately before the Easter Rising, he gave retrospective support to Connolly's involvement; in 1919 he was enthusiastic about the calling of the first Dail.[40] The absence of Socialist members did not weaken his support for Irish Nationalism. He seemed to believe that Connolly's dream of an Irish Socialist Republic was feasible. His explanation of the vitality of the independence movement lay in its working-class roots:

No international worker can afford to leave out of his calculations the success of Irishmen in slowly crushing British rule out of Ireland, for that success is not due to the Irish intellectuals or to the Sinn Fein members of the propertied class. Ireland's new fight started in 1907 during the Belfast dock strike, after which James Larkin commenced the Transport Workers' Union to embrace all Irish workers not in the old craft unions or attached to British unions.[41]

This characterisation lent a deceptive continuity to Irish labour developments since the 1907 dispute. Arguably the absorption of Labour's identity into the national struggle was not as inevitable as it can seem retrospectively. But Maclean's hopes for future developments were wildly unrealistic in the context of 1920:

Ireland cannot stop at a republic; Ireland's one big union will before the republic has really started convert it into a socialist republic.[42]

This was based on an inflated estimate of trade union strength and informed by a belief that the space for a capitalist stabilisation was very limited. The prognostication utilised an argument similar to one employed by Connolly in his historical writings. The transition to Socialism would be facilitated in Ireland since links could be formed with pre-capitalist traditions:

These workers are revolutionary in outlook and are bound on the establishment of a Republic to convert it into a Socialist Republic with Celtic Communist tradition as a mighty driving force.[43]

Like Connolly, Maclean placed emphasis on a contentious romanticised interpretation of the past. He ignored the complex problem of how far the Ireland of 1920 contained bases for a significant socialist development.

His interest in Irish Nationalism not only suggested similarities to and divergences from the Scottish situation. Both cases should be placed in the context of British imperialism. The impact of an Irish revolt on the

British Empire had been one strand in Connolly's justification for Easter 1916. Maclean in the Summer of 1920 made a similar claim. Some Socialists saw only the political intentions of Sinn Fein; they failed to examine the consequences of the Irish conflict:

The Irish situation obviously, is the most revolutionary that has ever arisen in British history, but unfortunately lads who fancy themselves the only revolutionaries are too stupid or too obsessed with some little crochet to see the tight corner the Irish are placing Britain in.

The Irish Sinn Feiners, who make no profession of socialism or communism and who are at best non-socialists, are doing more to help Russia and the revolution than all we professed Marxians in Britain.[44]

It could be the first step in the disintegration of the Empire, a process which Maclean saw as conducive to the success of British Labour. At this point there is a significant divergence from the ultimate position of Connolly. The latter had come to despair of a sympathetic response from the British Labour Movement on any Irish topic. The disillusions of 'Dublin 1913' and of 'August 1914' left their marks. In contrast Maclean continued to envisage a mutually-beneficial relationship. Irish revolt could help British Labour by weakening the British Government; the British Left could provide effective support for the Irish cause.[45] This hypothesis was never tested. Working-class radicalism diminished in Britain as unemployment rose; the distinctive Labour element within Nationalist Ireland became increasingly marginal.

Yet any attempt to connect Irish events with the hopes of British socialists faced an overwhelming obstacle. Maclean had been made very aware of this during a visit to Dublin in August 1919. At a meeting of the Socialist Party of Ireland:

one man desired to know why the Gordons came to Ireland after refusing to go to India. Hot stuff like that was poured into me.[46]

Scottish regiments were involved prominently in Ireland. Maclean might argue that this was 'Ireland's tragedy, Scotland's disgrace', but it raised a major difficulty for any hope of Gaelic unity against British – or perhaps English – imperialism. A further threat came from the impact of the Irish crisis on religious divisions in the West of Scotland. McShane has recalled how Maclean and his small group campaigned vigorously on the Irish issue following the split with the BSP. The commitment could provoke an equally vigorous response:

We held great open-air meetings on Ireland. In June 1920 we held one in Motherwell, which was always an Orange centre; the Orangemen smashed the platform, but some of the Irish came and fought them off ...[47]

There was also violent opposition at Port Glasgow and Partick. Episodes such as these did little to facilitate working-class unity. They could strengthen a desire to keep divisive national issues out of Socialist politics.

Beneath the conflict of Orange and Green, there lay a more fundamental problem which could block Maclean's hopes for a Scottish initiative towards Socialism and independence. Although Nationalists argued forcibly that English control had damaged Scotland both economically and culturally, the industries of Central Scotland owed much to the British connection. The prospects of those who worked in them were dependent on Britain's overseas trade. Throughout much of Ireland, the rural economy provided the basis for a Nationalist movement that had fused agrarian and political grievances. The Highlands were too small in relative terms to play this role. Elsewhere there was an industrial working class exploited by capitalists, but not so patently in 1918–21, a victim of the English connection.[48]

Despite the marginality of Highlands' radicalism, Maclean placed a significant emphasis on agrarian issues. Behind this lay the experiences of his own family and also the tendency for Scottish Socialists to seek alliances with rural radicals. It was in this context that he emphasised the idea that 'Celtic Communism' was an accurate characterisation of traditional Scottish society. Articles on this theme by Erskine were included in the *Vanguard*, and later on Maclean's suggestion in the SLP's paper, the *Socialist*.[49] The historical judgement led to Maclean proposing the slogan 'back to communism and forward to communism'. The relevant example was drawn not from Celtic historiography, but from the Bolshevik success:

The communism of the clans must be re-established on a modern basis. (Bolshevism, to put it roughly, is but the modern expression of the communism of the *mir*).[50]

This put it very roughly but at least in Russia, an avowedly socialist revolution had occurred in a society where communal peasant institutions had survived. Maclean's hope rested on little more than a dubious historical claim.

Yet the events of 1920 showed that agrarian radicalism was not yet dead. Maclean's interest was caught by the activities of land raiders on the Isle of Lewis, a mobilisation fired by opposition to the ill-fated modernisation programme of Lord Leverhulme.[51] The involvement of Maclean with the Lewis raiders is sometimes presented as idiosyncratic[52] but it reflected a longstanding enthusiasm on the Scottish Left. Labour's 1918 electoral strategy had demonstrated a wish to link industrial and rural struggles and Maclean was not the only Scottish Socialist to make a pilgrimage to Lewis in the Summer of 1920. Thomas Johnston was frequently at odds with Maclean over strategy and priorities; on this occasion, he responded similarly. Crofters had come home after the War. The old desire for land had been strengthened by the memory of sacrifices in France, or the encounter with new political ideas in the workshops.

Leverhulme's projects were models of modernisation; in material terms, the people of Lewis would benefit. But Johnston saw an opposition that a Socialist could support. Leverhulme:

has run headlong against something that is more permanent than Capitalism, and that something is soil-hunger and the freedom to till not for profit, but for use ... he is not going to be allowed to destroy the last remnants of an independent peasantry.[53]

Yet this revolt should not be dismissed by Socialists as a last stand against modernisation. Johnston argued that the seizures contained a Socialist potential; private ownership of land could not provide an acceptable standard of living:

they will, I hope, develop their Cooperative and Communist practices. They must cooperate to secure the latest appliances. For them, non-Cooperative effort means toil and scarcity and poverty; they must have common action.[54]

The argument depended not on belief in a distant communal past, but on a claim that contemporary rigours would demonstrate the obsolescence of individualism.

Maclean's justification for supporting the land raiders placed much more emphasis on an international theme. He provided a machiavellian interpretation of the Lewis modernisation:

Leverhulme is preparing Lewis and Harris for the navy in case of war with America.[55]

The expectation that capitalist rivalries would generate conflict between Britain and the United States was a recurrent theme in Maclean's post-war writings. It emerges most thoroughly in the pamphlet, *The Coming War With America*. This threat could be used as a powerful argument for Scottish independence:

The preparations to use the Scottish coast for Scottish lads in John Bull's fight forces on us the policy of complete political separation from England. Hence a Scottish Communist Party.[56]

This expectation – so spectacularly misplaced – can be used to diminish not only Maclean's case for Scottish independence, but his overall political judgement. Yet his argument about British–American rivalry included a significant perception. Just when the acreage of the British Empire was at its maximum, economic power was shifting across the Atlantic. It was a development ignored by many British politicians as they sought a return to pre-1914 conditions.[57]

The weakness in Maclean's argument came when he argued that this economic development would have a predictable political outcome – unless an effective revolutionary movement intervened. Such a dichotomous choice suggests a mechanistic element within his Marxism.

He criticised any fatalistic optimism that suggested capitalism would collapse of its own accord. A revolutionary intervention was essential. Yet he thought that lack of revolutionary success would leave a predicament where political options were limited rapidly by economic constraints. It was understandable given memories of 1914 that he should see politicians and capitalists as propelled inexorably into war to safeguard their interests. But such an appraisal was simplistic. It offered little scope for the facility with which ruling groups could redefine their essential interests – nor could it offer an effective appreciation of the complex relationship between constraint and agency.

The connection between Maclean's flawed conception of international developments and his advocacy of Scottish independence was a significant one. But his justification of a Scottish Workers' Republic did not rest on this one claim. It was supplemented by the argument that a significant revolutionary movement in Scotland should work in the same direction as the Republicans in Ireland:

Since the British Empire is the greatest obstacle to Communism, it is the business of every Communist to break it up at the earliest moment. That is our justification for urging a Communist Republic in Scotland.[58]

This presentation of self-determination for Scotland as an effective aid to revolution was complemented by other contingent claims. His rejection of the leadership of the BSP and later of the British Communist Party helped to produce his unsuccessful attempts to establish a separate Scottish Communist Party. His claim that such an organisation could be viable was supported by assertions about the advanced state of working-class opinion in Scotland – it was a country 'firmer for marxism than any other part of the British Empire'.[59] His diagnosis by late 1920 was based not on effective workplace organisation, but on the collapse of basis industries: 'the pressure of poverty is driving Scotland leftwards'.[60]

It would be tempting but misleading to see Maclean's attachment to independence as pragmatic. From this standpoint, support for separatism justified an attempt to build a Scottish Communist Party that would be independent of the British leadership that he rejected. Given the International's insistence on just one party in each country, an alternative organisation could be legitimate, if Scotland was accepted as a separate nation.[61] Similarly, the argument that Scottish independence should be justified as a contribution to the disintegration of the British Empire was a claim that appeared to support national independence, only insofar as it served an anti-imperialist purpose.[62]

Such emphases were important for Maclean as they had been for Connolly. But these did not exhaust his arguments. He focussed on what he hoped were potential bases for radical or revolutionary developments

that were distinctively Scottish. Such analyses again have their counterparts in Connolly's writings. Maclean had an awareness of his identity
that was specifically Scottish. This was not as marked as Connolly's
continued emphasis on the Irish content of his Socialism, yet even in
his pre-1914 writings, Social Democratic orthodoxies were decorated
with distinctively Scottish sentiments. Under pressure both Socialists
could articulate affirmations of national identity that assumed the
existence of distinctive and significant racial characteristics. Connolly
reacted in these terms to the Parliamentary Party's support for the War;
Maclean claimed the existence of a Celtic identity when expressing his
hopes that Scotland could emulate and ally with Ireland – and that
within Scotland Scots and Irish could unite in a common cause:

Irishmen must remember that communism prevailed amongst the Irish clans
as amongst the Scottish clans, so that, in lining up with Scotsmen, they are but
carrying forward the tradition and instincts of the Celtic race.[63]

Occasionally Maclean's sympathy and admiration for Irish Republicans
and his hopes for the Scottish Left produced a denunciation of English
superiority paralleling those made by Connolly after August 1914.

An independent Scotland would refuse to let her lads fight the battles of the
maniac English who hold the obsession that the world was made by God for them
to rule and rob.[64]

Maclean also combined national and class condemnation; responsibility
for the attack on the Irish people lay with 'the English, cold, calculating
capitalists'.[65]

    His nationalism is not reducible to a series of pragmatic responses
precipitated by ideological and organisational developments inside the
Revolutionary Left, nor shaped by the expectation of imminent international conflict. It owed much to optimism about the radical potential
secreted within a distinctively Scottish social structure. Maclean's
heightened interest in Scottish independence and the links he established
with other Nationalists cannot be understood outside the context of the
Irish struggle. This furnished both an urgent problem, and an attractive,
if misleading, exemplar. Moreover, Maclean had a relatively uncritical
perception of Scottish identity – and held to an uncomplicated belief
in distinctive racial characteristics.[66]

    These diverse roots did not provide a ready synthesis of nationalist
and socialist claims. Unlike Connolly, Maclean never made any attempt
to produce a reconciliation. His responses are of interest for what they
reveal about elements within the British Left that became buried under
subsequent developments. They belong to a moment when the Irish crisis
was still central to British politics and the structure and the identity of
the left beyond the Labour Party was not set solidly within the parameters

of the Russian model. The Labour Party was not yet a major parliamentary force. The full corrosive impact of depression in traditional industries had not had its full impact on trade-union organisations and working-class self-confidence. Soon, durable patterns of working-class politics would be firmly established. How inevitable was the loss of Maclean's distinctive combination of revolutionary socialism and Scottish nationalism?

One response is to examine the ebbing enthusiasm within the Scottish Left for a distinctive national response to working-class problems. Admittedly the dominant emphasis was on Home Rule but it is plausible to argue that the factors reducing support for this in favour of British initiatives would have relevance for the surivival of Maclean's more radical variant.[67] By November 1922 the Labour Party had emerged not just as the dominant force on the Scottish Left, but as a major presence in the nation's electoral politics. Initially this breakthrough could strengthen demands for Home Rule on the grounds that progressive Scotland was handicapped by conservative England.[68] But this argument was weakened with the early advent of a Labour Government. The failure of a Home Rule Bill to make headway during its brief period of office was perhaps a harbinger of a gradual shift of emphasis amongst Scottish Labour Members.[69]

This change was based on more than the promise of a majority for Labour within a British Parliament. Perhaps more decisively, the plight of Scottish industry confounded Home Rule aspirations. Throughout the twenties unemployment was higher than the average for Britain. Union membership fell and the number of distinctively Scottish trade unions declined. In 1925 seventy-five per cent of Scottish trade unionists belonged to British organisations. The difficulties faced by some Scottish workers could secure some redress perhaps, if they belonged to organisations that also operated in the more prosperous South. Significantly, this wa a judgement shared by Maclean at the time when he was propagandising for a Scottish Workers' Republic. In January 1921, he urged a response to unemployment that would entail a demand for full pay for all backed by the threat of a general strike. This could not be effective if restricted to a Scottish initiative:

Scotland alone is impotent; but if Scotland is united on this and brings full pressure to bear on the Special British Congress ... there is a sporting chance that British Labour may be united to save the unemployed.[70]

Scottish Labour leaders might argue that Scottish workers were suffering disproportionately, but the moral was likely to be an alliance with stronger sectors rather than separate action. Thus Scottish miners fought unsuccessfully alongside their English and Welsh colleagues in both 1921 and 1926. Their purpose was to defend the principle of national (British) wage agreements. In Scotland, as in Wales, the part of the 'Home Rulers' was played by the coal owners who favoured decentralised – and cheaper – wage bargaining.

Inevitably, this general history incorporated its own variants. When railway amalgamations were under discussion after 1918, the original Government proposals included one for a single Scottish company. This was changed following objections from the existing Scottish managements who claimed that such a combination would be unprofitable. Instead, two cross-border amalgamations were created. This occurred despite opposition from Scottish railway trade unionists who claimed that English-based companies would cut Scottish facilities. The fear was realised quickly as the newly-formed London Midland and Scottish Railway cut back on Scottish workshops. One consequence was a keen and continuing commitment to Home Rule amongst many Scottish activists within the NUR and the Railway Clerk's Association.[71] Yet, as the impact of these early cutbacks receded, so this enthusiasm faded. As railway workers everywhere became concerned to protect wage-levels and jobs in the face of recession and road competition, so an all-British response both industrially and politically became the priority. Maclean might have hoped that recession would shift the Scottish working class towards the left and towards separatism. The leftward move ended for most with the Labour Party; once there, the remedy was increasingly sought not in Scotland but in Britain.

Hopes that agrarian discontent might leave its mark on Scottish Socialism and Nationalism were similarly unfulfilled. The Coalition Government, ready to buy off grievances, wherever this seemed feasible, introduced legislation late in 1919.[72] This provided more extensive facilities for the State to establish crofts on previously large farms. Although the machinery worked slowly, the cumulative impact was significant. After a few years, the underlying land hunger was assuaged. Once again, the complexities of agrarian radicalism were evident. Maclean and Johnston had seen a Socialist potential in the crofters' actions, but one official assessment held that an amicable settlement could have a stabilising effect:

A landholder has no time for revolution ... the holder feels he has a stake in the country and his face is turned towards stability and security.[73]

This outcome could be seen in the increasingly conservative Irish peasantry, alongside aggrieved landless labourers and emigrants conscripted by economic necessity. In Scotland, the issue was much more marginal; a settlement was available.

The image of an independent and Socialist Scotland hit against powerful and unyielding realities. The recession eroded both enthusiasm for Home Rule, and whatever radical potential there had once been.

Increasingly the emphasis lay with all-British industrial strategies for economic defence, and with the Labour Party at Westminster for political influence. Yet it is an insensitive history which by telling it as it was, implies that that was how it had to be. Certainly the increasing weight of the mainstream institutions and preoccupations of British Labour seem overwhelming. It is easy to see why Scottish Labour politics took the shape that it did. The consequence was a significant contribution to an increasingly promising 'Forward March'. Yet need this dominance have been so total? Could some of the sentiments associated with Maclean have survived as a minority yet significant current?

Following his breach with the BSP, Maclean continually faced the problem of establishing a distinctive and significant political base. His attempts to form a separate Scottish Communist Party foundered on organisational rivalries and personal acerbities.[74] Most fundamentally, the CPGB offered not simply opposition but the attraction of the author-ised version. Subsequently he worked for a while in close co-operation with the Socialist Labour Party after some of that group's leading figures had left to join the Communist Party. This period was punctuated by imprisonment in the Summer of 1921 but his educational work and his agitations for the unemployed were backed up by a significant level of popular support. He stood as a candidate in the Kinning Park Ward in the Municipal Election of November 1921, and secured 2,000 votes. The Labour candidate was pushed down into third place.[75]

This result was achieved despite Maclean's arrest during the campaign. Yet his imprisonment for the next twelve months weakened his posi-tion. Perhaps his absence was decisive; more likely it simply accelerated an isolation that would have occurred anyway. McShane, previously a loyal follower of Maclean, was arrested himself in the summer of 1922. This exposed the brittleness of Maclean's organisational resources:

... although we had conducted the best propaganda and agitation in the West of Scotland, we had left no organisation behind us. When I was arrested there was no one else to carry on the work except the Communist Party or the Labour Party. Realising this, I thought I must make a choice about what I was going to do. I decided to join the Communist Party.[76]

This decision came from someone who had been involved in the rivalry between Maclean's followers and the Glasgow Communist Party. Whilst he had accepted the validity of Maclean's criticisms of the CPGB he felt ultimately that he must join that organisation. The pressure to work within some sort of established group proved decisive. As the Labour Party developed an extensive electoral base, and the Communist Party demonstrated its attraction for working-class radicals such as McShane, the political space left for Maclean became very limited. As his isolation increased, so did his resentment at what he characterised as personal treachery. Released from Barlinnie, he plunged into the Gorbals election of November 1922:

On my release, I had to start in Gorbals without committee, money or anything. I had been betrayed by McShane and Co. whilst in B.[77]

Candidates included a National Liberal/Conservative and an Independent Liberal, but his most powerful opponent was the official Labour representative, George Buchanan.

Labour support had grown significantly in Glasgow since December 1918. The progression had not been uninterrupted nor untroubled. Unemployment and poverty might produce a Labour commitment but they could damage party organisation, and generate what one Labour commentator described as 'social pessimism'.[78] Nevertheless, in November 1922, the Party's relevance was heightened perhaps by the damage that depression and defeat had wreaked on industrial organisations. Housing remained a crucial issue. The victory of 1915 had demonstrated the potential strength of working-class organisation. The shambles that was housing finance could be presented as symptomatic of capitalism's irrationality, inefficiency and inhumanity. Glasgow Labour activists had organised another rent strike in the summer of 1920. In immediate terms, it was unsuccessful, but two years later an unanticipated legal decision ruled that increases were invalid since they had not been preceded by notices of removal. This judgement stemmed from a Labour initiative. The Party could appear as the articulator of an important working-class demand. Moreover the risk of a damaging amendment to existing legislation suggested the importance of a Labour vote as a protective response. Although Maclean had involved himself in the housing question, the Labour Party had always played the dominant part. Predictably the high priority given to the issue in working-class communities helped to ensure that Labour became their principal political instrument.

The Labour Party also benefitted from another and more complicated change. Maclean had been notable amongst Scottish Socialists for the support that he had given to the Irish struggle for self-determination. In contrast, Scottish Labour had not found it easy to secure reliable support amongst the Irish community before 1914, and some sections of the Party had responded slowly to political developments after Easter 1916. Nevertheless, by 1922, the relationship between Scottish Labour and the Irish electors was closer than ever before. In part this reflected a belief that the National Question was more or less resolved, and that class could now have more influence on voting; but also Labour had gradually shown itself more receptive to the case put by newer Irish leaders. On class and to a lesser degree on national grounds, Labour could appear as an appropriate representative for Irish working-class electors. In the Gorbals, Labour had worked with Irish organisations since 1906; these developments strengthened this connection. It was a major obstacle for Maclean who had invested so much energy into the Irish question.

George Buchanan was the beneficiary of significant trends in Labour's favour. He emphasised unemployment – work or full maintenance; housing – a block on all rent increases; pensions – Labour's proposed Capital Levy could help here.[79] Despite these emphases on economic and social themes, he did not ignore nationalist questions. He urged the need to protect Irish freedom and supported self-government for Scotland. Policy was backed by effective organisation. After he had won, Buchanan claimed that his victory was one for Socialism. The Rent Question might have dominated discussion, but a more fundamental conclusion could be drawn:

We never hid our Socialist and anti-Militarist views, and the result proved that the working people are sick both of Capitalism and War.[80]

Maclean faced a very different challenge to that posed by Barnes in 1918. Buchanan's 16,479 votes and the accompanying triumphs of Labour candidates elsewhere in Glasgow and through industrial Scotland suggest the forging of a durable political link between many Scottish workers and the Labour Party. Alongside this success story, Maclean can appear as an irrelevant individual.

Isolation and a sense of grievance left their marks on his election address. Alongside the bitterness was the principle:

I stand in the Gorbals and before the world as a Bolshevik, alias a Communist, alias a Revolutionist, alias a Marxian. My symbol is the Red Flag, and it I shall always keep floating on high.[81]

His perspective was that of the contradictions of international capitalism, and in particular of the British Empire. A Scottish Workers' Republic would be a means to revolutionary action, a strategy which would require industrial organisation on a British basis:

I wish a Scottish workers' republic, but Scottish workers to be joined in one big industrial union with their British comrades against industrial capitalism.[82]

The objective was a revolutionary's dream of democracy, abundance and harmony:

When all empires are broken up and the workers by political control start to make land and wealth-producing property common property, when of the wealth produced all get sufficient to give them life abundantly with leisure and pleasure and education added thereunto, then all the independent workers' republics will come together into one great League or Parliament of Communist peoples, as a stage towards the time in the future when inter-marriage will wipe out all national differences and the world will become one.[83]

It would be easy to dismiss his campaign with its imprints of sectarian antipathies, its concentration on international developments, and its idealism, as politically irrelevant. This would be mistaken. The *Glasgow Herald* – hardly an impartial witness – saw Maclean continuing 'to plough his lonely furrow of Communism', standing 'alone in the Party sense'. But the *Herald* acknowledged that he drew large audiences and during the campaign he polled 4,287 votes in a municipal contest. This, however, was in the absence of a Labour candidate; in Gorbals the *Herald* estimated that he could secure 2,000 votes.[84] In fact, he obtained 4,027, far behind Buchanan, but hardly the vote of an irrelevant romantic sectarian.

A significant proportion of Gorbals' electors had chosen to vote for Maclean rather than Buchanan, although one had minimal organisation and the other an effective machine. In part, Maclean's vote probably reflected sympathy with his past campaigns and deprivations. But voters were choosing a self-proclaimed revolutionary who preferred to talk of international capitalist crisis rather than of rents and who urged abstention from Westminster. Maclean emphasised these aspects in a private assessment of his campaign:

I staggered the people by saying that I wouldn't go to the London H. of C. but would remain in Scotland. I refused to talk on rent, taxes or cap levy. I kept to the question of trade and the world political and economic complications.[85]

At least it can be argued that in Gorbals in November 1922, many were ready to support this position rather than that of the Labour Party. How far this indicated a distinctive bloc of support for Scottish independence is unclear. In 1922, attachment to variants on this theme remained widespread on the Scottish Left and included Buchanan as well as Maclean. The vital distinction was probably over Maclean's strong advocacy of communism and revolution. As yet, at least in Glasgow, the Communist Party had not established a secure monopoly over such sentiments.

Maclean's assessment was that it would fail to do so, and therefore would leave space for a specifically Scottish organisation. He saw his task as to 'create a keen desire' for a Scottish Workers' Republic:

and so lay the basis for a Scottish Communist Party or a Scottish Workers' Party. In due course a monthly or weekly paper could be issued and branches opened up all over the country. The CP is getting 'rocky' and as it fades the ground will be cleared for a real fighting party independent of outside dictation and finance.[86]

Two difficulties undermined this prognosis. The 'creation' of support for Scottish Independence, let alone a Workers' Republic had never made much headway. Connolly's prospectus, whatever its limitations, could build at least on a deep-seated and institutionalised separatist sentiment. But the post-War support for Scottish Home Rule was declining by 1923.

Maclean's judgement that major difficulties faced the Communist Party was reasonable, but these problems were not ascribable simply to 'outside dictation and finance'. Many would be faced by any revolutionary organisation in a non-revolutionary situation. 'A real Marxian organisation in Scotland'[87] would not be exempt. Moreover the international credentials of the Communist Party provided some defence against repeated disappointments and helped to ensure the continued adherence of a significant number of working-class activists.

These unpropitious circumstances provided the environment in which Maclean attempted to build a Scottish Workers' Republican Party. His rationale was a distillation of arguments that he had expounded since his separation from the BSP:

I'm certain London will never lead the Clyde or Scotland, so we must lead ourselves. A separate republic is justifiable as a step to keep Scotland out of future wars involving England; and breaking up the Empire that most retards Communism.

A working alliance with Ireland and Russia would give Scotland a great leverage in the period of transition.[88]

The organisation has left few traces: one branch minute book, references in Maclean's correspondence, press reports of municipal contests, hostile journalistic portraits.[89] It seems to have been limited to Glasgow. Members came often from those who had been active in unemployment agitations, but had not joined the Communist Party. McShane had moved from such campaigns into the CPGB but remained sympathetic to Maclean. His retrospective assessment of the SWRP was dismissive:

It had some queer people that I didn't like – they had never been to John's economics classes, they knew nothing about socialism or revolutionary work. Even if I had not joined the Communist Party, I could never have joined with that crowd.[90]

Maclean too was not always happy with his recruits. In June 1923, the SWRP fought a municipal election in North Kelvin. The candidate Mark O'Donnell joined the Party after he had entered the contest. Maclean's judgement was scathing:

He was very weak in brain and character ... he issued a leaflet proclaiming moderation in all things. We simply kept him off the platform and ran a *Red* propaganda campaign on our own, hardly mentioning his name.[91]

Such weakness provided material for Labour ridicule of the SWRP as a futile organisation which could nevertheless syphon off Labour voters. One manifestation was a self-righteous portrait that capitalised on SWRP brashness and inexperience:

if mere talking could bring us nearer the Socialist Commonwealth, then the Socialist Workers' Republican Party are the fellows to get us there at record speed.

If facility in the use of 'dams' and 'bloodies' and other choice epithets could do it, they would have had us there already. But the SWRP have been at the job for some time now, and as their practical achievements on behalf of the workers are so far *nil*, it would appear that windy oratory and bad language are not the chosen instruments of the social revolution.[92]

Throughout the summer and autumn of 1923, the SWRP contested municipal vacancies without success. On one occasion Maclean polled more than 2,000 and demoted the Labour candidate into third place. But apart from him, the Party had no significance and he was now ill and impoverished.[93] His involvement with the unemployed was much less as the Communist Party established its position within this field. Perhaps most wounding of all, he had broken his connection with the Scottish Labour College when its National Committee rejected his draft constitution.[94] He was a principled, often suspicious, revolutionary trapped in a harshly non-revolutionary world. As McShane recalled:

John was weak, living on one or two pounds a week without enough food or warm clothing – he was desperately anxious for the mass movement of workers to break out.[95]

He remained optimistic about the possibility of revolutionary developments, but in November 1923, the municipal elections spotlighted the SWRP's weakness. None of its twelve candidates came anywhere near victory. Some votes were derisory. In the two wards comprising the Gorbals' constituency, the SWRP candidates achieved a total of 480 votes. Even Maclean in his Kinning Park contest polled only 623 out of a total of 8,190.[96] It was an inauspicious prelude to his third Gorbals contest terminated prematurely by his illness and death. Despite his almost perpetual optimism and his personal appeal it seems clear that his vote would have declined significantly compared with 1922.

From one viewpoint, the ending is one of illness, poverty, isolation, disappointed hopes, the destruction of a revolutionary and thereby arguably the exposure of revolutionary naivete. Yet this process of isolation and defeat had been a complex one. It would be facile to see Maclean's position as a coherent and readily feasible option, yet obviously the state of the Scottish Left was more complex than some simple images of the inexorable rise of Labour might suggest. There is also the question of what alternative visions were lost in this growth of Labour dominance. In his last address to the Gorbals electorate Maclean repeated the familiar argument that a Scottish parliament would be a predominantly working-class one and that a socialist transition could be achieved more rapidly in Scotland. This was linked to an assessment of the early activities of Clydeside Labour MPs at Westminster:

Last year I told you I would not go as I could get nothing there. So you sent George Buchanan to get your rents back. Buchanan and his friends have spent a fruitless year, and have returned home empty of hand. So after all I was right. Had the Labour men stayed in Glasgow and started a Scottish Parliament, as did the genuine Irish in Dublin in 1918, England would have sat up and made concessions to Scotland just to keep her ramshackle empire intact ...[97]

The same sentiments were expressed vigorously after Maclean's death by Hugh MacDiarmid – but between the Wars, his combination of separatism and Marxist Socialism remained almost unique.[98] The writer, Edwin Muir, provided a more typical response. In the Summer of 1934, he made a *Scottish Journey*. He finished, depressed at the state of Scotland's economy. His diagnosis rejected the orthodox Nationalist case:

The Scottish proletariat have been denationalised not by English influence or English rule but by the operation of an industrial system conducted on a basis of individualism ... they are the results of a general process which no national frontiers could have shut out.[99]

The response should be to abolish capitalism; against this the question of political independence was trivial:

A hundred years of Socialism would do more to restore Scotland to health and weld it into a real nation than a thousand years ... of Nationalist government ... Scotland freed from capitalism would be a nation, but it would not care very much whether it was called a nation or not.[100]

Muir had once been a member of the Glasgow ILP.[101] The terms of his choice reflected the characteristic Scottish Labour position of the thirties.

Until the Popular Front period, Scottish Communists returned a blank on the National Question.[102] Scottish contingents participated in 'national' hunger marches to London. At the end of Lewis Grassic Gibbon's trilogy, *A Scots Quair*, the young Communist Ewan Tavendale leaves 'Duncairn' on such a march:

the windy five hundred miles to London ... the EC had given its instructions for Ewan and intended keeping him down there in London as a new organiser, right in the thick.[103]

Right in the thick – that was one attraction that had appealed to the new Clydeside Labour MPs in November 1922.

Part III

John Wheatley

Chapter 1

Roots

Wheatley's politics defy simple categorisation through a conventional label or a compelling image. This elusiveness was experienced by several contemporaries who found him enigmatic. Egon Wertheimer, the German Socialist was so often an acute observer of that generation of Labour politicians, but his characterisation of Wheatley was superficial. He presented him as the antithesis of a passionate Socialist rhetorician; certainly Wheatley displayed 'fanaticism' but this came:

> not from the warmth of his heart, but from the ice of his brain ... when he speaks, he often gives the impression of an automaton, mechanically developing his argument, inhibited by no trace of human weakness ... unpopular and mistrusted even by his closest friends ... a rootless Radical.[1]

The image of a cold aloof intellectual was misleading. Beneath an austere facade Wheatley apparently had a warm personality, hidden from all but a few by a deep reserve. When he retailed the harsh details of working-class poverty, his political statements became charged with emotion. This was especially true when he wrote of the mining industry where analysis was informed by his own experiences.[2] But more significantly Wertheimer's portrait failed to recognise the sharpness of Wheatley's intellect. His responses to the economic problems of the 1920s contained little that was conventional amongst Labour parliamentarians. Significantly it was Sir Oswald Mosley, often feted with hindsight as a creative thinker on these same issues who claimed a parallel retrospective significance for Wheatley: 'the only man of Lenin quality the English (sic) Left has ever produced'.[3]

In at least one respect Mosley had it badly wrong; Wheatley was emphatically not a product of the *English* Left. Equally, Wertheimer was adrift in describing him as a 'rootless Radical'. This judgement ignored the richness and the complexity of the national, cultural and class experiences that informed Wheatley's politcal development.[4] They helped to move him from Glaswegian Irish politics through the Catholic Socialist Society and the ILP into the Glasgow Council Chamber, then to the House of Commons and into the Cabinet. The sequence reads like a synopsis for one of those Labour autobiographies produced by several of Wheatley's contemporaries: provisional title 'From Coalface to Cabinet'. But in his case, Ministerial office was not the end. Wheatley then shifted to the position of left-wing critic. As such this can provide a significant Socialist biography in which rectitude triumphs over the lure of office. Yet this development had a nationalist complement. Although he quit the United Irish League for Labour and Socialist politics, Wheatley relinquished neither his Irish identity nor his Catholicism. Yet by the 1920s he saw the British State as the decisive instrument for Socialist politics; the prime beneficiary should be the British working class. Exploration of this combination of socialism and nationalism requires an initial understanding of Wheatley's attempt to move to Socialism without abandoning national and religious commitments.

His responses and his difficulties articulated the more general predicament of young working-class Irish Catholics in late Victorian Scotland.[5] How could their national and religious identities be related to a developing awareness of their class position? The former were expressed through religious cultural and political institutions that were formally separate but which often merged together in practice. These could provide a sense of identity and some hope of mutual protection in an environment that was sometimes hostile and always uncertain. The consequential cohesion could blur class differences within the Irish–Catholic community; electors should vote in the interests of Ireland, or in local elections to safeguard the educational concerns of the Church. But against this complex of communal institutions with their attendant priorities, there were counterposed the experiences of the Catholic–Irish worker, in the pit, as a railway ganger, on the docks, or as a council labourer. Some elements of industrial experience could strengthen communal identity, since it was painfully clear that Irish–Catholics had difficulty in entering the more skilled, more secure, better paid trades.[6] But equally, the vast majority of Irish–Catholics in Scotland were working class. Despite the contributions of ethnic and religious prejudices to divisions within this class, industrial experiences provided some basis for common action with other Scottish workers. An initial concern with trade unionism could carry political implications; by 1900, these were likely to have an Independent Labour or even a Socialist character. At that point, for the active minority the tensions between communal and class loyalties could become acute.

The difficulty was compounded because of the international character of the Catholic Church.[7] Alongside its role as a badge of Irish identity, its doctrinal responses were influenced by political events on the Continent. There, the Church had been often aligned with Conservatives against the forces of Liberalism, let alone those of socialism. From 1903, the Papacy was occupied by the highly conservative Pius X; he offered no new guidance on such issues. Instead the benchmarks were provided by his predecessor, the relatively liberal Leo XIII. In particular, his 1891 Encyclical *Rerum Novarum* was an inevitable reference point for

Catholics who attempted to argue for the acceptability of Socialism.[8] This had attempted to salvage something from the dominant equation of Catholicism with reaction by distinguishing between Socialism and social reform. The latter was deemed acceptable; but the former was identified with anti-clericalism, the abolition of private property and revolution. Simplisitic images of Continental Socialism were dominant, but this left British Catholics free to appeal to the distinctive tradition of British Socialism, as gradualist, legal and specifically concerned with economics. It was a Catholic counterpart to the claims made by the leaders of the ILP that Britain was equipped to follow a privileged peaceful evolutionary path to Socialism. Already it is possible to see some of the factors that led Wheatley to choose the ILP as a political instrument.

He came to this organisation from a political apprenticeship in conventional Nationalism. Already he was developing the organisational skills that he would bring to Glasgow Labour politics. He served as President of the United Irish League's Shettleston Branch; by May 1903 this claimed one of the highest memberships in Britain.[9] His Nationalism was turned to predictable purposes including the mobilisation of the Irish vote for the 1900 Election. Part of the exercise involved ascertaining that the Liberal candidate was sound on Home Rule.[10] Branch organisation was employed to celebrate those anniversaries that helped to strengthen a particular view of Irish identity. In 1903, the Shettleston Branch commemorated the centenary of Robert Emmet's execution with a march. All UIL members wore green rosettes; Wheatley was one of the marshalls.[11] In his *Labour in Irish History*, Connolly would commend Emmet as a Nationalist whom Irish Socialists should honour. But Wheatley in his UIL years seems to have made no discrimination between politically-acceptable and -unacceptable patriots; his Nationalism was uncomplicated.

Yet the complexities of Radical politics in Western Scotland could help to erode the conventional relationship between Nationalists and Liberals. If individual Liberal candidates distanced themselves from any commitment to Home Rule, then the UIL might look more favourably at Labour candidates. One such instance came in September 1901 when the League supported Robert Smillie rather than an unsympathetic Liberal at the North-East Lanark by-election. As a principled Socialist, Connolly had deplored the alliance between Labour and the capitalist United Irish League, but for a working-class Nationalist such as Wheatley, such a tactical arrangement might have a radicalising significance. Once again in January 1906, he supported the Labour candidate in North West Lanark, rather than his Liberal opponent. Of itself, this once again reflected UIL policy. Joseph Sullivan of the Scottish Miners was a Catholic; the Liberal was equivocal on Home Rule.[12] But for Wheatley electoral support for Labour was followed rapidly by an explicit attempt to reconcile the pressures of community and class. He declared himself a Socialist and claimed the compatability of this with his Catholicism.[13]

Although Wheatley and Connolly both encountered this problem, they came equipped with divergent experiences and different priorities. Behind their contrasting responses to sporadic deals between Labour and the United Irish League lay the legacies of their political apprenticeships. Connolly had been schooled as a Socialist and had then encountered the Nationalist challenge in Dublin. Thus he applied demanding Socialist criteria to any alliance between Labour and an Irish organisation that he dismissed as reactionary. In contrast, such electoral arrangements provided one of the incentives that led Wheatley to look towards the Labour Movement as a means of improving the conditions of the Irish working class. Differing ideological preoccupations were paralleled by their very different experiences. Connolly's life was scarred by poverty and marked by wanderings. Typically, his involvement was much more in a network of Socialists, than in the often self-sufficient world of Irish institutions. But Wheatley explored the political tensions within Clydeside politics, attempting to maintain a position in both Catholic and Socialist communities.

His attempt at reconciling conventionally divergent claims acquired institutional form in October 1906 when he chaired the inaugural meeting of the Catholic Socialist Society. He argued that far from being incompatible the doctrines could benefit from one another:

It was only after a Catholic understood and believed in Socialism that he saw the real meaning and beauty of Catholic doctrines ... In this organisation they would have Socialism preached in an atmosphere free from any irreligious taint.[14]

Judged by its membership figures the CSS was a marginal group. Its Glasgow membership never exceeded one hundred and attempts to form durable branches elsewhere had little success. Its activities conformed with those of other Edwardian Socialist groups; indoor meetings on Winter Sundays, tea parties and Summer outings.[15] Yet the Society made its mark on the Glasgow left. Its activities were reported regularly in *Forward*. The hostile responses of some priests produced polemical exchanges. Some of this was in pamphlet form: most notably Wheatley's *The Catholic Working Man* published in 1909;[16] but there were also long-running debates in the Catholic *Glasgow Observer*. The most celebrated was an exchange between Wheatley and the Belgian priest Father Puissant. This attracted considerable attention in Scottish Catholic circles during the Summer and Autumn of 1907.[17] The controversy persuaded at least one other Catholic to begin his shift towards Socialism:

I read the debate ... avidly. It went on for months ... The priest actually wasn't a match for him, but he was a Belgian and claimed that he knew more about continental socialism than Wheatley. Wheatley made mince-meat of him, but all the letters said the opposite, and I became very annoyed about it ... I started being convinced by Wheatley's arguments, even though I wasn't a socialist ...[18]

The most thorough presentation of Wheatley's position can be found in his pamphlet *The Catholic Working Man*. The text demonstrated the need to combat both Irish and Catholic objections and was preceded by a brief statement of the Catholic Socialist Society's position. This included two features that were central to Wheatley's argument. The definition of socialism was narrowly economic:

public Ownership of Land and Capital. This does not mean the abolition of all private property.

Such a claim could hopefully circumvent the Papal prohibition in *Rerum Novarum*; it also fitted in with the dominant approach within the British Labour Movement. Narrow definition was followed by a specific political recommendation:

The Society is in hearty agreement and cooperates with the Independent Labour Party.[19]

The pamphlet opened with a characterisation of capitalism, typical of Edwardian ILP propagandists. Britain was a grotesquely unequal society. The few were unable to usefully consume the whole of their income; the many experienced poverty and the fear or actuality of unemployment. The capitalists' increasing utilisation of trusts demonstrated that they at least appreciated the redundancy of the competitive principle.[20]

Despite this bleak portrait, Wheatley, like other ILP contemporaries, believed that powerful forces were promoting Socialism. The very development of capitalism was conducive: the move away from competition, increasing mechanisation, the dependence on co-operation in the productive process:

Now that by increased power and cooperation in labour, we can compel the earth to yield us plenty, there is no necessity for any scramble. Cooperation in the distribution of wealth which we collectively produce wil be the final blow to that system which makes every man his brother's enemy.[21]

This optimism echoed that of Ramsay MacDonald declaring in that same year 1909 that it was 'a Springtime of Society'.[22] Despite such fundamental optimism, Wheatley's Irish Catholicism meant that his belief in Socialist evolution had to be placed against the problems posed by nationality and religion.

In terms shared by Connolly, he presented the Irish 'nation' not simply as the object of British oppression, but as the victim of 'native landlordism and the rule of British Capitalists'.[23] The state of many of the

Irish in Britain was appalling.[24] Wheatley emphasised that this was not a unique example. Irish migrants were equally victims of capitalism in the United States.[25] Whilst it seemed unlikely that such experiences would promote acquiescence in existing society. Wheatley acknowledged that as yet Irish workers showed only limited signs of industrial radicalism. His optimistic expectation was that any of them who understood Socialism would support it – but there were two major obstacles:

In the mind of the non-Socialist Irishman there are two strong reasons for his remaining outside the Socialist movement. Firstly, he considers that his political duty is to gain Home Rule for Ireland; and secondly that Catholics may not support Socialism.[26]

Discussion of the political blockage began by examining changes in Ireland since Gladstone first adopted the Home Rule policy. Certainly Wheatley did not regard the Irish as a harmonious community unaffected by economic conflicts; he considered the position of the farmers to have been transformed by Government policy, but the condition of the rural labourers remained bleak.[27] The heart of his analysis concerned the British interest in Ireland; at this point his argument became crudely reductionist. Wheatley claimed that all British Governments were hostile to Home Rule and that such opposition must reflect the economic benefits of the Union. These preferences reflected the interests of the Few, since popular impact on Government policy remained slight despite the widening of the franchise:

you do not eliminate slavery from the minds of people the moment you loosen their chains ...[28]

Thus, the exising Party system institutionalised an artificial conflict:

For strategical reasons, the wealthy people – landlords and capitalists – are divided into two parties called Liberal and Tory. The Leaders of both are determined to uphold the present system ...[29]

But a radical change was in prospect:

To-day, this inherited servility is passing away and, in proportion as it disappears, we have Labour representation in the Government of the country.[30]

Labour would have no reason to block Home Rule:

The Socialist or Labour party will have nothing to gain by ruling Ireland. They will come into power to destroy rent, profit and interest. Profit being abolished, English Government of Ireland could no longer be a paying business.[31]

Wheatley's insistence that Socialism was concerned only with economic issues appeared to leave room for a variety of opinions in other areas; but in this instance he was prepared to reduce a conflict concerned with nationality and institutional forms into simplistic economic terms.

His characterisation of the Tory–Liberal conflict as essentially diversionary hardly fitted the bitter exchanges of 1912–14 when Home Rule served as a symbol for tensions that went far beyond the economic. Typically for his Socialist generation, Wheatley's argument paid no attention to the ideological ramifications of the issue – the degree to which in Britain, it could be presented as a question of national identity or of imperial virility. Equally, it failed to consider whether a Labour movement formed in the same national culture would be wholly exempt from such sentiments. Wheatley's crudely mechanistic analysis of the essential harmony between Home Rule and Labour politics demonstrated the characteristic myopia of Second International Socialists towards the tenacious grip of national identities. This limitation facilitated acceptance of an optimistic gradualism in which the anticipated dominance of class politics would make such controversies redundant.

When Wheatley turned to a consideration of the plight of the Irish working class in Britain, his recommendation of a Socialist response had to face the question of clerical antagonism. Once again his argument indicated how far his basic position was typical of an orthodox ILP member. Socialism was presented almost as uncontroversial. The key technique was public ownership of the means of production and distribution; the strategy assumed that existing political institutions would be effective as instruments for such a transformation:

the first important step ... is the return of Members to Parliament and to our administrative bodies who are in favour of it.

This presentation should exorcise the spectres employed by opponents:

It is not confiscation nor robbery nor the destruction of family life ... It is simply a scheme to abolish poverty.[32]

If properly understood, it should not arouse the opposition of the Catholic Church, not least since the underlying principles had been applied already. At this point, Wheatley's evolutionary case achieved a thorough presentation:

If the Catholic clergy were to prohibit Catholics from supporting British Socialism, they would commit themselves to a policy more reactionary than is advocated by the most extreme Conservative cranks. Every Socialist principle has been already accepted in British legislation.[33]

The same point – and what should be in Catholic terms a decisive contrast – had been made by Wheatley in his very first Socialist intervention:

it was the duty of Catholics to oppose the revolutionary confiscatory anti-religious methods of the early, modern Continental Socialists. But ... the methods and aims of the legal evolutionary Socialism of Great Britain do not merit opposition ... Socialism in Great Britain means the substitution of the public – the municipality or the State-ownership for private ownership.[34]

Wheatley's case that Catholics should support Socialism was not just a matter of working with the apparent grain of historical developments. Christian principles could not be realised under capitalism. Education would facilitate the decisive confrontation: 'Are you for or against poverty?'[35] Socialist developments were not only compatible with traditional Catholic principles; Wheatley argued that they would actually permit their more complete realisation. When he defended his views in a debate with Hilaire Belloc in November 1909, he claimed that state and municipal ownership would end poverty and allow a flowering of family life. His presentation suggested that he had been wholly untouched by contemporary arguments about the place of women:

people would have what they miss most now – security in life ... And the men would work, while the children were being educated and the mothers attended to their homes.[36]

Sentiments such as these demonstrated how far Wheatley remained influenced by orthodox Catholic social doctrines. His writings bear evidence of an acquaintance with Francesco Nitti's, *Catholic Socialism*, the work of a Neapolitan professor available in English translation from 1895.[37] Its influence could be seen in a claim voiced also by Connolly that historically Catholicism was a collectivist doctrine; capitalist individualism was a Protestant sentiment.[38] Despite such arguments and despite his continuing involvement in religious practices, Wheatley secured at best a grudging acceptance from his Church. Although he was ready to quote Archbishop Maguire of Glasgow in support of his views, in fact the latter seems to have had little sympathy. In private a Diocesan Committee on Socialism referred to Wheatley as 'a malcontent Catholic'.[39] More dramatic manifestation of orthodox hostility came in July 1912 when a crowd encouraged by an anti-Socialist sermon met outside Wheatley's house to burn his effigy. Yet in Glasgow such a clash was a-typical; the clergy like Wheatley had to respond to diverse pressures – the close identity of Catholicism with Irish Nationalism, the thorough anti-Socialism of Continental missionary priests, but also the need to retain the loyalty of congregations who were predominantly working class.[40]

Wheatley's shift to Socialism lacked any acquaintance with Marxism. The decisive text seems to have been Robert Blatchford's *Britain for the British* which he referred to in 1906 as 'the "text-book" of Socialism'.[41] The contrast with John Maclean who had begun with Blatchford, but then moved onto Marxism was fundamental. This was apparent on one occasion when Maclean spoke to the Catholic Socialist Society on historical materialism:

Wheatley tapped him and explained that this was a catholic audience. John said that he had given this talk to protestant audiences and if they didn't want it he would go away.[42]

The ex-Calvinist Marxist and the Catholic ILPer had little in common.

In the years before 1914, the Glasgow ILP grew in influence, and Wheatley occupied an increasingly significant place within it. His advocacy of this organisation as the appropriate vehicle for Irish working-class aspirations led to a position that was resolutely anti-sectarian. Catholic values and Irish issues might be important but a commitment to Labour meant an involvement in the struggles of a wider working-class body. It was such an appeal that had initiated his controversy with Father Puissant:

Your interests and those of your fellow Protestant workers are identical. Your enemies are their enemies. Workers of every race and creed must unite. When you capture Parliament and the local Councils, you will be in a position to raise yourselves. This can only be done by building up in these bodies a strong Labour Party.[43]

The arguments against such a strategy were weaker in municipal contests where the claim that Liberals should be supported to advance Home Rule, was irrelevant. Significantly in this instance, the *Glasgow Observer* agreed with Wheatley's contention:

in Municipal elections where the devotion to the Catholic cause or the cause of Ireland leaves them a free hand ... the Irish electors ... ought to vote Labour.[44]

There is evidence of some shift in Catholic working-class voting loyalties at the municipal level, although in parliamentary contests traditional sentiments were strengthened perhaps by the expectation of a decisive clash over Home Rule. In November 1910, Wheatley was elected to the Lanarkshire County Council; two years later with the extension of the City boundaries, he entered the Glasgow Council where Labour had a nucleus of twelve councillors.

The growth of Labour's municipal representation was paralleled by the slow formation of a Glasgow Labour Party equipped with its own municipal programme. This development occurred in a distinctive environment. Working class living conditions were often appalling, but the extent of municipalisation was unusual – water, gas, electricity, lighting and tramways. These achievements perhaps influenced Wheatley's sanguine expectations about the inevitability of gradualism, but they provided a strategic problem for Labour councillors. Nevertheless, from about 1910, the Glasgow ILP began to provide a more effective challenge, not least because of a highly talented leadership including Wheatley, James Maxton and Tom Johnston. The plausibility of a strategy for municipal socialism left little scope for the appeal of Direct Action. The strategic implications of the pre-War industrial struggles left relatively little mark on the Glasgow ILP.[45]

Wheatley applied his gradualist perspective to the housing crisis. In 1914, he produced a pamphlet, *Eight Pound Cottages for Glasgow*

Citizens, arguing that decent working-class housing could be provided at low rents using the profits of the municipal tramways. Municipalisation in one area could provide the basis for a further improvement in standards. The proposal met with obstruction in the Council, and eventually the Town Clerk's ruling that the proposal involved an illegality. Despite such obstacles, and the fact that Labour remained firmly in the minority on the Council,[46] Wheatley remained optimistic about the prospects for Socialism In One City. Early in 1915, he presented the vision of a Socialist Glasgow based on better housing, clean air, improved education and the reconstruction of the city through municipal programmes. Already Wheatley was demonstrating an awareness of the problem of overseas trade. A Socialist city would have to exchange goods with the outside world. The municipality would have to set up departments for home and foreign trade; these could give preference to other Socialist cities.[47] Perhaps there was a hint that any community developing a Socialist character would have to manage its external relationships carefully, otherwise any Socialist achievements could be destroyed. Yet the feasibility of such achievements within one city remained an open question. As yet the lack of progress in Glasgow could be attributed to the absence of a Labour majority, but such an explanation ignored the complex challenges raised by an attempt to establish a Socialist city within a capitalist environment.

Inevitably the outbreak of War forced Wheatley to consider wider issues. He rapidly expressed his opposition to British involvement but generally focussed on the need for specific material responses to working-class difficulties. Thus, he urged the nationalisation of food supply industries.[48] His position was characteristic of many British Labour leaders who sought harmony on specific problems in order to avoid divisive discussions on the principle of British involvement. But inevitably, Wheatley's wartime politics were marked by the distinctive and complex events within Glasgow. He was a significant participant in the Rent agitations of 1915. Already an acknowledged expert on housing, his Shettleston base became one of the centres of the protest. The blend of patriotic and anti-authority sentiments epitomised the wartime position of the Glasgow ILP. It was relatively easy for Wheatley to combine agitation in the community with a campaign inside the City Council.[49]

His involvement in the activities of the Clyde Workers' Committee was more equivocal. Unlike his Council colleagues, he advised the Shop Stewards on tactics, but in particular he influenced David Kirkwood, a member of the ILP and eventually a key figure in the collapse of the CWC's opposition to dilution.[50] Even the politically hostile Gallacher retrospectively acknowledged Wheatley's role:

He was the only one of the outstanding Labour Leaders who participated in any way in our activities, always of course from the outside. But if he ever was wanted for advice, encouragement or help of any kind, his services were at our disposal day or night.[51]

Such services demonstrated Wheatley's sympathy for those who were ready to stand out against State coercion. They did not represent support for the political priorities of many CWC leaders. He remained committed to the ILP's strategy for Socialism. By the last two years of the War, this choice seemed to be producing some results. After the deportations and gaolings of Spring 1916, the Party clearly dominated the Glasgow Left. Support had been mobilised through the Rent Campaign; however much leading members disagreed over the legitimacy of the War and the proper degree of resistance to it, they could unite in campaigns for better housing and against conscription. In 1917, and in 1918, the membership of the Glasgow ILP showed a significant growth.[52] This organisational development proved to have much more relevance than the increased prominence of Clydeside Marxists such as Maclean and the SLP Shop Stewards' activists. Yet their activities were a challenge to the ILP. Wartime confrontations and punitive responses by the State had publicised their ideas. Early accounts of the Bolshevik Revolution placed revolutionary sentiments back on the political agenda. Often the content and significance might be obscure, but in such a climate Socialist assessments of what was feasible and desirable could change rapidly. Despite their expanding influence, the leaders of the Glasgow ILP could find themselves under pressure, as Party members responded to revolutionary sentiments.

Wheatley reacted to this situation of organisational optimism and ideological uncertainty by a considered statement of his evolutionary socialist position. This was presented early in 1918, in a series of *Forward* articles. The continuities with his pre-War position were considerable, but wartime experiences and challenges left their marks. The basic theme of his case was that Socialists had to capture control of conventional political institutions; it was there that the decisive battle would be waged.

He began by opposing those who relied on organisation in the workshop and so dismissed political action as a waste of time.[53] There had been a time when the workshop was 'the seat of exploitation' but more recently exploitation of the consumer had become the more significant. The cause lay in the development of the American food trusts. Initially the impact on food prices was barely noticed, but wartime inflation had changed this:

The employer continues, of course, to exploit the worker, but he is hopelessly outpaced by the food merchant. All or nearly all, the increased exploitation of the past three years has been *outside* the workshops, and all the agitations inside have been for war wages and war bonuses to meet this.

Wheatley therefore saw control of food supplies as essential to any Socialist project. This would include a transfer of resources from destructive to constructive tasks: 'the gunmakers and shellmakers shall become producers of food'. One necessary step integrated a traditional Scottish Radical sentiment into an evolutionary Socialist outlook:

This transformation ... requires the abolition of private landlordism, and this can be accomplished by an Act passed by a Socialist Labour Party.

For Wheatley, the crucial arena for Socialist initiatives was ceasing to be the Council Chamber and becoming the nation-state. Alongside the specific problem, he made two more general claims that would come to occupy central places in his politics.

Already he was querying the benefits of unregulated Free Trade – at least in food:

Whatever portion we must import can best be dealt with also by political action. It should be purchased by national and not by trading or sectional representatives.

The focus on national policies raised the problem of uneven development and led Wheatley to consider the attraction of a specifically British Socialism:

Must we wait until a perfect industrial organisation in Parkhead is linked up not only with every union of workers in Britain, but with perfect industrial organisations in India, China and Africa? And meantime, are we to rejoice in our accumulating misery and reject paltry palliatives?[54]

The implications of these questions would be developed in subsequent writings; they would then encounter internationalist opposition within the ILP. But in 1918, Wheatley having rhetorically raised the question moved on to a defence of the ILP's political strategy.

This involved a justification of the ILP's decision to work together with the unions in a Labour Alliance. The strategy had required tolerance, but was based on a compelling vision:

a powerful Labour movement guided by Socialist principles and using both political and industrial weapons.[55]

Since 1906 this had come closer to realisation as more unions had effectively accepted the ILP programme. Yet for Wheatley such progress was flawed by a crucial equivocation. Certainly he saw any successful Socialist strategy as involving a revolutionary transformation; but the proper method often remained wrapped in ambiguity. He presented the choice dichotomously; on the one side, 'by the force of arms and bloodshed, if necessary', and on the other 'to rely ... on reason and constitutional methods'.

Despite the dramatic changes that the War had wrought on the expectations of many Socialists, Wheatley remained committed to his pre-War position:

... I am opposed to the use of armed force in the establishment of Socialism in this country because I regard it as immoral and impracticable.

The question of principle was presented partly as a question of democracy contrasted with elitism:

What right have we as Socialists, to impose our views by force on the majority of our fellow-citizens?

Wheatley also echoed a criticism that Francis Sheehy-Skeffington had made when considering Thomas MacDonagh's resort to force as a means of national emancipation. Methods that utilised violence had a fundamental exclusiveness that would affect the quality of whatever was achieved:

Are women to be deprived of all share in the shaping of a new society?

These objections appeared even more starkly since franchise reform had just removed a major obstacle to an evolutionary strategy:

The workers may, if they desire, have during the present year, a Socialist Labour Government.

This option would provide a democratic, and so Wheatley implied, an effective answer to any capitalist resistance:

Should the capitalists of this country challenge its decisions, then this Government would have on its side, not only right, but the majority of the people.[56]

Quite apart from matters of morality and the feasibility of an alternative, he suggested that any armed revolution would be doomed to failure. So long as capitalists held political power, revolts would be quixotic. Strategies founded on industrial action alone would be sterile:

The workers ... control nothing but their labour. This they may withold but only for a very limited period, as Capitalism from the moment they 'down tools' subjects them and their families to starvation.[57]

In contrast to the syndicalists he held political power to be decisive. Connolly had once dismissed the struggle for control of conventional political institutions as 'only the echo of the real battle'. But for Wheatley it was in these institutions that the decisive conflicts would be waged; all else would be a tragic diversion of energies leading to heroic but meaningless defeats:

... this idea of emancipation from Capitalism by a bloody revolution, while Capitalists hold political power is the very wildest dream, the propagation of which can only benefit Capitalism by distracting the minds of our youth from the vulnerable spot in the enemy stronghold and leading them to Featherstone or Tonypandy.

The analysis was not the work of someone who opposed all force as an absolute principle. Although his argument suggested that he saw little hope for a Socialist movement that found itself compelled to use violence, he clearly supported such a tactic against an illiberal regime:

I would have regarded armed revolt against the Government of the Czar as a sacred obligation.[58]

More broadly, he was ready to see force used in an attempt to prevent the invasion of fundamental liberal principles. But crucially he continued to see the situation of British Socialists as relatively advantaged. There was the possibility of a peaceful evolution towards Socialism founded on consent; this should be pursued.[59]

Wheatley might have proclaimed that the extension of the franchise had opened the way for 'a Socialist Labour Government', but the December 1918 Election provided a rapid riposte to easy optimism. Wheatley was expected by many to be the Member for the new Shettleston seat, but he was defeated by 74 votes. Nevertheless, the Labour cause in Glasgow gained support in the succeeding years. Industrial defeat and depression, the continuing importance of housing conditions and rent levels, and the mass transfer of Irish working-class electors all played their parts. Both the Irish and the housing elements highlighted themes that had concerned Wheatley before 1914. He continued to argue that Glasgow's housing crisis could not be settled within a capitalist frame-work. There was no way that working-class tenants could pay an economic rental.[60] Wartime and post-War experiences indicated that no purely municipal solution seemed feasible. A 'Socialist' housing policy required control of the national Government.[61]

The prospects for Labour in Glasgow parliamentary elections were enhanced by the shift of Irish voters to Labour. Wheatley's own reaction to Irish developments from the Easter Rising to the end of the War of Independence was discriminating. He condemned the executions of May 1916, but continued to express conventional Socialist reservations about Sinn Fein's brand of nationalism. Nevertheless, he shared in the general Labour opposition to British policy from 1919 onwards and participated in Glasgow meetings which blended labour and nationalist themes. His attachment to a Catholic characterisation of Irish Nationality was revealed perhaps in his thorough opposition to Partition.[62]

Wheatley thus maintained his Irish Socialist identity and in the 1924 Election, he was to be the victim of viciously xenophobic attacks by his Conservative opponent; but he was now committed to activity within the British political arena. What mattered there was an effective Labour Party dedicated to Socialist principles. By 1922, the judgement was shared by many of Glasgow's working-class Catholics. It helped to ensure the return of ten Labour Members, including Wheatley. His evolutionary socialism remained optimistic despite the industrial setbacks of the immediate post-War years. As yet he had not encountered the limitations of Labour's parliamentary Leadership; like many of his ILP contemporaries he had a naive view of the constraints faced even by a cautious Labour Government; his earlier comments had hinted at but had not explored the problems of seeking to develop Socialist priorities in one society. In November 1922, Wheatley appeared as a conventional ILP figure sanguine about the chances of constructing 'British Socialism', now this outlook would be put to the test.

Chapter 2

Labour and the nation

The demonstration that signalled the departure of the Clydeside Labour Members for London was a dramatic manifestation of a much wider optimism. An appreciation of this broader context is essential for an understanding of Wheatley's subsequent political development. The November 1922 Election established the Labour Party as a much more credible parliamentary force with strongholds in Central Scotland, parts of Northern England and South Wales. Such electoral successes inevitably raised hopes of further growth. Facts and dreams combined to marginalise alternative strategies for socialism.

Earlier events had produced some marginalisation and had boosted Labour support. The predicament faced by John Maclean in his last years highlighted crucial features. The Irish controversy now seemed a relatively minor question for the British Left. This was reflected not just in Labour's equation of socialism with economic and social improvements but also in the increasing readiness of Irish electors in Britain to support Labour candidates. If the Party's credibility was heightened by the diminishing political relevance of communal priorities, it was boosted further by depression in traditional industries. Unemployed miners and engineers could swell Labour's electoral base; so could those who remained in work, but who faced short-time working and attacks on wage levels. Such pressures eroded the plausibility of radical industrial initiatives. Engineers' shop-stewards' movements and miners' unofficial Reform Committees had offered some hope of progress through 'Direct Action'. But such workers' resources and self-confidence were weakened by depression. Leaders were victimised. The pursuit of a parliamentary majority for the Labour Party could appear as a credible alternative.[1]

Certainly, Labour's electoral achievement in November 1922 was the gateway to a spectacular advance, not in electoral support, but rather in the feasibility of a Labour Government. Conservative and Liberal divisions and the vagaries of three-party competition under a first-past-the-post electoral system contributed much towards the formation of a Labour Government in January 1924; nevertheless the fact of such a Government propelled the question of its desirability to the centre of political argument. Nothing demonstrated this more sharply than the style of the Conservative's 1924 election campaign. Whilst the Zinoviev Letter might be stigmatised by Labour politicians as a fraud, it was also

evidence that their Party had arrived and must be taken seriously. Even
with the cacophony of this Red Scare, Labour's total vote grew by more
than a million. Sceptics could note that the Party were running ninety
more candidates than in December 1923, but such an increase was a
sign of future ambitions. Despite the early loss of office, it was the
apparent signs of inexorable Labour advance that seemed often to be more
significant.[2]

Achievements and hopes could strengthen the appeal of electoral
politics pursued through the Labour Party: ballot box, parliament and
council chamber, political control over Whitehall and local administration. Wheatley's chosen political instrument was the Independent
Labour Party; his defence of its approach has been analysed. The dominant
Labour strategy in the 1920s was compatible with the assumptions on
which the ILP had been developed. But there was not a simple, uncon-
tested continuity. We have seen how the experiences of some Socialists
produced scepticism about electoral and parliamentary strategies.
Connolly had expressed themes central to the syndicalist critique of the
dominant outlook: the centrality of workers' power at the point of production, the need for some rank and file response to the oligarchic tendencies of trade union and party leaders; the linking of such irresponsibility
to deradicalisation. Such arguments connected with the optimistic
conclusion that the innate radicalism of the rank and file could be given
effective and durable organisational form. Depression and industrial
defeat promoted a more sombre verdict.

The legacy of the Russian Revolution was also crucial. The emergence
of the Communist Party as the vehicle for those who rejected the cautious
reformism of the Labour Party provided a political home for several who
had advocated a syndicalist response. They became increasingly aware
of Third International orthodoxy on the role of the Party. Whilst there
were often continuities of location and personnel between enthusiasm
for 'Direct Action' and support for the Communist Party, these masked
decisive changes of principle and of practice. Although the isolation of
the Soviet Union enhanced the plausibility of Russian orthodoxy in the
eyes of the committed, British Communist support remained meagre.
The confrontations of 1926 led to a temporary expansion, but ultimately
the events of that year served to weaken the Left beyond the Labour Party
still further.[3] The lingering appeal of 'Direct Action' seemed to have
been exorcised. As Idris Davies, the poet from the Rhymney expressed it:

Do you remember 1926? The great dream and the swift disaster ...[4]

The consequence of these developments was that by the late 1920s
the British Left was dominated industrially and politically by a sizeable
and hopeful Labour Party that combined appeals to class and to nation.
It was regarded widely as an innovative force but acted typically with

an anxious concern for established procedures and policies. From November 1922 to August 1931, Labour was symbolised for many by its Leader, Ramsay MacDonald. This was obscured subsequently by vilification of those who became members of the National Government. Yet in the 1929 General Election one eventual critic made a rather different judgement:

> Outstanding is the affection of the working classes for Mr MacDonald and Mr Snowden. I have met it everywhere; they are clarion names. They represent for the workers the triumph of character and ability over circumstance, and the confidence in them of humble men and women is a tremendous responsibility to bear.[5]

Such sentiments were a significant aspect of Labour's vitality during those years of optimism. Whatever political space remained on the Left was occupied by the Communist Party, small, increasingly locked in to the decisions of the International and by the end of the decade, formally, and often effectively, committed to the sectarianism of the 'Class Against Class' period. Yet despite its weaknesses and failures, as John Maclean discovered, the Party could secure the loyalty of a significant number of trade union and unemployed activists.

Almost everything else had been squeezed out. This narrowing of the British Left did not just involve a marginalisation of alternative strategies; it also involved an assumption typically tacit but sometimes overt, that the task for Socialists should be to work through the British State with the goal of achieving Socialism on an all-British basis. Equally the Communist Party accepted that Britain should define the scope of the Party's activities. The two organisations Labour and Communist disagreed vehemently about so much, but they accepted that the road to Socialism should be a British one.

For Labour, such a belief seemed to be supported by the prevalent assessment of the Party's electoral prospects. Already there were strongholds in industrial areas. There seemed no obstacle to the development of equivalent support elsewhere leading firstly to a majority of seats, then to a majority of voters and thereby the basis for a transition to socialism. Such an assessment of electoral prospects was naive in the extreme. It was a projection, not just of an old hope that the future lay with Progressive politics, but of the belief that occupational and cultural diversities would be irrelevant when measured against a growing recognition that Labour was the best promoter of the public interest. Whilst the Party's electoral performance in the 1920s might seem superficially to signpost such a forward march, in fact the record was very uneven. Labour strengthened its position in many areas of traditional industry, often where a relatively well-established trade unionism was confronted by depression, but it remained very weak in many rural, small-town and suburban areas. The 1929 result could strengthen the optimism of the faithful who focussed on the twenty seats needed for an overall majority. But some of the growth in seats was attributable to the electoral system and in some places Labour was weaker in 1929 than it had been in 1922.

Even before the crisis of 1931, hopes of a steady electoral progression towards Socialism on an all-British basis were naive. But quite apart from this misleading electoral position, Labour's strategy for a Socialist Britain raised its own problems. In its 1918 programme, *Labour and the New Social Order*, the Party had committed itself to a collectivist road forward through welfare reforms and public ownership. This was supplemented in 1928 by *Labour and the Nation*. The title was revealing – the dearth of references to socialism and class, the claim that Labour was a national party. Moreover, the title implied that there was one nation, Britain, that was the appropriate forum for action. The document itself was a lengthy, moralistic argument for parliamentary socialism with sixty-five proposals and an abundance of rhetoric. Hoping, in traditional radical style, to unite all industrious people against the few parasites, it advocated the public ownership of basic utilities, taxation reform, a reduction in arms spending and improvements in social services. Such predictable proposals were supplemented by a commitment to a reduction in unemployment. In 1929, Labour sloganised: 'The Works are Closed! but the Ballot Box is Open'.[6] It was a succinct statement of the economic decay and the political response that had marked Labour's growth over the previous decade.

Superficially, the appeal might be contrasted with the prevalence of orthodox economic remedies. In 1921, the collapse of the post-War boom had resulted in unemployment reaching nineteen per cent; during the rest of the decade, it settled at around ten per cent. This 'intractable million' were concentrated heavily in the traditional exporting sectors: coal, engineering, shipbuilding and textiles. Many politicians and economists claimed that dislocations in trading and financial relationships were responsible. The appropriate policy therefore should be a return to the pre-1914 world, whatever the short-term costs. Thus Britain reverted to the Gold Standard in 1925; the consequence was not prosperity but further deflation. 'The Economic Consequences of Mr Churchill' included the 1926 coal lock out, and a paucity of credit for industrial restructuring.[7] If the commitment to return to 1914 seemed increasingly like an economic 'cul-de-sac', then perhaps the attraction of Labour's proposals would be enhanced. But at this point, the Party's problems began.[8]

From one angle, the difficulties facing sections of British industry could be seen as a legacy of its early start. How could restructuring remove some of the problems of obsolescence? Labour with its declared readiness to employ the State for the achievement of economic objectives might be thought to offer something in this field. Certainly *Labour and the New Social Order* built on the growing economic involvement of the Wartime State and hoped to extend such interventions in peacetime. Equally, the deprivations of the working class had long stimulated discussions about the ending of poverty which had implications for the unemployment of the 1920s. Fundamental tensions remained unresolved however. One was between the ultimate commitment to socialism, and proposals to modernise industry. Would such modernisation provide a vital step in any transition to socialism, or could it serve to rehabilitate a malfunctioning capitalism? Similarly, unemployment and poverty were seen as basic to any socialist indictment of capitalism. Poverty was a consequence of inadequate employment opportunities. Typically, the remedy was presented as the elimination of capitalism; only then would the problem be solved. Thus both the question of modernisation and the issue of poverty raised the problem of strategy for the transition. No attempt was made to offer a substantive answer.

Most Labour leaders in the 1920s suggested that any transition would be protracted; but such gradualism had to be reconciled with the need to meet some immediate demands. These were expressed most sharply through the trade-union presence in the Party, but also through the obvious need to secure and retain electoral support. Thus socialism was offered as the only real answer – a distant, vague alternative to the unappealing present – yet alongside this, there was a desire, both pragmatic and moral, to achieve something in the immediate future for working-class supporters. The fundamentalist rejection of any solution under capitalism co-existed with immediate proposals for public works and for decent levels of unemployment benefit. Capitalism was the villain; it had to be replaced, but in the interim, Labour was committed to making working-class life a little more tolerable. Official doctrine was typically rendered schizophrenic by the failure to consider how one commitment might affect the other. Yet ultimately it was not the separation of Labour aspirations into separate compartments that proved the most damaging feature. Good intentions were destroyed by more orthodox attachments.

The Party leadership's hopes seemed immune from any suspicion that such aspirations could conflict with commitments to Free Trade, the Gold Standard or the orthodoxy of the balanced budget. Attachments to such icons were strong within the Party. Many Labour politicians combined a rhetorical devotion to socialism with an unthinking – or on occasions – zealous attachment to traditional liberal economics. Such a dualism connected with their lack of any substantive view on a transition from capitalism to socialism; it reflected that many had served political apprenticeships as Radical Liberals in the hey-day of Gladstonian economic orthodoxy. The ethical style of this economic position complemented elements of their own career: the concern for self-help and self-respect, the manner in which individual social mobility could license generous verdicts about the flexibility of the class structure, the increasing orthodoxy that came with the metamorphosis of propagandists into councillors, MPs and Ministers. Perhaps, above all, support for Free Trade could be justified by reference to the basic Socialist value of internationalism. The language of harmony was employed to express support for an economic doctrine that had symbolised the dominance of nineteenth century British capitalism. Some of the traditionally best-organised trade unions had an apparently vested interest in a Free Trade system. The big battalions of Coal and Cotton had been organised in industries where a strong export trade had often boosted workers' standards and expectations – and thereby had facilitated perhaps the task of trade union organisation.

But in the 1920s, such beliefs encountered harsh pressures. Continuing depression in the overseas markets for coal and cotton could induce scepticism about Free Trade. Queries could be muffled however by the association between this economic doctrine and other Liberal sentiments that had left their profound marks on British Labour. Before 1914 Labour speakers referred often to the supposed contrast between Britain and Germany regarding workers' living standards and the democratic credentials of the two societies. Protection was associated with elitism, reaction and corruption. Free Trade was not just economically superior; adherence to it provided an indice of national maturity. Such economic and patriotic sentiments led several Labour politicians to make highly conventional assessments of the prospects for economic recovery. Improvement would depend on a decline in international tensions and a trade revival. In effect, some who saw themselves as Socialists saw the best hope for the working class as lying in the resurrection of a lost capitalist world in which Britain would once again dominate international markets – a utopian capitalist hope to put alongside a utopian socialist one.[9]

This conventional expectation allied to the acceptance of orthodox budgetary precepts effectively prevented many Labour leaders – most notably Philip Snowden – from adopting any policies that would aid the unemployed. Typically, such passivity was justified by national or communitarian rhetoric. MacDonald, Snowden and several of their colleagues asserted frequently that Labour was dedicated to the welfare of the whole community and not just that of a class or of a section. At a critical moment in August 1931 the argument was employed to justify policies that were damaging to the unemployed.[10] Clearly during the 1920s as in subsequent decades, Labour's leaders could use the language of British nationalism so as to strengthen socialist suspicions of such rhetoric as a mere cloak for capitalist interests.

Labour's opinion in the late 1920s cannot be divided neatly however into a cautious patriotic Right and a radical class-conscious Left.

Many on the left themselves lacked any clear perception of a transitional strategy. Their criticisms of opponents within the Party tended to stick at the level of rhetoric. More significantly, some who claimed to be on Labour's Left developed diagnoses of the plight of British capitalism, that faced the problem of the transition to socialism within one advanced industrial society. They attempted to make coherent connections between a Socialist objective and the need to act immediately and radically against unemployment. Equally, they argued that the enhanced wellbeing of the working class was critical for the revival of the British economy. In one crucial respect, they departed from Labour's internationalist rhetoric. Believing that a transitional strategy for Britain was both urgent and feasible, they deprecated the view that a transition had to be an international affair. Instead, British workers would require protection from the international capitalist system during the transitional period.

Interest in the suppressed alternative of Labour Protectionism has tended to emphasise the views of Sir Oswald Mosley, ex-Tory, future Fascist, and in the late 1920s, an advocate of a radical credit policy and of an insulated economy. For a brief period, he was the principal hope of some of the Labour Left.[11] Although Mosley's arguments incorporated distinctive emphases, his general position was not unique. His claim that hopes for economic recovery should not be dependent on a revival of international trade, and his emphasis on the need to expand domestic purchasing power were made by others within the Independent Labour Party. The details might vary; the preferred mechanism might differ, but nevertheless here was a stock of ideas, that could offer some alternative to the nostrums of the Party Leadership.

Curiously, the recent emphasis on Mosley's ideas has not been matched by any equivalent assessment of John Wheatley's views. Yet he too argued for a national solution to economic difficulties that would involve the elevation and protection of working-class living standards. Perhaps it provides a revealing sidelight on some English historiography that the Winchester-educated baronet enjoys something of a political resurrection in his pre-Fascist guise; in contrast the Catholic Irish miner turned prosperous Scottish businessman still lingers on the margins of historical debate. Indeed Wheatley's arguments were developed by someone who had been a longstanding member of an avowedly socialist organisation. Mosley, the recent recruit to Labour, often argued as if economic and social modernisation were the relevant objectives; concern with their socialist content was 'theological'. In contrast, Wheatley's case remained linked tightly to a view of what socialism was, and how it could be achieved. The modernisation of Britain was envisaged as a decisive element in an effective and early transition to socialism.

Despite the preponderant identification of Labour and Free Trade, those who argued in the 1920s for some form of Labour Protectionism could have pointed to some relevant exemplars.[12] In one sense, trade union activities could be characterised as inherently Protectionist. As workers succeeded in raising living standards, or improving working conditions, the danger of foreign competition could intensify. In the late 1880s and early 1890s, the 'Tory Socialist' Henry Hyde Champion had argued that a successful campaign for the legislative eight-hour day would not mean the end of the issue. If as a result, foreign producers benefited from lower costs, then it would be necessary to protect British workers' newly-won standards against cheap imports. Any significant improvement of the condition of a national working class necessitated some form of Protection so long as an international capitalist economy continued.

Champion became a forgotten figure within Labour's political development. His overt Protectionism made it difficult for him to cultivate sympathy amongst Liberal Trade Unionists; his proprietorial attitude towards working-class political initiatives provoked resentment amongst those for whom the creation of Labour and Socialist organisations was in part a protest against the manipulative proclivities of bourgeois politicians. Yet in the 1890s, Champion's arguments struck responsive chords amongst some groups of workers faced by competition from cheap imports, and by employers keen to respond to such a challenge by introducing new machinery. Threats to employment and to work practices could produce reactions that extended beyond concern with imports, to allegations about the impact of immigrants on living standards. The National Union of Boot and Shoe Operatives combined a formal commitment to socialism with a wish to block immigration. Sometimes the economic argument became interwoven with the use of racial stereotypes, and allegations that 'England' was being invaded by 'aliens'. Against such xenophobia, Socialists and trade unionists often emphasised a commitment to internationalism or recalled a national tradition which pictured Britain as a sanctuary for European refugees. As yet the strength of Radical Liberalism proved effective, supported in the years prior to 1914 by an apparent economic revival.

From 1921 however, the staple industries suffered a continuing depression that might corrode Free Trade optimism and offer scope for the development of Labour Protectionism. Perhaps such arguments could connect with left-wing pressures for an effective strategy for a transition to socialism; or alternatively the incorporation of nationalist priorities and racist stereotypes within a Protectionist strategy could be the decisive and regressive factor. Certainly the politics of the 1920s and especially Wheatley's contribution provide illuminating material on the perennial and complex theme of the relationship between Labour's Socialism and British Nationalism.

Chapter 3

Radicalisation

It was not only perceptions of Labour's political prospects that were transformed by the Election of November 1922. Wheatley added an individual retrospective claim. The campaign and the emotional departure of the Glasgow MPs had changed his assessment of what was politically feasible. He suggested that as a Glasgow Councillor he had tailored his proposals according to a cautious estimate of public opinion:

I held the view strongly that public opinion was not ready for large-scale Socialist proposals, and I shaped my policies accordingly. The election has changed all that and convinced me I was wrong.

When I saw on that Sunday night after the election, when we left Glasgow for London, the streets lined with hundreds of thousands of people cheering the new MPs, when I saw the square in front of the station jammed tight with over a hundred thousand citizens madly enthusiastic not for the MPs themselves, but for the Socialism for which they stood, it was proved to me beyond doubt that the people were ready to respond to a bold Socialist lead. And so I gave expression to my changed view in Parliament.[1]

Whatever the precise significance of this Glasgow demonstration, it symbolised a decisive shift not just in the politics of the city, but also in Labour's national aspirations. Wheatley's response was influenced also by the judgement that the expectations of Labour supporters required a bold response, otherwise a vital opportunity would be lost.

Yet his assessment posed problems. Some stemmed from the cautious, respectable priorities of the Party's leaders. This constraint would become increasingly galling to Wheatley. But in his first Parliament, there seemed a more immediate obstacle. If the demands of Glasgow's working class necessitated an all-British response, then effective action required the achievement of similar enthusiasm elsewhere. For the moment, a Conservative Government ruled with a comfortable majority. It was likely to be 1926 or 1927 before Labour could hope to change this. No one could imagine that the first Labour Government was little more than a year away.

The frustrations of Opposition could be compounded if the Glasgow Labour Member began to witness, or perhaps experience, the deradicalising charms of parliamentary rituals and cameraderie. Wheatley might have decided that the pursuit of working-class interests necessitated a journey to Westminster, but this should be a passage free from such seductions. At the 1923 ILP Conference he moved a resolution recommending that Labour MPs should not accept the hospitality of political opponents.[2] Already some had been taken up by gossip columnists and society hostesses. Equally effective in the long run would be the relative ease with which a rhetorical Socialist such as James Maxton could be accommodated within the 'best club in Europe'. His would become eventually a predictable turn without practical significance. Perhaps Wheatley was a different matter.

A contrast emerged in the celebrated parliamentary scene of 27 June 1923.[3] Maxton, his emotions very much on the surface, refused to withdraw his description of a Tory MP as a 'murderer' for supporting a reduction in the Scottish Health Estimates. For Maxton, the issue had a painful personal significance. His wife had died recently, exhausted after the long illness of their young son. Eventually, Maxton was suspended from the Commons. Wheatley repeated the offence and was similarly dealt with. So too were two other Glasgow Members.

The demonstration attracted widespread criticism within the Party. MacDonald was appalled; H. N. Brailsford, recently appointed editor of the *New Leader* distinguished privately between those involved:

What Maxton did was trivial; the serious thing is Wheatley's deliberate theory of scenes, and his determination to follow his own tactics.[4]

Publicly Brailsford attacked those involved. They had weakened the credibility of Parliament, 'with all its faults ... the instrument to which we look for change'; they had damaged MacDonald's authority: 'the one possible leader ... Whatever weakens his position is an injury to the Socialist cause'. Most fundamentally, Brailsford argued that the use of the 'scene' was a blind-alley:

such scenes would soon pall if they become frequent. To keep up the stimulus, you must increase the dose. From scenes you must soon move on to violence, and transfer your activities to the streets. To that, one answer would be the parallel growth of a Fascist movement, and the ruin of any type of fundamental change by democratic means.

He acknowledged that the tactic could be justified as an effective means for dramatising the class struggle, but such theatre would not produce an informed following committed to constructive socialism:

... by raising the masses by crude methods, you may create behind yourselves a mob which will demand of you not a constructive policy of change, but a programme of smashing and destruction as crude as your own methods.[5]

The contrast was made repeatedly by Labour Leaders in the 1920s and at other times: the distinction between steady, unspectacular work and flashy counter-productive stunts, a juxtaposition that could feed on long-standing fears about the irrational impulses of the masses.

The contrast was misleading if applied to Wheatley. He was attracted by constructive arguments. They linked with his municipal experiences, and from the early months at Westminster he contributed forcefully and effectively to Commons debates on questions such as housing. But given the Conservative majority and his assessment of Glaswegian radicalism this seemed an insufficient strategy. All too easily it could collapse into a series of concessions at first verbal, later perhaps practical; all sanctified by the concern to appear 'reasonable'. Contributions to such discussions should not rule out the use of parliament as a pulpit from which to articulate the sentiments of the dispossessed. For the practical politician who wished to renew constantly a Socialist commitment, one should not veto the other.

Wheatley responded to criticism of the 'scene' by offering a justification in class-terms:

What are called 'scenes' in Parliament shock only those who are out of touch with the realities of working-class life, and who forget the scenes in the homes of the workers. The workers owe nothing to a Capitalist Parliament, and wish to pay it exactly what they owe.[6]

The claim was bolstered by a contrast that recalled some of Keir Hardie's early speeches:

I cannot help wondering what would have happened if those lost infants had been the children of the upper classes. Had the mourning occurred in Buckingham Palace, in the mansions of Britain or even among the middle class of Belgravia and Bearsden, would the action of the Labour MPs and their indignation have been so severely condemned?

But 'respectable' outrage underlined social inequalities:

as there is already a surplus supply of workers the ruling classes in their callous stupidity are unmoved by this dreadful tragedy.

In the one case the loss is thought of as only statistics; in the other case there would have been a day of national mourning for a loss of princes.[7]

The strategy had been employed infrequently by Labour politicians. Rather it was a demonstration much more characteristic of the Irish Party in its Parnellite hey-day. Significantly Maxton emphasised, with hindsight, a national dimension to his protest:

You are not nearly at the end of trouble in the House of Commons through Scotsmen ... we mean to tell them they can do what they like about English children but that they are not to suffer Scottish children to die and thousands of Scotsmen to suffer the starvation of unemployment.[8]

For the Scottish Left, this emphasis became less persuasive with the achievement of a Labour Government. It was an argument which Wheatley never used. Committed to an advance towards Socialism on an all-British basis, he was already considering the problem of the transition.

It is debatable how far Wheatley was ever an original thinker. Many of his views had been formulated previously by others, although his presentations had their distinctive connections and emphases. Thus at some point, probably during 1922, Wheatley accepted a thoroughgoing under-consumptionist analysis of poverty and unemployment in Britain. Broad sentiments of this kind had provided a recurrent strand in socialist critiques of capitalism. They had been given a more sophisticated form in the writings of the Radical Liberal economist, J.A. Hobson. In the early 1920s, he was moving closer to the ILP and in 1922 he published a new statement of his views, *The Economics of Unemployment*. This explained the experience of periodic recessions in terms of a lack of consumption produced by a heavily inegalitarian structure of incomes:

For these periodic movements of over-accumulation of capital, over-production, congestion of the machinery of industry, stoppages and unemployment ... there can be no real remedy except a removal of the surplus elements in large incomes which brought about the disproportion between saving and spending.[9]

Post-War dislocations had exacerbated and shaped the current depression, but they were not the fundamental cause:

The war wounds to our economic system call for emergency measures. But these ... are of the nature of first aid, and must not be regarded as substitutes for the remedial treatment which deeper diagnosis of the disease demands.[10]

It seems likely that this book influenced Wheatley. Already in the 1922 Election he was rejecting the conventional claim that the key to any reduction in unemployment must be found in the revival of the export trades:

In their search for a market for great stores of goods, the capitalists screamed about the necessity of putting Germany on its feet, Austria on its feet, Russia on its feet, and talked about granting credits which would enable those countries to purchase from us, so clearing our markets and setting our industries going. But why not set Glasgow on its feet, Dundee on its feet, Lanarkshire on its feet? Couldn't the people in these places use more goods if they had the power to purchase them?[11]

Wheatley diagnosed the maldistribution of wealth as critical:

the poverty of the workers is due to the embarrassing wealth of the country.[12]

These emphases were developed early in 1923 in a pamphlet *Starving in the Midst of Plenty*.

The under-consumptionist claim was joined by the argument that British industry was under challenge from cheaper producers whose industrial plant had been supplied by Britain. Any response that placed the primary emphasis on the revival of the export trade would involve downward pressure on wages. Not only would workers' standards be reduced, the strategy would be self-defeating, since it would provoke a similar response from competitors. The moral for Wheatley was clear: 'Reconstruct Britain First'. The strategy required a redistribution of purchasing power.

If this policy were to succeed, political action would be essential. Wheatley at this stage, did not suggest that trade-union action could prevent an effective onslaught on wage levels. In early 1923, after recent industrial defeats such pessimism seemed plausible. Yet throughout the inter-War years, trade unions retained some capacity to withstand wage cuts. Many employers would note carefully the cost to the coalowners of the lengthy 1926 dispute. Wheatley's analysis had value in its scepticism about any hopes for employment that depended on export revival, but it was simplistic in its assessment that single-minded employers would be able or willing to pursue this chimera to the exclusion of other objectives.

Even in this early form Wheatley's economic arguments could encounter objections from Socialists. Any programme that proclaimed 'Reconstruct Britain First' ran the risk of utilising racial stereotypes to advance its case. At the very least it claimed that the first priority should be the well-being of the British working class. It was necessary to end that state of affairs where 'the Coolies are busy, the Britishers are at the 'Buroo'.[13] At least Wheatley followed up this contrast by emphasising that the competitive lowering of wage-rates would damage workers of all nationalities.[14] Nevertheless, this awareness of the international ramifications of a deflationary spiral was succeeded by another racist innuendo. He noted that one consequence of raising unemployment through depressing wages was to stimulate demand for emigration:

the workers are told they must leave their native land. Frequently, as was remarked by one of my colleagues in the House of Commons, emigration is insolently advocated by men who speak English with difficulty.[15]

Such presumably anti-Semitic hints were not uncommon on the British Left especially when they could be linked to suggestions about the rootless cosmopolitan power of finance. Certainly the use of racial prejudices was not limited to those who were developing a Protectionist response to the economic problems of the British working class. Self-proclaimed internationalists could employ similar stereotypes, as when some attacked the French use of Negro troops in the occupation of the Ruhr.[16]

This episode provided an occasion for attacks on Wheatley's nationalism at the 1923 ILP Conference. Charles Roden Buxton, one of the ILP's recruits from the Radical wing of the Liberal Party had visited the Ruhr, and had recommended that the coalfield be restored to Germany. He had been followed there by a group of Clydeside MPs, including Wheatley. They had suggested that the area be placed under international control. This response was more in harmony with the basic tenets of the ILP than was the overt Francophobia of some who argued restoration to Germany. But the Clydesiders related their analysis of the Ruhr to the British situation and concluded that despite everything, the German miners were better off than their West of Scotland counterparts. The controversy emerged at the Conference in a fashion that connected views on the Ruhr, remedies for British unemployment and visions of Socialism.

Wheatley's argument came straight from the pages of Hobson's book with just the addition of an explicit anti-capitalism:

He did not agree with the argument that the ruin of Europe was responsible for the unemployment and misery in Great Britain. The cause was British competitive capitalism. The enemy was not beyond the sea; it was here at home ... the British workers were starving for ... goods and the reason was the shortage of purchasing power.[17]

Within this discussion, Wheatley's political solution was not narrowly British. He envisaged the inauguration of a European 'super-parliament' as an institutional response to the instabilities of a competitive economic system. The justification for this proposal was unclear; at the very least it required Socialist majorities across Europe if it were to be effective. Its Utopianism contrasted with Wheatley's growing insistence that action had to be taken in Britain as a matter of urgency. Perhaps he emphasised this wider community because he viewed it as an appropriate instrument for an under-consumptionist strategy within an ILP debate.[18] Its inclusion did not prevent controversy. Clifford Allen, the Party's Chairman, his health undermined by imprisonment as a Conscientious Objector, was viewed widely as the embodiment of the Party's internationalist conscience. His criticism of Wheatley owed something to conflicting economic analyses. Allen placed much more weight on international factors in his explanation of British unemployment. More fundamentally, Allen wished to argue a principle:

If they began to take a selfish view of Socialism, a national view, they would see growing up in the ILP the beginning of a national jingoism ... They stood for certain great moral ideas. They did not believe in geographical boundaries. They believed their ideas were international and must be adopted by the workers of all nations simultaneously.[19]

Within the ILP the argument was potent especially when delivered by someone with Allen's record. Wheatley might hint at the possibility of some improvement for British workers through a redistributive policy, perhaps one that could have some socialist potential. The internationalist position remained blank on the politics of transition. Yet this seemed not to matter for many within the ILP.

Such indifference was likely to be important for Wheatley, since any attempt to promote his ideas as a coherent programme would seek to employ the Party as a key instrument. When the 1918 Labour Party

Constitution incorporated provision for Divisional Parties with individual membership, the ILP was forced to seek a new role. In the early 1920s it retained a sizeable membership with several leading figures ready to debate policy and theoretical issues. Indeed, in 1923, the Party under Allen's Chairmanship was embarking on its most intellectually vital period. During the previous year, Allen had initiated a series of reforms. He had pleaded for financial backing from wealthy friends; the old *Labour Leader* had become the *New Leader* under Brailsford's editorship. Later, attempts were made to formulate coherent policies through the work of Study Groups.

The success of these initiatives was mixed. Financial requests produced some significant contributions but these were not complemented by the development of a high regular income from the branches. The *New Leader* gained critical approval and readers, but also hostility from some Party members who viewed its content as preciously intellectual and only weakly related to working-class priorities. Innovations by a London-based elite were greeted with suspicion by local ILP leaders. Beyond these problems there was disagreement about the proper role of the ILP. Should it function as a socialist think-tank or as an aggressive propaganda body? Could the tasks be reconciled? Should the Party take a clear position in wider Labour Party controversies?[20]

Despite such disputes and unresolved problems, the persistence of unemployment began to leave its mark on ILP policy documents. *The Socialist Programme*, published in 1923, was clearly influenced by Hobsonian analysis with its advocacy of a more equal wealth distribution as a means of expanding and stabilising domestic demand. Already the conception of a 'Living Wage' was starting to develop within ILP discussions.[21] But at this point in the development of Wheatley's – and the ILP's – ideas, the vagaries of the electoral system, plus ironically, the potency of a Free Trade appeal brought Labour into office and Wheatley into the Cabinet as Minister of Health.[22]

The ten months of the first Labour Government allowed Wheatley to develop a reputation as an effective administrator. Beatrice Webb responded positively to one of his early speeches from the Government Front Bench:

A new star in House of Commons dialectics, logical and humorous with first-rate delivery.[23]

His Housing Act could be counted as a modest success. It built on Coalition and Conservative legislation and offered a limited but significant response to the perennial problems of inadequate supply and low standards. Snowden's austere view of public expenditure commitments was circumvented by the fact that for some years little central Government finance would be needed. The Act was the most significant single achievement of the Government. It was certainly not a radical innovation but rather an attempt to achieve something within the limits of an orthodox attitude to public spending. Wheatley was demonstrating the administrative 'realism' of his Glasgow Council years rather than any attempt to initiate radical measures based on his more recent assessment of the temper of Labour's working-class support.

His attempts to inject a more distinctive character into his Ministerial activities were less successful. His attempt to rescind a 1921 Order forbidding the Poplar Board of Guardians to pay more than the nationally approved levels to claimants threatened the Government's life and ended in ambiguity. Moreover it left unclear Wheatley's own attitude to 'Poplarism'. Out of office he might express strong sympathy; in Government he set his face against unlawful over-spending.[24] A greater muddle resulted from his attempt to respond to predominantly left-wing Labour demands that evictions on the grounds of non-payment due to unemployment should be prevented. The resulting Bill foundered in a mass of political criticisms and procedural arguments. This time Beatrice Webb contrasted Wheatley's parliamentary skills with the politically-damaging consequences of his Departmental decisions:

Another example of Wheatley getting the Government into a deep hole, climbing out of it himself in a brilliantly successful speech, leaving the Government still deeper down in the hole which he had made.[25]

Predictably Wheatley's record in office was more mixed than some commentators have suggested. Nevertheless he could point to limited achievements; this in itself contrasted sharply with the records of many colleagues, and helped to heighten his dissatisfaction with Labour's existing leadership.

The Government's response to the problem of unemployment was minimal. Snowden's budget was impeccably orthodox. Although absorbed in Departmental tasks, Wheatley clearly felt that little was being achieved. Some years later John Scanlon recalled that in August 1924 Wheatley had told him that he would resign from the Cabinet once outstanding housing legislation had been passed:

He had seen the futility of trying to do anything of permanent value to remedy the defects of Capitalism in a Government composed of men who did not believe in Socialism.[26]

Immediately after losing office, he juxtaposed socialist principle and the constraints of Government: 'We have lost office. We have gained the right to be ourselves.'[27] In his case, this was much more than a rhetorical requiem.

Even before the Labour Government had been defeated at the polls, Wheatley had begun to elaborate his own view of Socialist strategy. He saw moral and national requirements combined in a programme for expanding purchasing power and argued that such a policy would necessitate an advance towards socialism:

the means of distribution should be cooperatively controlled and managed ... the land, the workshops, ... you should increase your output so long as it is necessary for the levelling up of conditions.

Early action was essential as the collapse of British capitalism was imminent. Such a debacle would reduce drastically the range of feasible socialist responses:

There is no time to lose. Within less than ten years, probably within five years, your capitalist system in Britain will fall about your ears, and it will be impossible to reform it in a constitutional way. We have got to remove capitalism as quickly as possible.

This imperative was linked to that prevalent belief on the British Left that Socialism could come as much from the achievements of capitalism as from its failures. But such a belief should not engender a passive attachment to the inevitability of gradualism. Instead decisive action was required:

We want to get through the period of transition in an orderly and peaceable way, but we want to get through it quickly. We do not want to have to bring about the revolution in the midst of starvation. We do not want to collapse into Socialism. We want to flourish into Socialism.[28]

By the end of 1924, Wheatley was equating Socialism with national reorganisation:

A general increase in the purchasing power of the people can be brought about only through national organisation ... Under the system of a national pool, nationally controlled, (which might in our case become an Empire pool) industries that are now neglected, because they provide no private profit, could be worked to the national benefit as part of a national scheme. This national pool of resources in men, materials and knowledge is Socialism, and nothing else is Socialism.[29]

This presentation inevitably raised the issue of Free Trade. Soon afterwards Wheatley elaborated his views; he began by highlighting the political problem: 'Labour is in difficulties on this question. Liberal Free Trade is the official policy of the Party'.[30] The strength of the attachment to this doctrine meant that heteredox opinions would meet with wide opposition, but Wheatley wished to argue that any effective Socialist strategy could not co-exist with a continuing adherence to Free Trade. His case was an extension of the point developed by him two years earlier about the disastrous consequences of international capitalist competition. It came complete with a racial stereotype. The argument was presented as one applicable to both capitalist and socialist governments. For both, the national organisation of trade was vital; if a Labour Government were committed to an advance towards socialism, then retention of a Free Trade system would kill this hope:

The methods of production in the nationalised steel industry of Britain may be as perfect as knowledge makes possible. But the workers here have a standard of life that approaches the Socialist ideal and are paid wages sufficient to maintain that standard. The Indian ... is still satisfied with his rice and his dug-out. What is to happen under Free Trade? Only one thing can happen. Until the cost of production in India is raised to the British level, the standard of living in the socialised steel industry of Britain must go down. The only alternatives are a national subsidy or a closing of the works. If Socialism is to be established piecemeal, it must be protected from capitalism as it is erected.[31]

The Conservative remedy of tariffs, he rejected as inadequate. Really cheap producers would surmount the barrier and the objective should be to protect working-class standards against sweated competition whatever its source: 'the sweater across the street may do more damage than the sweater across the sea'.[32] Yet the prevalence of cheap foreign imports made the trade question into a vital one. Liberal Free Trade doctrine was blind to the challenge; trade unions in their practice, if not always in their formal doctrine, offered an alternative:

Trade unions exist for the express purpose of preventing free competition. If free competition is good, trade unionism is bad.[33]

If Wheatley sought to base his criticism of Free Trade on Socialist advocacy of public ownership and trade unionists' inherent Protectionism, he coupled this with an attack on the prevalent if vague belief that progress towards Socialism could, and should, be on an international basis:

If every section of the human race were at a uniform stage of evolution towards Socialism and were certain to keep in step in their progress towards Socialism there would be no need to shelter one section or one country from another. But universal Socialism is not coming and cannot come in this way. We in Britain are centuries ahead of certain peoples, and although, with our aid, they may complete the journey to our stage at a quicker rate than we travelled, we cannot sit still till they arrive. We want Socialism now, and our problem is to convert Britain, or the British Empire, into a Socialist state in the midst of a Capitalist world.[34]

The riposte to one form of Socialist Internationalism also hit at the Radical Liberalism that had moulded the outlooks of so many Labour politicians. It was no doubt even more unpalatable to many on the left on account of its presentation of the British Empire as a possible basis for Socialist development. Such an emphasis appeared regularly in the writings of other Labour figures. Hardie had hoped for closer co-operation between the Empire's Labour and Socialist organisations as a foundation of a more democratic association.[35] Wheatley also took this aspect seriously. In the Summer of 1925, some Clydeside MPs voted in favour of Imperial Protection, and he produced a more thorough examination of the role of Empire. He began with the self-consciously realistic claim that whatever its failings, the Empire was an unavoidable political fact.

Any attempt to dismantle it could produce only more national rivalries based on competitive capitalism. For Wheatley this would epitomise the barren quality of the liberal alternative:

Liberalism stands for industrial competition, not only among persons, but among nations. It views the individual, like the nation, as free units whose best interests are served by competition. This leads and can only lead to anti-social ends – to man against man, nation against nation.

With the collapse of the liberal order Wheatley's assessment of contemporary developments emphasised some of the features that had inspired Joseph Chamberlain's Protectionist campaign more than twenty years earlier:

The era of free competition is past. We are now in a period of mighty combinations, of trustified capital and groups of people are massed under the control of mighty imperial states.[36]

The task was to transform such industrial giants into organisations that would serve communal needs, under the overall supervision of a Socialist state. The Empire, and especially the strong Labour Movements in some of the Dominions could play a vital role in such a transformation. Such 'a bloc against world capitalism' might prove attractive as an ally for Soviet Russia. Not only did this presentation indicate wishful thinking about Soviet priorities, more fundamentally it seemed blind to the harsh exploitation that was so central to British – and other – imperialisms.

Such traits demonstrated how far Wheatley's perceptions of Socialism had been marked by the traditionally privileged position of British capitalism. Yet he combined these characteristics with an insistence that class interests should be the vital yardstick for deciding policies. Thus he concluded his defence of the Empire's progressive character by emphasising that each issue should be considered 'both nationally and internationally from a purely working-class and anti-capitalist standpoint'.[37] His emphasis on a national route to Socialism did not dilute his fierce defence of working-class claims. This became very apparent as he, along with other Socialists, faced the industrial consequences of Britain's return to the Gold Standard.

Even before the situation in the mining industry became critical in the Summer of 1925, Wheatley argued that the diversity of production and marketing conditions for coal necessitated an overall plan. Relatively prosperous Yorkshire could balance impoverished Lancashire:

The tendency is towards double-shifts in Yorkshire and doles in Lancashire. Socialists propose that the Yorkshire and Lancashire and other British coalfields should be treated as one and indivisible. If this were done, the rich field would balance the poor field.[38]

This had been the hope of the Miners' Federation as they had sought to build on wartime advances. The defeat of 1921 and the subsequent depression especially in the exporting fields had shattered this dream. At least at the end of July 1925 the threat of sympathetic action prevented a further erosion of miners' wages. Wheatley welcomed the Baldwin Government's decision to grant a nine-month subsidy to the industry. Faced with a direct challenge, the Government had moved away from strict orthodoxy:

The granting of a subsidy is a shocking blow to Free Trade principles.

Moreover 'Red Friday' could give some hope to an embattled working-class:

Capitalism was winning in the commonest of canters. It had complete control of Parliament and could afford to nod complacently and patronisingly to the powerless Labour Party.[39]

Wheatley believed that now the Government would use the nine months respite to prepare for the impending conflict. The potential damage would not be limited to the working class: 'Should we sacrifice the nation to preserve a musty, academic theory?'[40] But he was hopeful that this class, benefitting from appropriate racial characteristics would defend the long-term interests of the nation:

… workers because they are Britons and not a servile Eastern race will prepare to meet this onslaught with … enthusiasm and determination … It looks like evens on a clash.[41]

The alternative, he suggested, would be disastrous:

It is now or never. If the workers are defeated here and driven to a lower standard of living I can see no hope of a successful rally … the very existence of the nation is menaced. You cannot depress seventy per cent of the population to barbarism without national disaster.[42]

Equipped with this bleak prognostication, and no doubt remembering his own years in the Lanarkshire coalfield, Wheatley forcefully supported the miners' case in the Spring and Summer of 1926. Once the Federation were left to fight on alone, he pictured them as the custodians of the national interest:

The miners are fighting alone, but they are fighting the battle of the nation. If they lose, we all lose.[43]

They had qualities that fitted them for such a task:

In courage, and to a considerable extent in culture, they represent all that is best in the British race.[44]

His analysis of what was at stake in the dispute helped to produce a vigorous reaction against the behaviour of many Labour leaders during the General Strike:

From the first moment of the struggle, and indeed before it, prominent Labour leaders were whining and grovelling.[45]

Such condemnations were commonplace on the Left of the Labour Movement; in Wheatley's case, they served to distance him further from his former Cabinet colleagues. Already late in 1925, Wheatley had been defeated in the elections to the Parliamentary Committee.[46] Yet although his attacks on the leadership during 1926 seemed likely to reduce his support still further, he saw one lesson of the industrial battle as a demonstration of the indispensability of political action. This was a prevalent emotion within the Party in the years after 1926, but Wheatley's emphases were distinctive. Many dismissed an industrial strategy for political influence as inherently dangerous. It would destroy all hope of constructive socialism; it would strengthen forces to the Left of the Labour Party. In contrast, Wheatley saw the problem not as 'Direct Action' but as the cautious qualities of any likely leadership:

I cannot see how a General Strike constitutionally conducted can attain its object. To be successful it would require to be swift and complete and backed by unconstitutional action.[47]

Such a possibility was remote:

While human nature remains as it is, the workers must be prepared for timid leadership in moments of crisis.[48]

Wheatley's acknowledgement that decisive political action was the only feasible strategy for Socialism in Britain was essentially a reaffirmation of his recurrent emphasis on a constructive but rapid transition. But this judgement meant that he faced up to the problem of the Labour Party as an appropriate instrument. By the Autumn of 1926, such a role seemed implausible to him. He reacted sceptically to the caution of the Party leadership:

We are anxious, almost painfully anxious, to disassociate ourselves from young men in a hurry. No word must be breathed that would be regarded as revolutionary by our most timid drawing-room friends.[49]

Could this be changed? In particular, did the ILP in the circumstances of 1926 have the potential to act as an organisation that could mount an effective Socialist challenge?

Chapter 4

Defeat

ILP activists had greeted Labour's unexpected arrival in office with a blend of enthusiasm and scepticism – enthusiasm that it had happened at all, and that there were sizeable ILP contingents in the Government and on the backbenches, but scepticism about the likely achievements of a minority administration.[1] Inevitably, cracks appeared within the ILP ranks over the degree of tolerance that should be extended to Ministers. Some suggested that the Government should place a bold Socialist programme before the Commons; most maintained that the ILP's task should be to campaign for a future Labour majority. Some specific disputes reflected the ILP's internationalist and pacifist traditions, as the Government revealed itself to be disconcertingly 'national'. Frustration at the failure to act over unemployment developed although some sections responded uncritically to the Gladstonian rectitude of Snowden's budget.

Some of the burgeoning discontent focused on Clifford Allen who was personally close to MacDonald and who was attracting criticism that would help to precipitate his resignation from the Party Chairmanship.[2] Yet, ironically, Allen combined his appeals for a tolerant attitude towards the Government's difficulties with a view of representative democracy that would be taken up by his critics on the Left. This could be related to Wheatley's demands for a bold and effective strategy.

Allen denied that an adventurous policy could be proposed only if there seemed already to be an electoral majority in its favour. Instead, at the ILP Conferences in 1924 and in 1925 he argued that a Labour Government should not allow itself to be constrained by such a limitation. The radical initiative should come from politicians:

We should henceforth reject the notion that it is the function of democracy to initiate. If it will do so, of course, so much the better. Rather it is the business of democracy to check the use of power after schemes have been submitted to Parliament.

Present practice was stultifying. Fear of electoral consequences encouraged politicians to substitute private goals for public ones:

So long as the criterion of what it is politically wise to attempt is the chance we have of winning democratic support, so long will democracy remain uneducated and confused, and so long will politicians be in danger of drifting into the entangling pursuit of personal power.

Such majoritarianism should yield to a democratic practice in which government would act as educator. Burke's dictum about 'judgement' supplementing 'industry' should be applied not just to the relationship between representatives and electors, but also to that between government and electors. The rejection of bold proposals at the ballot-box could have educational value:

We shall not try to enforce our programme by dictatorship, but the time lost in this procedure, pending a full democratic awakening, will be far less than if we obscure our programme in the name of a false theory of democracy.[3]

This provided a coherent, if optimistic, response to the refrain of Labour leaders that there existed no majority for socialism. Paradoxically, it would be Allen who dropped out of ILP activity after he resigned the Party Chairmanship in October 1925. By the following Summer he saw little point in contributing to Party discussions:

I don't see what is the good of my coming to the meetings for I have little influence over the people concerned ... the present position seems to me too sad and hopeless – at least for the moment – for me to be able to do anything.[4]

The 'people concerned' included some Clydeside ILP MPs most notably Maxton and Wheatley. After Allen resigned from the Chairmanship he was replaced by Maxton and the ILP leadership's strategy and style became much more identified with those of this small group. However, this change did not mean that the ILP became an unambiguously left-wing faction within the Labour Party. Many rank and file members and some sponsored MPs had deep reservations about what they viewed as excessive criticism of the Labour Party leadership. Such disagreements had an impact on the development of an effective ILP policy on unemployment.

Work on a document began seriously in the spring of 1925. One of the Party's study groups was asked to produce a policy that would end poverty and make a significant contribution to the achievement of socialism. Its Chairman was Hobson; Brailsford who shared many of the former's economic views was Secretary. The other members were Arthur Creech Jones of the Transport Workers', and E. F. Wise. By the spring of 1926, work was sufficiently advanced for the publication of an interim report, *Socialism in our Time*; a supportive resolution was duly carried at that year's ILP Conference. Five months later, the final document appeared.

Its title, *The Living Wage* indicated the under-consumptionist core of the argument.[5] A 'Living Wage' was needed on grounds of both justice and economic efficiency. Its level would be determined through a commission representing the various sections of the Labour Movement. Hopefully, a future Labour Government would carry a Commons resolution supporting the basic principle; the policy could be advanced through both trade union efforts and supportive government actions. The latter would include the public ownership of the banks and of basic utilities.[6] Despite the slogan 'Socialism in our Time', the Study Group was cautious about any rapid nationalisation of other industries; instead it suggested the creation of an Industrial Commission that could reorganise industries in a radical fashion.[7] Attention was paid to the problem of foreign trade with the suggestion that State Import Boards could deal with food and raw materials.[8] Purchasing power should be expanded directly through a system of family allowances, financed out of direct taxation.[9] Overall, the document suggested substantive measures within a framework of gradualism. The first step was to create 'general prosperity':

... only in this atmosphere of well-being would a party ... attempt large constructive changes. Taking care before it joined the main battle over the hotly-contested issues of nationalisation to stimulate the nation's trade, it would then approach its more contentious work with the public in a mood of optimism and good temper.[10]

The proposals had clear affinities with Wheatley's developing ideas – the emphasis on the need to increase working-class purchasing power, the concern with industrial reorganisation, the perception that Britain's foreign trade presented a problem. Certainly his perspective was more radical. He argued for a more rapid and thorough socialisation of industry; he expressed much more concern about the international dimension. The Commission's proposals on imports were concerned simply with difficulties arising out of price fluctuations and shortages. But, at the 1926 ILP Conference, he strongly supported the new policy. Brailsford who had introduced this to the delegates, and who had prepared the way by a series of articles in the *New Leader* acknowledged the value of Wheatley's contribution:

a masterpiece of clear, cool exposition without a wasted word which emphasised the importance of distribution in any Socialist strategy, and based its defence on the under-consumptionist doctrine.[11]

Yet his advocacy of 'the wisest and most opportune policy', struck a characteristically urgent note that distanced him from some supporters of the under-consumptionist strategy:

I wish somebody would inform me what 'the complete reorganisation of society' means, so that the workers might have some idea how long they have to wait before they get an interim dividend from the Socialist Movement.[12]

But for the moment, the 'Socialism in our Time' resolution was accepted almost unanimously by the ILP Conference. It might seem that here was a coherent policy relevant to some of the most urgent problems that would face any future Labour Government. The 'Living Wage' doctrine offered an alternative to a sterile mixture of economic orthodoxy and pious rhetoric. Moreover it was backed by a political group that had been central to the Labour Party since its inception.

But the prospects of the 'Living Wage' proposals securing wide support within the Labour Movement were meagre. The obstacles were powerful and various; together they indicate the problems facing Wheatley and his call for a bold political initiative. They began within the ILP itself where significant disagreements existed over the content and the significance of the proposals.

Some of the disputes centered around Sir Oswald Mosley, now active within the ILP and beginning to develop his own arguments for national economic reorganisation.[13] One controversy was less fundamental than it might have appeared to some of the protagonists. During the 1926 ILP Conference debates, Mosley and his accomplice John Strachey had claimed that inadequate attention was given to the need for a socialist credit policy.[14] In fact, *The Living Wage* would contain a chapter on this aspect and Brailsford had already emphasised the need for the 'scientific management' of credit in his *New Leader* articles.[15] More accurately, the official ILP policy placed credit control as a complementary strategy to the redistribution of purchasing power.[16] Mosley's pamphlet, *Revolution by Reason* published the previous Autumn had presented the control of credit as the vital strategy for industrial reorganisation and working-class prosperity.[17] The divergence indicated the degree to which Mosley was influenced by Keynes, rather than by the underconsumptionists such as Hobson. For the latter, savings were processed automatically into investment; thus over-saving led inexorably to over-production, and thus to the claim that redistribution away from accumulators to consumers would be decisive. In contrast, the Keynesian account denied that the transfer from savings to investment was automatic; it was prevented by a restrictive financial policy. The response should not so much be one of redistribution as one of lower interest rates and government intervention.[18]

The credit question tended to separate Wheatley from Mosley; the former's inspiration was much more Hobsonian in its origins. This divergence between Mosley and most advocates of the ILP scheme was not crippling to its political credibility, although Mosley's flair for the dramatic tended to exaggerate differences.[19] A more fundamental problem existed over the trade question; here Wheatley and Mosley argued from a similar anti-liberal base. Already Wheatley had rejected Free Trade and had moved towards the idea of an insulated economy. Mosley in *Revolution By Reason* embarked on a similar path. He echoed Wheatley in his dismissal of the 'fetish worship of the present dimensions of our export trade'.[20] As yet his lack of enthusiasm for Free Trade was expressed obliquely. His principal onslaught on the international dimension of economic orthodoxy focused on the recently restored Gold Standard.

The terms of the denunciation highlighted Mosley's disenchantment with liberal trade and financial policies, and with the self-proclaimed Socialists who accepted them. The supposedly self-adjusting mechanism of the Gold Standard was not a proper subject for Socialist admiration. Acceptance of the dominion of market forces was:

surely a direct contradiction of Socialist doctrine. Socialism is the conscious control and direction of human resources for human needs.[21]

This claim that financial orthodoxy and rational planning were incompatible closely paralleled Wheatley's dismissal of Free Trade. It was buttressed by a piece of straight nationalism that again had overtones of Wheatley's emphasis on the need to protect British living standards:

How can we afford to place the supreme instrument of exchange and purchasing power at the mercy of these blind hazards of fortune? Is the employment of the British worker to be dependent upon a nigger digging up a lump of glittering metal in far-away Africa or upon the gold jugglery of foreign statesmen and international financiers? Surely a gold-standard Socialist is a contradiction in terms.[22]

Thus Wheatley and Mosley, the one by an emphasis on the ravages wrought by competitive trade, the other through an analysis of the destructive impact of the international financial system, were both arriving at the conclusion that the modernisation of the British economy necessitated its insulation.

Neither came from a family with any reason to love the liberal economy of the nineteenth century. It had destroyed the traditional economic and social power of the Mosleys; forced migration and the appalling conditions of the late nineteenth century Lanarkshire coalfield had been the lot of the Wheatleys.[23] The latter experience had been paralleled by many of those families who provided Labour activists in the 1920s, yet this did not produce a wide rejection of liberal economic orthodoxy. The extent to which Wheatley's economic nationalism jarred on the internationalism of many ILPers was demonstrated at the Party's 1926 Summer School. Wheatley introduced a session on the new policy and raised the trade question:

He boldly advocated subsidies for the export trades, if necessary to meet the competition of low-paid industries abroad and the prohibition of imported sweated goods. He disturbed a portion of the School by incidentally referring to the possibility of preventing sweated imports by cruisers ...[24]

This provoked a reaction from Fenner Brockway soon to become editor of the *New Leader*. He attacked Wheatley's tendency to 'economic nationalism as dangerous',[25] and at a later session he returned to the theme. This time he went wider than 'the Wheatley school of national socialists'; there had been:

a reaction from international idealism to concrete schemes for social betterment in this country ... it was ... time to revert to the old militant internationalism of the Socialist pioneers.[26]

In part this was a dispute about the relevance of Socialist internationalism, but it hinted also at a divergence over the function of the ILP. Should it be a propagandising vehicle for basic Socialist principles or an organisation concerned with the practicalities of a Socialist transition? Disagreement and doubt about the Party's role would weaken the emphasis given to 'the Living Wage' doctrine.

The details of the proposals implied that, despite the fervent internationalism of many ILPers, any transition to socialism would be a specifically British affair. The emphasis on planning through the British State was a sufficient guarantee of this. Nevertheless the conclusion that effective planning would require an insulated economy was not accepted by at least one of those responsible for the proposals. Soon after the Study Group had begun its task, Hobson had criticised this view. He acknowledged that the implementation of the 'Living Wage' doctrine might reduce the relative importance of the export trade, but only on account of expanded production for the home market. Such a success would not in Hobson's view reduce the reliance on imports:

The country fully and productively employed ... would require at least as large an import trade to satisfy it as now. It would have no spare labour to produce at home the goods we import ... The notion of approaching towards a self-sufficing Britain is ridiculous.

Hobson, the old Radical Liberal claimed that the trade problem, as highlighted by Wheatley, necessitated an international solution:

If we had 'a world under Socialism' things might be arranged quite differently. But so long as outside countries run a sweating capitalism in trades where we must compete, no purely British reform can be efficacious.[27]

The international dimension provided a basis for division amongst the Labour leadership's critics which would grow more significant as the economic crisis deepened. Down to August 1931, Socialists, appalled at the consequences of fiscal and monetary orthodoxy found themselves at odds with one another over the trade question.

Wheatley's concern with the international problem had been deepened by his belief that rapid action was essential and that the cloudy internationalism of many Socialists effectively vetoed an otherwise available strategy. Similarly he welcomed the ILP proposals since they seemed to offer the basis for an effective transition. Yet this aspect also produced disagreements within the ILP. On occasions Brailsford suggested that the policy's main justification was inspirational. Workers would come to believe that a 'living wage' could not be available widely under capitalism. The demand was:

a clear, human understandable cry, to which people would rally ... a Socialist Battering Ram with which the forces of capitalism would be attacked.[28]

Tactically the policy could generate a new harmony between unions and Party since each would have its part to play. There was the prospect of effective agitation inside and outside Parliament. Yet Brailsford also argued that the policy offered more substantive benefits:

a whole series of measures which would amount to laying the ground-plan of a Socialist society.[29]

This was the interpretation that appealed to Wheatley, the combination of a Socialist promise and an 'interim dividend'. Yet the proposals could carry an assessment that offered much less to Socialists. The dividend need not be 'interim', but rather a demonstration of the feasibility of a capitalist stabilisation, given appropriate policies and institutions. This interpretation was made by Hobson. He dismissed as unpersuasive the claim that agitation for a Living Wage could expose the unbending limitations of capitalism. Such a view involved credulity towards capitalists' disingenuous claims that wage rises were impossible:

It is not obvious that capitalism with certain special public controls and modifications cannot be made to pay this basic wage.[30]

The 'Socialist Battering Ram' might drive a path to a managed capitalism.

Hobson's relatively sanguine outlook contrasted with Wheatley's apocalyptic fears. Beneath the divergence there lay a fundamental difficulty for Socialists which would become all too apparent after 1945. If the immediate demands of Labour supporters seemed capable of satisfaction under a managed capitalism, then what would happen to the argument for Socialism?

If one problem stemmed from ambiguity over what 'the Living Wage' would offer towards a transition, another fed on the sentiment that Socialists had no need to bother with transitional strategies. Nothing worthwhile could be achieved until there was a widespread desire for Socialism – and that would come in its own time. As George Lansbury argued in 1925:

Once the mass of the people want Socialism, they will find the right way to get it.[31]

This view, expressed often by those who claimed to stand on the Left was effectively a prop for the orthodoxy of Labour's leaders. All could accept the rigours of capitalism whilst contemplating the Socialist nirvana.

This passivity linked with other attitudes: the longstanding priority given within the ILP to 'making Socialists' through propaganda, the optimistic belief in the inexorable growth of Labour support, a desire to avoid rocking the boat. Together they blunted the potentially disturbing impact of 'the Living Wage'. Even the ILP was a less than wholehearted advocate. In December 1926, John Paton, the Party's National Organiser acknowledged that:

there has not been the consistent and energetic propaganda of the new programme which might perhaps have been expected.

In part this reflected the priority which many ILP branches had given to work for the locked-out miners, but there was, in Paton's judgement, another factor:

Many branches have taken the programme too lightly and have imagined that support could be taken for granted; others have dismissed the proposals as 'stunts' and 'slogans'.[32]

The ILP with its propagandising ethos was unlikely to contain a preponderance of members who were ready to devote time to promoting such a specific policy.

One venue where the programme was discussed seriously, was the ILP Summer School. Although this might stimulate the participants, it was unlikely to generate a wider mobilisation. A Continental Socialist claimed: 'It is difficult to realise that one is attending the summer school of a proletarian party'. The idyllic country house setting was 'curiously out of keeping with the drab sordidness in which most of the comrades among whom we work are doomed to spend their lives'. But the setting was less at variance with the School's social composition: three or four industrial workers out of a total of sixty-five.[33] The style offered some basis for a simplistic, negative image of the ILP as a bourgeois clique, out of touch with the needs of the workers, a characterisation which could be used to kill sympathy for ILP proposals.

Support was limited amongst the trade unions anyway. Although 'the Living Wage' strategy had been intended to bring industrial and political wings closer together, few prominent trade union leaders expressed any enthusiasm. Indeed, after the events of 1926, the support given by the Miners' Secretary, A. J. Cook, was likely to antagonise some other Trade Union leaders.[34] After the collapse of the General Strike, most Union officials were preoccupied with rebuilding their own organisations; they did not wish to become involved in a series of aggressive industrial challenges. Moreover, the ILP as a distinctive organisation counted for little inside the major unions.[35] Factionalism had crystallised increasingly around the question of relationships with the Communist Party. So the case for a 'Living Wage' went largely by default in trade-union circles. An increasingly beleaguered Communist dominated section dismissed the proposals as at best naive and at worst pro-capitalist. The dominant trade union element looked forward to the return of a Second

Labour Government under MacDonald's leadership and stigmatised the ILP's proposals as one more disruptive initiative by the Left. The acceptance of MacDonald's leadership entailed underwriting his political judgements, including his immediate dismissal of the proposals in the interim statement 'Socialism in our Time', as 'flashy futilities'.[36] Tactical opposition could be supplemented by union criticism of specific items within the ILP proposals. The advocacy of Family Allowances was opposed by some unions who feared the implications for future wage negotiations, and reflected the sexism inherent in the conception of the male as family provider. More broadly the 'Living Wage' theme suggested a long-term shift away from competitive wage-bargaining. The implication was welcomed by Wheatley, but it could appear as a threat to a central trade union function.[37]

Such opposition, or at least, lack of enthusiasm, within the unions coupled with MacDonald's antipathy meant that the ILP had little hope of gaining a favourable verdict from the Labour Party Conference. At the 1926 gathering, it took the unambitious line of proposing an inquiry on the issue. MacDonald accepted this procedure on behalf of Labour's National Executive, but in terms that suggested little chance of a positive outcome.[38] Brailsford had no illusions:

Mr MacDonald shrugged his shoulders and continued in words, gestures and tones to convey something of this disdain he feels for our proposals.[39]

The implicit pessimism was justified. The committee of inquiry was not formed for almost a year, and then concentrated on the family allowance proposal. The 'Living Wage' strategy was effectively buried; so were many of Wheatley's hopes for decisive political action.

As the 'Living Wage' proposals became lost in the maze of Labour Party policy-making, Wheatley continued to publicise his ideas for a Socialist initiative. The coal dispute had stimulated some reactions that would become parts of his more general argument. The demand for wage cuts in the mining industry demonstrated how the traditional system of fixing wages could have disastrous national consequences:

We are to commit suicide as a nation to save the competitive system of fixing wages.

Instead, the conclusion should be that no industry could be considered in isolation. Once again his unit of reference was the British nation:

The mining industry is but one department of British industry. We want to think nationally, organise nationally in order that we may prosper nationally. In no other way can Britain survive.[40]

The theme was presented more thoroughly in a pamphlet, *Socialise the National Income*, published early in 1927. National economic reorganisation could have a Socialist potential:

Every industry must be looked on and treated as a department of one workshop ...
Every department will be judged by its national utility. The capacity of the nation
as a whole, and not of what we now call an industry, will determine wages.[41]

During the period of transition, income levels should be determined by
the State. Wheatley implied that those affected would not find such
authority onerous. The State directors should be disinterested; at least
they would protect majority interests. The method of selection remained
unclear, although Wheatley suggested wide consultation. This vagueness
was matched by optimism about the consequences:

All workers by hand and brain will have a say in the selection of the State directors.
Under the new system the worker's political power will extend to his industrial
conditions ... He will be economically as well as politically enfranchised.[42]

This prospectus was mute on any role for trade unions. It also seemed
oblivious to the problems posed for democratic practice by the inevitable
bureaucracy. Such emphases and silences offered a sharp demonstration
of the predominant pattern of British Labour politics in the 1920s and
for several decades afterwards. The expectation that the British economy
planned through a centralised State could provide a basis for Socialism,
contrasted vividly with an alternative tradition. This had emphasised
decentralisation founded on vigorous and durable rank and file participation as the essential basis for a Socialist advance. Wheatley's optimism
about the benevolence of 'State directors' had not been shared by syndicalists such as the authors of *The Miners' Next Step*: nor in many of his
writings was it echoed by James Connolly. For them, the character of
leadership provided a fundamental problem for Socialists. The risk of
separation from the sentiments of the rank and file was ever present.
Since syndicalists tended to see the latter as essentially radical, such
irresponsibility seemed likely to have conservative consequences.
Wheatley was characteristic of many on the left in the late twenties, in
that he did not ponder this problem. Thus the quest for Socialism through
the British State did not simply marginalise alternative conceptions of
nationality; it also subordinated concern about bureaucracy and en-
trenched leadership to hopes for a rapid breakthrough towards a planned
economy.

Yet the consequences of Wheatley's proposals were unclear. Any
significant move towards their achievement would have involved a
radical departure from conventional characterisations of capitalism,
especially in Britain where capitalism was identified often with minimal
State intervention. Wheatley envisaged that the State would intervene
not simply to fix prices and incomes but also to redistribute resources:

Many occupations which are now extremely profitable to those engaged in them,
but which add nothing in substance to the national wealth will be scrapped, and
the people engaged in them released for additional *useful* production.[43]

Quite how utility would be determined was not revealed but Wheatley anticipated that many capitalists would welcome such an extension of State activity. They would see State control over wages and prices as acceptable if it meant the achievement of guaranteed markets. Wheatley also saw support for his alternative to Free Trade:

The policy will involve State regulation of imports and exports. The need for this is largely recognised now, even in capitalist circles. Many leading capitalists recognise the national value of a system of licences for imports and exports.[44]

He emphasised that his envisaged reorganisation of industry could be carried out under private ownership, but he claimed that the strategy offered hope to Socialists:

If the next Labour Government were to abolish the competitive system of fixing wages and prices, it would remove the greatest obstacle to nationalisation of the means of production ...[45]

Thus the prospects for Socialism were identified closely with those for the expansion of the public sector through State action. As with 'The Living Wage', Wheatley's arguments left open the problem of whether their enactment was more likely to produce a move towards Socialism, or towards a stabilised and managed capitalism. At least a readiness to raise such a question contrasted with the rhetoric and underlying passivity of many Labour politicians in the late 1920s. He at least perceived the perennial problem of reconciling pursuit of a Socialist objective with the need to ensure that the economic system maintained short-term viability. Already he anticipated the failure of 1929–31. However inadequate Labour's policies might be, the Party's electoral support was growing once again. If Labour's leaders regained office and relied on Socialist rhetoric without relevant proposals, then the Party's supporters would be bitterly disillusioned:

Labour is now wandering in a dark alley, and yet the nation is steadily rallying to its side. Its millions of supporters expect it to abolish poverty now and not when they are dead.[46]

Equally, Wheatley's 1927 proposals raised in sharp terms the question of how far a national economic strategy could provide a basis for Socialism in One Country. He continued to speak forcefully on the need to protect British living standards against cheap competition. The language was reminiscent of that employed by Champion almost forty years earlier:

I would use the navy were I in power, to sink the ship that brought from abroad the product of sweated labour to reduce the standard of life here.[47]

He continued to deride any economic solution that depended on an export revival:

... I think the country will want to know from the party opposite why they cannot devote some attention to the improvement of our own customers in our own country; why they reserve all their solicitude for every country but their own?[48]

Such sentiments clearly separated Wheatley from most on the Labour Left. Typically, their commitment to Socialism had a principled if often vague internationalism as one of its most basic elements.

Wheatley's isolation was not only at the level of ideas. In 1927 he became involved in an unsuccessful libel action. The accompanying publicity led to his contemplating resignation from Parliament. This intrusion has been assessed as a vital factor that derailed Wheatley's campaign against Labour's leadership and policy.[49] This assessment is implausible, based as it is on the assumption that Wheatley could have controlled sufficient resources to make a significant impression on Party decisions. The weaknesses of the ILP have already been analysed. The constraints facing any critical Left within the Labour Party were revealed sharply in the Cook–Maxton Manifesto Campaign of 1928.

The roots of this agitation were varied; its purpose remains ambiguous.[50] Wheatley had admired the campaigns waged by Arthur Cook since his election as Secretary of the Miners' Federation; many within the ILP had been involved heavily in the events of 1926. Yet this link, affording the ILP Left a friend amongst trade union leaders was likely to estrange others who saw Cook as an erratic maverick. The distance between the ILP and many leading trade unionists grew, as some officials reacted to defeat by preaching the virtues of industrial conciliation. Cook's open and outspoken dissent from the General Council's strategy of discussion with leading industrialists led to his own near-isolation within the TUC. One consequence was a meeting at the House of Commons early in June 1928. This brought together the Miner's leader and the Glasgow ILP MPs, along with the Communist Willie Gallacher. One result was the publication of the Cook–Maxton Manifesto.

Although the title pointed to the two signatories, Wheatley was thoroughly involved in this initiative. His emphasis on a national solution to economic crisis had never led him to relinquish the claim that the working class was vital to any Socialist strategy. Even as he was arguing for a national reorganisation of industry early in 1927, he was stressing the inevitability of class politics:

Our movement, whether we like the description or not, is a class movement as distinct from a national movement.[51]

Later in the year he characterised recent developments within the Labour Movement as corrosive of working-class radicalism:

The workers are in a state of apathy, almost of hopelessness, and there is no doubt in my mind that there is a close connection between this and the industrial policy now being advocated.[52]

Such sentiments were articulated in the Manifesto, with its aggressive anti-capitalism, its belief in the necessity of self-emancipation by the working class and its unqualified hostility to conciliatory strategies within the Labour Movement.[53] The presentation allowed for no nuances; its lack of concern for immediate complexities was far removed from both Wheatley's economic proposals and those of the 'Living Wage' document.

The Manifesto's advent must be placed also in the context of political uncertainties within the ILP. Many members seemed unsure how to react to recent political developments. John Strachey sensed such doubts at the 1928 Easter Conference:

> ... there was a feeling of uncertainty, of indecision ... The ILP point of view has always been an affair of instinct, an attitude of mind, rather than a clear-cut theoretical doctrine. But how was this distinctive attitude of mind, true and vital though it remained, to be applied to the bewilderingly new situation which had arisen?[54]

Imposed on this lack of direction, there was the dispute between those whose primary loyalty lay with the wider Labour Party led by MacDonald and those who were keen to use the ILP as a vehicle for an aggressive Socialist policy. When the National Administrative Council discussed the Campaign, several members were critical. In part the disquiet was organisational since the initiative had ignored official Party channels; but it was also political. The agitation could be seen as a divisive tactic just when Labour's electoral prospects seemed to be improving. After a lengthy discussion the NAC passed a supportive resolution by just one vote.[55] One critic, Patrick Dollan saw this as a tribute to Maxton's popularity, not any indication of enthusiasm for the Campaign.[56] Within the ILP's Scottish Division even this formal acquiescence was not available. Its Council resolved that the Scottish ILP would take no official part in the agitation.[57]

Even the Campaign's leaders seemed ambiguous about the character of the exercise. The Manifesto declared that the purpose was to ensure that the Labour Party remained a Socialist body, yet some who were close to events have suggested that John Wheatley was contemplating the possibility of an organisational initiative. His part-time Secretary John Scanlon claimed later that Wheatley was interested in developing a network of local groups prepared to support only those Labour candidates who would work for Socialist measures. His assessment of most Labour MPs was pessimistic; until they were replaced, any Labour Government would be worthless.[58] In contrast, Maxton explicitly denied any intention of setting up a new political organisation and emphasised the need for a Socialist revival.[59] Whereas Wheatley's bleak expectations about any likely Labour Government meant that for him the electoral implications of a critical campaign had little relevance Maxton remained sensitive to any suggestion that criticism would damage Labour's electoral prospects. This cautious position was more typical of opinion on the Labour Left. Unhappiness about the drifts of policy combined with stubborn optimism about the future; the result was a readiness to limit criticism in the pursuit of office. Such restraint was demonstrated by Maxton at the Campaign's inaugural Glasgow meeting.[60] Wheatley apparently reacted by tearing up a cheque intended to finance the Campaign; but such doubts were swallowed and the agitation continued, essentially on Maxton's terms.

As such it achieved nothing. A programme of meetings left no durable leaders; yet involvement even in such a limited critical campaign during a pre-election year could lower participants' standing even further in the eyes of Party loyalists. In part the Campaign's failure was a testimony to the perennial dilemma faced by Labour critics – on one side the promptings of Socialist principle, but as a counter, the persuasive claim that outside the Labour Party there was only political insignificance.

The specific circumstances of 1928 intensified the difficulties. Any left-wing initiative faced the question of relationships with the Communist Party. Early support from the Communists could discredit the Campaign even further in the eyes of Labour Party and trade union officials who were conducting intensified attacks on Communist influence in the aftermath of 1926. Moreover links with the Communist Party compounded the problems over the Campaign's purpose, a complexity removed only when Communists ceased to participate, and subsequently with the adoption of the 'New Line', shifted to a hostile position. Beneath the specific issues of Communist involvement and later opposition there was an unpalatable fact for those who wished to use the ILP as a radical Socialist organisation. The feasibility of such an exercise was constrained by the existence of the Communist Party. Although it was small in numbers, it had some trade-union presence and could compete for the allegiance of Socialists.

Such rivalry was more crippling on account of a further, perhaps even more intractable factor. The Cook–Maxton Campaign – and the Left's wider hopes for the ILP were predicated on a belief in the existence of a radical working-class, cruelly betrayed by political and industrial leaders, but ready to respond to a Socialist lead. Apart from a scattering of radical pockets, this was, in 1928, a misleading assumption on which to base a political campaign. The ILP's own assessment in the Spring of 1928 was less optimistic:

The last year has been one of exceptional difficulty ... The prolonged unemployment, part-time employment and low wages prevailing over the areas from which the Party draws its chief support has limited the activities of many of our branches, and led to the closing down of a number of those most seriously affected.[61]

An even bleaker appraisal could be found within the trade unions. Ernest Bevin, a critic of the ILP and of Cook responded to their case at the 1928 TUC:

It is all very well for people to talk as if the working class of Great Britain are cracking their shins for a fight, and a revolution, and we are holding them back. Are they? There are not many of them as fast as we are ourselves.[62]

This was the dominant sentiment amongst trade-union leaders, as they swallowed their doubts about Labour's political representatives and anticipated the election of a second Labour Government. The weakness of the Left, and especially of Wheatley in such a climate, was evident at the Labour Party's 1928 Conference. He attacked 'Labour and the Nation'; its proposals would take years to carry out. They would not produce Socialism:

No one suggests that you are doing any more than undertaking to run capitalism successfully.[63]

But the major unions were committed to support of the programme. When Wheatley attacked Labour's plans for the mining industry, J. R. Clynes could retort that these had the support of the Miners' Federation.[64] Against the backdrop of conflicts in the coalfields since 1918, the exchange offered insight into the weakness of the Labour Left. Whatever the harsh character of industrial experiences, decisive votes in the Labour Party were determined by an alliance between parliamentary leaders and the officials of major trade unions. Sections of the working class certainly moved leftwards in the 1920s, but the shift terminated with support for MacDonald's Party. Wheatley's scepticism about the likely achievements of such a Party distanced him not only from the mass of Labour voters and MPs but even from those on the Left who were prepared to subordinate criticism to electoral calculations, and then to give the 1929 Government a fair trial.

In June 1929 Wheatley was an isolated figure. Denied office, he appeared to new hopeful MPs as a cassandra prophesying doom for the Government, unless decisive action was taken rapidly:

Today the Government could do anything. Today the Government are not showing the courage that their supporters on these benches expect. If they displayed that courage and went on with their own policy, the parties opposite would not dare to wound them, however willing they might be to strike; but after the Government have disappointed their friends by twelve months of this halting half-way legislation ... and have been discredited in the country, then twelve months from now, there will be no party in this House poor enough to do them honour.[65]

Wheatley, as a senior parliamentary figure, might gain attention but it was MacDonald who secured the cheers and the votes at Party meetings.[66] Such loyalty survived early setbacks. By the end of 1929, the Government's defects were more apparent. Wheatley savaged J. H. Thomas's woolly expectations about employment. In one cutting phrase, Ministerial hopes about new ship-building orders were dismissed as 'Ships that pass in the night'.[67] But outside a small group of largely ILP MPs, any doubts remained strictly private. Beatrice Webb who had admired Wheatley's ministerial record painted a portrait of a pessimistic critic:

As a rebel in the Party, he has been a failure. His expression is sullen, his words are bitter. He says that he has lost his faith in political democracy; the common people have no will of their own; they are swayed backwards and forwards. He would be a Communist, if he were not a pious Catholic.[68]

Three months later he was dead; eighteen months later rejections of MacDonald's leadership and of the consequences of financial orthodoxy were general within the Labour Party.

The contrast with Wheatley's isolation in the Spring of 1930 is ironic, but many former loyalists limited their criticism to accusations of conspiracy and betrayal. Often critical assessment of political strategy remained slight. It would be disingenuous to see Wheatley's death as a factor that prevented an early generation of support for his ideas in the aftermath of August 1931. The obstacles had been overwhelming in the late 1920s; many of these constraints continued to limit the influence of the Labour Left, as a chastened Party embarked on a post-mortem. Moreover, Wheatley's politics were distinctive and should not be collapsed into a predictable Left-wing response. His arguments raised fundamental and difficult problems about the pursuit of a Socialist strategy through the British State, and more basically within one national community. But he became a largely forgotten politician, remembered for his brief Ministerial career or as one of the Clydeside rebels. His ideas, if considered at all, were assimilated into the conventional terms of Labour Left politics.

A past for a future

This history is one of failure, political isolation and subsequent misunderstanding. Connolly gambled that a nationalist revolution in wartime Ireland would have a Socialist significance; Maclean, inspired by the Bolshevik success, hoped that Scottish separatism would facilitate Socialist revolution. Neither dream left much mark on later political developments. The Free State combined the legacy of nationalist revolution with social conservatism; the Scottish working class responded to economic depression by, at most, supporting a Labour Party committed to a Unionist and gradualist strategy. Wheatley supported this response but insisted that the welfare of the British working class necessitated a vigorous transitional programme. Even the disaster of 1931 did not produce this.

These failures can promote neglect or the prevalence of simplistic and misleading images. Such fates fall far short of what is deserved. All three encountered forbidding challenges – poverty, indifference, and bigotry. Their political expectations were frustrated frequently. Connolly and Maclean confronted the authoritarianism of the wartime State. They knew the isolation and the vulnerability that came from dogged adherence to principle. Wheatley too came to know isolation as the cost of principle; not the isolation of the marginal weak organisation, but the loneliness that came from persistent defeats at the hands of a majority who were disinclined to consider awkward arguments.

No doubt as individuals, they could be difficult. Connolly and Maclean engaged in bitter polemics and sometimes injected personal acerbities into political controversies. Wheatley was classed by some as an aloof manipulative machine politician. Their visions of Socialism paid little attention to the oppression of women. Connolly was at best ambivalent, Maclean uninterested, and Wheatley reactionary.[1] All subscribed to a patriarchal culture where women often bore the heavy costs of male commitment to Socialist principle. Yet set against this, there were positives. Both Connolly and Maclean exhibited implacable heroism; all demonstrated a tough honesty. Their political expectations had been formed largely by the sentiments and assumptions of pre-1914 Socialism. Each confronted the destruction of this Socialist world and in doing so went beyond conventional reactions.

Their frustrations owed something to the lack of political space.

Connolly faced the domination of Irish Nationalist politics by a well-established Parliamentary Party. However conservative most of its leaders might be on social questions, they had credibility as the political custodians of Nationalist interests. Sinn Fein posed a similar problem for Connolly's successors. Like other British Marxists, Maclean had to come to terms with a working-class politics whose principal institutional expression was the Labour Party. The Social Democratic Federation, the British Socialist Party and the Communist Party all faced the problem of a rival whose position seemed to be as secure as its policies were judged inadequate. Although Wheatley belonged to this dominant organisation, he rejected the policies of its leadership, but found that critics had little influence. The alliance between the Parliamentary leaders and the officials of major unions normally held firm. Left initiatives were deflected, discredited, or when necessary, crushed.

Emphasis on the constraints suggests that hopes of alternatives were naive. Awareness of such limitations is important, yet within the seemingly inexorable patterns, there were moments perhaps when the connections were less certain. The transition from the dominance of Redmond's Party to that of Sinn Fein with the continuing marginalisation of Labour politics was not as simple as hindsight might suggest. The hegemony of the British Labour Party can appear inescapable – yet there were critical moments. The original decision to inaugurate a Socialist-trade union alliance had involved the defeat of those who preferred an overtly Socialist Party. Once this basic choice was made, alternatives became even less feasible. Nevertheless the survival of the Labour Party, more or less intact, throughout the 1914–18 War requires explanation. This durability can appear as a tribute to trade-union pragmatism, but the possibility of a rupture often seemed present. By the mid 1920s, Labour's identity and procedures seemed much more stable. This was the inhospitable prospect facing John Wheatley.

The narrowing of options was not just a consequence of Labour dominance. It also reflected the emergence of the Communist Party as the only significant Left-alternative. Revolutionary Socialists were attracted to a Party which could claim the authority of an apparently successful revolution, the more so when other revolutionary opportunities seemed to have vanished. The establishment of Third International orthodoxy meant either the canalisation and metamorphosis, or the disparaging, of alternative revolutionary strategies. One body of sentiment, largely absorbed by and transformed within the British Communist Party was the syndicalist current that had flowed through the trade-union Left since 1910. Connolly had articulated this; Maclean eventually had been influenced by it. To some degree, its decline reflected widely-perceived inadequacies. An emphasis on workplace organisation seemed to have little credibility when such initiatives had been pulverised by depression and victimisation. The results of post-War confrontations suggested that syndicalist optimism about the by-passing of State power was naive. But much was lost or changed out of recognition – the belief in and emphasis on participatory democracy, a sceptical appraisal of leadership as potentially irresponsible and conservative – but above all, a fundamental optimism about working-class creativity. Perhaps such optimism was incongruous in the political landscape of the 1920s. Certainly it found itself squeezed between the dominant alternatives: Social Democracy or Communism. The choice reflected the legacies of revolution and then of the subsequent capitalist stabilisation.

One area where there could be agreement across this divide was on the need for political initiatives to have a British basis. Only in the late 1930s, when the Popular Front strategy suggested the desirability of relating to radical national traditions did the Communist Party express support for Scottish and Welsh self-determination. One reason for the earlier agreement had been that trade-union experiences seemed to recommended all-British strategies. Even before 1914 miners and railwaymen had embarked on their first 'national' strikes. Noah Ablett, Syndicalist, a product of the Rhondda and the Central Labour College, responded to industrial conflict in the South Wales coalfield by declaring in May 1911 – 'we are out for a national movement'.[2] The local struggle over abnormal place payments developed into a national campaign for a minimum wage. The 'national movement' would be British in scope; its vehicle would be the Miners' Federation of Great Britain; an early objective to persuade the British Government to introduce legislation on wages. These parameters seemed compelling in those years when industrial militants were optimistic. Maclean urged Scottish miners to support their Welsh colleagues; Connolly hoped for British support to help locked-out Dublin workers. Often such solidarity proved elusive or brittle. But the achievements seemed to justify the strategy. The arguments seemed even more compelling in the dark years after 1921. Miners fought to salvage the remnants of national agreements. As recession devastated exporting coalfields, a united defence by Scottish, Welsh and English miners seemed the most credible response. It was the coalowners who favoured 'Home Rule' as the basis for negotiations. The argument could be extended readily. If Britain was the appropriate arena for industrial action, then the same should apply politically.

Historical analysis demonstrates how one strategy for Socialism in Britain became dominant. It indicates also how this outcome was the product of a complex history that included diverse responses on the theme of Nationalism and Socialism. Such an acount offers a temptation. The prospect that capitalism might be transformed through the Labour Party operating within the institutions of the British State has been corroded by the experiences of successive Labour Governments. So why not pick up those threads that were broken or knotted so many years ago? Why not link Socialist hopes with those for separatist Nationalisms within the United Kingdom?

But the examination of old complexities vetoes such a simple response. Connolly's arguments cannot be applied to the traumas of modern Irish politics. Maclean's principled stands provide no answer to the devastation of the modern Scottish economy. In part the objection is a basic historical one. These individuals, their ideas and their choices must be understood in their contexts as they responded to novel and sometimes misunderstood challenges.

Yet the difficulty goes deeper. Each of these Socialists offers insights into the complex problems of Nationalism and Socialist strategy. Whilst these are reminders of the diverse responses that have been available within the British Left, their illumination is as much of obstacles as of potentials. The case of Connolly provides stark testimony. The pre-occupation with the National Question ensured a divided Irish working-class, and helped to limit the development of Socialist politics. These divisions were exacerbated by the increasing emphasis on a Gaelic interpretation of Irish identity. This characterisation contained emphases that, from a Socialist viewpoint, might count as regressive.

An effective Socialist movement can develop only if it can make connections with the culture of the existing society. This includes elements that postulate a communal or national identity. Typically these will incorporate both progressive and regressive potentials. Connolly approached these issues in a relatively self-conscious fashion. He explored how an Irish Socialist movement should respond to, and then amend, pre-existing characterisations of Irish identity. His odyssey offers a perceptive if ultimately unsuccessful exploration of a perennial and inescapable problem.

Nations, after all, are 'imagined communities'.[3] Claims about their character and their extent are contestable. The results of such contests are likely to have far-reaching political consequences. Perhaps, this is particularly the case in a multi-national political system such as the United Kingdom.

The earlier history indicates a complex contemporary diagnosis. The politics of a multi-national State offer the possibility of alliances between subordinate Nationalisms and other radical movements. Arguments over self-determination, independence and devolution can puncture the self-confidence of elites and erode the power of conservative myths. Yet this radical prospectus must be handled cautiously.

Characterisations of Welsh, Scottish and Irish identity often contain significant radical emphases yet in each case, a thicket of progressive and regressive elements must be explored. This task must be complemented by a deflating awareness that the more radical characterisations need not enjoy widespread support. In the General Election of 1979, Wales moved sharply to the Right; despite four years of industrial devastation this shift was reaffirmed in 1983. Those who articulated a radical nationalism, that seemed to offer a wider Socialist hope, were exposed in a cruel isolation.[4] The brute force of electoral statistics destroyed any simplistic image of 'Radical Wales'. Yet in 1984, support for the Welsh miners transcended barriers of language and of geography.[5] Whether this marked the development of a popular radical characterisation of a Welsh community remains an open question; as yet the nagging doubt must remain.

Brooding over arguments about the complex relationships between Celtic Nationalisms and Socialism, there is the problem of the British State and its identification with a durable, conservative characterisation of British – or often English – identity. This State has always had a robust capacity for authoritarianism. The myth of unspotted liberalism survives only in official panegyrics and in the fanciful flights of some political scientists. This profile should be set alongside Wheatley's politics. These demonstrated the pressures that drove a Socialist, Irish by origin and Scottish by political apprenticeship to his belief that the British State offered the most likely instrument for Socialist advance. He did so without beginning to consider how far such a British identity and centralised strategy could be combined with a Socialist politics.

Attempts have been made to fill this gap. From the late 1930s Communist Party historians argued for a radical democratic English pedigree.[6] Michael Foot offered a characterisation of radical patriotism whose tragic denouement provided a starting point for this analysis. Edward Thompson faced the electoral torpor of 1983 and argued for a radical Britain to set against that of the authoritarian, philistine bully. He acknowledged an obstacle:

I am told by my friends in Wales and in Scotland that I have got it wrong. They say that the trouble with Britain has always been one thing: the English. And it is true that if the matter had been left to the choice of the Welsh and Scottish nations, we would long ago have had a non-nuclear island, and some other democratic improvements besides.[7]

The problem of course, is not 'the English' but the close connection between one presentation of English identity, and the characteristic ethos of the British State. Yet the easier dismissal is all too understandable. Many English Socialists – and some from elsewhere in the British Isles – have responded uncritically to such a presentation and such a style. The events of 1982 demonstrated that the British State and its culture pose an unavoidable problem for Socialists. Contestation of images of national identity is as vital for English Socialists as for their Celtic counterparts.

The centralised State is, in key respects, increasingly authoritarian. Gloomy testimony is provided by the fates of municipal revolts against rate-capping, of miners' pickets against a nationally-organised police force, and of much else. Such emphases readily promote a mirroring of Wheatley's arguments. If the British State is where decisive power seems to rest, then this should be the focus for radical politics. But it is not just the record of the Left during the last half-century that illuminates the difficulties with this response. In economic terms, the British State has become increasingly irrelevant. Capitalist organisations have shattered communities without attention to the interests of the 'nation'.[8] The responses of those affected have focused increasingly in arenas other than that of the State. Often the threat appears as a local one, felt intensely at the level of the knowable community.[9] So miners in 1984 reacted in terms of immediate traditional solidarities, but then often extended beyond the familiar relationships to a wider union that eroded old barriers of style, gender and place. The building blocks of resistance were variants on the complex theme of community. But the levels of oil and coal imports showed how the resources of capital were oblivious to national frontiers. In response miners' delegations crossed Europe seeking support.[10]

The most intense manifestations were local; the confrontation raised basic questions about the character of national communities – who after all was 'the enemy within?'; yet resistance required attempts to build international alliances; through it all, there ran a challenge to conventional economic and social priorities. Yet the power of the State could not be ignored – the road blocks, the arrests, the Ministerial comments – sometimes vindictive, sometimes misleading, often self-righteous; the indifference or worse of welfare services.[11]

This untidy spontaneous resistance, captured in so many images of 1984, demonstrated how, on the one hand, the points of pressure produced resistance that built outwards from the community into a network that went beyond the limits of the nation; and yet in the last analysis this web could not withstand the resources of the British State.

The Labour Party Leadership reacted in familiar terms. All should be subordinated to pursuit of electoral victory. The prize is the Government of Britain. That tired face of June 1983 has gone. But the strategy remains. A familiar film is remade yet again. Once it brought the crowds; now the script seems dated; the audience is sparse.

This analysis has highlighted a less familiar world when debates about Socialist politics were linked often with arguments about national identity. The British State mattered for Socialists, but it was not always their prime objective nor did it straitjacket thoughts on strategy. This is a history to work through facing difficulties and ambiguities honestly and avoiding simplistic responses.

Recovery of such a complex past is sufficient justification for a historical enterprise. The political legacy is a tangle; attempts to draw implications for the present may be often naive. Yet there is perhaps a significant perception. British Socialists should face up to the problem of how to characterise those national communities that are presided over by the British State. Through this, there may be some hope of creative relationships between national and communal movements, and a socialist politics informed by an ecumenical view of strategy.

In many parts of North-West England, in the sodden summer of 1985, there is not much hope.

Notes

Threads

1 Eric Hobsbawm (ed.), *The Forward March of Labour Halted?* (Verso, London, 1981).

2 'Cato', *Guilty Men* (Gollancz, London, 1940). For a discussion of an earlier example of radical–patriotism and its demise see Hugh Cunningham, 'The Language of Patriotism', *History Workshop Journal* (12), 1981, pp. 8–33.

3 A. J. P. Taylor, *English History 1914–45* (Clarendon, Oxford, 1965), p. 600. The adjective in the title of a book that covers Wales, Scotland and until 1922 Ireland, is perhaps significant evidence of the way in which these alternative national traditions have been written out of many historical accounts. More recently, Welsh, Scottish and Irish historians have begun to redress this situation with a series of rigorous and creative works. Scottish and Irish sources appear in later chapters – for Wales see Kenneth O. Morgan, *Rebirth of a Nation: Wales 1880–1980* (University Presses of Oxford and Wales, 1982). Gwyn Williams, *When Was Wales?* (Penguin, Harmondsworth, 1985); plus a collection of essays David Smith (ed.), *A People and a Proletariat* (Pluto, London, 1980). Michael Foot's view of 1945 can be found in his *Aneurin Bevan; 1945–60* (Davis-Poynter, London, 1973), pp. 1–3; for a later gallery of radical-patriotic heroes, see his *Debts of Honour* (Picador, London, 1981).

4 Significant responses to these developments can be found in the writings of Tom Nairn. See his *The Left Against Europe?* (Penguin, Harmondsworth, 1973) and *The Break-Up of Britain* (New Left Books, London, 1977). For one critical response to the latter work see Eric Hobsbawm, 'Some Reflections on "The Break-Up of Britain"', *New Left Review* (105), 1977, pp. 3–23. For an analysis considering the merits of various approaches, Jim Bulpitt, *Territory and Power in the United Kingdom* (University Press, Manchester, 1983).

5 Speech at Cheltenham, 3 July 1982, cited in Anthony Barnett, 'Iron Britannia', *New Left Review* (134), 1982, Sections I–III of this article are especially valuable for the issues raised in this chapter.

6 For examples of the range of responses see Stuart Hall and Martin Jacques (eds.), *The Politics of Thatcherism* (Lawrence and Wishart, London, 1983), Section III – the contributions by Hobsbawm, Robert Gray and Nairn.

7 *The Communist Manifesto* reprinted in Karl Marx, *The Revolutions of 1848* (Penguin, Harmondsworth, 1973), p. 78.

8 *Ibid.*, p. 84.

9 For a discussion utilising many examples from this period, see Eric Hobsbawm, 'What Is the Workers' Country?' in his *Worlds of Labour* (Weidenfeld, London, 1984), pp. 49–65; published originally as 'Working Classes and Nations', *Saothar* (8), 1982, pp. 75–85.

10 On the general theme of Marxist responses to nationalist questions see Michel Lowy, 'Marxism and the National Question' in Robin Blackburn (ed.),

Revolution and Class Struggle: a Reader in Marxist Politics (Fontana, London, 1979). See also Nairn, *The Break-Up of Britain*, pp. 82–91, and his 'Internationalism: a critique', *Bulletin of Scottish Politics*, 1 (autumn 1980), pp. 101–25.

11 Cited in Peter Nettl, *Rosa Luxemburg* (University Press, Oxford, 1969), p. 502. The original source was a letter to Kautsky dated 7 February 1882. Nettl pp. 500–502 summarises Marx and Engels' attitude to Polish nationalism.

12 See *ibid*, Appendix, 'The National Question', pp. 500–519.

13 See Lowy, Marxism ...; for other summaries of his view see Leszek Kolakowski, *Main Currents of Marxism 2: The Golden Age* (University Press, Oxford, 1981), pp. 285–290; John Breuilly, *Nationalism and the State* (University Press, Manchester, 1982), pp. 322–323. There is a brief extract from Bauer's work in Tom Bottomore and Patrick Goode, *Austro–Marxism* (University Press, Oxford, 1978), pp. 102–117.

14 Cited in Tom Bottomore, *Sociology and Socialism* (Wheatsheaf, Brighton, 1984), pp. 43–44, original source Bauer, 'What is Austro–Marxism?' (1927).

15 For discussions of Lenin's views see Neil Harding, *Lenin's Political Thought, Vol. 1, Theory and Practice in the Democratic Revolution* (Macmillan, London, 1977), pp. 296–302 for his pre-war polemic with Luxemburg; *Vol. 2, Theory and Practice in the Socialist Revolution* (Macmillan, London, 1981), pp. 59–68 for his analysis of national–liberation movements in the context of imperialism.

16 George Orwell, 'The Lion and the Unicorn' in his *Collected Essays and Letters Volume 2* (Penguin, Harmondsworth, 1971), p. 88; for a critical analysis see Raymond Williams, *Orwell* (Fontana, London, 1971), Chapter 2, and for a discussion of Orwell's life during this period, Bernard Crick, *George Orwell* (Secker, London, 1980), Chapter 12.

17 On the EEC and on the Communist position towards this controversy see Nairn, *The Left Against Europe?* For Benn see for example his *Parliament, People and Power* (Verso, London, 1982) especially Section II, 'The British State and Democracy' and Section III 'Britain's Crises'; for the idea of a British Liberation struggle see pp. 107–108.

18 For a description of this confrontation see E. P. Thompson, *William Morris: From Romantic to Revolutionary* (Merlin, London, 1977), pp. 482–495.

19 This and preceding quotations from Marx to Sigfrid Meyer and August Vogt, 9 April 1870 in K. Marx and F. Engels, *Ireland and the Irish Question* (Progress Publishers, Moscow, 1971), pp. 292–294.

20 See Teodor Shanin, 'Marx and the Peasant Commune', *History Workshop Journal* (12), 1981, pp. 108–128.

21 For a discussion see Ellen Hazelkorn, 'Reconsidering Marx and Engels on Ireland', *Saothar* (9), 1983, pp. 79–88.

22 The choice of individuals will hopefully be justified by what follows. The case of Wales raises problems that are distinctive – not least that of the continuing relevance of the language question. For a Welsh Socialist who did take the national question seriously see Robert Griffiths, *S. O. Davies: A Socialist Faith* (Gomer Press, Llandysal, 1983); also the same author's *Turning to London: Labour's Attitude to Wales, 1898–1956* ('Y Faner Goch', Cardiff, n.d.); The question of why the Welsh-speaking quarrymen of Gwynedd combined a strong national identity with trade unionism but not with political separatism in the years before 1914 is discussed in R. Merfyn Jones, *The North Wales Quarrymen, 1874–1922* (University of Wales Press, Cardiff, 1982), pp. 55–71, especially from p. 69. The parallel between this analysis and Bauer's emphasis on cultural autonomy, perhaps under a multinational state, is striking.

23   This theme is analysed in Dai Smith, *Wales! Wales!* (Allen and Unwin, London, 1984), Chapter 4.

PART I

The red and the green

1   See particularly the most thorough published biography, C. Desmond Greaves, *The Life and Times of James Connolly* (Lawrence and Wishart, London, 1976); also the profile by Desmond Ryan, *James Connolly* (Labour Publishing Company, London, 1924), and the sketch by him in J. W. Boyle (ed.), *Leaders and Workers* (Mercier Press, Cork, 1978), pp. 67–75. A more conceptual work is provided by Bernard Ransom in *Connolly's Marxism* (Pluto Press, London, 1980), with its theme of the Hibernicisation of Marxism.

2   For two contrasting analyses of the broader problems, see Michael Farrell, *The Orange State* (Pluto Press, London, 1976); Belinda Probert, *Beyond Orange and Green* (Academy Press, Dublin, 1978).

3   Originally in his *The Story of the Irish Citizen Army* – first published in 1919; see also his *Drums Under the Windows* (Macmillan, London, 1946), p. 315 on Connolly – 'His fine eyes saw red no longer, but stared into the sky for a green dawn'.

4   See for example, Austen Morgan, 'Socialism in Ireland – Red, Green and Orange' in Austen Morgan and Bob Purdie, *Ireland: Divided Nation, Divided Class* (Ind Links, London, 1980); John Newsinger, 'James Connolly and The Easter Rising', *Science and Society*, Summer 1983, Vol. 47, pp. 152–177.

Chapter 1: Edinburgh

1   For material, see Bernard Ransom, 'James Connolly and the Scottish Left' (unpublished Edinburgh PhD, 1975), hereafter Ransom *Thesis*, Chapter 1; C. Desmond Greaves, *The Life and Times of James Connolly* (Lawrence and Wishart, London, 1976), Chapters 3 and 4; Ruth Dudley Edwards, *James Connolly* (Gill and Macmillan, Dublin, 1981), Chapter 1.

2   The occupational structure is discussed in R. Q. Gray, *The Labour Aristocracy in Victorian Edinburgh* (Clarendon Press, Oxford, 1976), pp. 19–26.

3   *Justice*, 12 August 1893.

4   See Gray, *op cit*, especially pp. 169–81; see also especially for the impact of the rail strike John Gilray, 'Early Days of the Socialist Movement in Edinburgh', *NLS. Acc. 4965*, hereafter Gilray, *MS.*

5   See Jim Smyth, 'Socialism in Scotland; the Beginnings' in *Radical Scotland*, No. 7, Feb/March 1984; also Gilray, *MS.*

6   For this theme see Ransom, *Thesis*, pp. 29–30.

7   For records of these developments see Scottish Labour Party, Edinburgh Central Branch Minutes, *NLS. Acc. 3828 (Microfilm)*; and Independent Labour Party, Edinburgh Central Branch Minutes, Edinburgh Public Library.

8   *Justice*, 12 August 1893.

9   *Edinburgh Labour Chronicle*, 5 November 1894.

10   *Ibid*, 1 December 1894.

11   *Ibid*.

12   *Ibid*, 5 November 1894.

13   See *ibid*, 15 October 1894.

14   *Ibid*, 1 December 1894.
15   *Ibid*.
16   *Ibid*.
17   See for example the exchanges at the Mid-Lanark By-Election of April 1894 as cited in David Howell, *British Workers and the Independent Labour Party 1888–1906* (University Press, Manchester, 1983), pp. 154–6.
18   Cited in Gray, *op cit*, pp. 98–9; original source Royal Commission on Housing in Scotland, Q. 19273.
19   *Ibid*, p. 178.
20   For background, see Greaves, *op cit*, pp. 38–9; 50.
21   John Leslie, *The Irish Question* (Reprint, Cork Workers' Club, 1974), p. 3.
22   *Ibid*, pp. 4–5.
23   *Ibid*, pp. 5–6, including an attack on John Mitchel for his anti-Socialism.
24   *Ibid*, p. 8.
25   *Ibid*, p. 9.
26   *Ibid*, p. 23. In contrast, note at pp. 24–5 the attacks on Davitt, then intervening on behalf of Liberal candidates, including the case of Mid-Lanark.
27   *Ibid*, p. 13 – note on p. 14 the claim that only through Socialism can Ireland become a manufacturing nation without brutal exploitation.
28   Connolly to Hardie, 8 and 19 June 1894. Copies in William O'Brien Papers *NLI*, MS 13933. Originals of this correspondence in *ILP Archive*, 1894. See also Edinburgh Central ILP Minute Book for 1894 for relevant discussions.
29   Connolly to Hardie 3 July 1894 – copy in O'Brien Papers, MS 13933.
30   *Edinburgh Labour Chronicle*, 5 November 1894.

Chapter 2: Dublin

1   See D Keogh, *The Rise of the Irish Working Class: The Dublin Trade Union Movement and Labour Leadership 1890–1914* (Appletree Press, Belfast, 1982), Chapter 1.
2   *Ibid*, Chapter 2.
3   For Connolly's Dublin years, see Greaves, *op cit*, Chapters 5–8; R. Dudley Edwards, *op cit*, Chapter 2.
4   William O'Brien, *Forth the Banners Go* (Three Candles, Dublin, 1969), p. 4.
5   *Workers' Republic* (hereafter *WR*), 7 October 1899.
6   O'Brien, *op cit*, pp. 30–5 for election details.
7   *Ibid* p. 5.
8   *ISRP Minute Book*, 12 February 1900, William O'Brien Collection, National Library of Ireland, MS 16265.
9   For details see Greaves, *op cit*, pp. 75–7.
10   For the SDF view see *Justice*, 14 May 1892.
11   For the Irish Party in the 1890s, see F. S. L. Lyons, *The Irish Parliamentary Party 1890–1910* (Faber and Faber, London, 1951).
12   For these developments, see F. S. L. Lyons, *Culture and Anarchy in Ireland 1890–1939* (University Press, Oxford, 1982), Chapters 3 and 4.
13   *Shan Van Vocht*, October 1896.
14   The text of the original pamphlet can be found in three articles – 'Ireland for the Irish' in *Labour Leader*, 10, 17 and 24 October 1896. The pamphlet went through successive editions in which some amendments were made in the direction of a more exclusivist Socialism. To avoid confusion, all references here are from the *Labour Leader* articles.

15   *Labour Leader*, 10 October 1896.

16   For discussions of this, see Teodor Shanin, 'Marx, and the Peasant Commune' and Haruki Wada, 'Marx and Revolutionary Russia', both in *History
Workshop Journal* (12), 1981.

17   *WR*, 23 September 1899.

18   *WR*, 1 July 1899.

19   *Shan Van Vocht*, January 1897.

20   *WR*, 20 August 1898.

21   *Ibid*, 12 May 1900.

22   *Labour Leader*, 17 October 1900.

23   *Shan Van Vocht*, 1 January 1897.

24   *Labour Leader*, 26 March 1898 (unsigned review of Gavan-Duffy's, *My
Life in Two Hemispheres*).

25   *WR*, 5 August 1899.

26   *Labour Leader*, 17 October 1896.

27   See Nancy Cardozo, *Maud Gonne* (Gollancz, London, 1979), pp. 126–30;
also W. B. Yeats, *Autobiographies* (Macmillan, London, 1955), p. 366.

28   Greaves, *op cit*, pp. 97–100; R. Dudley Edwards, *op cit*, p. 26.

29   *WR*, 3 September 1898, reprinted from *L'Irlande Libre*.

30   *Ibid*.

31   *Labour Leader*, 17 October 1896.

32   See Greaves, *op cit*, pp. 101–5; R. Dudley Edwards, *op cit*, p. 25; for Maud
Gonne's part, Cardozo, *op cit*, pp. 145–52.

33   *Labour Leader*, 17 October 1896.

34   *WR*, 27 August 1898.

35   *Ibid*, 24 September 1898.

36   *Labour Leader*, 24 October 1896.

37   *WR*, 10 June 1899.

38   *Ibid*, 22 September 1900.

39   See K. Marx, 'The Civil War in France', in *The First International and After*
(Penguin, Harmondsworth, 1974), especially pp. 206–12.

40   *Labour Leader*, 24 October 1896.

41   *Ibid*.

42   *Labour Leader*, 22 January 1898; for Marx's emphasis on Anglo–Irish
differences as a key element in capitalist domination see his letter to Meyer and
Vogt, 9 April 1870, cited in Marx and Engels *Ireland and the Irish Question*.

43   *Labour Leader*, 22 January 1898.

44   *Ibid*, 24 October 1896.

45   *WR*, 2 September 1899.

46   *Ibid*, 12 August 1899.

47   *Ibid*, 4 November 1899.

48   *Ibid*, 1 July 1899.

49   *Ibid*, 15 December 1900.

50   *Ibid*, 3 September 1898.

51   *Shan Van Vocht*, November 1896.

52   See *WR*, 22 July 1899.

53   *Ibid*, 27 August 1898 for hope; and 16 September 1899, for criticism.

54   *Ibid*, 20 August 1898.

55   *Ibid*, 19 August 1899.

56   *Ibid*, 4 November 1899. For Marx, see 'The British Rule in India' in *Surveys
from Exile* (Penguin, Harmondsworth, 1977), pp. 301–6).

57   On theme of British Socialists and the South African War, see D. Howell,
op cit, Chapters 15 and 16 passim.

58   *WR*, 19 August 1899.
  59   See Greaves, *op cit*, pp. 113–25; R. Dudley Edwards, *op cit*, pp. 31–5; Cardozo, *op cit*, Chapters 19–22; for Griffith, see R. P. Davis, *Arthur Griffith and Non-Violent Sinn Fein* (Anvil Books, Dublin, 1974).

Chapter 3: Sectarianism

  1   James Connolly, *Erin's Hope – The End and the Means* (Sphinx Publications, Dublin, nd. but probably 1936) – both quotations from p. 15 of this edition.
  2   *WR*, 5 August 1899.
  3   For details see W. O'Brien, *op cit*, pp. 30–1; also D. Keogh, *op cit*.
  4   *WR*, 27 August 1898.
  5   *Ibid*, 16 September 1899.
  6   *Justice*, 31 March 1900; these comments were in response to an article by Bruce Glasier in *Clarion*, 17 March 1900, describing his Irish tour under Fabian Society auspices.
  7   *WR*, March 1901.
  8   *Ibid*, October 1901.
  9   See R. Dudley Edwards, *op cit*, p. 36; W. O'Brien, *op cit*, p. 27.
  10   For example, the complexities surrounding Quelch's contest at Dewsbury early in 1902. See Greaves, *op cit*, pp. 139–40.
  11   On the SDF see C. Tsuzuki, *H. M. Hyndman and British Socialism* (Heinemann and Oxford University Press, London, 1961); Henry Collins, 'The Marxism of the Social Democratic Federation' in Asa Briggs and John Saville (eds.), *Essays in Labour History 1886–1923* (Macmillan, London, 1971), pp. 47–69.
  12   On this see Raymond Challinor, *The Origins of British Bolshevism* (Croom Helm, London, 1977), pp. 9–10.
  13   On these campaigns see *Justice*, 22 and 29 June, 13 and 27 July, 21 September, 5, 12 and 19 October 1901; 17 May, 12 and 19 July, 9 and 30 August 1902.
  14   James Connolly to J. C. Matheson, 14 March 1902, William O'Brien Papers (NLI), MS 13906.
  15   *Ibid*, 14 July 1902, *loc cit*.
  16   Quoting Sutton of Salford, *ibid*.
  17   On these developments, see Challinor, *op cit*, chapter 1; Ransom, *Thesis*, pp. 94–141 passim.
  18   Connolly to Matheson, 21 March 1903, William O'Brien Papers, MS 13906.
  19   See Greaves, *op cit*, pp. 146–159; Dudley-Edwards, *op cit*, pp. 43–6.
  20   See *The Socialist*, July 1903 for report of inaugural conference. Delegates attended from Glasgow, Edinburgh, Leith.
  21   On this see Tom Bell, *Pioneering Days* (Lawrence and Wishart, London, 1941), pp. 40–1.
  22   *The Socialist*, June 1903.
  23   See letter from Connolly to the American, SLP, 31 March 1899, quoted in C. Tsuzuki, 'The Impossibilist Revolt in Britain', *International Review of Social History* (1), 1956, p. 377.
  24   Greaves, *op cit*, pp. 104–5.
  25   *WR*, 10 February 1900.
  26   *Ibid*, August 1902.
  27   Letter from Bridgeport Conn. 23 September 1902, W. O'Brien Papers, MS 13906.

28   Connolly to Matheson, February 1903, *loc cit.*
29   See particularly on De Leon, L. G. Seretan, *Daniel De Leon: The Odyssey of an American Marxist* (Harvard UP, Cambridge, Mass. 1979).
30   Morris Hillquit 'Loose Leaves from a Busy Life', (NY, 1934), p. 34, cited in L. G. Seretan, 'The Personal Style and Political Methods of Daniel De Leon: A Reconsideration', *Labor History*, Spring 1973, p. 163–201.
31   *The Socialist*, June 1903.
32   Daniel De Leon, *Reform or Revolution* (SLP Press, Edinburgh 1906), p. 8.
33   *Ibid*, p. 9.
34   *Ibid*, pp. 14–15.
35   *Ibid*, p. 26.
36   *The Socialist*, June 1903.
37   For the Party's weakness, see Challinor, *op cit*, p. 28.
38   *The Socialist*, June 1903.
39   Connolly to Thomas Lyng from Providence, RI, 29 September 1902, *William O'Brien Papers*, MS 13912(ii).
40   See John Laslett, 'De Leonite Socialism and the Irish Shoe Workers of New England', in his *Labor and the Left* (Basic Books N.Y. 1970).
41   Silverman of the Boot and Shoe Workers Union, 24 April 1898, in debate with De Leonites cited *ibid*, p. 69.
42   On this point see Seretan, *Daniel De Leon: The Odyssey of an American Marxist*, pp. 157ff.
43   *Weekly People*, 9 April 1904 reprinted in *The Connolly–De Leon Controversy on Wages, Marriage and the Church* (The Cork Workers' Club, Cork, nd.).
44   Connolly to Matheson, July 1904, *W. O'Brien Papers*, MS 13906.
45   *Ibid*, 19 November 1905 (from Newark), *loc cit.*
46   *Ibid*, 10 June 1906, *loc cit.* See also his letter of 28 January 1907 to Secretary, Irish Socialist Party, *O'Brien Papers*, MS 13940.
47   Connolly to Matheson, 27 September 1907, *W. O'Brien Papers*, MS 13906.
48   *Ibid*, 6 April 1907, *loc cit.*
49   *Ibid*, 30 January 1908, *loc cit.*
50   *Ibid*, 7 May 1908, *loc cit.*
51   *Ibid*, 10 June 1909, *loc cit.*

Chapter 4: Syndicalism

1   For the IWW see Melvyn Dubofsky, *We Shall Be All* (Quadrangle Books, Chicago, 1969); Philip Foner, *History of the Labor Movement in the United States, Vol. IV, The Industrial Workers of the World* (International Publishers, New York, 1965). Material on Connolly's involvement in the organisation can be found in Carl Reeve and Ann Barton Reeve, *James Connolly and the United States* (Humanities Press, Atlantic Highlands, NJ, 1978), Chapters 9–15.
2   Connolly to Matheson, 1 March 1908, *William O'Brien Papers*, MS 13906.
3   For this, Reeve and Barton Reeve, *op cit*, Chapters 9–11 and also material on Connolly's involvement in the New York IWW can be found in the *Industrial Unionist Bulletin* (reprinted by Greenwood, Westport Conn, 1970) – under the heading 'Notes From New York'.
4   See Seretan *op cit*, pp. 175ff; Dubofsky, *op cit*, part 2, passim.
5   Daniel De Leon's address at Minneapolis, 10 July 1905, published as *The Preamble of the Industrial Workers of the World* (later as 'Principles of Industrial Unionism'), pp. 24–5.

6 See Dubofsky, *op cit*, pp. 83–4.

7 As suggested in Connolly to Matheson, 19 November 1905, *loc cit*.

8 *Ibid*, c April 1907.

9 *Ibid*, 27 September 1907.

10 For WFM, see the appropriate chapter in John H. M. Laslett, *Labor and the Left*; also Dubofsky, *op cit*, esp. Chapters 3 and 4.

11 Cited in Dubofsky, *op cit*, p. 109.

12 See his letter to Matheson, 27 September 1907, *loc cit*.

13 For the inaugural convention and the IWW's first year, see Dubofsky, *op cit*, pp. 71–115; for the background to Debs's early involvement see Nick Salvatore, *Eugene V. Debs: Citizen and Socialist* (University of Illinois Press, 1982), pp. 200–12.

14 Connolly to Matheson, c April 1907, *loc cit*.

15 *Ibid*, 8 October 1908.

16 Dubofsky, *op cit*, pp. 131–2; p. 141.

17 Connolly to Matheson, April 1908, *loc cit*.

18 *Ibid*, 7 May 1908, *loc cit*.

19 Original statement in Western Federation of Miners, Proceedings of the 1907 Convention and cited in Dubofsky, *op cit*, p. 135.

20 From Industrial Unionist Bulletin, April 1908, cited in Dubofsky, *op cit*, p. 136; Connolly saw himself largely in agreement with Williams – except for the latter's underestimating 'the necessity of fully utilising the political structure of capitalism as a propagandist basis' – see his letter to Matheson, 8 April 1908, *loc cit*.

21 See Reeve and Barton Reeve, *op cit*, pp. 123–32.

22 Dubofsky, *op cit*, pp. 136–41.

23 Connolly to Matheson, 27 September 1907, *loc cit*.

24 *Ibid*, 27 September 1908, *loc cit* (written during the Chicago Convention). Connolly's presence at the 1908 Convention, although not as a voting delegate can be traced in *Industrial Unionist Bulletin*, 10, 24 October, 7 November 1908.

25 *Ibid*. Connolly's political development can be traced in *The Harp*, January, May and June 1908. See also the recollections of John Lyng, *O'Brien Papers*, MS 13929.

26 The cover design for the original was drawn by Ralph Chaplin – see his *Wobbly: the Rough and Tumble Story of an American Radical* (University of Chicago Press, 1948), p. 150 'The Cover I drew was full of runic decorations, shamrocks and an Irish harp'.

The other relevant writings are 'Ballots, Bullets or – ', *International Socialist Review*, October 1909; 'A New Labour Policy', *The Harp*, January 1910; 'Industrialism and the Trade Unions', *International Socialist Review*, February 1910.

27 *Socialism Made Easy* (The Plough Book Service Dublin, 1971), p. 38.

28 *Ibid*, p. 44.

29 *Ibid*, p. 45.

30 *Ibid*, p. 47.

31 *Ibid*, p. 38.

32 *Ibid*, p. 39.

33 *Ibid*, p. 40.

34 For this strategy see Sally M. Miller, *Victor Berger and the Promise of Constructive Socialism 1910–20* (Greenwood Press, Westport Conn, 1973).

35 Connolly, *Socialism Made Easy*, p. 40.

36 *Ibid*.

37   *Ibid*, p. 41.

38   For the way in which such experiences could lead to pessimistic conclusion, see David Beetham, 'From Socialism to Fascism: The Relation between
Theory and Practice in the work of Robert Michels, *Political Studies*, 1977,
pp. 3–24, 161–81.

39   For a characteristic example see Connolly to Matheson April 1908, *loc cit*
– 'Our loathing for De Leon did not turn us to anti-ballotism but did set our mind
to work to discover the method by which the working class could control its own
political party, and put the non-working class elements where they belong'.

40   'Ballots, Bullets or – ', *International Socialist Review* October 1909,
reprinted in Ryan (ed.), *The Workers' Republic*, p. 67. See also *Labour, Nationality
and Religion* (New Book Publications, Dublin, 1972), p. 55.

41   *The Miners' Next Step Being a Suggested Scheme for the Reorganisation
of the Federation Issued by the Unofficial Reform Committee* (1912), see
especially 'Ch IV Constitution', and 'Ch V Policy'.

42   Eg. *Socialism Made Easy*, pp. 39–40 or *Labour, Nationality and Religion*,
pp. 43–4.

43   For a discussion of this theme see E. J. Hobsbawm, 'Bolshevism and the
Anarchists' in his *Revolutionaries* (Quartet, London, 1977), pp. 57–70.

44   For the first complete English translation see Werner Sombart, *Why is there
No Socialism in the United States?* (trans. P. M. Hocking and C. T. Husbands),
(Macmillan, London, 1976); for recent discussions of the topic, see Jerome
Karabel, 'The Failure of American Socialism Reconsidered', *Socialist Register
1979*, Mike Davis, 'Why the US Working Class is Different', *New Left Review*,
123, September–October 1980, pp. 3–44; Eric Foner, 'Why is There No Socialism
in the United States?', *History Workshop Journal* (17), Spring 1984, pp. 57–80.

45   For an example of the longevity of some of these discussions see the
quotation from E. L. Godkin dated 1867 in Eric Foner, *op cit*, p. 58.

46   Sombart, *op cit*, p. 106.

47   See for example, *The Harp*, May 1908.

48   For a discussion of the variable impacts of ethnic and communal ties on
the development of class solidarities see John T. Cumbler, *Working Class Community in Industrial America: Work, Leisure and Struggle in Two Industrial
Cities, 1880–1930* (Greenwood Press, Westport, Conn, 1979).

49   For material on this see Salvatore, *op cit*; David A. Shannon, *The Socialist
Party of America: A History* (Macmillan, N.Y. 1955). Ira Kipnis, *The American
Socialist Movement 1897–1912* (Greenwood Press, New York, 1968). H. Wayne
Morgan, *Eugene V Debs Socialist For President* (University Press Syracuse, 1962).

50   For these years in the IWW, see Dubofsky, *op cit*, Chapters 8–11.

51   Sombart, *op cit*, p. 119.

52   'A New Labour Policy', *The Harp*, January 1910 reprinted in Ryan, ed.,
The Workers' Republic, p. 73.

53   Philip Foner, *op cit*, pp. 281–95 paints a positive portrait of the IWW's
impact at McKees Rocks; Dubofsky, *op cit* draws attention to a wider range of
factors and is less sanguine about the IWW's achievements – see pp. 198–209.
For Connolly's initial pessimism about impact of craft–union sectionalism see
The Harp August 1909.

54   Cited in Dubofsky, *op cit*, p. 206.

55   *Ibid*, p. 209 notes that an attempt to reorganise the IWW local showed only
20 signatories of members.

56   Reeve and Barton Reeve, *op cit*, Chapter 17 chronicles Connolly's involvement. Dubofsky refers to dispute in one sentence on p. 208. Philip Foner, *op cit*,

discusses it at pp. 299–303 with particular reference to early months of the dispute.

57 In 'Industrialism and the Trade Unions', *International Socialist Review*, February 1910, reprinted in Ryan (ed.), *The Workers' Republic*, p. 85. See also *Socialism Made Easy*, pp. 33–6, and *Industrial Unionist Bulletin*, 28 December 1907.

58 'Industrialism and the Trade Unions' at p. 78 in Ryan volume.

59 *Ibid* – the argument is developed at pp. 78–80 in *op cit.*

60 *Ibid* at p. 80 in *op cit.*

61 *Ibid* at pp. 80–81 in *op cit.*

62 For a discussion of the historiographical debates surrounding the Knights see Davis *op cit*, pp. 26–29 especially p. 28 and the accompanying footnote 41.

63 Chicago Socialist 23 December 1905 cited in H. W. Morgan *op cit*, p. 87.

64 On its vicissitudes see William M. Dick, *Labor and Socialism In America: The Gompers Era* (Kennitat Press, Port Washington, NY, 1972), esp Chapters 2, 3 and 5; Marc Karson, *American Labor Unions and Politics 1900–1918* (Southern Illinois UP, Carbondale, Ill, 1958), Chapters 2, 3 and 6. Lasswell, *op cit.*

65 Cited in Dick, *op cit*, p. 129.

66 'Industrialism and the Trade Unions', p. 81 in Ryan collection.

67 See Laswell, *op cit*, and also analysis in Dick, *op cit*, pp. 67–80.

68 *Socialism Made Easy*, p. 40.

69 For material on repression see Dubofsky, *op cit*, pp. 191–5 for San Diego free speech fight, 1912; Chapters 15–17 for the War and its aftermath; also William Preson Jr, *Aliens and Dissenters: Federal Suppression of Radicals 1903–1933* (Harvard UP, Cambridge, 1963).

70 For this optimism see his letter to Matheson, 27 September 1908, *loc cit.*

71 For these developments viewed from various positions see Salvatore, *op cit*, pp. 242–58; Miller, *op cit*, Chapters 3 and 6, and Kipnis, *op cit*, especially Chapters 17 and 18.

72 The sources cited in FN71 all give analyses of the split: they disagree on whether any link should be made between the exodus of members and the victory of the Right. Compare Miller at pp. 109–10 and Kipnis at p. 418.

73 *The Harp*, February 1908.

Chapter 5: Socialism and the 'Gael'

1 See David Doyle, 'The Irish and American Labour 1880–1920', *Saothar* I, 1975, pp. 42–53.

2 *The Harp*, January 1909.

3 For emphases on the divisive impact of ethnic loyalties on socialist perspectives, see Karabel, 'The Failure of American Socialism Reconsidered', and Davis, 'Why the US Working Class is Different'.

4 As exemplified in Cumbler, *Working Class Community in Industrial America*.

5 Cited in Elizabeth Gurley Flynn, *I Speak My Own Piece* (Masses and Mainstream, New York, 1955), p. 65.

6 *The Harp*, May 1908.

7 *Ibid*, September 1908.

8 *Ibid*, May 1909.

9 Cited as in Doyle, *op cit*, p. 46.

10   See the chapter on the Shoe Workers in J. Laslett, *Labor and the Left*. For the stereotype, Marc Karson, *American Labor Unions and Politics 1900–1918*, Chapters 9 and 10.

11   See Flynn, *op cit*, pp. 65–6.

12   Connolly claimed that De Leon's hostility had some significance. See his letter to William O'Brien, 13 April 1907, *O'Brien Papers*, MS 13908.

13   See his letters to O'Brien, 13 November and 6 December 1909, *loc cit*.

14   Flynn, *op cit*, p. 66.

15   Circular dated January 1907 following foundation of Irish Socialist Federation in *O'Brien Papers*, MS 13908.

16   See copy of a piece by Connolly for *Weekly People*, 2 March 1907 in *loc cit*, MS 13928.

17   *The Harp*, January 1908.

18   *Ibid*, January 1909.

19   *Ibid*, September 1908.

20   *Ibid*, August 1909. See Connolly's comment in the Foreword to *Labour in Irish History* (hereafter LIH) that Alice Stopford Green's book was 'the only contribution to Irish history we know of which conforms to the methods of modern historical science', *LIH*, p. 1. Edition used here (Three Candles, Dublin, nd.), published as part of *Labour in Ireland*.

21   *LIH*, p. 1.

22   For his emphasis that the loss of a communal social system went along with the loss of the language see *ibid*, pp. 2, 4–5.

23   *Ibid*, p. 8.

24   *The Reconquest of Ireland* (New Book Publications, Dublin, 1972), Foreword.

25   *Ibid*, p. 40.

26   *Ibid*, p. 41.

27   *Ibid*, p. 129–30.

28   See Raphael Samuel, 'British Marxist Historians', *New Left Review*, (120), 1980, pp. 34–7; 58–9.

29   *LIH*, pp. 7–8.

30   *Ibid*, pp. 120–1.

31   *Ibid*, p. 80.

32   See J. C. Beckett, *The Making of Modern Ireland* (Faber, London, 1966), Chapter 13; T. Pakenham, *The Year of Liberty* (Hodder and Stoughton, London, 1969).

33   *LIH*, p. 60.

34   *Ibid*, p. 46.

35   *Ibid*, pp. 79–80.

36   *The Socialist*, August 1903.

37   *LIH*, p. 132.

38   *Ibid*, p. 139.

39   Mitchel, cited in *LIH*, p. 141.

40   John Mitchel, *Jail Journal* (Gill, Dublin, nd.), p. 78, including the comment 'Socialists are something worse than wild beasts'.

41   For a much more complete publication of his writings, see James Fintan Lalor, *Collected Writings* (Talbot Press, Dublin, 1947).

42   *LIH*, p. 148.

43   Cited in F. S. L. Lyons, *Ireland Since the Famine* (Fontana, London, 1968), pp. 111–12; Thomas Luby, *Irish People*, 19 December 1863, the original source.

44   Cited in T. W. Moody, 'The Fenian Movement in Irish History' in his edited collection *The Fenian Movement* (Mercier Press, Dublin and Cork, 1978), p. 105.

45   *LIH*, pp. 159–64.
46   *The Harp*, January 1909.
47   *LIH*, p. 135.
48   For the comparison see Neal Ascherson, *The Polish August* (Penguin, Harmondsworth, 1981), pp. 86–7. See also Emmet Larkin 'Church, State and Nation in Modern Ireland', *American Historical Review*, 1975, pp. 1244–76.
49   *Forward*, 9 May 1913.
50   For a discussion of this aspect see F. S. L. Lyons, *Culture and Anarchy in Ireland*, Chapter 3.
51   Tom Bell, *Pioneering Days*, p. 51.
52   For discussions of this aspect of Connolly's thought see Ransom, *Connolly's Marxism*, Chapter 4; Owen Dudley Edwards, *The Mind of An Activist: James Connolly* (Gill and Macmillan, Dublin, 1971).
53   *Labour Leader*, 18 January 1896.
54   *Ibid*, 15 February 1896.
55   *The People*, 9 April 1904, reprinted in *The Connolly–De Leon Controversy*.
56   See Chapter 9 of *News From Nowhere*.
57   Americanism and Fordism in Antonio Gramsci, *Selections From the Prison Notebooks*, ed. Q. Hoare and G. Nowell-Smith (Lawrence and Wishart, London, 1973), pp. 304–5.
58   See for example Chapter 6 of *The Reconquest of Ireland*.
59   For the growing anti-socialism of the Catholic Church in Ireland pre-1914, see Emmet Larkin, 'Socialism and Catholicism in Ireland', *Church History*, 1964, pp. 462–83.
60   *The Harp*, September 1908.
61   *Labour Nationality and Religion*, Chapter 2.
62   *Ibid*, pp. 50–60.
63   *Ibid*, p. 58.
64   See Samuel, *op cit*.
65   *Forward*, 2 August 1913.

Chapter 6: Unionism and the working class

1   See R. Dudley Edwards, *op cit*, pp. 86–102; C. Desmond Greaves, *op cit*, Chapter 15; Austen Morgan, 'Politics, the Labour Movement and the Working Class in Belfast, 1905–1923', Queens University Belfast PhD, 1978, (hereafter Morgan *Thesis*), Chapter 8; Henry Patterson, *Class Conflict and Sectarianism: The Protestant Working Class and The Belfast Labour Movement, 1868–1920* (Blackstaff Press, Belfast, 1980), Chapter 4.
2   *Forward*, 3 May 1913.
3   See ATQ Stewart, *The Ulster Crisis: Resistance to Home Rule 1912–14* (Faber, London, 1967).
4   Connolly to William O'Brien, 29 July 1913, *O'Brien Papers*, MS 13908.
5   See Patterson, *op cit*, pp. 80–4.
6   See *ibid*, p. 82.
7   *Irish Worker*, 6 June 1914.
8   *Forward*, 25 July 1914.
9   *Ibid*, 23 August 1913; 3 May 1913.
10   Connolly to O'Brien, 7 December 1911, *O'Brien Papers*, MS 13908.
11   *Workers' Republic*, 12 February 1916.
12   *Forward*, 2 August 1913.
13   *Ibid*, 13 March 1911.

14   Cited in Appendix 1 of Brian Inglis, *Roger Casement* (Coronet Books, London, 1974), p. 426.

15   *Forward*, 3 May 1913.

16   *Ibid*, 2 August 1913.

17   *Ibid*, 27 May 1911.

18   *Ibid*, 23 August 1913.

19   *Ibid*, 5 July 1913.

20   See the sources by Patterson and Morgan already cited; see also Peter Gibbon, *The Origins of Ulster Unionism* (University Press, Manchester, 1975); Paul Bew, Peter Gibbon and Henry Patterson, *The State in Northern Ireland 1921–72* (University Press, Manchester, 1979); Belinda Probert, *Beyond Orange and Green*; Tom Nairn, *The Break-up of Britain*, Chapter 5; also some of the publications of the British and Irish Communist Organisation proposing the 'Two Nations' thesis such as *Connolly and Partition* (1972); See also Chapter 5 of Lyons, *Culture and Anarchy*.

21   For a critical discussion of this tendency see the Introduction to Patterson, *Class Conflict and Sectarianism*.

22   These developments are considered in the early chapters of Patterson's book.

23   On the place of the Belfast dispute, see David Howell, *British Workers and the Independent Labour Party 1888–1906*, p. 87.

24   For a discussion of Walker, to supplement the treatment in Patteson *op cit*, and in Morgan *Thesis*, see J. W. Boyle, 'William Walker', in his (ed.), *Leaders and Workers* (Mercier Press, Cork, 1978), pp. 57–65.

25   September 1905, Dixon Unionist 4,440 Walker LRC 3,966 Maj 474 January 1906 Dixon Unionist 4,907 Walker LRC 4,616 Maj 291.

26   This time, the vote was Clarke, Unionist 6,021, Walker 4,194, Maj 1,827.

27   On this theme, see Patterson, *op cit*, pp. 40–1.

28   On sectarianism and occupations see *ibid*, pp. xiii–xv; also the comment in Morgan, *thesis*, pp. 32–3.

29   Probert, *op cit*, Chapter 1 places a very strong emphasis on this element; for a vigorous characterisation of this culture see Geoff Bell, *The Protestants of Ulster* (Pluto, London, 1976).

30   These developments are discussed in Patterson, *op cit*, especially pp. 43–6, and in his 'Independent Orangeism and Class Conflict in Edwardian Belfast', *Proceedings of the Royal Irish Academy*, Vol. 80, Section C, No. 4 (1980), pp. 1–27. For detailed analysis of Sloan's campaign and of the IOO, see J. W. Boyle, 'The Belfast Protestant Association and the Independent Orange Order', *Irish Historical Studies*, XIII (1962–63), pp. 117–52.

31   *Labour Leader*, 30 August 1902.

32   See Patterson's criticism of Probert's failure to consider this component in *Saothar*, No. 5 (1979), pp. 50–55; also his discussion of the theme in *Class Consciousness and Sectarianism*, pp. 46–51.

33   *Belfast Labour Chronicle*, November 1904.

34   See Boyle, 'William Walker', pp. 61–2. He said 'Protestantism means protesting against superstition, hence true protestantism is synonymous with labour'.

35   See, for example, Pete Curran's letter in *Belfast Labour Chronicle*, 23 September 1905.

36   As argued by Walker and reported in *Irish News*, 23 August 1905, cited in Patterson, *Class Conflict and Sectarianism*, pp. 56–57.

37   As predicted in the leader article, *Belfast Labour Chronicle*, November 1904.

38   *Ibid*, 14 October 1905. This is in the context of a leader on the Irish language.

39   *Ibid*, 7 October 1905.

40   *Ibid*, July 1905.

41   *Ibid*.

42   *Ibid*, 7 October 1905.

43   Some contemporary examples are discussed in Patterson, 'Independent Orangeism and Class Conflict in Edwardian Belfast'.

44   The occasion was a debate at the 1911 Irish TUC on this question when for the last time the Belfast Labour Unionists were successful, *ITUC Report of Proceedings* 1911, pp. 39—42. The polemic is in *Forward*, 27 May, 10 June, 1 July 1911 (Connolly's contributions); 3 June, 17 June and 8 July 1911 (Walker's contributions). All have been reprinted as *The Connolly—Walker Controversy — On Socialist Unity in Ireland* (The Cork Workers' Club, nd.).

45   *Forward*, 27 May 1911.

46   At a meeting to support Walker's proposed candidacy reported in *Belfast Labour Chronicle*, May 1905.

47   The Belfast disputes of 1907 are discussed in Patterson, *Class Conflict and Sectarianism*, pp. 66—72; his 'James Larkin and the Belfast Dockers' and Carters' Strike of 1907', *Saothar* 4, pp. 8—14; John McHugh, 'The Belfast Labour Dispute and Riots of 1907', *North West Group for the Study of Labour History. Bulletin*, No. 4, 92—129; Emmet Larkin, *James Larkin* (Routledge, London, 1965), pp. 26—40; Morgan, *Thesis*, Chapter 3.

48   Larkin, *op cit*, p. 27.

49   Indeed, Emmet Larkin despite the earlier quotation seems to accept this: 'In the long run Larkin achieved little of a tangible nature in Belfast, not because he was something less than what he should have been, but because his enemies were too powerful and circumstances too adverse', *ibid*, p. 40.

50   *Forward*, 7 June 1913.

Chapter 7: Lock Out

1   Lord Askwith, *Industrial Problems and Disputes* (John Murray, London 1920), p. 259.

2   On the development of the ITGWU in Dublin see C. Desmond Greaves, *The Irish Transport and General Workers' Union: The Formative Years, 1909—1923* (Gill and Macmillan, Dublin 1982); Emmet Larkin, *James Larkin*; D. Keogh, *The Rise of the Irish Working Class*, especially Chapters 6 and 7; C. Desmond Greaves, *The Life and Times of James Connolly*, Chapter 17; for a view from the employers' side, see Arnold Wright, *Disturbed Dublin* (Longmans, London, 1914). See also the Essays in Review by Emmet O'Connor, 'An Age of Agitation, *Saothar* (9), 1983, pp. 64—70, and by John Newsinger in *Bulletin of the Society for the Study of Labour History* (49), Autumn 1984, pp. 69—71.

3   James Connolly, *The Reconquest of Ireland*, p. 30.

4   See Larkin, *op cit*, p. 109.

5   *Ibid*, pp. 74—6.

6   Keogh, *op cit*, pp. 154—5.

7   New Statesman, 6 September 1913 — a piece headed 'Anarchism in Dublin'.

8   Connolly to William O'Brien, 13 September 1912, *O'Brien Papers*, MS 13908.

9   For a study of this conflict see Dermot Keogh, 'William Martin Murphy and the Origins of the 1913 Lock Out', *Saothar* (4), 1978, pp. 15–34.

10   For the escalation of the confrontation see *ibid*, also Larkin *op cit*.

11   The MP was Handel Booth reported in *Manchester Guardian*, 1 September 1913.

12   For a discussion of this relationship see Bill Moran, '1913, Jim Larkin and the British Labour Movement', *Saothar* (4), pp. 35–49.

13   For examples, see Keogh, 'William Martin Murphy', pp. 30–1.

14   For detail on Connolly's role, see Greaves, *op cit*, Chapter 17.

15   For presentations of this type of thesis see Moran, *op cit*, especially pp. 46–8; E. Strauss, *Irish Nationalism and British Democracy* (Methuen, London, 1951), pp. 223–8.

16   For the programme, see Larkin, *op cit*, pp. 61–3; and then pp. 95–6 for a consideration of the attachment to compulsory arbitration.

17   *Irish Review*, October 1913, p. 391.

18   *The Miners' Next Step*, Chapter 1.

19   For the political legacy of the British experience, see David Howell, *British Workers and the Independent Labour Party*, Chapter 6.

20   See 'Report of the Dublin Disturbances Commission', Command 7569, p. 13 in *Parliamentary Papers* (1914), Vol. XVIII.

21   ITUC, 1912, *Report*, pp. 12–19 for resolution and debate.

22   For Larkin's loss of interest see R. Dudley Edwards, *James Connolly*, pp. 96–7.

23   The basis for the projected Irish Labour Party restricted itself to 'labour representation'. Socialism was not mentioned. See ITUC *Report*, 1912, p. 12.

24   See Larkin, *op cit*, pp. 100–106, for background.

25   *Forward*, 31 January 1914.

26   *Dublin Trades Council Minutes*, 26 January 1914.

27   *British Trades Union Congress Report*, 1913, p. 67.

28   *British TUC, Minutes of Parliamentary Committee*, 19 November 1913.

29   These developments were chronicled in the *Daily Herald*.

30   For reports see *Daily Herald*, 16–22 September 1913; 3–9 December 1913.

31   For Connolly's response to this episode, see *ibid*, 6 December 1913.

32   *Ibid*, 13 October 1913, reporting Larkin's speech at Birmingham.

33   Interview, *ibid*, 31 October 1913.

34   *Ibid*, 17 November 1913.

35   Reports can be found in *Daily Herald*, and *Manchester Guardian*, both for 10 December 1913; also *Labour Leader*, 11 December 1913. The decisive vote was on an amendment moved by Jack Jones of the Gasworkers favouring the 'blacking' of Dublin goods. This was defeated by 2,280,000 to 203,000.

36   *Daily Herald*, 10 December 1913.

37   Cited with critical comments in *ibid*, 23 September 1913; see also Snowden's statements of his position, and Hardie's criticisms in *Labour Leader*, 25 September, 2, 9 and 23 October 1913. Note also Philip Snowden, *Socialism and Syndicalism* (Collins, London, nd).

38   Speech at Manchester cited *Daily Herald*, 17 November 1913.

39   *Daily Herald*, 12 December 1913.

40   See piece from Labour Press Agency in *ibid*, 27 November 1913.

41   For a discussion of Tillett's motivation, see Jonathan Schneer, *Ben Tillett* (University of Illinois Press, Urbana, 1983), pp. 166–72.

42   See *Manchester Guardian*, 24 November and 3 December 1913.

43   *Ibid*, 18 September 1913.

44 *Daily Herald*, 17 September 1913.

45 *Forward*, February 1914.

46 *Ibid*.

47 For affirmations of his continuing faith in Industrial Unionism, see *ibid*, 21 February, 14 March 1914.

48 See for example, *Daily Herald*, 3 November 1913 for an attack by Williams on NUR officials' opposition to 'sympathetic strikes', *ibid*, 13 December 1913 on his barring from the Special Congress.

49 This and immediately preceding quotations from 'Old Wine in New Bottles', *New Age*, 30 April 1914.

50 Speech at Victoria Park, East London, reported in *Manchester Guardian*, 15 September 1913.

51 For a discussion of these disputes see Schneer, *Ben Tillett*, pp. 150–163.

52 *New Age*, 30 April 1914.

53 *Forward*, 23 May 1914.

54 *Irish Worker*, 29 November 1913.

55 *Forward*, 2 May 1914.

56 See for example, *ibid*, 18 April 1914.

57 A case put in *ibid*, 11 April 1914.

58 *The Reconquest of Ireland*, p. 61.

59 One exception was Stephen Gwynn, see *Daily Herald*, 21 November 1913.

60 Dillon to T. P. O'Connor, 15 October 1913, cited in F. S. L. Lyons, *John Dillon* (Routledge, London, 1968), p. 335.

61 See generally Emmet Larkin, 'Socialism and Catholicism in Ireland', *Church History*, 1964.

62 *Daily Herald*, 7 November 1913.

63 Catholic Bulletin, November 1913 cited in P. J. O'Farrell, *Ireland's English Question* (Batsford, London, 1971), pp. 269–70.

64 For Griffith and Sinn Fein, see Richard P. David, *Arthur Griffith and Non-Violent Sinn Fein*.

65 See *The Harp*, April 1908, and *Irish Nation*, 23 January 1909.

66 *Ibid*.

67 See Davis, *op cit*, for examples of this response.

68 This and the preceding quotes from Griffith's article, 'Sinn Fein and the Labour Question', *Sinn Fein*, 25 October 1913.

69 Moreover a leader article in *Sinn Fein*, 27 September 1913 had referred to Connolly as 'the man in the Leadership of the Transport Union with a head on his shoulders'. Note also *Irish Worker*, 13 December 1913, praising Griffith's attitude to police treatment of strikers.

70 For one response by Sheehy-Skeffington to the issue of the children, see *Daily Herald*, 28 October 1913.

71 *Irish Worker*, 1 November 1913.

72 *Irish Times*, 8 October 1913.

73 *Daily Herald*, 3 November 1913.

74 Connolly subsequently used Russell's work on Co-operation – see Chapter 8 of *The Reconquest of Ireland*.

75 *Irish Worker*, 1 November 1913.

76 For his career until then see Ruth Dudley Edwards, *Patrick Pearse: The Triumph of Failure* (Faber, London, 1979).

77 'From a Hermitage October 1913', in Padraic H. Pearse, *Political Writings and Speeches* (Talbot Press, Dublin, 1962), pp. 173–4.

78 *Ibid*, p. 176.

79   *Ibid*, p. 180.
80   For MacDonagh, see his evidence to the Commission on the Dublin
Disturbances, Command 7269, *Parliamentary Papers* (1914), Vol. XVIII; for
Markiewicz, see her involvement in Larkin's appearance in O'Connell Street,
31 August 1913 – see Larkin, *op cit*.
81   *Irish Worker*, 15 November 1913.
82   At a meeting on 13 November 1913, cited in W. O'Brien, *Forth the Banners
Go*, p. 120.

Chapter 8: The choice

1   For Tillett in wartime, see J. Schneer, *Ben Tillett*, Chapter 9; for Stanton
see the entry in Joyce Bellamy and John Saville, *Dictionary of Labour Biography*,
Volume 1 (Macmillan, London, 1972), pp. 311–12. An illuminating discussion
covering both figures' pre-1914 styles is Peter Stead, 'The Language of Edwardian
Politics', in D. Smith, *A People and a Proletariat*, pp. 148–65.
2   The ambiguities of MacDonald's position are explored in David Marquand,
Ramsay MacDonald (Cape, London, 1977), Chapters 9–10. There is no adequate
biography of Snowden but see Colin Cross, *Philip Snowden* (Barrie and Rockliff,
London, 1966).
3   Original sources, Burns Diary 29th October 1914, cited in K. D. Brown, *John
Burns* (Royal Historical Society, London, 1977), p. 187.
4   For examples of Connolly's response to the policy of the Parliamentary
Party, see *Irish Worker*, 8 August and 12 September 1914.
5   For the Volunteers, see F. X. Martin (ed.), *the Irish Volunteers 1913–1915:
Recollections and Documents* (James Duffy, Dublin, 1963); Michael Tierney,
Eoin MacNeill Scholar and Man of Action, 1867–1945 (Clarendon Press, Oxford,
1980), Chapters 7–10; for the Redmondite response see Denis Gwynn, *The Life
of John Redmond* (Harrop, London, 1932). Key aspects are discussed in Charles
Townshend, *Political Violence in Ireland: Government and Resistance Since 1848*
(Clarendon Press, Oxford, 1983), Chapter 5.
6   From Redmond's speech at Woodenbridge, 20 September 1914, cited in
Martin (ed.), *The Irish Volunteers*, p. 148. Part IX of the same volume gives
material on the response of the Irish Volunteers to Redmond's activities.
7   For estimates see Tierney, *op cit*, p. 154 citing Bulmer Hobson's calculations
as his source.
8   The problems confronting the Parliamentary Party are examined in Gwyn,
op cit, Chapters 10–12.
9   For discussions of these divergences, see Tierney, *op cit*, Chapters 11,
13–15; Townshend, *op cit*, Chapter 6; R. Dudley Edwards, *Patrick Pearse*,
Chapter 6.
10   This was Alderman Lawrence Kettle – see the brief reference in Martin
(ed.), *op cit*, p. 29. On the disturbance, see also R. M. Fox, *The History of the
Irish Citizen Army* (James Duffy, Dublin, 1944), p. 9.
11   For the ICA, see material in *William O'Brien Papers*, MS 15673. Also, Fox
op cit; Sean O'Casey. *The Story of the Irish Citizen Army* (Reprint, Journeyman
Press, London, 1980); the discrepancies in this account are discussed in C.
Desmond Greaves, *Sean O'Casey: Politics and Art* (Lawrence and Wishart,
London, 1979), Chapter 6. Note also the analysis in Townshend, *op cit*, pp. 283–5
and in F. X. Martin, '1916: Myth, Fact and Mystery', *Studia Hibernica*, 1967,
pp. 76–79.

12 *Forward*, 15 August 1914.
13 *Ibid*, 22 August 1914.
14 For these developments, see Ransom, *Thesis*, p. 311; also Tom Bell, *Pioneering Days*, pp. 49–50.
15 *International Socialist Review*, March 1915.
16 *Workers' Republic*, 24 July 1915.
17 *Ibid*, 21 August 1915.
18 *Ibid*, 8 April 1916.
19 *Ibid*, 18 September 1915.
20 *Ibid*, 29 May 1915 for a statement by Connolly of the union's current position.
21 See *ibid*, 12 June 1915 for the decision to contest. There is a reprint of Farren's manifesto in Ryan (ed.), *The Workers' Republic*, pp. 181–2.
22 *Workers' Republic*, 19 June 1915.
23 *Ibid*, 5 February 1916.
24 *Irish Worker*, 8 August 1914.
25 *Workers' Republic*, 22 January 1916.
26 *Irish Worker*, 29 August 1914.
27 *Ibid*, 31 October 1914.
28 Cited in Leon O'Broin, *Dublin Castle and the 1916 Rising: The Story of Sir Matthew Nathan* (Helican, Dublin, 1966), p. 23. Original source gives as Nathan MS 462, 11 November 1914 (Bodleian Library).
29 *Forward*, 22 August 1914.
30 *Irish Worker*, 29 August 1914.
31 *Workers' Republic*, 18 March 1916.
32 For Connolly's response to this claim, see *Irish Worker*, 12 September 1914; also *ibid*, 8 August 1914 for claim that military support for a German army in Ireland would be justified because of its damaging consequences for the British Empire.
33 *Workers' Republic*, 8 August 1916.
34 Full text in R. Dudley Edwards, pp. 280–1; prefaced by the claim that it was 'mainly *Pearse's* work' (p. 279).
35 See *ibid*, pp. 217–18, which includes the recollection of William O'Brien that at a conference on 9 September 1914, 'Connolly advocated making definite arrangements for organising an insurrection, and … getting in touch with Germany, with a view to military support'.
36 These looked at lessons of earlier European insurrections – see *Workers' Republic*, 24 July 1915 for a summary.
37 The preparations for the funeral are discussed in R. Dudley Edwards, *op cit*, pp. 235–8; the speech at the graveside by Pearse is in his *Political Writings and Speeches*, pp. 133–7 and is prefaced by 'a character study', pp. 127–32. These can be compared with Connolly's praise of Rossa in *Workers' Republic*, 7 August 1915. For the authorities' attitude to the funeral demonstration, see O'Broin, *op cit*, pp. 52–3.
38 This strand is very prominent in *Workers' Republic* during the last months of 1915 – see for example, his emphasis on Mitchel in issue of 13 November.
39 *Ibid*, 13 November 1915.
40 *Ibid*, 20 November 1915.
41 *Ibid*, 13 November 1915.
42 *Ibid*, 18 December 1915.
43 *Ibid*, 22 January 1916.
44 *Ibid*, 29 January 1916.

Chapter 9: Might-have-beens

1   Eric Hobsbawm, 'Some Reflections on "The Break-Up of Britain"', *New Left Review* (105), 1977.
2   *Lenin on Ireland* (New Books, Dublin, 1974), pp. 32–3 – originally written in July 1916 and published October 1916.
3   Sean O'Casey, *The History of the Irish Citizen Army*, p. 52.
4   *Workers' Republic*, 7 August 1915.
5   *Ibid*, 18 March 1916.
6   *Ibid*, 22 January 1916.
7   Pearse, *Political Writings and Speeches*, p. 340.
8   *Ibid*, p. 341. For a discussion of this last pamphlet of Pearse see R. Dudley Edwards, *op cit*, pp. 257–261. It is worth noting the contemporary verdict of James Stephens in his *The Insurrection in Dublin* (Maunsel, Dublin, 1916), pp. 96–7: 'The Reputation of all the leaders of the insurrection, not excepting Connolly, is that they were intensely patriotic Irishmen, and also, but this time with the exception of Connolly, that they were not particularly interested in the problems of labour.'
9   'Peace and the Gael' in Pearse, *Political Writings and Speeches*, pp. 213–218, passage cited is at p. 216.
10   *Workers' Republic*, 25 December 1915.
11   *Forward*, 22 August 1914.
12   *Workers' Republic*, 5 February 1916.
13   For the problem of interpretation see F. X. Martin, 'The 1916 Rising – a Coup d'Etat or a "Bloody Protest"?', *Studia Hibernica*, 1968, pp. 106–37, also Townshend, *op cit*, Chapter 6.
14   'The Rose Tree' – text taken from Roger McHugh (ed.), *Dublin 1916* (Arlington, London, 1976), p. 332.
15   *Irish Work*, 19 December 1914. (This was an abortive attempt to replace the banned *Irish Worker*.)
16   Letter published in *The Socialist*, 17 April 1919.
17   Cited in R. Dudley Edwards, *op cit*, p. 250 – original source Bulmer Hobson, MSS (NLI).
18   See Hannah Sheehy-Skeffington, 'A Pacifist Dies', in McHugh (ed.), *op cit*, pp. 276–88. See also the piece by his son Owen Sheehy-Skeffington in O. Dudley Edwards and F. Pyle (ed.), *1916: The Easter Rising* (MacGibbon and Kee, London, 1968), pp. 135–48, and Roger McHugh, 'Thomas Kettle and Francis Sheehy-Skeffington' in Conor Cruise O'Brien (ed.), *The Shaping of Modern Ireland* (Routledge, London, 1960), pp. 124–39.
19   Stephens, *The Insurrection in Dublin*, pp. 50–1.
20   Cited by Owen Sheehy-Skeffington in Edwards and Pyle, *op cit*, p. 144.
21   A point made by Owen Dudley Edwards in his *The Mind of an Activist*, Chapter 4, 'The Lost Heir'.
22   Reprinted in Dudley Edwards and Pyle, *op cit*, pp. 149–52; originally printed in the *Irish Citizen*, May 1915.
23   *Ibid*, p. 150.
24   *Ibid*, p. 151.
25   *Ibid*, p. 152.
26   *Labour Leader*, 27 April 1916 – the same paper on 11 May 1916 referred to the rebellion as 'a crime'.
27   Tierney, *Eoin MacNeill* is a thorough biography.

28   See F. X. Martin, 'Eoin MacNeill on the 1916 Rising' in *Irish Historical Studies*, Vol. XII, 1960–61, pp. 226–71. This includes an Introduction and very detailed footnotes. Two memoranda are reproduced. The crucial one for the present analysis is Memorandum 1 at pp. 234–40; footnotes pp. 240–5. (The second memorandum dealt with MacNeill's role in the events leading up to the Rising.) Both documents were found in the Hobson Papers.

29   *Irish Historical Studies*, Vol. XII, p. 236.

30   *Ibid.*

31   *Ibid*, p. 239.

32   *Ibid*, p. 240.

33   See for example his celebration of the Manchester Martyrs, *Workers' Republic*, 20 November 1915.

34   Thus he saw this failure as characteristic of most leaders in 1848 – see for example, *Workers' Republic*, 13 November 1848 – a view that depended on a belief that the leaders consistently betrayed a more militant rank and file. This view was reiterated after he had committed himself to the Rising. See *ibid*, 11 March 1916.

35   *Ibid*, 8 April 1916.

36   A point made by Townshend, *op cit*, especially pp. 313–21.

37   This point is made in MacNeill's Memorandum of February 1916, *IHS*, Vol. XII, pp. 239–40.

38   *Lenin on Ireland*, pp. 33–4.

39   For some discussion see Conor Cruise O'Brien, 'The Embers of Easter: 1916–1966' in Edwards and Pyle, *op cit*, especially pp. 225–28. The changing political situation in one county, Clare, is discussed in David Fitzpatrick, *Politics and Irish Life, 1913–1921: Provincial Experience of War and Revolution* (Gill and Macmillan, Dublin, 1977).

40   See *ibid*, especially Chapter 7. For one trade union involvement in the War of Independence see C. Townshend, 'The Irish Railway Strike of 1920; Industrial Action and Civil Resistance in the Struggle for Independence', *Irish Historical Studies* (XXI), 1979, pp. 265–82. An earlier general survey is Patrick Lynch, 'The Social Revolution That Never Was', in Desmond Williams (ed.), *The Irish Struggle, 1916–1926* (Routledge, London, 1966), pp. 41–54.

41   On this paticular confrontation see Emmet O'Connor, 'Agrarian Unrest and the Labour Movement in County Waterford, 1917–1923', *Saothar* (6), 1980, pp. 40–58.

42   This argument was set down on 10 March 1922. It is reproduced in J. Anthony Gaughan, *Thomas Johnson* (Kingdom Books, Dublin, 1980), pp. 192–3, footnote 5. The original source was *Voice of Labour*, 18 March 1922; the context, an argument with British Communists about the feasibility of revolution in Ireland.

43   The original publication had been signed 'J'.

44   Townshend, *op cit*, pp. 338–39 considers how far there was widespread participation and reaches a relatively sceptical conclusion.

45   For discussions on this scheme see Brian Farrell, 'Labour and the Irish Political Party System: A Suggested Approach to Analysis', *Economic and Social Review*, 1970, pp. 477–502; and Peter Mair, 'Labour and the Irish Party System Revisited: Party Competition in the 1920s', *Economic and Social Review*, 1977, pp. 59–70.

46   Text in R. Dudley Edwards, *op cit*, pp. 261–2.

PART II

A disputed legacy

1 For a brief account of Maclean's career see the entry in William Knox (ed.), *Scottish Labour Leaders 1918–39: A Biographical Dictionary* (Mainstream, Edinburgh, 1984), pp. 179–92.

2 See W. Gallacher, *Revolt on the Clyce* (Lawrence and Wishart, London, 1936); also his *Last Memoirs* (Lawrence and Wishart, London, 1966); Tom Bell, *John Maclean: Fighter for Freedom* (Communist Party Scottish Committee, Glasgow, 1944). For an earlier study from a different political tradition – anti-parliamentary communism – see Guy Alfred, *John Maclean: Martyr of the Class Struggle* (Strickland Press, Glasgow, 1932).

3 See for example Gallacher, *Revolt on the Clyde*, Chapter 9.

4 For MacDiarmid's views, see the discussion of Maclean on his *The Company I've Kept* (Hutchinson, London, 1966); his reference to him in his introduction to P. Berresford Ellis and S. MacA-Ghabhainn, *The Scottish Insurrection of 1820* (Gollancz, London, 1970), and his two poems. 'John Maclean (1879–1923)' and 'Krassivy, Krassivy.' in his *Complete Poems 1920–76* (Martin, Brian and O'Keefe, London, 1978).

5 For an account informed by this emphasis see John Broom, *John Maclean* (Macdonald, Loanhead, 1973); the biography by Maclean's daughter Nan Milton, *John Maclean* (Pluto, London, 1973), shares similar concerns.

6 The best example of this genre is perhaps Walter Kendall, *The Revolutionary Movement in Britain 1900–21* (Weidenfeld, London, 1969).

7 For this judgement see Iain McLean, *The Legend of Red Clydeside* (John Donald, Edinburgh, 1983) especially Ch. 12 – and for a counter-claim the review of this book by Sean Damer, in *History Workshop Journal*, No. 18, Autumn 1984, pp. 199–203.

8 For a selection see Nan Milton (ed.), *In the Rapids of Revolution* (Alison and Busby, London, 1978).

Chapter 1: A model Social Democrat

1 For an account of his early Socialist career see Milton, *John Maclean*, Chapters 2–7.

2 For an analysis of the relative impacts of Socialist and Labour organisations in pre-1914 Glasgow see Joyce Smith, 'Commonsense and Working-class Consciousness: Some Aspects of the Glasgow and Liverpool Labour Movements in the Early Years of the Twentieth Century' (unpublished PhD Thesis, University of Edinburgh, 1980), especially pp. 301–38, and 409–44, hereafter Smith *Thesis*. Some of her principal points are summarised in her 'Labour Traditions in Glasgow and Liverpool', *History Workshop Journal* (No. 17), Spring 1984, pp. 32–56.

3 See his argument with Tom Johnston in the columes of *Forward* in the Summer of 1910. Extracts are in N. Milton (ed.), *In the Rapids of Revolution*, pp. 37–42.

4 Thus, he supported Tom Gibb in the South Lanark by-election late in 1913. See for example *Justice*, 1, 8 and 22 November 1913. Note also the post-mortem *ibid* 20 December 1913.

5 See *Forward*, 6 August 1910 – 'had it not been for the NAC of the ILP the socialist forces would have been fused prior to the birth of the LRC and the present political chaos of the workers undoubtedly avoided.'

6 *Justice*, 9 December 1911.

7 Under the pseudonym 'Gael' and the title 'Scottish Notes'.

8 *Justice*, 24 February 1912.

9 *Ibid*, 3 May 1913.

10 See for example his claim that the Miners' strike ballot early in 1912 offered an excellent opportunity to make a Socialist case, *ibid*, 27 February 1912.

11 *Ibid*, 4 January 1913.

12 *Ibid*, 4 October 1913.

13 *Ibid*, 15 April 1913.

14 *Ibid*, 11 January 1913.

15 For analysis of the BSP's position, see Smith, *Thesis*, pp. 420–6; also H. McShane and Joan Smith, *No Mean Fighter* (Pluto, London, 1978), Chapters 3–5.

16 For an analysis of the general weakness of the BSP see Dylan Morris, 'The Origins of the British Socialist Party', *North West Group for the Study of Labour History, Bulletin*, No. 8, 1982–3, pp. 29–42.

17 See for example his attempt at the 1914 BSP Conference to put *Justice* under Party control.

18 For a discussion of Scottish politics see Henry Pelling, *Social Geography of British Elections 1885–1910* (Macmillan, London, 1967), Ch. 16.

19 On this see *Justice*, 31 May 1913.

20 For his view of Smillie and the miners, see *ibid*, 20 July 1912; for his appraisal of Scottish railway workers' organisation, *ibid*, 23 November 1912; 25 May 1913; for criticisms of STUC, *ibid*, 4 May 1912; 10 May 1913; for a general assessment of Scottish trade unionism, *ibid*, 4 May 1913.

21 On the Scottish economy pre-1914, see Christopher Harvie, *No Gods and Precious Few Heroes* (Edward Arnold, London, 1981), Chapter 1; Tony Dickson (ed.), *Scottish Capitalism: Class, State and Nation from before the Union to the Present* (Lawrence and Wishart, London, 1980), Chapter 6.

22 For this emphasis see Smith *Thesis*, pp. 136–7; for her emphasis on Glasgow's skilled base and the political consequences, pp. 138–75.

23 For the housing issue see Joseph Melling, *Rent Strikes: Peoples' Struggle for Housing in West Scotland, 1890–1916* (Polygon, Edinburgh, 1983).

24 For an early example, see his letters to the Pollokshaws News, 25 March and 8 April 1904 cited in Milton (ed.), *In the Rapids of Revolution*, p. 50; later contributions can be found in *Justice* 15–29 March; 11 October 1913.

25 *Ibid*, 24 August 1907. See also the later attack on Carson and Orange politics, *ibid* 21 June 1913.

26 *Ibid*, 29 July 1911. For a stimulating analysis of some issues raised by this dispute that emphasises its distinctive qualities, see Dai Smith, *Wales, Wales?*, Chapter 4.

27 *Justice*, 27 July 1912.

28 These and preceding quotations all from *ibid* (his Gael column, *Justice*, 27 July 1912).

29 For background see James Hunter, *The Making of the Crofting Community* (John Donald, Edinburgh, 1977); also his 'The Gaelic Connection: Highlands, Ireland and Nationalism, 1873–1922', *Scottish Historical Review*, 1975, pp. 178–204.

30 See Hunter, *The Making of the Crofting Community*.

31 A point emphasised by Tom Nairn, *The Break-Up of Britain*, especially at pp. 147–8.

32 See D. W. Crowley, 'The Crofters' Party 1885–92', *Scottish Historical Review*, 1956, pp. 110–26.

33   *Justice*, 1 January 1914.

34   *Ibid*, 31 May 1913.

35   See for example *ibid*, 30 December 1911.

36   Michael Keating and David Bleiman, *Labour and Scottish Nationalism* (Macmillan, London, 1979), p.70.

37   *Justice*, 26 March 1914.

38   *Ibid*, 12 February 1914.

39   For an outline of Erskine's early career see H.J. Hanham, *Scottish Nationalism* (Faber, London, 1969), pp.123–6.

40   Both this and the preceding quotation in *Justice*, 31 August 1913.

41   *Ibid*, 13 December 1913.

42   See for example *ibid* 4 January 1913, arguing for a change in propaganda tactics but not in the message.

43   *Ibid*, 6 August 1914.

Chapter 2: Internationalism

1   *Justice*, 17 May 1913.

2   *Ibid*, 10 September 1914 – although see also his comment in *Forward* 8 May 1915 where he describes a recent meeting in Pollokshaws as perhaps the first in Scotland advertised definitely as anti-war.

3   On early responses to the War within the Glasgow Labour Movement, see Smith *Thesis*, pp.445–98.

4   *Justice*, 17 September 1914. See also *ibid*, 1 October 1914, where the Pollokshaws Branch of the BSP was reported as having repudiated the Executive Manifesto advising participation in recruiting meetings. For a later intervention by Maclean see his defence of Peter Petroff, *ibid*, 30 December 1915.

5   *Forward*, 8 May 1915.

6   It occurred alongside the suppression of *Forward*. See McLean, *The Legend of Red Clydeside*, p.59.

7   For a full report of his trial see *Forward*, 20 November 1915. It is worth noting Sheriff Lee's comment that Maclean 'had been using diligence not to give offence, not to interfere with recruiting, which on principle he could not approve of. But on these two occasions he had allowed himself to slip.'

8   For material on the dismissal, see *Maclean Papers*, NLS, Acc 4251.

9   On the rent agitation see Melling, *Rent Strikes*, Chapters 5–11; also his 'Scottish Industrialists and the Changing Character of Class Relations in the Clyde Region c 1880–1918' in Tony Dickson (ed.), *Capital and Class in Scotland* (John Donald, Edinburgh, 1982), pp.61–142; McLean, *The Legend of Red Clydeside*, Chapter 2; Smith *Thesis*, pp.469–79.

10   For the CWC, see James Hinton, *The First Shop Stewards' Movement* (Allen and Unwin, London, 1973), Chapters 3 and 4; also his 'The Clyde Workers' Committee and the Dilution Struggle' in A. Briggs and J. Saville, *Essays in Labour History 1886–1923* (Macmillan, London, 1971), pp.152–84; McLean, *op cit*, Chapters 3–7; Smith *Thesis* especially pp.484–92.

11   *Vanguard*, October 1915.

12   *Ibid*, November 1915. For an account of Petroffs career see the entry in W. Knox, *Scottish Labour Leaders*, pp.224–30.

13   For the theme of illiberality see *Vanguard*, October 1915.

14   *Ibid*, December 1915.

15   *Ibid*.

16   *Ibid.*
17   See Melling, *Rent Strikes* passim.
18   In fact the politics of the Glasgow Trades Council were relatively cautious at the time – and notably more so than its Govan counterpart. See Smith *Thesis*, p. 455. For the particular incident, see Melling, *op cit*, p. 91.
19   *Vanguard*, December 1915.
20   There are accounts of most of the leading figures in Knox, *Scottish Labour Leaders*; Gallacher, pp. 113–21; Kirkwood, pp. 161–4; MacDougall, pp. 170–5; Muir, pp. 214–16.
21   For an analysis of the CWC's response see Hinton, 'The Clyde Workers' Committee and the Dilution Struggle', pp. 167–71. The relevant document is in *The Worker*, 15 January 1916.
22   *Vanguard*, December 1915.
23   *The Socialist*, February 1916.
24   Extract from the suppressed January 1916 number of the *Vanguard*. The advanced proofs were seized in a raid on the Civic Press during the suppression of *Forward* on 2 January 1916. The *Vanguard* extracts appear in typescript with a brief section repeated in long hand in *MUN 5/70/324/18*. Some passages are also contained with slight alterations within two leaflets in the same folder – 'Warning to Clyde Workers' produced by the Free Speech Committee and a BSP item 'Clyde Workers Beware'.
25   Maclean's position is discussed in Hinton, *op cit*, pp. 169–70. This particular point was made in the suppressed number of *Vanguard*.
26   *Ibid.* The row between Maclean and the CWC leadership is discussed in McShane and Smith, *op cit*, pp. 77–9; also for an early account blaming Petroff, Gallacher, *op cit*, pp. 58–62.
27   *Vanguard* extracts from January 1916 number.
28   David Kirkwood, *My Life of Revolt* (Harrap, London, 1935). The point was made also by Maclean at his trial in 1918 cited in Milton, ed., *op cit*, p. 101.
29   *Vanguard*, extract from January 1916 number.
30   For example, *Vanguard*, December 1915 for hopes of the escalation of working class protest. However, Maclean's *Vanguard* writings are shot through with foreboding about the dire consequences of a failure to revolt.
31   Gallacher, *op cit*, p. 55.
32   McShane and Smith, *op cit*, p. 74.
33   Christopher Harvie, 'Labour and Scottish Government: The Age of Tom Johnston' in *The Bulletin of Scottish Politics*, No. 2, Spring 1981, p. 1. See also his discussion in Chapter 1 of *No Gods and Precious Few Heroes*. McLean, *The Legend of Red Clydeside* fits into the same framework whilst Kendall, *The Revolutionary Movement in Britain*, Chapter 7 presents a naive view of Scottish radical potential.
34   In the sources cited above in footnote 9.
35   *The Socialist*, April 1916.
36   On the responses of Government, see McLean, *op cit*, Chapters 3–7.
37   J. Paterson to Llewellyn Smith, 17 January 1916 cited in *ibid*, p. 105. Paterson was Clydeside Labour Officer for the Ministry of Munitions; Llewellyn Smith, the Ministry's Permanent Secretary.
38   For one analysis of this strand, Hinton, *The First Shop Stewards' Movement*.
39   See Smith *Thesis*, p. 460, for this emphasis.
40   One aspect was the SLP's focus on struggle in the workplace, *ibid*, p. 467.
41   In a photograph within Melling, *Rent Strikes*.

Chapter 3: Revolution?

1   For an account of this, see Kendall, *The Revolutionary Movement in Britain*.
2   For material on the agitation for his release, see *Maclean Papers*. Liberal MPs active in the campaign were Charles Trevelyan, Joseph King and J. M. Hogge.
3   Paper by George Barnes, *CAB 24/70*. Document GT6379, 26 November 1918.
4   Report of Ministry of Labour on the Labour Situation for Week Ending 13 November 1918, *loc cit*, Document GT6323.
5   See Milton, *In the Rapids of Revolution*, pp. 107–8 for his allegations at his May 1918 trial.
6   For a discussion of the evidence, G. Rubin, 'A Note on the Scottish Office Reaction to John Maclean's Drugging Allegation', *Scottish Labour History Society Journal* (14), 1980, pp. 40–5.
7   McShane and Smith, *No Mean Fighter*, p. 100. Also Gallacher, letter to John Broom, 14 June 1962 in *Maclean Papers*.
8   For his Fife propaganda see the reports of meetings at Bowhill in *The Call*, 11 October 1917; 14 February 1918; For Glasgow propaganda, *ibid*, 31 January and 21 March 1918.
9   Gallacher, *Revolt On The Clyde*, p. 171.
10 *The Call*, 7 February 1918.
11 *CAB 24/44*, Document GT3838, Appendix B. Memorandum by Lt. General J. Ewart of Scottish Command, 27 February 1918.
12 *Forward*, 18 May 1918.
13 For ILP's growth in Glasgow see Smith, *Thesis*, pp. 498–504.
14 For the text of the Leeds debates see *British Labour and the Russian Revolution* with an introduction by Ken Coates (Spokesman Books, Nottingham, n.d.).
15 For Maclean's experience at the abortive attempt to set up a Council for London, see Milton, *John Maclean*, p. 142; note also his references to attempts to develop the policy in Glasgow, *The Call*, 2 and 9 August 1918.
16 *BSP Conference Report*, 1918, p. 9.
17 *Ibid*, p. 16.
18 *Ibid*, p. 17.
19 See for example his piece 'Clyde Labour', *The Call*, 11 October 1917.
20 For an analysis of how the changes came about and their significance see Ross McKibbin, *The Evolution of the Labour Party 1910–24* (Clarendon Press, Oxford, 1974); for a critical assessment of this analysis, Stuart MacIntyre, 'Socialism, the Unions and the Labour Party after 1918' *Bulletin of the Society for the Study of Labour History* (31), Autumn, 1975, pp. 101–11.
21 *BSP Conference Report*, 1918, p. 30.
22 Kendall, *The Revolutionary Movement in Britain*, p. 133.
23 *BSP Conference Report*, 1918.
24 R. Page Arnot, *The Scottish Miners* (Allen and Unwin, London, 1955), has very little on wartime developments in the coalfields. But see I. MacDougall (ed.), *Militant Miners* (Polygon Books, Edinburgh, 1981), Chs 3–5; Stuart MacIntyre, *Little Moscows* (Croom Helm, London, 1980), pp. 53–5.
25 See especially, 'The Lanarkshire Movement', *The Call*, 6 September 1917; including the programme of the Reform Committee; by April 1918, it was claimed that 24 branches had affiliated to the Committee, *ibid*, 11 April 1918. See also MacDougall's piece, 'The Scottish Miners', *ibid*, 15 August 1918.
26 See *The Call*, 2 August 1917.

27 For an analysis of the limits to wartime radicalisation even in South Wales, see M. Woodhouse, 'Rank and File Movements among the Miners of South Wales, 1910–26' (Oxford, D Phil, 1969), pp. 133–45.

28 On these developments see Hinton, *The First Shop Stewards' Movement*, especially Ch. 10.

29 For an analysis of the election, see K. O. Morgan, *Consensus and Disunity: The Lloyd George Coalition Government* (Clarendon Press, Oxford, 1979), Ch. 2.

30 *The Call*, 24 January 1918.

31 For discussions of the Gorbals case see *Labour Party National Executive Committee Minutes*, 9 April, 8 May, 7 and 27 November 1918 and Minutes of the Organisation and Elections Sub-committee, 30 October 1918. See also the account of Gallacher in *Last Memoirs*, p. 116.

32 See *The Call*, 12 December 1918 for a post-release statement by Maclean.

33 Tom Bell, *John Maclean*, p. 79.

34 A letter from a local Party member to Clifford Allen, 28 June 1921, cited in Arthur Marwick, *Clifford Allen: The Open Conspirator* (Oliver and Boyd, Edinburgh and London, 1964), p. 74.

35 *Forward*, 23 November 1918.

36 *Glasgow Herald*, 12 December 1918.

37 For an account by Dora Montefiore, see *The Call*, 12 December 1918.

38 See *ibid* for reports of enthusiastic Irish and Jewish meetings for Maclean.

39 *Forward*, 21 December 1918.

40 *Glasgow Observer*, 4 January 1919.

41 See *The Call*, 19 December 1918 for an account of Sinn Fein and Irish Transport Workers' support for Walton Newbold in Motherwell.

42 *Forward*, 4 January 1919.

43 For Barnes's stress on Bolshevism, see *Glasgow Herald*, 30 November and 6 December 1918.

44 *Forward*, 23 November 1918. At least one Glasgow Labour candidate the old Radical Home Ruler G. B. Clark distinguished himself from Maclean on the question of revolution, *Glasgow Herald*, 11 December 1918.

Chapter 4: Retrenchment

1 *Forward*, 4 January 1919.

2 On the Forty Hours' Strike see McLean, *op cit*, Chapters 10 and 11; Smith *Thesis*, pp. 568–74; McShane and Smith, *op cit*, Chapter 9; Gallacher, *Revolt on the Clyde*, Chapter 10.

3 This statement is cited in Morgan, *Consensus and Disunity*, p. 48.

4 Gallacher, *op cit*, p. 234; similar judgements can be found at pp. 220–1; 233; but on pp. 223–4 he emphasises the isolation of the Clyde strikers.

5 For material on his English tour see *The Call*, 6 February 1919 for Workington, Whitehaven, Barrow and Manchester; *ibid*, 13 February 1919 for London's Albert Hall. The early speeches are discussed in one of Sir Basil Thompson's fortnightly Reports on revolutionary organisations – for the period ending 10 February 1919 – 'people came away from all his meetings at Barrow saying that his gospel was too extreme for Englishmen and expressing surprise that he is allowed out of prison ...', *CAB 24/75*, Document 6816.

6 *The Call*, 23 January 1919.

7 *Ibid*.

8 *Ibid*.

9   *The Call*, 30 January 1919.

10   Cited in *Glasgow Herald*, 28 January 1919.

11   For the MFGB's wartime relationship with the State, see M.W. Kirby, *The British Coalmining Industry 1870–1946: A Political and Economic History* (Macmillan, London, 1977), Chapter 2. The division within the MFGB between advocates of state ownership and advocates of workers' control is discussed in M. Woodhouse, 'Mines for the Nation or Mines for the Miners', *Llafur*, 1978, pp. 92–109.

12   On events in the coalfields, for the Hamilton demonstration, see *Glasgow Herald*, 30 January 1919; MacDougall on the Fife demands in *The Call*, 6 February 1919; *The Worker*, 8 and 15 February 1919 discusses problems faced by the Left in both coalfields.

13   See Smith, *Thesis*, p. 574.

14   For discussions of industrial developments during this period, see Kirby, *op cit*, pp. 36–48; Morgan, *op cit*, pp. 46–66.

15   *The Call*, 27 March 1919.

16   For Smillie, see for example *The Call*, 2 October 1919.

17   *The Worker*, 31 May 1919.

18   On the Miners' strategy see *The Call*, 2 and 23 October 1919.

19   *Ibid*, 9 October 1919.

20   See *ibid*, 28 August 1919.

21   *Ibid*, 23 October 1919. For a later statement of faith in the BSP, *ibid*, 11 December 1919.

22   See *Forward*, 12, 19, 26 July; 2 August 1919.

23   For an outline of some significant aspects, see Hinton, *The First Shop Stewards' Movement*, Chapter 12.

24   *The Call*, 12 June 1919. Rothstein wrote as often was the case under the pseudonym 'John Bryan'. For a discussion of Rothstein's politics, see John Saville's introduction to the reprint of Rothstein's *From Chartism to Labourism* (Lawrence and Wishart, London, 1983), pp. v–xvii.

25   *The Call*, 24 April 1919.

26   *Ibid*, 17 April 1919.

27   Hinton, *op cit*, pp. 307–8.

28   *The Call*, 24 April 1919.

29   *Ibid*, 19 February 1920.

30   McShane and Smith *op cit*, p. 112. See Saville, *op cit*, pp. xii–xvi for a critical assessment of other judgements that Maclean had made about Rothstein's wartime activities. Maclean later claimed that he had been 'secretly' expelled. See *The Socialist*, 6 February 1921.

31   For Cecil l'Estrange Malone see the entry by David Martin and John Saville in Joyce Bellamy and John Saville (eds.), *Dictionary of Labour Biography*, Vol. 7 (Macmillan, London, 1984), pp. 159–65.

32   *Vanguard*, December 1920.

33   *Ibid*, May 1920.

34   McShane and Smith, *op cit*, pp. 111–12. McShane emphasises the negative role of a party organiser, Ernie Cant, 'He looked at our bookshop, took notes of this and that, but it was obvious he had no politics at all'. For Cant's view of the Glasgow BSP, see *The Call*, 18 December 1920.

35   McShane and Smith, *op cit*, p. 113.

Chapter 5: Isolation

1 For accounts of this period see the biographies by Milton and Broom. McShane and Smith *op cit* offers some useful insights, Chs 10 and 11 – and also in Ch 12, pp. 150–52. For an account that emphasises Maclean's isolation and eccentricity see Iain McLean, *The Legend of Red Clydeside*, pp. 144–53.

2 For an attack on Gallacher as 'that communist clown' see his November 1922 Gorbals election address reprinted in Milton (ed.), p. 235.

3 *The Socialist*, 3 February 1921 – Maclean's 'Open Letter to Lenin'.

4 *Vanguard*, December 1920.

5 *Ibid*, May 1920.

6 *Ibid*. For a claim that this programme was naive in the circumstances of 1920, see McLean, *op cit*, p. 152.

7 Tom Bell, *John Maclean*, p. 103.

8 *Vanguard*, August 1920.

9 *Ibid*.

10 See McShane and Smith, *op cit*, pp. 115–16.

11 *Vanguard*, May 1920.

12 *Ibid*, July 1920.

13 *The Socialist*, 6 February 1921.

14 See Smith, *Thesis*, pp. 320–30 for 1908 unemployed demonstrations.

15 See for example McShane and Smith, *op cit*, pp. 120–2 for reminiscences. McShane's contemporary accounts can be found in *The Socialist* – for example, 8 and 20 January 1921; for Maclean's account of the start of the campaign see *Vanguard*, November 1920.

16 The numerical estimates are in *The Socialist*, 10 February 1921; the qualification in *ibid*, 27 January 1921.

17 *Ibid*, 3 February 1921.

18 *Vanguard*, December 1920.

19 For background see Hanham, *op cit*, pp. 138–9.

20 *The Call*, 9 January 1919.

21 Hanham, *op cit*, p. 139.

22 *The Call*, 30 January 1919.

23 Including the traditionally moderate cotton workers, see *The Call*, 20 March 1919.

24 For an account of these developments see Keating and Bleiman, *Labour and Scottish Nationalism*, Ch. 3. For an example of the type of resolution favoured see *Report of the Labour Party Scottish Advisory Council Conference*, 1916, pp. 43–4.

25 *Ibid*, for 1919, p. 6, gives the Scottish Labour Party Programme for the 1918 Election.

26 *Ibid*, 1918, p. 8, for a reference to the development of a general understanding on candidates.

27 In a letter to W. Gillies, Secretary of the Comunn nan Gaidheal cited in *Scottish Review* (Summer 1918), p. 172.

28 *Ibid* (Winter 1918), pp. 544–5.

29 See *Report of the Labour Party Scottish Advisory Council Conference*, 1918, p. 30, for Duncan's criticisms – followed (pp. 30–1) by Smillie's response.

30 See *ibid*, 1919, pp. 18–20 for discussion of the HLL's weakness.

31 See for example the speech of Ramsay MacDonald in *Ibid*, pp. 33–4 where more effective representative government is presented as a way 'to avoid the class struggles and enmity which might involve the state in a disaster that all of us would deplore'.

32   The development of his ideas can be traced in Hanham, *op cit*, p. 136–40.

33   *Scottish Review* (Spring 1918), pp. 20–1.

34   Cited in Hanham, *op cit*, p. 137; source *Scottish Review* (1919), p. 10.

35   See his 'The Future of the Scottish Labour Party' in *Scottish Review* (Summer 1918).

36   *Ibid*, p. 174.

37   The contrast is cited in Hanham, *op cit*, p. 138; the original source was *Scottish Review* (1919), pp. 390, 400.

38   As emphasised by Hanham, *op cit*, on p. 136. The evidence is in *Scottish Review* (1916), pp. 354–74. See also the hostile obituary of John Redmond in *ibid* (Spring 1918), pp. 145–6 where the Nationalist leader is condemned for conservatism and lack of vision.

39   A proposal emphasised by Hanham *op cit*, p. 135. It appeared in *Scottish Review* (1917).

40   Milton, *op cit*, p. 196 for a recollection of Maclean's reaction.

41   *Vanguard*, June 1920.

42   *Ibid*.

43   *Ibid*, August 1920.

44   *Ibid*.

45   This hope is central to his 1920 pamphlet, *Ireland's Tragedy: Scotland's Disgrace*.

46   *The Worker*, 23 August 1919.

47   McShane and Smith, *op cit*, pp. 116–18; see also *Vanguard*, August 1920 for disturbances by Orange supporters at Maclean's Motherwell meetings; for another recollection see the comments of John McArthur in MacDougall (ed.), *Militant Miners*, pp. 43–4.

48   For an attempt to argue the dissimilarity of the two cases, see Tom Bell, *John Maclean*, pp. 151–2.

49   See, for example, *Vanguard*, September, November and December, 1920; *The Socialist*, 20 January 1921.

50   From the leaflet 'All Hail, The Scottish Workers' Republic' first published in August 1920, reprinted in Milton (ed.), pp. 217–18.

51   The events are discussed in Hunter, *The Making of the Crofting Community*. See also his 'The Gaelic Connection'.

52   For example by Iain McLean, *The Legend of Red Clydeside*, p. 152.

53   *Forward*, 15 May 1920.

54   *Ibid*.

55   *Vanguard*, September 1920.

56   *Ibid*, December 1920.

57   For a similar emphasis from the 1920s, Leon Trotsky, 'Where is Britain Going?' in *Leon Trotsky on Britain*, (Monard Press, New York, 1973).

58   *Vanguard*, September 1920.

59   *Ibid*, December 1920.

60   *Ibid*, September 1920.

61   See for example, Maclean's argument in *Vanguard*, December 1920 that since Scotland was a 'definite country' it could have its own Communist Party and still comply with the conditions of the Communist International.

62   For the view that Maclean's nationalism should be seen in instrumental terms see John McHugh and Brian Ripley, 'John Maclean: The Scottish Workers' Republican Party and Scottish Nationalism', *Scottish Labour History Society Journal*, 1983, pp. 43–7.

63   'All Hail. The Scottish Workers' Republic', at p. 218 in the Milton collection of Maclean's writings.

64   *Vanguard*, September 1920.

65   *Ibid*, November 1920.

66   Thus his reference to 'a high-spirited race like the Irish', *Vanguard*, July 1920; such stereotyping was of course common amongst Socialists, eg. Marx's reference to 'the more passionate and more revolutionary character of the Irish compared with the English' (letter to Meyer and Vogt, 9 April 1870) in Marx & Engels, *Ireland & the Irish Question*.

67   See Keating and Bleiman *op cit*, pp. 79–101 for the Scottish Labour Movement's declining interest in Home Rule in the 1920s. Also Thomas Johnston in *Forward*, 1 September 1923.

68   See for example James Maxton's speech at a Wallace Memorial Meeting in Glasgow, August 1923. *Glasgow Herald*, 27 August 1923.

69   For this see 5th Series *HCDeb*, Vol. 173, Cols 789–874 (9 May 1924).

70   *The Socialist*, 20 January 1921.

71   For the railway case see Keating and Bleiman, *op cit*, pp. 88–91.

72   See Hunter, *The Making of the Crofting Community*, pp. 195–206.

73   Allotments and Smallholdings Files, AF66/57, Memo on Land Settlement, nd, in Scottish Record Office, Edinburgh, cited in Hunter, *The Making of the Crofting Community*, p. 195.

74   Most dramatically in the confrontation between Maclean and Gallacher, at a meeting to form a Scottish Communist Party in December 1920. See McShane and Smith, *op cit*, pp. 123–4.

75   See *ibid*, pp. 133–5 for an account of this campaign. Also *Maclean Papers*, NLS Acc 4251 for a copy of his election address.

76   *Op cit*, p. 140.

77   Maclean to James Clunie, 24 November 1922, *Maclean Papers*, NLS Acc 4334.

78   For an exhaustive analysis of the growth of the Labour vote in Glasgow see I. McLean, *op cit*, Chs. 13 and 14. The comment comes from *Forward*, 18 November 1922.

79   For Buchanan's economic proposals see *Glasgow Herald*, 9 November 1922.

80   *Forward*, 9 December 1922.

81   See Election Address, November 1922, in Milton collection of his writings, p. 234.

82   *Ibid*, at p. 237.

83   *Ibid*, at p. 239.

84   See *Glasgow Herald*, 6 November 1922, noting Maclean's independence and his large audiences 'who may not all however accept the gospel he preaches', 8 November for his municipal result; 13 November for estimate of Maclean's vote as 2,000.

85   Maclean to James Clunie, 24 November 1922, *Maclean Papers*. Acc 4334.

86   *Ibid*.

87   *Ibid*.

88   Maclean to Clunie, 24 April 1923, *loc cit*.

89   For an account see McHugh and Ripley, *op cit*.

90   McShane and Smith, *op cit*, pp. 150–1.

91   Maclean to Clunie, 13 June 1923, *Maclean Papers*.

92   *Forward*, 25 August 1923.

93   Accounts of the by-elections can be found in his letters to Clunie, for example that of 4 June 1923 give details of his Kingston contest and his vote of 2,008.

94   His letters to Clunie, 29 January and 5 October 1923 gives references to the dispute over the SLC Constitution. See also Milton, *op cit*, pp. 284–5, 295.
95   McShane and Smith, *op cit*, p. 151.
96   For results see *Glasgow Herald*, 7 November 1923.
97   1923 Election Address reprinted in Milton Collection of writings – quotation at p. 248, original in *Maclean Papers*, NLS Acc 4335.
98   See for example his articles under the by-line of C. M. Grieve in *Forward* during 1928; for example on 23 June which includes the comment: 'It is amusing to find Scottish Socialists busily disavowing any intention of taking their orders from Moscow (and thus admitting the nationalist principle) and at the same time supinely taking them from London'.
99   Edwin Muir, *Scottish Journey* (reprint, Mainstream, Edinburgh, 1979), p. 248.
100   *Ibid*, p. 233; p. 249.
101   On Muir's career see the introduction by Christopher Smout in *ibid*, pp. vii–xx.
102   See for example McShane and Smith, *op cit*, pp. 224–7 for the Communist Party change of policy.
103   Lewis Grassic Gibbon (James Leslie Mitchell) *Grey Granite* in *A Scots Quair* (Pan, London, 1978), p. 214.

PART III

Chapter 1: Roots

1   Egon Wertheimer, *Portrait of the Labour Party* (Putnams, London, 1929), p. 296.
2   See for example, *How the Miners Are Robbed: The Duke in the Dock* (Glasgow, 1908) and *Miners, Mines and Misery* (Glasgow, 1909).
3   Oswald Mosley, *My Life* (Nelson, London, 1968), p. . For the political relationship between Wheatley and Mosley in the late 1920s see Robert Skidelsky, *Oswald Mosley* (Macmillan, London, 1981), pp. 168–9.
4   For an examination of this see Ian S. Wood, 'John Wheatley, The Irish and the Labour Movement in Scotland', *Innes Review*, 1980, pp. 71–85; the religious background is examined in David McRoberts (ed.), *Modern Scottish Catholicism 1878–1978* (Burns, Glasgow, 1978); see also J. E. Handley, *The Irish in Modern Scotland* (University Press, Cork, 1947).
5   On these themes see Wood, *op cit*; for one working-class Catholic's experience, Harry McShane and Joan Smith, *No Mean Fighter*, Chapters 1–3.
6   *Ibid*, pp. 19–20.
7   For this aspect see Sheridan Gilley, 'Catholics and Socialists in Glasgow 1906–12', in K. Lunn (ed.), *Hosts, Immigrants and Minorities* (Dawson, Folkestone, 1980), pp. 160–200.
8   Thus Harry McShane recalled 'I became an expert arguing against *Rerum Novarum* and I still own several editions of it'. McShane and Smith, *op cit*, p. 17.
9   *Glasgow Observer*, 23 May 1903.
10   *Ibid*, 14 July, 29 September 1900.
11   *Ibid*, 5 September 1903.
12   For UIL support for Sullivan, see *ibid*, 13 January 1906.
13   See the letter by 'Catholic Socialist' in *ibid*, 24 February 1906.
14   *Ibid*, 3 November 1906 for the report of the inaugural meeting and 20 and 27 October 1906 for his letters justifying the formation of the Society.

15 For discussion see Wood, *op cit*, p. 76; Gilley, *op cit*; pp. 178–9 for an attempt by Wheatley to explain its position to Socialists see his 'The Catholic Socialist Movement in Britain', *Socialist Review* (April 1912), pp. 138–44.

16 Also his *A Christian in Difficulties* (Glasgow, 1912).

17 See *Glasgow Observer* beginning with Wheatley's letter of 13 July 1907; for a discussion of Puissant's views see Gilley, *op cit*, pp. 180–3.

18 McShane and Smith, *op cit*, pp. 17–18.

19 This, and the preceding quotation, from John Wheatley *The Catholic Workingman* (Catholic Socialist Society, Glasgow 1909), p. 2.

20 *Ibid*, pp. 5–8.

21 *Ibid*, p. 8 and p. 10.

22 *ILP Conference Report*, 1909, p. 39.

23 *The Catholic Workingman*, p. 10.

24 *Ibid*, pp. 11–13.

25 *Ibid*, pp. 14–17.

26 *Ibid*, p. 17.

27 *Ibid*, pp. 17–18.

28 *Ibid*, p. 18.

29 *Ibid*.

30 *Ibid*.

31 *Ibid*, p. 19.

32 *Ibid*, p. 22.

33 *Ibid*, p. 28.

34 *Glasgow Observer*, 24 February 1906.

35 *The Catholic Workingman*, p. 32.

36 *Forward*, 27 November 1909.

37 Francesco Nitti, *Catholic Socialism* (Swan Sonnenschein, London, 1895).

38 *Glasgow Observer*, 24 February 1906.

39 Thus Wheatley cited Maguire at length in *the Catholic Workingman*, pp. 13–14. For a discussion of Maguire's attitude and the comment cited see Gilley, *op cit*, pp. 184–8.

40 Gilley discusses the complex origins of this confrontation, pp. 188–93.

41 *Glasgow Observer*, 14 July 1906.

42 McShane and Smith, *op cit*, p. 55.

43 *Glasgow Observer*, 13 July 1907.

44 *Ibid*.

45 See Samuel Cooper, *John Wheatley, A Study in Labour History* (unpublished Glasgow PhD, 1973), hereafter Cooper, *Thesis*, Chapter 3; Smith 'Labour Tradition in Glasgow and Liverpool', pp. 34–9.

46 For the Glasgow ILP's pre-War involvement in the housing question see Jospeh Melling, *Rent Strikes*, Chapter 4.

47 *Forward*, 6 February 1915.

48 *Ibid*, 15 August 1914; see Smith, *Thesis*, pp. 448–53 on Glasgow ILP divisions over War.

49 For one example of Wheatley's involvement in an anti-eviction protest see Melling, *op cit*, pp. 66–7.

50 The role of Wheatley is discussed in James Hinton, 'The Clyde Workers' Committee and the Dilution Struggle', pp. 172–3; especially the accompanying footnote 86.

51 Gallacher, *Revolt on the Clyde*, p. 142.

52 See Smith, *Thesis*, pp. 500–4.

53 *Forward*, 12 January 1918. The series had the general title 'An Examination of Some Current Criticisms of ILP Policy'. This one was presented as 'Political Action is a Waste of Time'.

54   This and preceding quotations all in *ibid*.
55   *Ibid*, 19 January 1918.
56   *Ibid*, 26 January 1918 for this and preceding quotations.
57   *Ibid*, 12 January 1918.
58   This, and the preceding quotation, *ibid* 26 January 1918.
59   The series also included a piece by Wheatley in *Forward* for 9 February 1918 arguing for the representation of consumers as well as workers in socialist institutions; a reply on 23 March from the Parkhead Marxian Study circle and a final piece by Wheatley on 6 April entitled 'The Policy of the ILP'. this reiterated the point that progress towards socialism would occur on a national basis.
60   See his comments reported in *Forward*, 9 August 1919.
61   For a discussion of the post-War Coalition's housing policy see Kenneth Morgan, *Consensus and Disunity; the Lloyd George Coalition Government 1918–22*, pp. 88–98; 105–8. For Wheatley's response in Glasgow, see Cooper *Thesis*, Chapter 5.
62   For Wheatley's post-1916 responses to Irish issues see Wood, *op cit*, pp. 80–1.

Chapter 2: Labour and the nation

1   For the complexities of electoral politics in the 1920s see Michael Kinnear, *The British Voter* (Batsford, London, 1981), pp. 40–9; 84–5; 104–13; 116–26.
2   For one interpretation of reactions to this see Maurice Cowling, *The Impact of Labour 1920–4* (University Press, Cambridge, 1971).
3   The intellectual aspects are analysed in Stuart Macintyre, *A Proletarian Science: Marxism in Britain, 1917–33* (University Press, Cambridge, 1980).
4   From Idris Davies, 'The Angry Summer' cited in Gwyn Williams, *When Was Wales?*, p. 267.
5   Harold Laski in *New Leader*, 31 May 1929.
6   This 1929 poster is reproduced in Robert Skidelsky, *Politicians and the Slump: The Labour Government of 1929–31* (Macmillan, London, 1967), facing p. 67.
7   See Sidney Pollard (ed.), *The Gold Standard and Employment Policies Between the Wars* (Methuen, London, 1970).
8   For Labour's economic policies, see Skidelsky, *op cit passim*; also Ross McKibbin, 'The Economic Policy of the Second Labour Government 1929–31', *Past and Present* (68), August 1975, pp. 95–123; Ben Pimlott, *Hugh Dalton* (Methuen, London, 1985), Chapter 8. More general contemporary accounts of the Party are Egon Wertheimer, *Portrait of the Labour Party*, and John Scanlon, *Decline and Fall of the Labour Party* (Peter Davies, London, 1932).
9   Some of the background assumptions are discussed in R. Skidelsky, *Oswald Mosley*, Chapter 2, 'The Challenge to Liberalism'.
10   The emphasis is very apparent in David Marquand, *Ramsay MacDonald*, Chapters 26 and 26.
11   See Skidelsky, *Oswald Mosley*, Chapters 7–12.
12   These examples are discussed in David Howell, *British Workers and the Independent Labour Party*, pp. 373–88.

Chapter 3: Radicalisation

1 John Paton recalling Wheatley's statement after the latter's death, *New Leader* (*NL*), 16 May 1930.

2 *ILPCR*, 1923, p. 142–3.

3 See 165 *HCDeb* 5th Series, Cols 2377–2404, 27 June 1923. For descriptions see Middlemass, *The Clydesiders*, (Hutchinson, London, 1965), pp. 128–30 & C. L. Mowat, *Britain Between the Wars 1918–40* (Methuen, London, 1955), pp. 154–5.

4 H. N. Brailsford to Clifford Allen, 2 July 1923, *ILP Archive*, 1923/44.

5 *NL*, 6 July 1923.

6 *Ibid*, 29 June 1923.

7 *Glasgow Eastern Standard* (*GES*), 14 July 1923.

8 *Glasgow Herald*, 27 August 1923.

9 J. A. Hobson, *The Economics of Unemployment*, (Allen and Unwin, London, 1924), p. .148. For a discussion of Hobson's views in the 1920s see P. F. Clarke, *Liberals and Social Democrats* (University Press, Cambridge, 1978), Chapter 7, especially pp. 222–34.

10 Hobson, *The Economics of Unemployment*, p. 150.

11 *Glasgow Herald*, 30 October 1922.

12 *Forward*, 28 October 1922.

13 John Wheatley, *Starving in the Midst of Plenty* (1923), p. 3.

14 *Ibid*, p. 5.

15 *Ibid*.

16 See for example the examples cited in C. A. Cline, *Recruits to Labour* (University Press, Syracuse, NY, 1963), pp. 78–9.

17 See *ILPCR*, 1923, p. 89.

18 *Ibid*, p. 90.

19 *Ibid*. For Allen see Martin Gilbert, *Plough My Own Furrow* (Longmans, London, 1965); Arthur Marwick, *Clifford Allen: The Open Conspirator*. Note also Brailsford's discussion of this debate in *New Leader*, 6 April 1923.

20 For a discussion of these reforms see R. Dowse, *Left in the Centre*, (Longmans, London, 1966), Ch. 7.

21 Developments in ILP policy are discussed carefully in Adrian Oldfield, 'The Independent Labour Party and Planning 1920–26', *International Review of Social History*, 1976, pp. 1–29.

22 For discussions of Wheatley as a Minister see Cooper, *Thesis*, Chapters 7 and 8; R. Lyman, *The First Labour Government* (Chapman and Hall, London, 1957); and most critically, Iain McLean, *The Legend of Red Clydeside*, pp. 211–18.

23 Beatrice Webb Diary entry for 29 February 1924, cited in M. Cole (ed.), *Beatrice Webb's Diaries 1924–32* (Longmans, London, 1956), p. 11.

24 See the contrasting views noted in McLean, *op cit*, pp. 213–14.

25 Beatrice Webb Diary entry for 7 April, 1924, cited in Cole (ed.), *op cit*, p. 19.

26 John Scanlon, *Decline and Fall of the Labour Party*, pp. 72–3.

27 *NL*, 30 October 1924.

28 *Ibid*, 23 October 1924.

29 Speech at Cambridge Union, cited in *ibid*, 12 December 1924.

30 *GES*, 21 February 1925.

31 *Ibid*.

32 *Ibid*, 7 March 1925.

33 *Ibid*, 21 March 1925.

34   *Ibid*.
35   See the discussion in K.O. Morgan, *Keir Hardie: Radical and Socialist*, (Weidenfeld, London, 1984), pp. 188–200.
36   *GES*, 27 June 1925 – the text of an interview with the *Sunday Worker*.
37   *Ibid*.
38   *Ibid*, 28 March 1925.
39   *Ibid*, 8 August 1925.
40   *Ibid*, 15 August 1925.
41   *Ibid*, 8 August 1925.
42   *Ibid*, 22 August 1925.
43   *Ibid*, 29 May 1926.
44   *Ibid*, 17 July 1926.
45   *Forward*, 22 May 1926.
46   For a discussion of this episode see Scanlon, *op cit*, pp. 87–9; see also David Marquand, *Ramsay MacDonald*, pp. 428–9.
47   *Forward*, 30 October 1926.
48   *GES*, 30 October 1926.
49   *Ibid*.

Chapter 4: Defeat

1   For ILP reactions to the Labour Government see Dowse *op cit*, Chs. 9 & 10.
2   For his resignation see Marwick, *Clifford Allen*, Chapter 11; especially his letter to Maxton, 21 October 1925 cited at pp. 100–1.
3   Clifford Allen, *Socialism and the Next Labour Government* (1925).
4   Clifford Allen to Francis Johnson, 17 July 1926, *ILP Archive*, 1926/31.
5   See *The Living Wage* (1926) – for example at pp. 11–12.
6   For banks, see *ibid*, pp. 18–19; for basic utilities, p. 37; for overall strategy, p. 33.
7   *Ibid*, pp. 37–8.
8   *Ibid*, p. 42.
9   *Ibid*, Chapter 4.
10   *Ibid*, p. 54.
11   *NL*, 9 April 1926.
12   Cited in *ibid*.
13   For Mosley, see Robert Skidelsky, *Oswald Mosley*, Chapter 7.
14   See contributions cited in *NL*, 9 April 1926; for Strachey, see Hugh Thomas, *John Strachey* (Eyre Methuen, London, 1973), Chapter 4.
15   See for example, *NL*, 29 April 1924.
16   See *The Living Wage*, Chapter 3.
17   Oswald Mosley, *Revolution by Reason*, for example at page 7.
18   This is discussed by Skidelsky, *op cit*, pp. 140–1.
19   Thus Brailsford on Mosley's speech at the 1926 ILP Conference 'the ablest speech in opposition … a formidable cavalry charge, but … somewhat exaggerated, and at some points not altogether accurate in its description of the scheme', *NL*, 9 April 1926.
20   *Revolution by Reason*, p. 27.
21   *Ibid*, p. 22.
22   *Ibid*, p. 23 – a contrast with the claim in *The Living Wage* at p. 17, that an 'enlightened' credit policy was possible even under the Gold Standard.
23   For family backgrounds, see Cooper *Thesis*, Chapter 2; Skidelsky, *op cit*, Chapter 1.

24 *NL*, 6 August 1926.

25 *Ibid.*

26 *Ibid*, 13 August 1926.

27 *Ibid*, 10 July 1925. Hobson also reassured MacDonald privately in October 1926 that he was unhappy about some of the political conclusions drawn from *The Living Wage* by leading members of the ILP. See Marquand, *Ramsay MacDonald*, p. 455.

28 *NL*, 14 August 1925. See also Brailsford's comment in *ibid* 3 April 1925: 'we realise, as plainly as our critics, that the demand cannot be met as things are to-day.'

29 *Ibid* 4 September 1925.

30 *Ibid*, 3 July 1925.

31 *Ibid*, 18 September 1925 – in a debate with Brailsford on the role of the ILP.

32 *Ibid*, 10 December 1926; for a discussion of the ILP attitudes to the policy, see Dowse, *op cit*, pp. 136–7.

33 *NL*, 5 August 1927.

34 For Cook's support see *ibid*, 26 November 1926.

35 Ernest Bevin's antagonism to Brailsford and the *New Leader* in June 1926 is demonstrated in Alan Bullock, *The Life and Times of Ernest Bevin*, Vol. I (Heinemann, London, 1960), p. 350.

36 *Socialist Review*, March 1926; on the complexities of MacDonald's responses see Marquand, *Ramsay MacDonald*, pp. 450–62.

37 For example, in his speech to the 1926 ILP Conference, cited in *NL*, 9 April 1926.

38 *LPCR*, 1926, pp. 259–61.

39 *NL*, 22 October 1926.

40 *GES*, 3 July 1926.

41 *Socialise the National Income* (1927), p. 9. The material was published also in *GES* beginning 15 January 1927. Note also Mosley's review of the pamphlet in *NL*, 1 April 1927.

42 *Socialise the National Income*, p. 11.

43 *Ibid.*

44 *Ibid.*

45 *Ibid*, p. 14.

46 *Ibid.*

47 220 *HCDeb* Col 1176 (Complete speech cols 1170–1180, 24 July 1928).

48 222 *HCDeb* Col 543 (Complete speech cols 538–546, 12 November 1928).

49 See for example Middlemass, *The Clydesiders*, pp. 209–12.

50 See for example the discussions in Scanlon, *Decline and Fall of the Labour Party*, Chapter 7; Middlemass, *op cit*, Chapter 9; J. Paton, *Left Turn*, (Secker & Warburg, London, 1936), pp. 294–305.

51 *GES*, 12 March 1927.

52 *Ibid*, 22 October 1927.

53 The complete text is in Scanlon, *op cit*, pp. 107–9.

54 *NL*, 13 April 1928.

55 On the NAC's response see material in *ILPCR*, 1929, pp. 36–7; also Paton, *op cit*, p. 305.

56 *Forward*, 7 July 1928; this piece by Dollan was headed 'Why I Disagree With Maxton'; see also the entry on Dollan in Knox (ed.), *Scottish Labour Leaders*, pp. 95–6.

57 See the discussion by Dollan in *Forward*, 14 July 1928; also McNair, *James Maxton*, pp. 172–3.

58   Scanlon, *op cit*. pp. 110–11; Paton, *op cit*, pp. 300–1 recounts a conversation with Wheatley where the latter expressed similar ideas; he adds that although the genesis of the Campaign was much more haphazard, Wheatley did want an organisational initiative (pp. 301–2).

59   See interview with Maxton, *Forward*, 30 June 1928.

60   See Paton, *op cit*, pp. 302–4; Scanlon, *op cit*, pp. 111–12; also the report in *Forward*, 14 July 1928.

61   *ILP Report of the National Administrative Council to be Presented to the Annual Conference 1928*, p. 3.

62   Cited in A. Bullock, *The Life and Times of Ernest Bevin, Vol. 1, Trade Union Leader 1881–1940*, p. 401.

63   *LPCR*, 1928, p. 213. Complete speech is at pp. 212–14.

64   *Ibid*, p. 216.

65   230 *HCDeb* Col 98 (complete speech cols 89–98, 15 July 1929).

66   See F. Brockway, *Inside the Left*, (New Leader, London, 1947), pp. 197–8 for a recollection of Wheatley and MacDonald at an early PLP meeting during the 1929 Parliament.

67   233 *HCDeb* Col 1807 (complete speech cols 1805–20, 20 December 1929). He had criticised Thomas's approach at the 1929 Party Conference. See *LPCR*, 1929, pp. 182–3.

68   Entry for 14 February 1930 in M. Cole (ed.), *Beatrice Webb's Diaries 1924–32*, p. 235.

A past for a future

1   Connolly's relatively sensitive chapter on women in *The Reconquest of Ireland* must be set against the views and assumptions demonstrated in his polemic with De Leon. Wheatley, as Minister of Health, maintained that Department's obstructive attitude on the availability of birth-control information. See Jill Liddington, *The Life and Times of a Respectable Rebel: Selina Cooper 1864–1946* (Virago, London, 1984), Ch. 18.

2   Note of Meetings of the Unofficial Reform Committee, 27 May 1911 – material presented in David Egan, 'The Unofficial Reform Committee and the Miners' Next Step: Documents from the W. H. Mainwaring Papers, With An Introduction and Notes', *Llafur*, 1978, p. 71.

3   See Benedict Anderson, *Imagined Communities: Reflections On the Origin and Spread of Nationalism* (Verso, London, 1983).

4   Williams, *When Was Wales?*, pp. 296–7; pp. 302–3.

5   See Hywel Francis, 'Mining The Popular Front', *Marxism Today*, February 1985, pp. 12–15.

6   See Eric Hobsbawm, 'The Historians' Group of the Communist Party', in Maurice Conforth (ed.), *Rebels and Their Causes: Essays in Honour of A. L. Morton* (Lawrence and Wishart, London, 1978), pp. 21–47; Bill Schwarz, '"The People" in history: the Communist Party Historians' Group 1946–56' in Centre for Contemporary Cultural Studies, *Making Histories* (Hutchinson, London, 1982), pp. 44–95.

7   E. P. Thompson, *The Defence of Britain*, (END/CND, London, 1983), p. 33.

8   For a discussion of these themes see Raymond Williams, *Towards 2000* (Penguin, Harmondsworth, 1985), pp. 178–99.

9   For examples see Angela Williams, 'A Kind of Angry Poetry', *Planet 51*, especially pp. 15–16.

10   See the chapters by Kim Howells, Doreen Massey and Hilary Wainwright, and Loretta Loach in Huw Beynon (ed.), *Digging Deeper: Issues in the Miners' Strike* (Verso, London, 1985), pp. 139–79.

11   See Bob Fine and Robert Millar (ed.), *Policing the Miners' Strike* (Lawrence and Wishart, London, 1985); Jim Coulter, Susan Miller and Martin Walker (eds.), *A State of Siege* (Canary Press, London, 1984).

Bibliography

Manuscript Sources

British Trades Union Congress
  Minutes of Parliamentary Committee
Cabinet Papers
  CAB 24/44; CAB 24/70–24/76 (Public Records Office)
Dublin Trades Council Minutes
  (National Library of Ireland, MS 12783)
Gilray, John
  'Early Days of the Socialist Movement in Edinburgh', (National Library of
  Scotland, Acc 4965)
Independent Labour Party
  Archive material – sometimes known as Francis Johnson Correspondence
  (microfilm, Huddersfield Polytechnic)
  Minutes of National Administrative Council (microfilm, City of Manchester
  Reference Library)
  Edinburgh Central Branch Minutes (Edinburgh Public Library)
Labour Party – National Executive Committee
  Minutes (microfilm, City of Manchester Reference Library)
John Maclean Papers
  (National Library of Scotland, Acc 4251, 4334, 4335)
Ministry of Munitions
  (Public Records Office, MUN 5/70)
William O'Brien Papers
  (National Library of Ireland) Material useful for Connolly includes: MS 13906,
  13908, 13912, 13913, 13928, 13929, 13933, 13937, 13939, 13940, 15673,
  15674, 16265, 16270.
Scottish Labour Party
  Edinburgh Central Branch Minutes (National Library of Scotland, microfilm
  Acc 3828)

Contemporary Newspapers and Periodicals

Belfast Labour Chronicle
The Call
Clarion
Daily Herald
Edinburgh Labour Chronicle
Glasgow Eastern Standard
Glasgow Herald
Glasgow Observer
The Harp

Industrial Unionist Bulletin
  (reprinted Greenwood, Westport, Conn, 1970)
International Socialist Review
Irish Review
Irish Times
Irish Worker
Justice
Labour Leader
Manchester Guardian
New Age
New Leader
New Statesman
Scottish Review
Shan Van Vocht
Sinn Fein
The Socialist
Vanguard
The Worker
Workers' Republic

Contemporary Printed Political Material

British Socialist Party
  Conference Reports
British Trades Union Congress
  Reports of Proceedings
House of Commons
  Parliamentary Debates, 5th Series
Independent Labour Party
  Annual Conferences, Reports of Proceedings
  Report of the National Administrative Council to be presented to the Annual
  Conference, 1928.
Irish Trades Union Congress
  Reports of Proceedings
Labour Party
  Conference Reports of Proceedings
Labour Party – Scottish Advisory Council
  Reports of Conferences
Report of the Dublin Disturbances
  Parliamentary Papers (1914), Vol. XVIII, Cmnd 7569
Scottish Trades Union Congress
  Reports of Proceedings

Books and Pamphlets

Aldred, Guy, *John Maclean: Martyr of the Class Struggle* (Strickland Press,
  Glasgow, 1932).
Anderson, Benedict, *Imagined Communities: Reflections on the Origin and
  Spread of Nationalism* (Verso, London, 1983).
Anderson, Perry, *Arguments Within English Marxism* (Verso, London, 1980).

Arnot, R. Page, *The Scottish Miners* (Allen and Unwin, London, 1955).

Ascherson, Neal, *The Polish August* (Penguin, Harmondsworth, 1981).

Beckett, J.C., *The Making of Modern Ireland* (Faber, London, 1966).

Bell, Geoff, *The Protestants of Ulster* (Pluto, London, 1976).

Bell, Geoff, *Troublesome Business: The Labour Party and the Irish Question* (Pluto, London, 1982).

Bell, Tom, *John Maclean: Fighter for Freedom* (Communist Party Scottish Committee, Glasgow, 1944).

Bell, Tom, *Pioneering Days* (Lawrence and Wishart, London, 1941).

Bellamy, Joyce and Saville, John (eds.), *Dictionary of Labour Biography* (Macmillan, London, dates various).

Benn, Tony, *Parliament, People and Power* (Verso, London, 1982).

Berresford Ellis, P., *A History of the Irish Working Class* (Gollancz, London, 1972).

Berresford Ellis, P. and Mac A-Ghabhainn, *The Scottish Insurrection of 1820* (Gollancz, London, 1970).

Bew, Paul, Gibbon, Peter and Patterson, Henry, *The State in Northern Ireland 1921–72* (University Press, Manchester, 1979).

Beynon, Huw (ed.), *Digging Deeper: Issues in the Miners' Strike* (Verso, London, 1985).

Bottomore, Tom, *Sociology and Socialism* (Wheatsheaf, Brighton, 1984).

Bottomore, Tom and Goode, Patrick, *Austro–Marxism* (University Press, Oxford, 1978).

Bowman, John, *De Valera and the Ulster Question 1917–1973* (Clarendon Press, Oxford, 1982).

Boyce, D. George, *Nationalism in Ireland* (Croom Helm, London, 1982).

Boyle, J.W. (ed.), *Leaders and Workers* (Mercier Press, Cork, 1978).

Breuilly, John, *Nationalism and the State* (University Press, Manchester, 1982).

British and Irish Communist Organisation, *Connolly and Partition* (1972).

Brockway, Fenner, *Inside the Left* (New Leader, London, 1947).

Broom, John, *John Maclean* (MacDonald, Loanhead, 1973).

Brown, K.D., *John Burns* (Royal Historical Society, London, 1977).

Brown, Terence, *Ireland: A Social and Cultural History 1922–79* (Fontana, London, 1981).

Bullock, Alan, *The Life and Times of Ernest Bevin: Volume 1, Trade Union Leader, 1881–1940* (Heinemann, London, 1960).

Bulpitt, Jim, *Territory and Power in the United Kingdom* (University Press, Manchester, 1983).

Cardozo, Nancy, *Maud Gonne* (Gollancz, London, 1979).

'Cato', *Guilty Men* (Gollancz, London, 1940).

Challinor, Raymond, *The Origins of British Bolshevism* (Croom Helm, London, 1977).

Chaplin, Ralph, *Wobbly: The Rough and Tumble Story of an American Radical* (University of Chicago Press, 1948).

Clarke, P.F., *Liberals and Social Democrats* (University Press, Cambridge, 1978).

Clarkson, J.D., *Labour and Nationalism in Ireland* (Columbia University Press, New York, 1925).

Cline, C.A., *Recruits to Labour* (University Press, Syracuse, NY, 1963).

Coates, Ken (ed.), *British Labour and the Russian Revolution* (Spokesman Books, Nottingham, no date).

Cole, Margaret (ed.), *Beatrice Webb's Diaries 1924–32* (Longmans, London, 1956).

Connolly O'Brien, Nora, *James Connolly: Portrait of a Rebel Father* (reprint, Four Masters, Dublin, 1975).

Coulter, Jim, Miller, Susan and Walker, Martin (eds.), *A State of Siege* (Canary Press, London, 1984).

Cowling, Maurice, *The Impact of Labour 1920–24* (University Press, Cambridge, 1971).

Crick, Bernard, *George Orwell* (Secker, London, 1980).

Cross, Colin, *Philip Snowden* (Barrie and Rockliff, London, 1966).

Cumbler, T., *Working Class Community in Industrial America: Work, Leisure and Struggle in Two Industrial Cities* (Greenwood Press, Westport, Conn, 1979).

Davies, D. Hywel, *The Welsh Nationalist Party 1925–45: A Call to Nationhood* (University of Wales Press, Cardiff, 1983).

Davies, John, *The Green and the Red: Nationalism and Ideology in 20th Century Wales* (Plaid Cymru, Aberystwyth, no date).

Davies, R. P., *Arthur Griffith and Non-Violent Sinn Fein* (Anvil Books, Dublin, 1974).

Dick, William M., *Labor and Socialism in America: The Gompers Era* (Kennitat Press, Port Washington, NY, 1972).

Dickson, Tony (ed.), *Scottish Capitalism: Class, State and Nation from Before the Union to the Present* (Lawrence and Wishart, London, 1980).

Dowse, Robert, *Left in the Centre: The Independent Labour Party 1893–1940* (Longmans, London, 1966).

Dubofsky, Melvyn, *We Shall Be All* (Quadrangle Books, Chicago, 1969).

Edwards, Owen Dudley (ed.), *Celtic Nationalism* (Routledge, London, 1968).

Edwards, Owen Dudley, *The Mind of an Activist: James Connolly* (Gill and Macmillan, Dublin, 1971).

Edwards, Owen Dudley, *The Sins of our Fathers: Roots of Conflict in Northern Ireland* (Gill and Macmillan, Dublin, 1970).

Edwards, Owen Dudley and Pyle K. (eds.), *1916: The Easter Rising* (MacGibbon and Kee, London, 1968).

Edwards, Ruth Dudley, *James Connolly* (Gill and Macmillan, Dublin, 1981).

Edwards, Ruth Dudley, *Patrick Pearse: The Triumph of Failure* (Faber, London, 1979).

Farrell, Michael, *The Orange State* (Pluto Press, London, 1976).

Fine, Bob and Millar, Robert (ed.), *Policing the Miners' Strike* (Lawrence and Wishart, London, 1985).

Fitzpatrick, David, *Politics and Irish Life, 1913–21: Provincial Experience of War and Revolution* (Gill and Macmillan, Dublin, 1977).

Flynn, Elizabeth Gurley, *I Speak my own Piece* (Masses and Mainstream, New York, 1955).

Foner, Philip, *History of the Labor Movement in the United States, Vol. V, The Industrial Workers of the World* (International Publishers, New York, 1965).

Foot, Michael, *Aneurin Bevan, 1945–60* (Davis-Poynter, London, 1973).

Foot, Michael, *Debts of Honour* (Picador, London, 1981).

Fox, R. M., *The History of the Irish Citizen Army* (James Duffy, Dublin, 1944).

Francis, Hywel, *Miners Against Fascism: Wales and The Spanish Civil War* (Lawrence and Wishart, London, 1984).

Francis, Hywel and Smith, David, *The Fed: A History of the South Wales Miners in the Twentieth Century* (Lawrence and Wishart, London, 1980).

Gallacher, William, *Revolt on the Clyde* (Lawrence and Wishart, London, 1936).

Gallacher, William, *Last Memoirs* (Lawrence and Wishart, London, 1966).
Gaughan, J. Anthony, *Thomas Johnson* (Kingdom Books, Dublin, 1980).
'Gibbon, Lewis Grassic' (James Leslie Mitchell), *A Scots Quair* (Pan, London, 1978).
Gibbon, Peter, *The Origins of Ulster Unionism* (University Press, Manchester, 1975).
Gilbert, Martin, *Plough My Own Furrow* (Longmans, London, 1965).
Ginger, Raymond, *The Bending Cross: A Biography of Eugene Victor Debs* (Rutgers, New Brunswick, NJ, 1949).
Gramsci, Antonio, *Selections from the Prison Notebooks* (ed.) Q. Hoare and G. Nowell-Smith (Lawrence and Wishart, London, 1973).
Gray, R.Q., *The Labour Aristocracy in Victorian Edinburgh* (Clarendon Press, Oxford, 1976).
Greaves, C. Desmond, *The Irish Transport and General Workers' Union: The Formative Years 1909–23* (Gill and Macmillan, Dublin, 1982).
Greaves, C. Desmond, *The Life and Times of James Connolly* (Lawrence and Wishart, London, 1976).
Greaves, C. Desmond, *Sean O'Casey: Politics and Art* (Lawrence and Wishart, London, 1979).
Griffiths, Robert, *S. O. Davies: A Socialist Faith* (Gomer Press, Llandysal, 1983).
Griffiths, Robert, *Turning to London: Labour's Attitude to Wales, 1898–1956* (Y Faner Goch, Cardiff, no date).
Gwynn, Denis, *The Life of John Redmond* (Harrop, London, 1932).
Hall, Stuart, and Jacques, Martin (eds.), *The Politics of Thatcherism* (Lawrence and Wishart, London, 1983).
Handley, J.E., *The Irish in Modern Scotland* (University Press, Cork, 1947).
Hanham, H.J., *Scottish Nationalism* (Faber, London, 1969).
Harding, Neil, *Lenin's Political Thought. Volume I. Theory and Practice in the Democratic Revolution* (Macmillan, London, 1977).
Harding, Neil, *Lenin's Political Thought. Volume II. Theory and Practice in the Socialist Revolution* (Macmillan, London, 1981).
Harvie, Christopher, *No Gods and Precious Few Heroes* (Edward Arnold, London, 1981).
Hechter, Michael, *Internal Colonialism. The Celtic Fringe in British National Development* (Routledge, London, 1978).
Hinton, James, *The First Shop Stewards' Movement* (Allen and Unwin, London, 1973).
Hobsbawm, Eric (ed.), *The Forward March of Labour Halted?* (Verso, London, 1981).
Holton, Bob, *British Syndicalism: 1900–14, Myths and Realities* (Pluto, London, 1976).
Howell, David, *British Workers and the Independent Labour Party 1888–1906* (University Press, Manchester, 1983).
Hunter, James, *The Making of the Crofting Community* (John Donald, Edinburgh, 1977).
Inglis, Brian, *Roger Casement* (Coronet Books, London, 1974).
Jones, Alun R. and Thomas, Gwyn (eds.), *Presenting Saunders Lewis* (University of Wales Press, Cardiff, 1983).
Jones, Merfyn R., *The North Wales Quarrymen, 1874–1922* (University of Wales Press, Cardiff, 1982).
Karson, Marc, *American Labor Unions and Politics 1900–18* (Southern Illinois University Press, Carbondale, Ill., 1958).

Keating, Michael and Bleiman, David, *Labour and Scottish Nationalism* (Macmillan, London, 1979).

Kendall, Walter, *The Revolutionary Movement in Britain 1900–21* (Weidenfeld, London, 1969).

Keogh, D., *The Rise of the Irish Working Class: The Dublin Trade Union Movement and Labour Leadership 1890–1914* (Appletree Press, Belfast, 1982).

Kinnear, Michael, *The British Voter* (Batsford, London, 1981).

Kipnis, Ira, *The American Socialist Movement, 1897–1912* (reprinted, Greenwood, New York, 1968).

Kirby, M.W., *The British Coalmining Industry 1870–1946: A Political and Economic History* (Macmillan, London, 1977).

Kirkwood, David, *My Life of Revolt* (Harrap, London, 1935).

Knox, William (ed.), *Scottish Labour Leaders 1918–39: A Biographical Dictionary* (Mainstream, Edinburgh, 1984).

Kolakowski, Leszek, *Main Currents of Marxism 2: The Golden Age* (University Press, Oxford, 1981).

Larkin, Emmet, *James Larkin* (Routledge, London, 1965).

Laslett, John, *Labor and the Left: A Study of Socialist and Radical Influences in the American Labor Movement 1881–1924* (Basic Books, New York, 1970).

Lenin on Ireland (New Books, Dublin, 1974).

Liddington, Jill, *The Life and Times of a Respectable Rebel: Selina Cooper 1864–1946* (Virago, London, 1984).

Lyman, R., *The First Labour Government* (Chapman and Hall, London, 1957).

Lyons, F.S.L., *Culture and Anarchy in Ireland 1890–1939* (University Press, Oxford, 1982).

Lyons, F.S.L., *Ireland Since the Famine* (Fontana, London, 1978).

Lyons, F.S.L., *The Irish Parliamentary Party 1890–1910* (Faber and Faber, London, 1951).

Lyons, F.S.L., *John Dillon* (Routledge, London, 1968).

McCann, Eamonn, *War and an Irish Town* (Second Edition, Pluto, London, 1980).

MacDiarmid, Hugh (C.M. Grieve), *The Company I've Kept* (Hutchinson, London, 1966).

MacDiarmid, Hugh, *Complete Poems 1920–76*, edited by M. Grieve and W.R. Aitken (Martin Brian and O'Keefe, London, 1978).

MacDougall, I. (ed.), *Militant Miners* (Polygon Books, Edinburgh, 1981).

McGovern, John, *Neither Fear Nor Favour* (Blandford Press, London, 1960).

McHugh, Roger (ed.), *Dublin 1916* (Arlington, London, 1976).

MacIntyre, Stuart, *Little Moscows* (Croom Helm, London, 1980).

MacIntyre, Stuart, *A Proletarian Science: Marxism in Britain, 1917–33* (University Press, Cambridge, 1980).

McKibbin, Ross, *The Evolution of the Labour Party 1910–24* (Clarendon Press, Oxford, 1974).

McLean, Iain, *The Legend of Red Clydeside* (John Donald, Edinburgh, 1983).

McNair, John, *James Maxton: The Beloved Rebel* (Allen and Unwin, London, 1955.

McRoberts, David (ed.), *Modern Scottish Catholicism 1878–1978* (Burns, Glasgow, 1978).

McShane, Harry and Smith, Joan, *No Mean Fighter* (Pluto, London, 1978).

Marquand, David, *Ramsay MacDonald* (Cape, London, 1977).

Martin, F.X. (ed.), *The Irish Volunteers, 1913–15: Recollections and Documents* (James Duffy, Dublin, 1963).

Marwick, Arthur, *Clifford Allen: The Open Conspirator* (Oliver and Boyd, Edinburgh and London, 1964).

Marx, Karl, *The First International and After* (Penguin, Harmondsworth, 1974).

Marx, Karl, *The Revolutions of 1848* (Penguin, Harmondsworth, 1973).

Marx, Karl, *Surveys from Exile* (Penguin, Harmondsworth, 1977).

Marx, Karl and Engels, Frederick, *Ireland and the Irish Question* (Progress Publishers, Moscow, 1971).

Melling, Joseph, *Rent Strikes: Peoples' Struggle for Housing in West Scotland 1890–1916* (Polygon, Edinburgh, 1983).

Middlemass, Keith, *The Clydesiders: A Left Wing Struggle for Parliamentary Power* (Hutchinson, London, 1965).

Miller, Sally M., *Victor Berger and the Promise of Constructive Socialism 1910–20* (Greenwood Press, Westport, Conn., 1973).

Milton, Nan, *John Maclean* (Pluto, London, 1973).

Mitchell, Arthur, *Labour in Irish Politics 1890–1930* (Irish Universities Press, Dublin, 1974).

Moody, T. W., *Davitt and Irish Revolution 1846–82* (Clarendon Press, Oxford, 1981).

Morgan, H. Wayne, *Eugene V. Debs: Socialist for President* (University Press, Syracuse, 1962).

Morgan, Kenneth O., *Consensus and Disunity: The Lloyd George Coalition Government* (Clarendon Press, Oxford, 1979).

Morgan, Kenneth O., *Keir Hardie: Radical and Socialist* (Weidenfeld, London, 1984).

Morgan, Kenneth O., *Rebirth of a Nation: Wales 1880–1980* (University of Wales Press and Oxford University Press, 1982).

Mosley, Nicholas, *Rules of the Game: Sir Oswald and Lady Cynthia Mosley 1896–1933* (Secker and Warburg, London, 1982).

Mosley, Sir Oswald, *My Life* (Nelson, London, 1968).

Mowat, C. L., *Britain Between the Wars 1918–40* (Methuen, London, 1955).

Muir, Edwin, *Scottish Journey* (reprint, Mainstream, Edinburgh, 1979).

Nairn, Tom, *The Break-Up of Britain* (New Left Books, London, 1977).

Nairn, Tom, *The Left Against Europe?* (Penguin, Harmondsworth, 1973).

Nettl, Peter, *Rosa Luxemburg* (University Press, Oxford, 1969).

O'Brien, Conor Cruise (ed.), *The Shaping of Modern Ireland* (Routledge, London, 1960).

O'Brien, Conor Cruise, *States of Ireland* (Hutchinson, London, 1972).

O'Brien, William, *Forth the Banners Go* (Three Candles, Dublin, 1969).

O'Broin, Leon, *Dublin Castle and the 1916 Rising: The Story of Sir Matthew Nathan* (Helican, Dublin, 1966).

O'Casey, Sean, *Drums Under the Windows* (Macmillan, London, 1946).

O'Farrell, P. J., *Ireland's English Question* (Batsford, London, 1971).

O'Riordan, Manus, *Connolly in America* (Irish Communist Organisation, Belfast, 1971).

Pakenham, Thomas, *The Year of Liberty* (Hodder and Stoughton, 1969).

Paton, John, *Left Turn* (Secker and Warburg, London, 1936).

Patterson, Henry, *Class Conflict and Sectarianism: The Protestant Working Class and the Belfast Labour Movement 1868–1920* (Blackstaff Press, Belfast, 1980).

Pelling, Henry, *America and the British Left: From Bright to Bevan* (Black, London, 1956).

Pelling, Henry, *Social Geography of British Elections 1885–1910* (Macmillan, London, 1967).

Pimlott, Ben, *Hugh Dalton* (Methuen, London, 1985).

Pollard, Sidney (ed.), *The Gold Standard and Employment Policies Between the Wars* (Methuen, London, 1970).

Preston, William Jr., *Aliens and Dissenters: Federal Suppression of Radicals 1903–33* (Harvard University Press, Cambridge, Mass. 1963).

Probert, Belinda, *Beyond Orange and Green* (Academy Press, Dublin, 1978).

Quint, Howard, *The Forging of American Socialism* (reprint, Bobbs-Merrill, Indianapolis, 1964).

Ransom, Bernard, *Connolly's Marxism* (Pluto Press, London, 1980).

Reeve, Carl and Reeve, Ann Barton, *James Connolly and the United States* (Humanities Press, Atlantic Highlands, NJ, 1978).

Rumpf, E. and Hepburn, A. C., *Nationalism and Socialism in Twentieth Century Ireland* (University Press, Liverpool, 1977).

Ryan, Desmond, *James Connolly* (Labour Publishing Company, London, 1924).

Salvatore, Nick, *Eugene V. Debs: Citizen and Socialist* (University of Illinois Press, Urbana, Ill., 1982).

Scanlon, John, *Decline and Fall of the Labour Party* (Peter Davies, London, 1932).

Schneer, Jonathan, *Ben Tillett* (University of Illinois Press, Urbana, Ill., 1983).

Seretan, L. G., *Daniel De Leon: The Odyssey of an American Marxist* (Harvard University Press, Cambridge, Mass., 1979).

Seton-Watson, Hugh, *Nations and States: An Enquiry into the Origins of Nations and the Politics of Nationalism* (Methuen, London, 1977).

Shannon, David A., *The Socialist Party of America: A History* (Macmillan, New York, 1955).

Skidelsky, Robert, *Oswald Mosley* (Macmillan, London, 1981).

Skidelsky, Robert, *Politicians and the Slump: The Labour Government of 1929–31* (Macmillan, London, 1967).

Smith, Dai, *Wales, Wales!* (Allen and Unwin, London, 1984).

Smith, David (ed.), *A People and a Proletariat* (Pluto, London, 1980).

Sombart, Werner, *Why Is There No Socialism in the United States!* (trans. P. M. Hocking and C. T. Husbands) (Macmillan, London, 1976).

Stewart, A. T. Q., *The Ulster Crisis: Resistance to Home Rule 1912–14* (Faber, London, 1967).

Strauss, E., *Irish Nationalism and British Democracy* (Methuen, London, 1951).

Summerfield, Henry, *That Myriad Minded Man: A Biography of George William Russell 'AE', 1867–1935* (Colin Smythe, Gerrards Cross, 1975).

Taylor, A. J. P., *English History 1914–45* (Clarendon, Oxford, 1965).

Thomas, Hugh, *John Strachey* (Eyre Methuen, London, 1973).

Thomas, Ned, *The Welsh Extremist* (Y Lolfa, Talybont, Dyfed, 1973).

Thompson, E. P., *The Defence of Britain* (END/CND, London, 1983).

Thompson, E. P., *William Morris: From Romantic to Revolutionary* (Merlin, London, 1977).

Tierney, Michael, *Eoin MacNeill: Scholar and Man of Action 1867–1945* (Clarendon Press, Oxford, 1980).

Townshend, Charles, *Political Violence in Ireland: Government and Resistance Since 1848* (Clarendon Press, Oxford, 1983).

Tsuzuki, C., *H. M. Hyndman and British Socialism* (Heinemann and Oxford University Press, London, 1961).

Wertheimer, Egon, *Portrait of the Labour Party* (Putnams, London, 1929).

Williams, Desmond (ed.), *The Irish Struggle 1916–26* (Routledge, London, 1966).

Williams, Gwyn, *The Welsh in Their History* (Croom Helm, London, 1982).

Williams, Gwyn, *When was Wales!* (Penguin, Harmondsworth, 1985).

Williams, Raymond, *Orwell* (Fontana, London, 1971).
Williams, Raymond, *Towards 2000* (Penguin, Harmondsworth, 1985).
Yeats, W. B., *Autobiographies* (Macmillan, London, 1955).
Young, James, *The Rousing of the Scottish Working Class* (Croom Helm, London, 1979).

Articles

Barnett, Anthony, 'Iron Britannia', *New Left Review* (134), 1982.
Beetham, David, 'From Socialism to Fascism: The Relation Between Theory and Practice in the Work of Robert Michels', *Political Studies* (1977), pp. 3–24, 161–81.
Boyle, J. W., 'The Belfast Protestant Association and the Independent Orange Order', *Irish Historical Studies* XIII (1962–3), pp. 117–52.
Brown, Kenneth D., 'Larkin and the Strikes of 1913: Their Place in British History', *Saothar* (9), 1983, pp. 89–99.
Collins, Henry, 'The Marxism of the Social Democratic Federation', in Asa Briggs and John Saville (eds.), *Essays in Labour History 1886–1923* (Macmillan, London, 1971), pp. 47–69.
Crowley, D. W., 'The Crofters' Party 1885–1892', *Scottish Historical Review*, 1956, pp. 110–26.
Cunningham, Hugh, 'The Language of Patriotism', *History Workshop Journal* (12), 1981, pp. 8–33.
Damer, Sean, Review of Iain McLean's *The Legend of Red Clydeside* in *History Workshop Journal*, No. 18, Autumn, 1984, pp. 199–203.
Davis, Mike, 'Why the US Working Class is Different', *New Left Review* (123), 1980, pp. 3–44.
Dickson, Tony, 'Marxism, Nationalism and Scottish History', *Journal of Contemporary History*, April 1985, pp. 323–36.
Doyle, David, 'The Irish and American Labour 1880–1920', *Saothar* (1), 1975, pp. 42–53.
Edwards, Owen Dudley, 'Connolly and the Irish Tradition', *The Furrow* 30 (7), July 1979, pp. 411–24.
Egan, David, 'The Unofficial Reform Committee and "The Miners' Next Step": Documents from the W. H. Mainwaring Papers with an Introduction and Notes', *Llafur* (1978), pp. 64–80.
Englander, David, 'Landlord and Tenant in Urban Scotland: The Background to the Clyde Rent Strikes, 1915', *Scottish Labour History Society Journal* (No. 15), 1981, pp. 4–14.
Farrell, Brian, 'Labour and the Irish Political Party System: A Suggested Approach to Analysis', *Economic and Social Review* 1970, pp. 477–502.
Fitzpatrick, David, 'Strikes in Ireland, 1914–21', *Saothar* (6), 1980, pp. 26–39.
Foner, Eric, 'Why is there no Socialism in the United States?', *History Workshop Journal* (17), Spring 1984, pp. 57–80.
Francis, Hywel, 'Mining the Popular Front', *Marxism Today* (February 1985), pp. 12–15.
Gallagher, M., 'Socialism and the Nationalist Tradition in Ireland, 1798–1918', *Eire-Ireland* 12(2), 1977, pp. 63–102.
Gallagher, Tom, 'Orangeism in Scotland Before 1914', *Radical Scotland* August/September, 1984, pp. 23–5.
Gallagher, Tom, 'Catholics in Scottish Politics', *The Bulletin of Scottish Politics*, Vol. 1, No. 2, (Spring 1981), pp. 21–43.

Gallagher, Tom, 'Red Clyde's Double Anniversary', *Scottish Labour History Society Journal* (No. 20), 1985, pp. 4–13.

Gilley, Sheridan, 'Catholics and Socialists in Glasgow 1906–12', in K. Lunn (ed.), *Hosts, Immigrants and Minorities* (Dawson, Folkstone, 1980), pp. 160–200.

Goldring, Maurice, 'Connolly Reassessed', *Saothar* (7), 1981, pp. 50–3.

Harvie, Christopher, 'Labour and Scottish Government: The Age of Tom Johnston', *The Bulletin of Scottish Politics*, No. 2, Spring 1981, pp. 1–20.

Harvie, Christopher, 'MacDiarmid the Socialist', *Scottish Labour History Society Journal*, No. 15, 1981, pp. 4–11.

Hazelkorn, Ellen, 'Reconsidering Marx and Engels on Ireland', *Saothar* (9), 1983, pp. 79–88.

Hinton, James, 'The Clyde Workers' Committee and the Dilution Struggle', in Asa Briggs and John Saville (eds.), *Essays in Labour History 1886–1923* (Macmillan, London, 1971), pp. 152–84.

Hobsbawm, Eric, 'Bolshevism and the Anarchists', in his *Revolutionaries* (Quartet, London, 1977), pp. 57–70.

Hobsbawm, Eric, 'The Historians Group of the Communist Party', in Maurice Cornforth (ed.), *Rebels and their Causes: Essays in Honour of A. L. Morton* (Lawrence and Wishart, London, 1978), pp. 21–47.

Hobsbawm, Eric, 'Some Reflections on "The Break-Up of Britain"', *New Left Review* (105), 1977, pp. 3–23.

Hobsbawm, Eric, 'Working Classes and Nations', *Saothar* (8), 1982, pp. 75–85, republished as 'What is the Workers' Country?', in his *Worlds of Labour* (Weidenfeld, London, 1984).

Hoffmann, J., 'James Connolly and the Theory of Historical Materialism', *Saothar* (2), May 1976, pp. 53–60.

Hunter, James, 'The Gaelic Connection: Highlands, Ireland and Nationalism, 1873–1922', *Scottish Historical Review* 1975, pp. 178–204.

Karabel, Jerome, 'The Failure of American Socialism Reconsidered', *Socialist Register*, 1979, pp. 204–27.

Keogh, Dermot, 'William Martin Murphy and the Origins of the 1913 Lock-Out', *Saothar* (4), 1978, pp. 15–34.

Kerevan, George, 'Arguments Within Scottish Marxism', *The Bulletin of Scottish Politics*, Vol. 1, No. 2, (Spring 1981), pp. 111–33.

Knox, Bill, 'The Scottish Labour Movement and Home Rule c 1880–1945', *Radical Scotland*, October–November, 1984, pp. 21–3.

Larkin, Emmet, 'Church, State and Nation in Modern Ireland', *American Historical Review*, 1975, pp. 1244–76.

Larkin, Emmet, 'Socialism and Catholicism in Ireland', *Church History* 1964, pp. 462–83.

Lowery, Robert, 'Sean O'Casey and the Irish Worker', *O'Casey Annual*, No. 3, 1984, pp. 33–114.

Lowy, Michel, 'Marxism and the National Question', in Robert Blackburn (ed.), *Revolution and Class Struggle: A Reader in Marxist Politics* (Fontana, London, 1977), pp. 136–60.

McHugh, John, 'The Belfast Labour Dispute and Riots of 1907', *North West Group for the Study of Labour History, Bulletin*, No. 4, pp. 92–129.

McHugh, John, 'The Clyde Rent Strike 1915', *Scottish Labour History Society Journal* (No. 12), 1978, pp. 56–62.

McHugh, John and Ripley, Brian, 'John Maclean the Scottish Workers' Republican Party and Scottish Nationalism', *Scottish Labour History Society Journal*, 1983, pp. 43–7.

MacIntyre, Stuart, 'Socialism, the Unions and the Labour Party after 1918', *Bulletin of the Society for the Study of Labour History* (31), Autumn 1975, pp. 101–11.

McKibbin, Ross, 'The Economic Policy of the Second Labour Government 1929–31', *Past and Present* (68), August 1975, pp. 95–123.

Mair, Peter, 'Labour and the Irish Party System Revisited: Party Competition in the 1920s', *Economic and Social Review*, 1977, pp. 59–70.

Martin, F.X., 'Eoin MacNeill on the 1916 Rising', *Irish Historical Studies*, Vol. XII, 1960–61, pp. 226–71.

Martin, F.X., '1916: Myth, Fact and Mystery', *Studia Hibernica*, 1967, pp. 7–126.

Martin, F.X., 'The 1916 Rising – a Coup d'Etat or a Bloody Protest?', *Studia Hibernica*, 1968, pp. 106–37.

Melling, Joseph, 'The Glasgow Rent Strike and Clydeside Labour – Some Problems of Interpretation', *Scottish Labour History Society Journal* (No. 13), 1979, pp. 39–44.

Melling, Joseph, 'Scottish Industrialists and the Changing Character of Class Relations in the Clyde Region c 1880–1918', in Tony Dickson (ed.), *Capital and Class in Scotland* (John Donald, Edinburgh, 1982).

Moody, T.W., 'The Fenian Movement in Irish History', in his *The Fenian Movement* (Mercier Press, Cork, 1978), pp. 99–111.

Moody, T.W., 'Michael Davitt and the British Labour Movement', *Transactions of the Royal Historical Society*, 1953, pp. 55–77.

Moran, Bill, '1913, Jim Larkin and the British Labour Movement', *Saothar* (4), 1978, pp. 35–49.

Morgan, Austen, 'A British Labourist in Catholic Ireland', *Saothar* (7), pp. 54–61.

Morgan, Austen, 'Socialism in Ireland – Red, Green and Orange', in Austen Morgan and Bob Purdie (eds.), *Ireland: Divided Nation, Divided Class* (Ind. Links, London, 1980).

Morris, Dylan, 'The Origins of the British Socialist Party', *North West Group for the Study of Labour History Bulletin*, No. 8, 1982–83, pp. 29–42.

Morris, R.J., 'Skilled Workers and the Politics of the "Red Clyde"', *Scottish Labour History Society Journal* (No. 18), 1983, pp. 6–17.

Munch, Ronald, 'Class and Religion in Belfast – A Historical Perspective', *Journal of Contemporary History*, April 1985, pp. 241–59.

Murray, Peter, 'Electoral Politics and the Dublin Working Class Before the First World War', *Saothar* (6), 1980, pp. 8–25.

Nairn, Tom, 'Internationalism: A Critique', *The Bulletin of Scottish Politics*, Vol. 1, No. 1 (Autumn 1980), pp. 101–25.

Newsinger, John, '"In the Hunger Cry of the Poor is Heard the Voice of Ireland", Sean O'Casey and Politics 1908–16', *Journal of Contemporary History*, April 1985, pp. 221–40.

Newsinger, John, 'James Connolly and the Easter Rising', *Science and Society*, Summer 1983, Vol. 47, pp. 152–77.

O'Connor, Emmet, 'An Age of Agitation', *Saothar* (9), 1983, pp. 64–70.

O'Connor, Emmet, 'Agrarian Unrest and the Labour Movement in County Waterford 1917–23', *Saothar* (6), 1980, pp. 40–58.

O'Connor, Lysaght, 'The Rake's Progress of a Syndicalist: The Political Career of William O'Brien, Irish Labour Leader', *Saothar* (9), 1983, pp. 48–62.

Oldfield, Adrian, 'The Independent Labour Party and Planning 1920–26', *International Review of Social History* (1976), pp. 1–29.

Orridge, A. W., 'Uneven Development and Nationalism', *Political Studies* 1981, pp. 1–15 and 181–90.

Orwell, George, 'The Lion and the Unicorn' in his *Collected Essays and Letters, Volume 2* (Penguin, Harmondsworth, 1971).

Parry, Cyril, 'The Independent Labour Party and Gwynedd Politics 1900–20', *Welsh Historical Review*, 1968, pp. 47–66.

Patterson, Henry, 'Independent Orangeism and Class Conflict in Edwardian Belfast', *Proceedings of the Royal Irish Academy* Vol. 80, Sec C, No. 4, 1980, pp. 1–27.

Patterson, Henry, 'James Larkin and the Belfast Dockers' and Carters' Strike of 1907', *Saothar* (4), 1978, pp. 8–14.

Patterson, Henry, 'Reassessing Marxism on Ulster', *Saothar* (5), 1979, pp. 50–55.

Purdie, Bob, 'Red Hand or Red Flag? Loyalism and Workers in Belfast', *Saothar* (8), 1982, pp. 64–9.

Rodgers, Murdie and Smyth, Jim, 'John Maclean: Organiser for the Socialist Revolution', *Radical Scotland*, December 1983/January 1984, pp. 20–2.

Rubin, G., 'A Note on the Scottish Reaction to John Maclean's Drugging Allegation', *Scottish Labour History Society Journal* (14), 1980, pp. 40–5.

Samuel, Raphael, 'British Marxist Historians', *New Left Review* (120), 1980, pp. 21–96.

Saville, John, Introduction to Theodore Rothstein, *From Chartism to Labourism* (Lawrence and Wishart, London, 1983), p. v–xvii.

Schwarz, Bill, '''The People'' in History: The Communist Party Historians' Group 1946–56', in Centre for Contemporary Cultural Studies, *Making Histories* (Hutchinson, London, 1982).

Seretan, L. G., 'The Personal Style and Political Methods of Daniel De Leon: A Reconsideration', *Labor History*, Spring 1973, pp. 163–201.

Shanin, Teodor, 'Marx and the Peasant Commune', *History Workshop Journal* (12), 1981, pp. 108–28.

Smith, Jim, 'Socialism in Scotland: The Beginnings', *Radical Scotland* No. 7, February/March 1984.

Smith, Joyce, 'Labour Traditions in Glasgow and Liverpool', *History Workshop Journal* (17), Spring 1982, pp. 32–56.

Stead, Peter, 'The Welsh Working Class', *Llafur* (1973), pp. 80–92.

Thompson, E. P., 'The Peculiarities of the English' in *The Socialist Register* (1965), reprinted in *The Poverty of Theory* (Merlin, London, 1978), pp. 35–91.

Townshend, Charles, 'The Irish Railway Strike of 1920: Industrial Action and Civil Resistance in the Struggle for Independence', *Irish Historical Studies* (XXI) 1979, pp. 265–82.

Trotsky, Leon, 'Where is Britain Going?' in *Leon Trotsky on Britain* (Monad Press, New York, 1973).

Tsuzuki, C., 'The Impossibilist Revolt in Britain', *International Review of Social History* (1), 1956, pp. 377–97.

Vestri, Paolo, 'The Rise of Reformism', *Radical Scotland*, April/May 1984, pp. 21–3.

Wada, Haruki, 'Marx and Revolutionary Russia', *History Workshop Journal* (12), 1981, pp. 129–50.

Williams, Angela, 'A Kind of Angry Poetry', *Planet* (51), June/July 1985, pp. 15–22.

Williams, Gwyn, 'Sardinian Marxist and Welsh Predicament', *Radical Wales*, Summer, 1985, pp. 18–21.

Williams, L. J., 'The Road to Tonypandy', *Llafur* (1973), pp. 41–52.

Wood, Ian S., 'Irish Immigrants and Scottish Radicalism 1880–1906', in Ian
    MacDougall (ed.), *Essays in Scottish Labour History* (John Donald, Edinburgh,
    no date), pp. 64–89.
Wood, Ian S., 'John Wheatley, the Irish and the Labour Movement in Scotland',
    Innes Review (1980), pp. 71–85.
Woodhouse, M., 'Mines for the Nation or Mines for the Miners', *Llafur* (1978),
    pp. 92–109.
Young, James D., 'John Maclean's Place in Scottish History', *Bulletin of the
    Society for the Study of Labour History* (39), 1979, pp. 80–4.
Young, James D., 'Marxism and the Scottish National Question', *Journal of
    Contemporary History*, 1983, pp. 141–63.
Young, James D., 'Nationalism, "Marxism" and Scottish History', *Journal of
    Contemporary History*, April 1985, pp. 337–55.

Unpublished Theses

Cooper, Samuel, John Wheatley, A Study in Labour History, Glasgow PhD, 1973.
McLean, Iain, The Labour Movement in Clydeside Politics, 1914–22, Oxford
    DPhil, 1971.
Morgan, Austen, 'Politics, The Labour Movement and the Working Class in
    Belfast 1905–23', Queen's University, Belfast, PhD, 1978.
Ransom, Bernard, 'James Connolly and the Scottish Left', Edinburgh PhD, 1975.
Smith, Joyce, 'Common Sense and Working-Class Consciousness: Some Aspects
    of the Glasgow and Liverpool Labour Movements in the Early Years of the
    Twentieth Century', PhD, University of Edinburgh, 1980.
Woodhouse, M., 'Rank and File Movements Among the Miners of South Wales,
    1910–1926', Oxford, DPhil, 1969.

Political Writings

The writings of the three principal figures can be found almost wholly in newspapers and pamphlets.

a. Connolly

Amongst the later collections note:

Desmond Ryan (ed.), *Socialism and Nationalism* (Sign of Three Candles, Dublin,
    1948).
Desmond Ryan (ed.), *Labour and Easter Week* (Sign of Three Candles, Dublin,
    1949).
Desmond Ryan (ed.), *The Workers' Republic* (Sign of Three Candles, Dublin,
    1951).
P. Berresford Ellis (ed.), *James Connolly: Selected Writings* (Penguin, Harmonds-
    worth, 1973).
Owen Dudley Edwards and Bernard Ransom (eds.), *James Connolly – Selected
    Political Writings* (Cape, London, 1973).

The pamphlets produced by the Cork Workers' Club:

The Connolly–Walker Controversy on Socialist Unity in Ireland (1974)
Ireland Upon the Dissecting Table – James Connolly on Ulster and Partition
    (1975)

The Connolly/De Leon Controversy on Wages, Marriage and The Church (1976)
Sinn Fein and Socialism (includes a piece by Connolly) (1977)

The principal works produced by Connolly with original date of publication:

Erin's Hope: The End and The Means (1897)
The New Evangel (1901)
Erin's Hope (Revised edition 1902)
Socialism Made Easy (1908)
Labour, Nationality and Religion (1910)
Labour in Irish History (1910)
The Reconquest of Ireland (1915)

b. *Maclean*

The most extensive collection is:

Nan Milton (ed.), *John Maclean: In the Rapids of Revolution: Essays Articles and Letters 1902–23* (Allison and Busby, London, 1978)

Pamphlets, with the original date of publication, include:

The Greenock Jungle (1907)
Cooperation and the Rise in Prices (1911)
The War After the War in the Light of Elements of Working Class Economics (1918)
Sack Dalrymple, Sack Stevenson. Let Labour Revenge Bloody Friday (1919)
The Irish Tragedy: Scotland's Digrace (1920)
The Coming War with America (1920)

c. *Wheatley*

The pamphlets include:

How the Miners are Robbed: The Duke in the Dock (1907)
The Catholic Working Man (1909)
Miners, Mines and Misery (1909)
A Christian in Difficulty (1912)
Eight-Pound Cottages for Glasgow Citizens (1913)
Municipal Banking: How the City of Glasgow Could Save Millions (1920)
The New Rent Act: A Reply to the Rent Raisers (1920)
Starving in the Midst of Plenty (1923)
Socialise the National Income (1927)

d. *Others*

Allen, Clifford, *Socialism and the Next Labour Government* (1925).
Askwith, Lord, *Industrial Problems and Disputes* (John Murray, London, 1920).
De Leon, Daniel, *The Preamble of the Industrial Workers of the World ... An Address* (SLP Press, Edinburgh, 1907).
De Leon, Daniel, *Reform or Revolution* (SLP Press, Edinburgh, 1906).
Green, Alice Stopford, *The Making of Ireland and her Undoing 1200–1600* (Macmillan, London, 1908).
Hobson, J.A., *The Economics of Unemployment* (Allen and Unwin, London, 1924).
Independent Labour Party, *The Living Wage* (1926).

Lalor, James Fintan, *Collected Writings* (Talbot Press, Dublin, 1947).
Leslie, John, *The Irish Question* (reprint, Cork Workers' Club, 1974).
Mitchel, John, *Jail Journal* (Gill, Dublin, no date).
Mosley, Oswald, *Revolution by Reason* (1925).
Nitti, Francesco Saverio, *Catholic Socialism* (Swan Sonnenschein, London, 1895).
O'Casey, Sean, *The Story of the Irish Citizen Army* (Journeyman Press, London, 1980).
Pearse, Padraic H., *Political Writings and Speeches* (Talbot Press, Dublin, 1962).
Snowden, Philip, *Socialism and Syndicalism* (Collins, London, no date).
Stephens, James, *The Insurrection in Dublin* (Maunsel, Dublin, 1916).
Unofficial Reform Committee, *The Miners' Next Step* (reprint, Puto, London, 1973).
Wright, Arnold, *Disturbed Dublin* (Longmans, London, 1914).

Index

Ablett, Noah, 283
Allen, Clifford
  on Ruhr question, 257
  and ILP revival, 258
  view of Socialist strategy, 265–6
  disenchantment with ILP, 266
American Federation of Labor (AFL)
  and Industrial Workers of the
    World, 53, 55–6
  and skilled workers, 66
  Connolly's dismissal of, 66–7
  socialist views on, 68–9
  politics of, 68
  Irish in, 76–7
Askwith, Sir George, 107
Asquith, H.H., 129

Barnes, George
  on campaign for Maclean's release
    (1918), 185
  and 1918 Gorbals election, 191–3
Bauer, Otto, 5–6
Belfast
  Marx's neglect of its politics, 10
  shipyard expulsions (1912), 94
  Labour Movement in, 94–5,
    99–106
  economic position of, 98
  Labour Representation Committee
    (LRC) in, 102–4
  Maclean on, 165
Belfast Dock Strike (1907), 105–6,
  165
Belfast Engineering Dispute (1895), 99
Belfast Labour Chronicle, 102–3
Belfast Trades Council, 94–100
Bell, Tom, 89, 157, 192, 204
Belloc, Hilaire, 236
Benn, Tony, 7
Berger, Victor, 65, 71
Bevin, Ernest, 278
Blatchford, Robert, 40, 161, 236
Bonar Law, Andrew, 130

Boot and Shoe Workers' Union
  (USA), 49, 77
Booth, Handel, 302
Bowen-Colthurst, Captain, 145
Bowman, Alexander, 99
Brailsford, H.N.
  opposition to parliamentary
    scenes, 253
  and ILP Study Group on Unem-
    ployment, 266–7
  on 'living wage' as myth, 270–1
  on Mosley, 322 n.19
Britain for the British, 236
The British Road to Socialism, 7
British Socialist Party
  Maclean as orthodox member of,
    167–71
  weakness of, in 1914, 163; in
    1918, 189–90
  Maclean's row with pro-war
    faction, 173–4
  Glasgow situation (1914–15),
    173–4
  party press on Maclean (1918), 186
  position in Glasgow (1918), 187
  outlook on revolution (1918), 188
  connection with Labour Party
    (1918), 188–9
  and 1918 election, 193
  and Maclean's involvement
    (1919), 199
  referendum on third international,
    200
  exit of Maclean, 200–1
  problem of political space, 282
British Trades Union Congress
  on 1913 Dublin riots, 110
  Sexton's speech (1913), 114
  Special Conference (December
    1913), 115–16, 302
  1915 Congress, 133
  views in late 1920, 272–3, 276
  1928 Congress, 279

Brockway, Fenner, 269–70
Bryan, William Jennings, 64
Buchanan, George, and Gorbals
    election (1922), 220–1
Burns, John, 128
Buxton, Charles Roden, 257

The Call, 201
Cambrian Combine strike
    (1910–11), 14, 166
Cant, Ernie, 314
Carson, Sir Edward, 128, 130
Casement, Roger, 96
Catholic Socialism, 236
Catholic Socialist Society, 232–6
The Catholic Working Man, 232–6
Ceannt, Eamonn, 130
Celtic Communism, 32, 211, 213
Central Labour College, 283
Champion, Henry Hyde, 251
Chaplin, Ralph, 295 n.26
Clark, G. B., 313 n.44
Clyde Workers' Committee
    on dilution and conscription, 174,
        176–8
    politics and strategy, 176–8
    SLP in, 179
    reformed, 191
    and John Wheatley, 238–9
Clynes, J.R., 279
coal dispute (1984), 14
Colum, Padraic, 126
The Coming War with America,
    214–15
Communist International, 200
The Communist Manifesto, 4–5
Communist Party (British)
    programme, 7
    attitude to John Maclean, 157–8,
        219
    pressures for formation, 200
    J. Maclean's criticism of, 203,
        222–3
    H. McShane's move to, 219
    early silence on Scottish
        Nationalism, 225
    position in 1920s, 245–6, 272,
        278, 282
    and syndicalism, 282–3
    views on Nationalism in
        Popular Front period, 225, 283,
        285

Connolly, James
    outline of career, 11
    episodes: Edinburgh politics,
        19–27; Dublin (1896–1903),
        28–41; Irish Socialist
        Republican Party, 28–9; visits
        USA (1902), 45–6; and Socialist
        Labour Party (British), 46;
        emigrates to USA (1903), 48;
        rows with De Leon, 50, 90; and
        Socialist Party of America, 58;
        New Castle strike, 66–7, 69,
        77; in Belfast, 93; polemic with
        William Walker, 104; and
        Dublin Lock Out, 110–27;
        outbreak of European War,
        130–1; journalistic changes
        during war, 131; ITGWU, 133;
        commitment to Easter Rising,
        138–9
    views on: Liberals, 21; Socialist
        strategy, 22, 38–9, 42–52,
        58–63, 113–14 (*see also*
        Industrial Unionism); Ireland
        (Edinburgh years), 23–6;
        Parnell, 25; Irish Parliamentary
        Party, 25, 121; Irish
        Nationalism (1896–1903),
        31–9; land nationalisation, 35;
        socialism in Ireland, 36; Polish
        independence, 36; relations
        between British and Irish
        Socialists, 37; materialist view
        of history, 38, 80–1, 91;
        violence (1890s), 39–41; trade
        unions (1890s), 39;
        international conflict, 39;
        Fabianism, 43; Labour Alliance,
        43–4, 56; Social Democratic
        Federation (early 1900s), 44–6;
    democratic practices in Socialist
        organisations, 50; Industrial
        Workers of the World, 53ff.;
        Industrial Unionism, 56–7,
        59–62, 76, 118–20, 141–2;
        McKees Rocks strike, 65–6;
        American Federation of Labor,
        66–7, 69; Knights of Labor,
        67–9; European and American
        Socialist prospects, 72; Irish
        identity, 74–92; Gaelic
        revival, 78–9, 88, 95; Daniel

O'Connell, 82; Wolfe Tone, 82–4; John Mitchel, 85; James Fintan Lalor, 85–6; Fenianism, 86; Roman Catholicism, 88–91; Unionism, 93–106; Orange Order, 94–8, 106; James Larkin, 108–9; British TUC (1913), 115, 116, 118; sympathetic strikes, 116; British working class (1913–16), 118, 120, 133, 135; Socialist support for the war, 131–2; war's impact on unions, 132–3; British TUC (1915), 133; British Imperialism, 135; Germany, 136–7, 305 n. 32; Republican heroes, 138; blood sacrifice doctrine, 143; Nationalist revolt, 144–5; F. Sheehy Skeffington, 145; insurrectionary view compared with that of Eoin Macneill, 149–50; patriarchal attitudes, 281
writings: *Erins' Hope*, 31–5, 42; *Socialism Made Easy*, 59–60; *Labour in Irish History*, 75, 78–87; *The Harp*, 77–9; *Labour Nationality and Religion*, 88–91
other: historiography on, 17–18; critical verdicts on, 140–1; comparisons with John Maclean, 159–60, 172, 210–11, 215–16, 281–5; comparisons with John Wheatley, 231–2, 274, 281–5
Cook, Arthur J.
and sympathy for ILP, 272
and position in Trade Union Movement, 276
involvement in Cook-Maxton Manifesto campaign, 276–9
Cook-Maxton Manifesto campaign, 276–9, 324 n. 58
Crofters' Members of Parliament, 168–9
Curragh Mutiny, 93

Daily Herald, 117
Davies, Idris, 245
Debs, Eugene, 55, 64–5, 68

De Leon, Daniel
career and character, 47
views on Socialist strategy, 48
rows with Connolly, 50, 90
Connolly's rejection of his leadership, 51–2
attitude to IWW, 53–7
Democratic Party, Connolly's view or, 75–6
Devlin, Joe, 105
Diack, William, 210
Dillon, John, 121
Doccan, Patrick, 277
Dublin
influence on Connolly (1896–1903), 28–41
occupational structure and trade unions, 28
housing, 28 (*see also* subsequent entries)
Dublin Lock Out (1913)
general, 14, 107–27;
problems of interpretation, 110–13
and British Labour opinion, 114–18
Connolly, reflections on, 118–21
Nationalist responses, 121–6
Dublin Socialist Club, 28
Dublin Trades Council
Craft unions on (1890s), 28
ITGWU and, 108
and 1915 College Green election, 133–4
Duncan, Joseph, 209

Easter Rising (1916)
and ideology, 17
proclamation, 137
Connolly's commitment to, 138–9
problems of characterisation, 143–4
Nationalist alternatives to, 144–50
possibly premature, 151–2
Scottish responses to, 159–60
and John Maclean, 184, 211
and 1918 Glasgow election, 193
influence on Ruaraidh Erskine, 211
and John Wheatley, 242

The Economics of Unemployment,
    255
Edinburgh
    Connolly's activities in, 19–27
    class structure, 19
    trade unionism in, 19–20
    Socialism in, 20–7
    Irish National League in, 26
Edinburgh Trades Council, 19–20
*Eight Pound Cottages for Glasgow
    Citizens*, 237–8
elections
    Edinburgh Central (1892), 20
    St Giles (1894), 21
    Edinburgh Poor Law (1895), 22–3
    Dublin municipal (1895), 22–3
    North-East Lanarkshire (1901),
        44, 231
    United States presidential (1900,
        1904), 49; (1908, 1912), 64–5;
        (1908), 75
    Belfast North (1885), 99; (1905,
        1906, 1907), 100
    Belfast South, 101
    Dublin municipal (1912–14),
        113–14
    College Green (1915), 133–4;
        Ireland (1918), 153; Glasgow
        (1918), 191–4, 242
    General (1919), record, 199
    Bothwell (1919), 199
    Scotland (1918), 208
    Glasgow Kinning Park (1921), 219
    Gorbals (1922), 220–2
    North Kelvin (1923), 223
    SWRP contests (1923), 224
    1900 election and Irish vote, 231
    North-West Lanarkshire (1906),
        231
    Wales (1979, 1983), 285
Engels, Frederick
    and Polish Nationalism, 5
    and influence of Lewis Morgan,
        81
Engineering Strikes (1919), 191
*Erin's Hope: The End and the
    Means*, 31–5, 42
Erskine, Hon. Stuart (the Hon.
        Ruardaidh Erskine of Mar)
    early career, 169–70
    Maclean's links with (post-1918),
        207

    on Russian Revolution, 210
    and Easter Rising, 211

Fairchild, E.C., 200
Farren, Thomas, 134
Fenianism
    John Leslie on, 24
    Connolly on, 86
Fife Miners' Reform Committee,
    190, 197
Fife miners' strike (1919), 197
Flynn, Elizabeth Gurley, 77
Foot, Michael
    electoral defeat (1983), 1
    part-author of *Guilty Men*, 1
    and South Atlantic crisis (1982),
        3
    historical views of, 285
Forty Hours' Strike (1919), 195–8
Forward
    Connolly piece for May-Day
        (1914), 120
    Connolly ceases to contribute, 131
    and diverse ILP views, 173
    and 1918 Glasgow elections,
        192–3
    attack on 'Direct Action' (1919),
        195
    Catholic Socialist Society and,
        232
    Wheatley's articles on strategy in
        (1918), 42
    C. M. Grieve/Hugh MacDiarmid
        in, 318 n. 98
Free Trade, as issue in Labour party,
    248, 249, 250–1, 260–2,
    268–9

Gaelic Athletic Association, 30
Gallacher, Willie
    on John Maclean, 157, 186
    and CWC, 176–8
    Harry McShane's view of, 178
    and 1918 election, 192
    on Forty Hours' Strike, 195
    object of Maclean's polemic, 203,
        315
    on John Wheatley, 238–9
    and Cook-Maxton Manifesto
        campaign, 276
General Strike (1926), 245, 263–4
George, Henry, 74

George Square riot (1919), 195
Glasgow
  economic situation pre-1914, 164
  housing situation, 165, 242
  war's impact on city's politics,
    173–4, 187
  assessment of wartime radicalism,
    178–83
  1918 election in, 192–4, 242
  1922 election in, 220–1, 253
  municipalisation in, 237–8
Glasgow Herald, 222
Glasgow Observer, 12, 193, 232, 237
Glasgow rent strike
  Maclean and, 175
  government response, 180
  political impact of, 181–2
  and John Wheatley, 238
Glasgow Trades Council, 175, 311
    n. 18
Glasier, J. Bruce, 293 n. 6
Gold Standard, 247–8, 268–9
Gompers, Sam, 68
Gonne, Maud, 34, 41
Gramsci, Antonio, 91
Grassic Gibbon, Lewis (Leslie
    Mitchell), 225
Griffith, Arthur, 41, 123–4
Guilty Men, 1
Guth na Bliadhna (the Voice of the
    Year), 170
Gwynn, Stephen, 303 n. 59

Hands off Russia campaign, 200–1
Hardie, James Keir, 25–6, 44, 100,
    110
The Harp, 77–9
Harvie, Christopher, 178–9
Hayes, Max, 68
Haywood, William, 71
Hobsbawm, Eric, 140
Hobson, Bulmer
  and anti-Redmond volunteers,
    130
  against Connolly on insurrection,
    144–5
Hobson, J. A.
  and under-consumptionist theory,
    225
  influence of, 255–7, 258
  and ILP Study Group on Unem-
    ployment, 266–7

concern about some inter-
    pretations of the 'living wage',
    270–1, 323 n. 27
Hogge, J. M., 312 n. 2
Highland Land League, 169, 208–9
Hyndman, H. M., 40, 44, 173

Independent Labour Party
  in Edinburgh, 20–1
  in Dublin, 28
  in Belfast, 99
  attitude to industrial militancy,
    116
  attitude to 1914–18 War, 147
  Maclean's view of, 161
  and Glasgow wartime experiences,
    173, 187, 238–9
  and Glasgow rent strike, 175–6
  supported by Wheatley, 233, 235,
    237, 239–42
  debate on Ruhr at 1923
    conference, 256–7
  revival of, 258
  response of Labour Government
    (1924), 264–5
  leadership in, 266
  policy on unemployment/'The
    Living Wage', 266–73
  Summer School (1926), 269–70;
    general, 272
  limits as vehicle for 'living wage'
    policy, 272
  lack of trade union support for
    ILP policy, 272–3
  response to Cook-Maxton
    Manifesto campaign, 277
  weakness of (1928), 278
Independent Labour Party (Scottish
    Division), 277
Independent Orange Order, 101–2,
    105
Industrial Workers of the World
    ('Wobblies')
  Connolly's support for, 53
  early divisions in, 54–8
  early weakness of, 55–6
  expulsion of De Leon, 57
  New Castle strike, 58, 66
  expansion of, 65
  McKees Rocks strike (1909),
    65–6
  and political legacy, 69–72

International Socialist Review, 131
Irish Citizen Army
    foundation, 127
    under Connolly's control, 130
    involvement with Republicans, 138
Irish National League, 23, 26
Irish Neutrality League, 137
Irish Parliamentary Party
    attitude of British Socialists
        towards, 23, 120–1
    Connolly's view of, 25, 34, 141
    problems in 1890s, 30
    attitude to Dublin Lock Out,
        121–2
    and 1914–18 War, 129–30
    problem for Irish Labour, 282
Irish Republican Brotherhood,
    Military Council, 139
Irish Socialist Federation, 77
Irish Socialist Republican Party,
    28–9, 44–5
Irish Trades Union Congress, 25, 27,
    94, 108, 113
Irish Transport and General Workers'
    Union
    Connolly as Belfast organiser, 93
    as new industrial force, 105
    impact on Dublin, 107–8
    membership, 108
    character in 1913, 110–11
    Connolly's leadership of, 133
    post-1916 growth, 151–2
    County Waterford strikes
        (1922–23), 152
Irish Transvaal Committee, 41
Irish Volunteers
    foundation, 125, 129, 130
    split in, 129–30
    Eoin MacNeill's position in,
        147–50
Irish Worker, 109, 131
Isle of Lewis land raids, 168, 213–14

Johnson, Thomas, probable author
    of contribution to *Voice of
    Labour*, 153
Johnston, Tom
    on Maclean, 187
    and Lewis land seizures, 213–14,
        218
    and Glasgow municipal politics,
        237

Jones, Arthur Creech, 266
Jones, Jack, 302
Justice, 46, 162–3, 173

Kautsky, Karl, 45, 170
Kendall, Walker, 189
Kettle, Lawrence, 304 n. 10
King, Joseph, 312 n. 2
Kirkwood, David, and CWC, 176–8,
    238
Knights of Labor, 67–8, 77

Labour Party
    electoral board, 1
    record in office, 2
    in August 1914, 4
    and nationalism in Britain, 7–8
    and Irish Parliamentary Party,
        120–1
    pre-1914 weakness in Scotland,
        163–4
    and 1918 election, 191–4
    NEC on Maclean's 1918
        candidacy, 191–2
    and Scottosh politics in 1920s,
        217–18
    and Glasgow housing, 220–1
    attack on Scottish Workers'
        Republican Party, 223–4
    development in Glasgow, 237–8
    electoral position in 1920s,
        244–52
    Free Trade, protection debate in,
        247–51
    1928 Conference, 279
Labour Party (Scottish Council),
    208–9
Lalor, James Fintan
    John Leslie on, 24
    Connolly on, 85–6
Lanarkshire Miners' Reform
    Committee, 190, 196–7, 312
Lanarkshire miners' strike (1917),
    190; (1919), 196–7
Lanchester, Edith, 89
Landis, Judge, 70
Lansbury, George, 271
Larkin, Emmet, 105, 301 n. 49
Larkin, James
    and 1907 Belfast dock strike,
        105–6
    personality of, 108

attitude to Irish Labour Party, 113
and James Sexton, 114
attacks on British trade union
leaders, 115
attacked by John Dillon, 121
leaves for USA, 133
Lawrence Textile strike (1912), 71
Leeds Convention (1917), 187
Lee, Sheriff, 310
Leith, 19, 21
Lenin, V.I.
on nationalism, 6
on Easter Rising, 140–1, 150–1
Leo XIII, 230–1
Leslie, John, and *The Present
Position of the Irish Question*,
24–5
Leverhulme, Lord, 213–14
Liebknecht, Karl, 136
List, Friedrich, 123
Little, Frank, 57
'Living Wage', 266–73
Lloyd-George, David, 191, 198
Luxemburg, Rosa, 5

McClennan, George B., 75
MacDermott, Sean, 130
MacDiarmid, Hugh (C.M. Grieve),
158, 225, 318 n. 98
MacDonagh, Thomas
and Dublin Lock Out, 126
and anti-Redmondite Volunteers,
130
'Open Letter' from F. Sheehy-
Skeffington, 146
MacDonald, Ramsay
and Belfast Labour politics, 100
against sympathetic strikes, 116
and 1914–18 War, 128
optimism of (1909), 233
appeal of in 1920s, 246, 279–80
against class politics, 249
antipathy to parliamentary
scenes, 253
attitude to 'Living Wage', 273
Home Rule as way of avoiding
disintegration, 315 n. 31
and Hobson on 'Living Wage',
323 n. 27
MacDougall, James
and CWC, 176
and miners, 190, 197, 198

McKees Rocks Steel strike,
Pennsylvania (1909), 65–6
McLean, Iain, 178
Maclean, John
outline of career, 11–12
episodes: disputes in BSP, 173–4;
gaoled and sacked, 174, 184–6;
Glasgow rent strike, 175;
position in April 1916, 182–3;
allegations about prison
treatment, 185–6; work in
Scottish coalfields, 186, 190–1;
Soviet Consul in Glasgow, 187;
distinctive position in BSP
(1918), 187–8; and 1918
Gorbals election, 191–4; BSP
activities (1919), 199; rift with
BSP, 200–1; personal situation
from 1921, 203; organiser of
unemployed, 205–6, 219;
Gorbals election (1922), 220–2,
(1923), 224; predicament in
1923, 224; electoral work
(1923), 224
views on: orthodox Social
Democrat pre-1914, 161–71;
antipathy to pre-war
syndicalism, 162–3; Scottish
trade unions, 164–5; Irish
religious tensions, 165; need
for British-based unions, 166;
Scottish Home Rule (pre-1914),
166–7; Scottish land question,
168–9, 170, 213–15, 218;
Triple Alliance, 170–1;
wartime strategy, 174–5; rent
strike, 175; CWC, 176–8;
Bolshevik revolution, 184;
Easter Rising, 184, 211;
changing views on strategy,
188–9; Forty Hours' Strike,
196; miners' demands (1919),
196, 198–9; Communist Party,
203, 222–3; concern over
Russian influence, 204;
strategic concerns (1921),
204–5; Industrial Unionism,
205; Scottish independence,
205–6, 209, 215–25; Sinn
Fein, 212; war with United
States, 214–15; patriarchal
views of, 281

Maclean, John (continued)
 other: historiographical debate
  over, 157–60; comparison
  with Connolly, 159–60, 172,
  210–11, 215–16, 218–85;
  exchange with Wheatley, 236
MacManus, Arthur
 and Connolly, 144
 and CWC, 176–7
MacNeacaill, H.C., 211
MacNeill, Eoin
 and Irish Volunteers split, 129–30
 on insurrectionary option, 147–50
McShane, Harry
 views on: CWC, 178; Maclean's
  rift with BSP, 201–2, 312;
  Maclean's 1921 propaganda,
  205; Maclean's unemployment
  campaign, 206; reason for
  joining Communist Party, 219;
  Scottish Workers' Republican
  Party, 223; Maclean's situation
  (1923), 224; Wheatley–Puissant
  controversy, 232–3
Maguire, Archbishop (of Glasgow),
 236
Malone, Cecil L'Estrange, 201
Markiewicz, Countess, 126
Marx, Karl
 and internationalism, 4
 and Polish Nationalism, 5
 and Ireland, 8–10
Matheson, John Carstairs, 45, 56
Maxton, James
 contrast with Wheatley, 13
 support for parliamentary scenes,
  253–4
 rise to ILP leadership, 266
 and Cook-Maxton Manifesto
  campaign, 276–8
Melling, Joseph, 179
Michels, Robert, 72
Miners' Federation of Great Britain
 minimum wage strike (1912), 166
 debates during 1914–18 War,
  190–1
 1919 programme and strategy,
  196–8
 increasing political attachment
  to Labour Party, 199–200
 and all-British strategy, 217–18,
  283

and crisis of, 1925–6, 262–4
 at 1928 Labour Party Conference,
  279
The Miners' Next Step, 111,
  119–20
Ministry of Labour, 185
Mitchel, John, 85, 298 n.40
The Molly Maguires, 77
Morgan, Lewis, 81
Morning Post, 115
Mosley, Sir Oswald
 on Wheatley, 229
 economic views in 1920s, 250
 view on 'Living Wage', 268–9
 Brailsford on, 322 n.19
Muir, Edmund, 225
Muir, John, and CWC, 176–7
Munitions Act
 Maclean on, 175
 Socialist view of, 179
Munro, Robert, 195
Murdoch, John, 167
Murphy, William Martin, 109

Nathan, Sir Matthew, 136
National Front, 2
National Union of Boot and Shoe
  Operatives, 251
National Union of Dock Labourers,
  105
National Union of Railwaymen, 210,
  218
New Castle Tinplate Strike,
  Pennsylvania (1910), 8–66
New Leader, 253, 267, 268
New Statesman, 108
Nitti, Francesco, 236

O'Brien, William, 28–9, 305 n.35
O'Casey, Sean, 18, 141, 142, 290
  (1st n.3)
O'Connell, Daniel, 82
O'Connell, Mark, 223
O'Neil, John, 55
Orange Order
 Connolly on, 94–8, 106
 working class and, 100–1
 opposition to Maclean, 212

Parkhead Marxian Study Circle, 320
  n.59
Partridge, William, 109

Parnell, Charles Stewart, John Leslie
  and Connolly's views on, 25
Paterson, J., 311 n. 37
Paton, John, 272, 324 n. 58
Pearse, Patrick
  and Dublin Lock Out, 125–6
  and anti-Redmond Volunteers,
    130
  and blood-sacrifice doctrine,
    142–3
  quotation from 'The Fool', 154
  contributor to *Guth na Bliadhna*,
    170
Petroff, Peter, on failure of Second
  International, 174
Pius X, 230
Plaid Cymru, 2
Plunkett, Joseph, 130, 142
Poland
  independence movement in, 5, 36
  comparison with Ireland, 88
Pollockshaw, 11
Poplar Board of Guardians, 259
*The Present Position of the Irish
  Question*, 24–5
Protestantism
  Connolly on, 91
  in North of Ireland, 94, 100–3
  and control of skilled Belfast
    trades, 100
Puissant, Father, 232–3

Railway Clerks Association, 218
Railway strikes in Birmingham,
  Liverpool and South Wales
  (1913), 115, 117, (1919), 198
The Reconstruction Society, 201
Redmond, John
  and Irish Volunteers, 129
  support for War, 129
  hostile obituary of, 316 n. 38
Rerum Novarum (Papal Encyclical,
  1891), 230–1, 233, 318 n. 8
Revolution by Reason, 268–9
Roberts, Lord, 173
Roman Catholicism
  and Socialism, 75
  Connolly's writings on, 88–91
  and Dublin Lock Out, 122
  Connolly's view of in 1913, 122
  influence on John Wheatley,
    230–6

attacks on John Wheatley, 236
The Rose Tree, cited, 144
Rothstein, Theodore, 200
Royal Commission on Housing in
  Scotland, 23
Russell, George 'A.E.', and Dublin
  Lock Out, 124–5
Russian Revolution
  influence on: Irish politics,
    150–1; John Maclean, 184;
    BSP (1919), 200; Scottish
    Nationalism, 210; Glasgow
    politics, 239; Left-Wing politics
    in 1920s, 245
  as argument for Celtic
    Communism, 213

St John, Vincent, 66
Sankey Commission, 198
Scanlon, John, 259, 277
Scheu, Andreas, 20
A Scots Quair, 225
Scottish Home Rule Association,
  208
Scottish Journey, 225
Scottish Labour College, 188, 199,
  210, 224
Scottish Labour Party, 20
Scottish Land and Labour League, 20
Scottish National Party, 2
Scottish Review, 210–11
Scottish Socialist Federation, 20
Scottish Trades Union Congress
  Maclean critical of, 164
  support for Home Rule, 208
Scottish Workers' Republican Party,
  223–4
Sexton, James, 114, 118
Shan Van Vocht, 30–1, 34
Sheeky-Skeffington, F.
  on Dublin Lock Out, 124
  and Easter Rising, 145–6
  'Open Letter' to Thomas
    MacDonagh, 146
Sherman, Charles, 55
Shipping Federation, 19
Shop Stewards' Movement
  (Engineering), 191
Singer strike, Clydebank (1911),
  162–3
Sinn Fein
  origins, 30

Sinn Fein (continued)
  Connolly on economic doctrines
    of, 123
  and Dublin Lock Out, 123–4
  post-1916 situation, 151–2
  early influence on Scotland, 169
  backed by Maclean, 212
  problem for Irish Labour, 282
  on Connolly (1913), 303 n.69
Sloan, Tom, 101
Smillie, Robert
  and North-East Lanarkshire
    by-election (1901), 44, 231
  and Dublin Lock Out (1913),
    115–16
  Maclean's admiration for, 164, 198
  support for Gaelic language, 208
  on Labour links with Highland
    Land League, 209
Snowden, Philip
  opposition to 'Direct Action',
    115–16
  and 1914–18 War, 128
  against class politics, 249
  in 1924 Labour Government, 258
  economic orthodoxy of, 258
Social Democratic Federation
  in Edinburgh, 20–1
  and Labour Alliance, 44, 282
  division in, 44–6
  and Ireland, 44
  Scottish District Council's
    criticisms of national
    leadership, 45
  Maclean's membership of, 161
Social Democratic Party, Austro-
    Hungarian Empire (SDP), 6
Social Democratic Party, Germany
    (SPD), 4, 89, 128
Socialise the National Income,
    273–5
Socialism in our Time, 266–7
The Socialist, 45, 213
Socialist International, Paris
    Congress (1900), 44–5
Socialist Labor Party (United
    (States)
  Connolly's changing views on,
    46–58
  electoral record, 49
  and IWW, 53–7
  attacked by John O'Neill, 55

Socialist Labour Party (British)
  foundation, 46
  in 1914–18 War, 173
  in CWC, 179
  in Glasgow, 187
  and Unity negotiations (1919–20),
    200
Socialist Party of America
  Connolly's views on, 49
  electoral record, 49
  Connolly joins, 58
  factionalism in, 58
  and Industrial Unionism, 70–2
  Irish Socialist Federation, 77
Socialist Party of Ireland, 92, 212
The Socialist Programme, 258
Socialist Trades and Labor
    Alliance, 48–50
Sombart, Werner, on American
    Socialism, 63–5
South Wales miners' strike (1915),
    132
South Wales Socialist Society, 200
Stanton, Charles, 128
Starving in the Midst of Plenty,
    255–6
Stephens, James, 145, 306
Stopford Green, Alice, 79, 298 n.20
Strachey, John, 268, 277
Sullivan, Joseph, 231
Synge, J.M., 89

Taylor, A.J.P., 2
Telfer, A.C., 23
Thatcher, Margaret
  record in office, 2–3
  on South Atlantic crisis (1982), 3
Thomas, Jimmy
  on Dublin Lock Out, 115, 119
  and 1919 rail strike, 198
Thompson, Sir Basil, 313
Thompson, Edward, 285
Tillett, Ben
  and Dublin Lock Out, 117
  jingoism of, 128
Tone, Wolfe, 82–4
Tonypandy riot (1910), 14
Trafalgar Square riot (1887), 8
Transport Workers' Federation
  and Dublin Lock Out, 117
  Connolly on, 118
Treasury Agreement, 179

Trevelyan, Sir Charles, 312 n. 2

Ulster Covenant, 93
Ulster Volunteer Force, 93
United Irish League, 44, 230–2
United Irishman, 41
United Mineworkers of America, 69

Vanguard, 173–4, 178, 213
Voice of Labour, 152–3

Walker, William
  in Belfast North Elections, 100
  political ideas, 102–4
  polemic with Connolly, 104
  on Protestantism, 300 n. 34
Webb, Beatrice, on John Wheatley,
  258, 259, 280
Weekly People, 46
Wertheimer, Egon, on John
  Wheatley, 229
Western Federation of Miners, 55
Wheatley, John
  outline of career, 12–13
  episodes: United Irish League,
    230–2; Catholic Socialist
    Society, 232–6; support for
    ILP, 233, 235, 237, 245;
    municipal career, 237–8;
    1914–18 War, 238–42; as
    Labour Minister, 258–9;
    estrangement from Labour
    Party leaders, 264; and
    Cook-Maxton Manifesto
    campaign, 276–9, 324 n. 58
  views on: Roman Catholicism,
    230–6; Irish Home Rule, 234;
    the family, 236, 281, 324 n. 1;
    Blatchford, 236; Maclean,
    236–7; ILP-style Socialism,
    236–7; Socialist strategy
    (1918), 239–42; Easter Rising,
    242; significance of 1922

election, 252; parliamentary
    scenes, 253–4; under-
    consumptionist theory, 255,
    257; Ruhr occupation, 256–7;
    strategic response to 1924
    Government, 259–60;
    opposition to Free Trade,
    260–2, 268–70, 272–6; State
    planning, 260–2, 273–5;
    General Strike tactic, 264;
    'Living Wage' policy, 267; on
    prospects of new Labour
    Government (1929), 279
  publications: *The Catholic
    Working-Man*, 232–6; *Eight
    Pound Cottages for Glasgow
    Citizens*, 237–8; *Starving in
    the Midst of Plenty*, 255–6;
    Socialise the National Income,
    273–5
  other: problems of interpretation,
    229–30, 281–5; comparison
    with Connolly, 231–2, 274;
    influence of J. A. Hobson, 255,
    257; comparison with Mosley,
    250, 268–9
Williams, Ben, 57
Williams, J. E., 115
Williams, Robert, 118, 363 n. 48
Wilson, Havelock, 115, 118
Wilson, John (Broxburn Miners'
    Agent), 20
Wise, E. F., 266
The Worker (1914), 131
The Workers' Republic, 29, 131,
    138–9
Workers' Socialist Federation, 200

Yeats, William Butler
  on Dublin Lock Out, 124
  'The Rose Tree' cited, 144

Zimmerwald Conference (1915), 174